MUTINOUS WOMEN

JOAN DEJEAN

MUTINOUS WOMEN

How French Convicts Became
Founding Mothers of the Gulf Coast

BASIC BOOKS

New York

Basic Books
Hachette Book Group
1290 Avenue of the Americas, New York, NY 10104
www.basicbooks.com

Printed in the United States of America

First Edition: April 2022

Published by Basic Books, an imprint of Perseus Books, LLC, a subsidiary of
Hachette Book Group, Inc. The Basic Books name and logo is a trademark of the
Hachette Book Group.

The Hachette Speakers Bureau provides a wide range of authors for speaking
events. To find out more, go to www.hachettespeakersbureau.com or call (866)
376-6591.

The publisher is not responsible for websites (or their content) that are not owned
by the publisher.

Print book interior design by Amy Quinn.

Library of Congress Cataloging-in-Publication Data
Names: DeJean, Joan E., author.
Title: Mutinous women: how French convicts became founding mothers of the
   Gulf Coast / Joan DeJean.
Other titles: How French convicts became founding mothers of the Gulf Coast
Identifiers: LCCN 2021057367 | ISBN 9781541600584 (hardcover) | ISBN
   9781541600591 (ebook)
Subjects: LCSH: Gulf States—History—To 1803. | Frontier and pioneer life—
   Gulf States. | France—Colonies—America—Biography. | French—Gulf
   States—Biography. | Women prisoners—France—History—18th century. |
   Female offenders—France—History—18th century. | Convict ships—France—
   History—18th century. | Mutine (Frigate)—History.
Classification: LCC F372 .D45 2022 | DDC 976/.02—dc23/eng/20211202
LC record available at https://lccn.loc.gov/2021057367

ISBNs: 9781541600584 (hardcover), 9781541600591 (e-book)

LSC-C

Printing 1, 2022

In memory of my grandmothers, Marie Aline Achée and Lilia Marie Salaun, and in memory of the mutinous women known by their descendants as their "first grandmothers"— Marie Avril, Marie Anne Benoist, Geneviève Bettemont, Marie Louise Brunet, Marie Daudin, Marie Anne Fourchet, Marie Anne Grise, Jeanne Mahou, Jeanne Pouillot, and Anne Françoise Rolland.

Mutin/Mutine, adjectif et substantif:
Qui se révolte contre l'autorité légitime. Les séditions commencent par
quelques mutins qui veulent secouer le joug des lois et des magistrats.

—Antoine Furetière, Dictionnaire universel *(1690)*

Mutinous, masculine and feminine, adjective and noun:
Someone who revolts against legitimate authority.
Seditions are begun by a few rebels who want to
throw off the bondage of laws and magistrates.

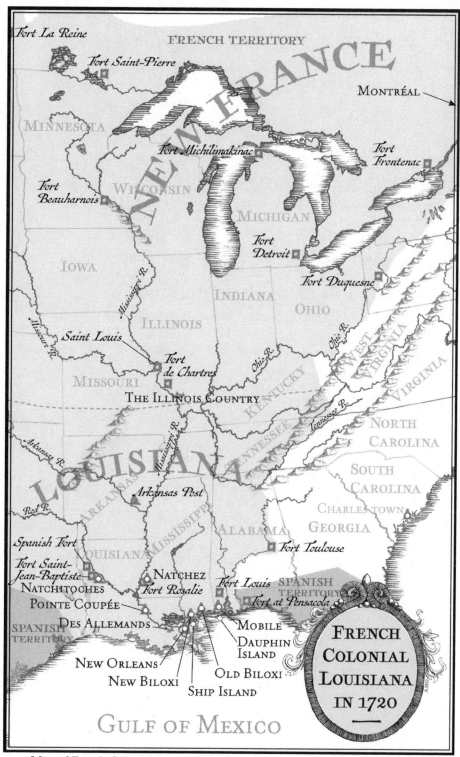

Map of French Colonial Louisiana in 1720. The names and frontiers of today's states have been indicated to provide a sense of scale and a perspective on the location of the original settlements in French Louisiana. Andrea Gottschalk.

Contents

Preliminaries

A Second Coast,
a Second Ship

IN THE POPULAR IMAGINARY, THIS COUNTRY'S EARLY COLONIZA-
tion is dominated by the Atlantic Coast. The second coast claimed
by a European power, the Gulf Coast, seems inconsequential by
comparison. The Eastern Seaboard's European settlement is almost
inevitably identified with what has become a cultural icon, the *Mayflower*, the ship that in 1620 carried 102 Puritans who chose to leave
their homeland in search of religious freedom. But the Gulf Coast
had an iconic ship of its own, *La Mutine*. This was the frigate that
in 1720 brought some 100 passengers from France to islands situated offshore from what are now the states of Alabama and Mississippi. *La Mutine*'s voyage marks the first time that a vessel sent to
the future United States transported solely women. *La Mutine*'s passengers were all female convicts, most of them accused of the same

1

crime—prostitution. And unlike those who crossed the Atlantic on the *Mayflower*, the women on *La Mutine* did not make the journey of their own volition.

In 1719, nearly two hundred women were taken from a prison in Paris. They were chained together for transport to French ports, where most were shackled in ships' holds. Unlike the *Mayflower*'s passengers, these women have mainly been forgotten—for over three hundred years. They have been almost entirely excluded from the historical record, and their stories have never been properly told. When they are remembered at all, the convict women of 1719 are often confused with women who later sailed from France to Louisiana and who are known as "casket girls" because, it is said, they were given personal effects and a small sum of money to be kept in a casket or chest to serve as a dowry when they reached their destination. Even when the women of 1719 are correctly identified, they are dismissed as mere "prostitutes" and blamed for many crucial problems of the fledgling French colony of Louisiana, from a low birth rate to a high crime rate.

This book tells the story of who the women of *La Mutine* really were. They were *not* prostitutes. They were instead in various ways victims of the endemic poverty that gripped France in the years prior to their journey—and also of the police corruption that gripped Paris in 1719. They accepted neither victimization passively.

Nearly all of them were ordinary women. The majority had been given what were then the most common names for girls: Marie and Marie Anne. Many of their family names were also common, the Smiths and the Joneses of France. Most were working women; they had struggled to earn a living at a moment when the vast majority of the French were cash-strapped. They had fended for themselves in what was then the most populous city in Europe and in one of the most dangerous times in Paris's history: in the process, they became streetwise. What happened to these ordinary Frenchwomen could have happened to virtually any woman who found herself in Paris in 1719. When these women fell into the clutches of the Parisian police, they talked back to corrupt officers of the law and defiantly resisted false arrests. Deportation was the price they paid for such defiance.

Across the ocean on the second coast, this country's French coast, a significant number of these rebelliously unconventional colonists realized a female version of "the American dream." The women of *La Mutine* were among the founding inhabitants of settlements from Natchez to New Orleans, where they built the earliest houses—often with their own hands. They became property owners and acquired considerable estates. They founded dynasties. Indeed, with each generation, their tens of thousands of descendants have spread ever more widely across this country. The women's accomplishments are all the more remarkable given that most had been born into extreme poverty, few had any formal education, and none had received an education worthy of her intelligence.

The biographies of the women loaded like cargo aboard a ship called *La Mutine*, or *The Mutinous Woman*, are among the earliest surviving records of this country's first European female settlers. I discovered them in documents preserved in archives in the homeland that rejected them, notably the French National Archives in Paris. This is fitting, for even though the latter part of the women's lives unfolded in what is now the United States, their story can only be understood in the economic and social context of early eighteenth-century France. They were Frenchwomen: born in France, they grew up there, wearing only French clothing and eating only French food. When they were forced out of their homeland and deported to a fledgling French colony across an ocean, they remained French subjects, under the rule of the French monarchy and French law. Their years in France are the chronicle of their families; of the villages and small towns where they were born; of the lives they made for themselves in their homeland; and in particular of one city, Paris, where many grew up and where they were all arrested. Their time in France ended when a ship sailed across the Atlantic, bearing them away in chains in its hold.

Next begins the story of Frenchwomen who found themselves in a far-flung French colony both vast and still largely uncharted, at a moment when the French remained uncertain about even the name of *La Mutine*'s destination. While the royal ministers who authorized their exile often referred to the place where the women they spoke of as "merchandise" were to be deposited as "Louisiana," the colonists who lived there still used the territory's earlier name, "Mississippi."* The lived reality of the second life that authorities in France forced upon these women was one that unfolded in a world that was mainly alien to them. When they emerged from the hold of the ship in which they had crossed the Atlantic, these women who until then had rarely met anyone not French-born found a land where the French were but a tiny minority, vastly outnumbered by Indigenous peoples. They found themselves surrounded by flora, fauna, and landscapes that were strange, forbidding, and at times even nightmarish to Parisians and women from the countryside near Paris. Bread made from French wheatflour, the food that had until then been their principal sustenance, was replaced by a new dietary staple: corn. These women from landlocked regions were now surrounded by strange waterways, especially bayous, in whose murky depths they had their first encounters with the predator Europeans considered most terrifying of all, the alligator.

When the women arrived, most of the towns and cities in which they would make new lives did not exist or barely existed; many of these places did not yet have fixed names. When New Orleans, for example, officially became "New Orleans" and acquired the very first shards of an identity, the women were instrumental in that process. The colony comes into focus, settlement by settlement, through the

---

* The French colony to which the women were sent included the modern state of Louisiana, significant portions of today's Mississippi and Alabama, and land now part of other states, including Arkansas, Illinois, and Missouri. In the following pages, I will refer to this vast French territory as "Louisiana," a name given it in honor of King Louis XIV.

eyes of some of the first Frenchwomen to live there, a view of the construction of French Louisiana that highlights the impact of the women of *La Mutine* and their families on the colony's development.

Everything about the process designed to rid France of these women was conceived and executed in great haste and confusion. No French authority had a clear idea of the identity of the alleged criminals being summarily judged: for them, these female prisoners were rarely individuals, merely members of a collective mass of undesirables. There were so many prisoners thus treated, so many voices never before heard, and so many stories to be recovered that readers may find the accounts blending together, just as they did for the French authorities who exiled the women. I hope, however, that these facts will always remain clear: the women of *La Mutine* were unjustly accused, unjustly convicted, and unjustly sentenced. Even more than that clarity, though, I hope above all to have restored as much as possible to these women voices and an individuality of which they were robbed by the homeland that had rejected them.

Part I

France

Chapter 1

False Arrests and
Trumped-Up Charges

BETWEEN SIX AND SEVEN A.M. ON TUESDAY, DECEMBER 28, 1700, detective chief inspector of the Parisian police Louis Jérôme Daminois was awakened with the news that a corpse had been found in a small street near one of the major gateways into Paris, the Porte Saint-Honoré, the entrance nearest the royal palace, the Louvre.[1] Daminois's lengthy report on the crime scene is a masterpiece of forensic observation.

Daminois "rushed instantly" to the scene, where he found several people clustered in front of the shop of Adrien Jonquet, a *marchand grenetier* who sold grain and hay. They were gathered around the body of a man of about thirty, "of average height" (then about five feet two or five feet three). The deceased had "blackish hair," "slightly curly" and worn short, and he was bearded. His black hat with silver trim lay at his side, along with a sword with a golden handle, still in its scabbard. He wore a *justaucorps* or long jacket in the then highly fashionable shade of brown known as musk, leather pants, and grey wool stockings. His pockets were empty, except for his jacket's left pocket, which contained "five small pieces of raw beef." The man's undergarment was soaked in blood, and "just over his right nipple" was "a wound with a very small entrance point."

Although Daminois and his officers interrogated witnesses and residents of the neighborhood for nearly three months, they never established with certainty the identity of the nattily dressed dead man. They most often referred to him as "Saint-Martin," first name unknown. Their failure to identify the victim was hardly surprising. Most of the witnesses who came forward lived in the area where the murder had occurred, a zone just outside the city's limits, the faubourg or agglomeration that had taken shape immediately beyond the Saint-Honoré Gate. In 1700, the Faubourg Saint-Honoré, while situated not far from the Place Vendôme and some of Paris's newest and most elegant architecture, was itself far from truly urban. It was sparsely populated and lightly built up, a transitional zone between the city and the countryside beyond rather than a true neighborhood. Most of those who passed through the Faubourg Saint-Honoré did so on their way into and out of Paris: residents had no reason to know the identity of these transients, most of whom they had never seen before and would never see again.

Numerous witnesses reported having spotted a man they believed to be the deceased late the night before or in the very early hours of that Tuesday morning, always in the company of three or four men, none of whom was ever arrested and only one of whom was ever identified. Within hours of the murder, however, the police's attention had been drawn to another suspect—a woman. One witness described having seen a woman "running down the street, terrified, carrying in her hands a sword with a gold handle in its scabbard." Two others claimed to have seen a woman walking in various locations with the men the police were already trying to identify. Still another witness, Catherine Forderet, a seventy-nine-year-old widow who spent her days "begging near the Porte Saint-Honoré," testified that she had heard a woman singing "the most depraved kind of songs." Forderet returned later that same day with additional information: "she had just heard that the wife of Bourdin [a neighborhood merchant] had told someone else that she had recognized the woman as '*la Bouquetière, une créature de mauvaise vie*'"—"the Flower Girl [*bouquetières* sold bouquets and cut flowers], a creature who lived a dissolute life."

At this point, the still-unidentified woman stood accused of nothing more than of having been seen in the company of men potentially involved in a crime and of singing "depraved songs." But a third-hand rumor repeated as an afterthought eventually condemned her to twenty years of misery, determined her life—as well as the destinies of several hundred other women—and ultimately changed the history of French Louisiana.

THE DAY AFTER THE MURDER, DECEMBER 29, THE POLICE WERE ON high alert: finding the woman known as "the Bouquetière" had become a top priority. On January 5, 1701, a town crier and a trumpeter marched around to the city's main squares and gates calling out the police's request for any information that could lead to her arrest. No one came forward.

Finally, on January 29, 1701, a full month after the fact, a widow named Marie Le Duc, who lived a considerable distance from the crime scene and near Paris's principal market, the Halles, walked in and volunteered the name of the man the police soon decided had murdered Saint-Martin. In her statement to Daminois, Le Duc testified that she had learned from the mother of someone Le Duc knew only as "Dubourg" that her son had wanted for a long time to kill a man named Saint-Martin because Saint-Martin "had it coming to him." Marie Le Duc added that Dubourg was "a good man," and ended her statement by reporting that his mother had also confided

11

that "people were saying that the Bouquetière was responsible for the murder." The public rumor machine—or at least the presumed assassin's mother—had at last explicitly connected the Bouquetière to the crime.

That same day, still another widow, Jeanne Ballet, came in to say she had known Saint-Martin well and that "she had learned that Dubourg had killed him at the instigation of the Bouquetière, who led a scandalous life and was involved in a *commerce de débauche* [debauchery] with Dubourg." This was the only time that anyone asserted that Dubourg and the Bouquetière had had a relationship; Ballet's allegation lent credence to Dubourg's mother's charge that the Bouquetière was "responsible" for the murder.

And then, on January 30, the police struck pay dirt with three witnesses who claimed to have direct knowledge of the by then infamous Bouquetière. Marguerite Baudin, the wife of merchant Bourdin and the original source of the rumors, came in to recount in person the story already repeated by Forderet. Baudin also described sighting the Bouquetière at five thirty a.m. on the day of the murder, although her testimony regarding time and place did not align with that of other eyewitnesses. And then there were the two soldiers who became the prime witnesses for the prosecution.

Claude Dubois was the first one in. He claimed to have seen Dubourg and the Bouquetière together on the evening before the murder and ended his testimony with a bombshell: "The Bouquetière had been boasting that she had had Saint-Martin killed, that she had had many others killed before him, and that she would have others killed in the same way." A second soldier, Thierry François, alleged that "a week or so ago," he and other soldiers had run into the Bouquetière when she was out with several friends. Upon seeing her, one of the soldiers exclaimed, "There's the bitch responsible for the death of that poor Saint-Martin." To which, he maintained, she replied, "Yes, you poor beggar, I had him killed. I've had many others killed, too, and I'll do the same to you." Next, when the Bouquetière and her friends left the place where they'd all been having a beer, her friends attacked the soldier who had insulted her, wounding him with a sword thrust "just above the right nipple." All the while, in François's words, the Bouquetière kept yelling, "Yes, I killed him." François closed by adding that "he'd also heard that about two months ago the Bouquetière had had one of the Swiss guards killed."

With those two witnesses, the Bouquetière was promoted from accessory to one murder to a very rare category in the annals of crime: a female serial killer. The signature to the crimes for which she was allegedly responsible was a single sword thrust just above the right nipple.

By February 2, the Bouquetière had been incarcerated. The following day, she was taken for questioning from For-L'Évêque prison on the banks of the Seine not far from the Halles to nearby police headquarters, the Châtelet. "Marie La Fontaine, age 20, residing on the place Ville-Neuve," reads the file identifying the suspect. That notation reveals that the police had dealt with their prime suspect so summarily that they had never bothered to make sure they were writing her name correctly. Had they inquired, she could have explained that her family name was in fact "Fontaine," rather than "La Fontaine," and that her friends and family knew her as "Manon," the diminutive of "Marie" that became wildly popular in the early eighteenth century.

The Parisian neighborhood where Manon Fontaine lived, the Ville-Neuve or New City, took shape in the first half of the seventeenth century in what is now Paris's second arrondissement or district. Unlike the winding alleyways of medieval Paris, the New City's streets were modern—straight and well aligned. They were also short and narrow and bustling with foot traffic from the merchants and artisans and working-class Parisians who populated the area and for whom it had been designed. Those streets were lined with the modest dwellings two and three stories high in which the New City's residents lived, as low-income workers of the day typically did, crammed

Bouchardon in.
A Paris Chés Joullain. Mon bel Oeillet. *C. S.*

Figure 1. The street vendors called *bouquetières*, or "flower girls," walked through Paris displaying the selection for sale that day in baskets strapped around their waists.

Pommes cuites au Four.

Figure 2. Other itinerant Parisian street vendors carried fruit for sale in these wide, flat baskets, known as *inventaires*, or inventories.

into tight quarters: a family of four or five might share a single room, at most two. The New City was well situated, within easy walking distance of the Halles market, as well as the royal palace, the Louvre, and the elegant and spacious streets that surrounded the palace and that were home to a clientele highly desirable for merchants and artisans, the aristocrats who frequented the court.

Manon Fontaine said she made a living as one of the city's countless street vendors. A *"fille vendante* [sic] *du fruit,"* she crisscrossed Paris's streets all day long hawking fruit carried in a large and deep basket strapped to her back, with a second basket, this one broad and flat and known as an *inventaire* or inventory, secured around her waist and extending out in front of her as a display space for her wares. As she moved along, she would have advertised the goods she had for sale by calling out to pedestrians, repeating continuously the names of the fruits in her basket that day. Manon explained that people knew her as "the Bouquetière" because she had formerly walked the city's cobblestones selling little bouquets, carrying and displaying her nosegays in the same manner. She also stated that she could neither read nor write, something that explains why she had not availed herself of her legal right to review her testimony and thus had not noticed the incorrect spelling of her name.

In eighteenth-century Paris, the chants of street vendors like Manon Fontaine—"carnations, carnations, my beautiful carnations"; "baked apples, apples baked in an oven"—reverberated incessantly through the streets. This was an age-old urban ritual: the calls of wandering sellers like Manon Fontaine were the heartbeat of the city, so basic to the soundscape of Paris that these chants were known as *"les cris de Paris,"* "the cries of Paris," as though the vendors were somehow the voice of the city itself.

Manon denied knowing any of the men she was alleged to have frequented; she denied the rumors about her conduct. She explained that in the early morning hours of December 28, she was asleep at home with her mother, with whom she would have shared not only a single room but also a bed. The police never bothered to verify her alibi, nor did they question her neighbors about her character, a procedure that would surely have proved instructive, for the New City, unlike the Faubourg Saint-Honoré, was a close-knit community in which residents lived in such tight proximity that they saw their neighbors all the time and knew them by sight. During Manon's interrogation, she also denied that she "had conspired with Dubourg and enticed Saint-Martin to follow her by promising him debauchery so that Dubourg could kill him." This question made it clear that Daminois was so eager to indict the Bouquetière as an accomplice to murder that he was floating hypotheses with no foundation in the evidence he had gathered.

On February 5, the prisoner was brought in again; this time, Daminois took a no-holds-barred approach. *Was she responsible for Saint-Martin's death? Had she ordered many men to be killed, as soldier Thierry François had alleged? Had one of her friends wounded François's fellow soldier with a sword thrust above the right nipple? Had she ordered the assassination of a Swiss guard?* Manon categorically denied all these accusations.

Daminois sent out a bailiff to round up still more witnesses, and on February 17, new depositions were recorded. Two of them provided highly incriminating testimony regarding Dubourg. A third witness, master cobbler Claude Martin, testified that on the day of the murder he "had seen two men between 5 and 6 a.m.," adding "but not their faces, so he would not be able to identify them." This was the first indication that the already fragile case would soon go up in smoke.

On Wednesday, February 23, the first of what were known as "confrontations" was staged at police headquarters. Accused and accusers were gathered together in the same room; under oath, they responded to questioning by Daminois and a team of officers, all of whom did their best to intimidate the accuser and, especially, the accused. Catherine Forderet, the first person to place Fontaine at the scene of the crime and to make allegations regarding her character, admitted that she neither knew nor recognized Manon Fontaine. One after another, numerous witnesses said the same thing. Only two, Ballet and Le Duc, said they could identify Manon as the woman called the Bouquetière. Neither of them, however, had placed her at the scene of the crime.

Later that same day, and when Manon was no longer present, Daminois gave the witnesses the chance to add new evidence. Only Forderet chose to modify her story, although not in the way the police were expecting: "She shouldn't have said that the woman was young and of average height, because she hadn't seen her face," Forderet's statement concludes. One key witness thereby disqualified herself.

Like cobbler Martin before her, Forderet forced the police to confront a fact that should have given them pause from the start: in a small byway outside the city limits and without Paris's sophisticated streetlighting, at five a.m. on the 28th of December, the night would have been pitch-black. None of the witnesses could have been sure of any identifications, of the many specific details they had offered up, not even really of the number of men and women they claimed to have seen. Indeed, already on December 28, Charlotte Travitz, one of the group gathered around the dead man when Daminois arrived on the scene, admitted that they hadn't been able to discern anything at all until "a woman carrying a candle happened along." By the light of that candle, they noticed for the first time the blood on the victim's clothing and realized they were dealing with a corpse.

On February 25, Manon was confronted with Marguerite Baudin, the source of the rumors that had put the police on her trail. When Baudin identified her as "the Bouquetière, of whom she had heard it said that she lived a dissolute life," Manon rejoined that she had never seen her accuser before. Once again, Daminois came up empty-handed.

From then on, it went steadily downhill for the police. On Monday, March 7, Manon Fontaine was confronted with the two soldiers, each of whom identified her as the Bouquetière and repeated his wild tales about her proud avowals of having been responsible for the murders of many men. Later that afternoon, however, one of them, Claude Dubois, retracted the core of his testimony: "He had heard only through hearsay that the Bouquetière had boasted of having had Saint-Martin killed." Ultimately, one of the only two witnesses to have offered evidence of the Flower Girl's complicity provided Daminois merely with still more neighborhood gossip.

On and on it went, as witness after witness brought in to confront the Bouquetière said the same thing: they did not know the accused, and their testimony had nothing to do with her. Finally, on March 23, 1701, after three months during which the Parisian police had questioned twenty-one witnesses and Manon Fontaine had been interrogated by prominent officers of the law on three occasions, had endured serious intimidation, if not some form of what would now be considered torture, and had "confronted" all witnesses at least once, the case officially known as "The Crown vs. Marie La Fontaine and four unidentified men" came to an end.

In the final decree, the men, three of whom remained anonymous, were convicted of "the murder of the person named Marin." (The first witness questioned on December 28 had mentioned hearing someone call out, "Hey, Marin," but that name never reappears in the extensive trial proceedings until it suddenly pops up again in the verdict.) The men were sentenced to hanging. Since they had been officially pronounced "fugitives," their punishment was merely staged, and a gallows was erected at the Croix du Tiroir, a major intersection near the Louvre, with an effigy representing them attached to it.

The Crown was also obliged to recognize that three months of the best efforts of Paris's finest police investigators had turned up nothing against the person who was at the center of their preoccupations, and the case against Manon Fontaine was dismissed for lack of evidence. "Because of her long detention, she shall be released from prison," the verdict began, although the presiding magistrate ordered the police "to continue to gather information." An ultimate decree made it clear that her troubles were far from over: "On the condition that she present herself every time and whenever she is ordered to do so." That "condition" ensured that Manon could not leave Paris and guaranteed that she could be put behind bars again at a moment's notice.

By then, Manon Fontaine knew well just how vulnerable an illiterate, working-class woman like herself was under the law. At the end of her second interrogation on February 5, Daminois had attempted to blindside Manon by enquiring "if she had ever been in prison before," a question to which he already knew the answer. Manon's response was to the point: "Yes," she said.

Exactly one year before the murder at the Porte Saint-Honoré, on December 2, 1699, the Parisian police came upon the body of a man subsequently identified only as "d'Autel," first name unknown. He had been killed by a single sword thrust. Unlike the second trial in early 1701, legal procedure was quickly dispatched in 1699. This time, the case was handled by lawyers representing the Parisian Parlement rather than the police. Already on December 22, 1699, the sole interrogations took place: the man purported to be the assassin and his two alleged accomplices each responded to a brief series of questions before being summarily convicted.

Pierre Chenillard, a nineteen-year-old soldier of the watch, denied that he had drawn his sword against the deceased; he had never taken it out of its scabbard. In Chenillard's account, the deceased had picked a fight with him and had struck him with his cane. Chenillard fought back, he claimed, not with his sword but merely with his baton. Chenillard also denied knowing the two women alleged to be his accomplices and asserted that the woman the police claimed had instigated the murder had in fact played no role whatsoever in the altercation earlier that month.

The woman considered Chenillard's principal accomplice was identified as "Marie La Fontaine, from Paris," profession: "selling merchandise here and there." No one bothered to follow standard

procedure and ask her age or address. Instead, the parliament's lawyers gave their version of the murder in question form. *Was she a
loose woman? Had she insulted d'Autel by calling him a "fucking pimp
who put on airs"?*[2] *Had d'Autel replied, "Get out of here, bitch, or I'll
beat you with my cane"? Had she then grabbed d'Autel's tie and cried
out, "Help me, Chenillard"? Had Chenillard then drawn his sword and
killed d'Autel?* Manon was characteristically brief, replying only
"that all of this was false."

The final interrogation was reserved for a woman identified only as
"Bourdin, age 27"—in fact, Anne Bourdin who worked as a servant
in Paris. The lawyers were hoping she would admit to having been a
witness to the crime, but she replied that she "knew nothing about
any of this."

That same day, December 22, 1699, a verdict was pronounced.
Chenillard was convicted of murder and sentenced to hanging, his
body to be left on the gallows for twenty-four hours. Fontaine and
Bourdin, convicted of "having participated in the assassination," were
sentenced to whipping, branding, and "banishment from the jurisdiction of the Parisian Parlement for five years." Bourdin was described
as "a debauched woman," but no such accusation was made against
Manon Fontaine.

All three appealed the verdict. Chenillard's and Bourdin's appeals
were quickly dismissed. Manon, however, had done her homework,
as she did in all her dealings with the judicial system, and it was decreed that she had legal grounds for an appeal. In her appeal, Manon
argued that the prosecution had produced no evidence to support any
of their claims. Royal prosecutors always sought to discourage appeals, which they saw as further clogging up already overburdened
legal machinery. To this end, they typically upheld the original verdicts, while imposing harsher sentences. In Manon's case, she was
now sentenced to be stripped naked in public and forced to watch
the execution with a noose around her neck, and then banished from
Paris—this time, permanently.

Manon Fontaine's first conviction was a case that might well be unique: a woman condemned as an accessory to murder because she was alleged to have cried out, "Help me."

Manon was flogged; she was branded on her right shoulder with a fleur-de-lys, symbol of the French monarchy, guaranteeing that for the rest of her life she would be easily recognized as a dangerous criminal. She left Paris, as she had been required to do, in early 1700. Manon explained what happened next in her response to Daminois's interrogation on February 5, 1701. She had been imprisoned first during what she termed "the d'Autel affair," and then "a second time because she had failed to respect her banishment from Paris." Daminois asked why she had not followed the rules of her banishment, and Manon replied that she had been in the countryside with every intention of remaining there, until she was called back to Paris on order from Louis Le Peletier, among the principal magistrates of the Parisian Parlement. She then produced the written decree.[3]

That order, which Manon had had the foresight to hold onto and to bring with her to prison, reveals that Le Peletier, one of Louis XIV's close advisers, had personally intervened in order to entrap an illiterate fruit vendor. And Le Peletier was surely involved in the case of Manon Fontaine at the request of Henri François d'Aguesseau, widely considered the finest legal mind of eighteenth-century France.

On September 24, 1700, d'Aguesseau was named the Parisian Parlement's *procureur général*, France's chief magistrate. Soon after, Manon received the decree ordering her to return to Paris—where she was quickly rearrested and convicted of failing to respect her banishment. She was released once more and resumed her life in the New City. Then on December 28, 1700, another man was killed with a single sword thrust. The Bouquetière became a person of great interest in early 1701 because of the similar circumstances under which the victims known as d'Autel and Saint-Martin died.

Manon's first trial had been presided over, as most often happened, by one of nineteen "substitute" or associate royal counsels, whereas beginning on day one, the investigation of the second murder was orchestrated by d'Aguesseau himself.[4] It was undoubtedly at d'Aguesseau's instigation that Commissioner Daminois tried so desperately to place Manon near the Porte Saint-Honoré on the night of the murder and to establish her complicity in the crime. D'Aguesseau issued orders that the records of all depositions and interrogations be brought to him directly. From then on, the Parisian Parlement's chief magistrate, the jurist Voltaire later described as "the most learned magistrate in French history," personally signed off on every decree in the proceedings of the Crown vs. Marie La Fontaine.[5]

A surprising number of those decrees do not mention the charges for which Manon was tried. Instead, they speak of the sole crime for which d'Aguesseau had evidence, that of returning to Paris. (They naturally fail to mention that Manon had done so only under orders from a high official of the very governing body that had issued the sentence.) And that is how d'Aguesseau finally managed to put a definitive end to Manon's life as a free woman in the country of her birth.

After the March 23, 1701 decree that closed the second murder investigation, Manon enjoyed a few months in Paris, before being arrested again. On Monday, December 12, 1701, her fourth trial began. This time, no one had been killed, and Manon was charged solely with "failure to respect the terms of her banishment" and with "having been found living in Paris with no employment." Once again, it was never mentioned that she had been ordered to remain in Paris and at the police's beck and call. D'Aguesseau personally signed off on the charges and added that "the King will be informed of her transgression." Even the Sun King, Louis XIV, was made aware of the crimes of "the Flower Girl."

Once more, witnesses were called, and there were depositions and confrontations. The business dragged on until March 23, 1702, when a verdict was entered: this time, the accused was identified only as "Marie." On March 27, d'Aguesseau signed the order condemning "Marie" to be taken immediately to the Salpêtrière prison's notorious Maison de Force (or House of Force), often called simply La Force—literally, strength, might, violence. There, she was to be "locked up in perpetuity." At the end of two and a half years during which she had been almost constantly incarcerated and standing trial, the Bouquetière's fate was sealed: she would spend the rest of her days in prison.

Manon's sentence was uncommonly harsh. Whereas typically women locked away in perpetuity were true repeat offenders, there was no blemish on her record either prior to her first arrest at age nineteen or during the periods between her trials. Manon's original punishment—banishment—was the most common sentence meted out in early eighteenth-century Paris. The police did not have the resources necessary to monitor all those sentenced to banishment, so it was also a punishment very rarely heeded. Exiles seemed always to return to Paris, if indeed they even bothered to leave. The fact that Manon had respected her initial banishment by leaving the city and staying away was highly unusual. Her actions demonstrate her respect for the law that condemned her.

The vast majority of those exiled were working-class men and women. How could an itinerant vendor or a flower girl have earned a living in a French village? In the exceptionally tough economic climate of the late 1690s and the early eighteenth century, when the French state was moving ever closer to bankruptcy because of Louis XIV's endless and increasingly costly wars, Paris was the only urban center in France with the density of population and the concentration of wealth necessary to guarantee employment for the 50,000 to 100,000 of the city's estimated 550,000 inhabitants who worked as domestic servants.[6] In these conditions, a life sentence to the brutal Maison de Force for failure to respect a decree of expulsion was unheard of.

THE LOCATION OF THE FACILITY TO WHICH MANON WAS CONFINED, the Hôpital Général or General Hospital, most often referred to as

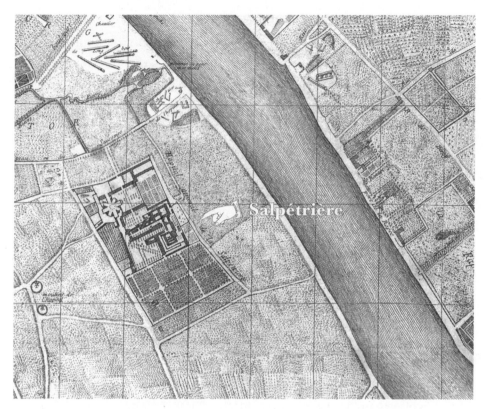

Figure 3. This detail from a 1728 map of Paris shows the Salpêtrière's isolated location.

the Salpêtrière, is now fully integrated into the urban fabric: railway stations, universities, and monuments such as the Panthéon are all within easy reach. But in the early eighteenth century, the setting was a no-man's-land. Prisoners in Paris's other penitentiaries such as the Bastille could at least hear the sounds of the city from their cells and feel a connection to the world outside. Surrounded by thirty-foot-high walls, the Salpêtrière was situated north, south, east, and west of, and across the Seine from, nothing. There were neither bustling streets nor residential neighborhoods nearby. The prison was bordered by a cemetery on one side, a huge garbage dump on another, and on a third by a fetid pool in which tanneries had long discarded their chemical waste—its water was so polluted that it was a breeding ground for rats and infectious diseases. Compared to this desolation, even the murder scene in the Faubourg Saint-Honoré positively teemed with street life. If prisoners in the Salpêtrière moaned or wailed or called out for help, there was no one to hear their cries.

There is still a Salpêtrière; it is now a vast, modern hospital complex. Still standing near its center is the section to which Manon Fontaine was confined, the House of Force. England had workhouses, in which the poor endured forced labor and malnutrition, but as its name implied, La Force was intended as a place where particularly brutal means of correction could be used on the women imprisoned there whenever this was deemed necessary. With its blank, utilitarian façade, still today, La Force—now a psychiatric ward—remains somehow terrifying.

Even the authorities who issed the orders confining women to La Force's cells considered its conditions grim. The building was dilapidated. Its foul odors and humidity were notorious, and there was no ventilation to speak of. Each cell had a single window, only two feet wide, with bars. Windows were up high near the ceiling, so prisoners might perhaps have glimpsed, at most, a fragment of sky.

La Force's overcrowding was as well-documented as the nauseating smells that filled its corridors. Up to six women shared a bed meant to sleep four, with two at the head and two at the foot. The inmates who had been incarcerated longest automatically claimed the spots on the bed, and those who found no room slept on the stone floor. Cells were barely wide enough to accommodate a bed, leaving hardly enough space to squeeze in two inmates on the floor. Prisoners sometimes divided the night in half and took turns sleeping in the bed in groups of three. Blankets were distributed only in winter.

The rhythm of daily life was dictated by the woman who was in charge of the facility during all the years of Manon Fontaine's confinement there, the prison's longest-serving director, the notoriously harsh *baillie* (warden), Marguerite Pancatelin. After the wake-up bell sounded at five a.m., prayers were held in the dormitory, and the prisoners then had a half hour to deal with "their personal hygiene." From six to seven, they attended Mass. They were next allotted fifteen minutes "to satisfy their personal needs" and given a little water to wash their hands. Work began immediately afterward. Most inmates spent their days at needlework: sewing, embroidery, lace-making. At eight a.m., they were authorized some wine and "a bit of bread." It was then back to work until eleven, when watery soup was distributed. Work then continued nonstop until seven p.m., at which time inmates were given their only water of the day to drink and a second "bit of bread." After prayers in the dormitory, at nine thirty, they went to bed. Sunday was a special day: they were awakened only at six.

Discipline was, in the words of one lieutenant general of the Parisian police, "severe," and the worst treatment of all was reserved for women incarcerated for prostitution. Not long after Manon Fontaine's stay in the Salpêtrière, a Parisian roofer named Michel Cotel had his eighteen-year-old daughter imprisoned there on prostitution charges. Three months later, he begged for her release because he had found her "in the most pitiful state conceivable." The conditions in the prison, Cotel wrote in his petition, were "so much worse than [he] ever could have imagined." He had hoped to have her behavior "corrected," he explained; instead, "she was in danger of losing her life."[7]

MANON FONTAINE'S LIFE CAN BE DIVIDED INTO THREE ROUGHLY equal periods. For nineteen years, she lived in Paris, the city of her birth, growing up in poverty and working at menial, back-breaking jobs. She spent the next nineteen years in prison, mainly in the Salpêtrière's squalor. The event that brought the second period to an end took place on November 22, 1718. By then, Manon had been incarcerated in La Force for nearly seventeen years.

During all those years, there was once again not a blemish on her record, but on that November day, she somehow incurred the wrath of the tyrannical Marguerite Pancatelin. Pancatelin was well established in her half-century of uncontested rule over women detained in the Salpêtrière. Her position guaranteed her an income, living quarters, and a degree of independence and status otherwise difficult to attain for an unmarried woman at that time. Pancatelin had even been able to supplement her revenue by selling, often at hefty prices, the finest needlework produced by inmates in her prison.[8] Prior to late 1718, even though numerous accounts confirm the image of a repressive and abusive warden, Pancatelin's absolute authority appears to have gone unchallenged.

Then, there came what Pancatelin termed the "sedition" that erupted in her prison. Pancatelin described the events of November 22 as "a seditious revolt," "a great uprising" organized by "three creatures armed with knives who had slashed fellow prisoners and guards alike." In a sensationalistic account of the uprising, Pancatelin conjured up a lurid vision: three blade-wielding "creatures" had revolted against their guards, one of whom had been wounded in the melee. According to Pancatelin's unverified version of what transpired, the seditious women had threatened corrections officers at knifepoint, all the while "swearing and screaming the kind of blasphemies against God that make one's hair stand on end." One of the revolt's instigators had tried to kill a second one and had succeeded in gashing her shoulder, before she herself had her head bashed in by the woman she had stabbed. Numerous prisoners had suffered injuries before the arrival of armed soldiers. Even with their vastly superior forces, the soldiers succeeded in "putting it down only with considerable difficulty."

Pancatelin's graphic evocation of a prison brawl is in no way coherent with either the prior or the subsequent records of the event's alleged ringleaders. The Bouquetière as serial killer invented by the soldiers at her 1701 trial might have become the woman who initiated a reign of terror in the Salpêtrière, but the real-life Manon Fontaine? Absolutely not. Yet when authorities took Pancatelin at her word, that mythic prison altercation became the foundation of France's first and only officially sanctioned program for the permanent banishment or deportation of female prisoners to its overseas colonies.

Pancatelin immediately had the three "creatures" placed in solitary confinement, chained to the floors of their cells, and limited their rations to bread, water, and "a small amount of soup." Pancatelin was aware that her treatment of the prisoners was exceptionally severe, so on November 23, she wrote to Louis Charles de Machault, who had been appointed lieutenant general of the Parisian police the previous January, to justify her actions. Machault was known as particularly uncompromising, a hard-liner who believed in cracking down on crime. He ran the Parisian police for only two years. It was during Machault's brief tenure that a radically new way of dealing with the women incarcerated in the Salpêtrière took shape.

In her appeal to Machault, Pancatelin called the revolt's leader "Manon Fontaine": this was the first time that a member of the French judicial system referred to "the Flower Girl" using her correct name.[9]

Since neither Machault nor d'Aguesseau's successor as *procureur général*, Guillaume François Joly de Fleury, had been active at the time of Manon Fontaine's arrest, Warden Pancatelin devoted the lion's share of her missive to an account of the crimes that had landed Fontaine in the Salpêtrière for life. Her report officially enshrined Manon Fontaine in the French judicial record as a dangerous repeat offender: "Entered [the Salpêtrière] by a royal decree dated March 27, 1702. This is a summary of that decree. This girl is accused of having assassinated the son of M. d'Autel by slashing him eighteen times with a knife, and of murdering several other men—a total of fifteen."[10]

On November 25, Machault assured Pancatelin that she had "done well" and that he would take the matter up with Maurepas—that is, Jean Frédéric de Phélypeaux, Comte de Maurepas, who earlier that year had been named at age seventeen head of the Maison du Roi, minister of the Royal Household. The Flower Girl had now attracted attention in the highest ranks of the government of a second king of France, Louis XIV's great-grandson Louis XV.

In the margin next to the purported summary of Fontaine's criminal past, Procureur Général Joly de Fleury wrote, "It will be necessary to obtain decrees of commutation of justice." Manon had been sentenced to life in the Salpêtrière, but after November 22 the king's lawyer began to consider substituting a brand-new option for the French judicial system—lifetime exile to a French colony across the Atlantic. This would be the ultimate form of permanent banishment from Paris, one from which there was virtually no return.

THE PLAN FOR LIFE SENTENCES IN LOUISIANA TOOK SHAPE IN December 1718. On January 2, 1719, Pancatelin addressed a formal request to the regent governing France until the eight-year-old Louis XV came of age, Philippe d'Orleans, for whom New Orleans had only recently been named. She "respectfully begged" authorization to "transfer" to the Salpêtrière's sister facility in the French port of Rochefort the three women guilty of insurrection on the grounds that they "were stirring up the other prisoners and encouraging them to revolt and threatening to knife her and her fellow officers to death."

The first of Fontaine's alleged accomplices was Marguerite Vallet, whom Pancatelin pronounced guilty of an extraordinary variety of crimes ranging from theft to being "the associate of counterfeiters and helping them bury the evidence of their crimes in Fontainbleau forest" and "an accomplice to all the murders committed in that forest." The second was Marie Anne Porcher, accused by Pancatelin of everything from theft to "public and scandalous prostitution in the streets [of Paris]," "cutting off the fingers of her arresting officers with a knife she had hidden in her sleeve," and setting her cell in the Salpêtrière on fire.

Pancatelin's initial request for a transfer from one royal prison to another was followed by a second such request, to move the three women from Rochefort to either of the principal French colonies in the Caribbean, Martinique or Saint-Domingue (today's Haiti). Joly de Fleury signed off on this request on January 3 and sent it on to Maurepas for the regent's signature.

By January 10, the regent had issued orders to the mayors and officials of all villages along the roughly three-hundred-mile route that separated Paris and Rochefort to supply food and fresh horses for a convoy; he also instructed the governor of Rochefort to hold the three women prisoner there until the first ship sailed "for the islands." Officials calculated the cost of sending three men—two armed guards and a soldier specially trained to deal with hardened criminals sentenced to the galleys—to accompany the three prisoners on a journey that they estimated would last eighteen days.

Once Pancatelin had managed to rid herself of three prisoners, her ambitions grew. Already on February 18, she submitted the names of fourteen additional candidates for exile "to the islands," "where it would be appropriate to detain them for the rest of their lives." As she explained, "This would disencumber the Salpêtrière and relieve the public of a burden." After Joly de Fleury approved this new list, Pancatelin went to him again, this time with the names of numerous other women incarcerated in her prison.

Pancatelin's ultimate list contains the names of 208 prisoners whom she pronounced "bonnes pour les îles," "fit for the islands." Whereas Warden Pancatelin piled on charges against Manon Fontaine and the other "seditious" women, almost every inmate on this list was described above all with one word: prostitute. On June 27, 1719, the regent officially approved the permanent exile from France of all 208 women, on the grounds of "their extraordinary moral depravity." By June 1719, however, even though official correspondence continued to read "the islands," the destination chosen as France's overseas penal colony had changed. When no ship sailing for the Caribbean islands had space for additional passengers, the women were redirected to a mainland settlement, an unspecified location in the vast and still largely undeveloped territory on the North American

31

continent named "Louisiana." In July, the three seditious women with whom the deportation project began, as well as the fourteen on Pancatelin's second list, were loaded onto a vessel named *Les Deux Frères*, *The Two Brothers*, bound for Louisiana. The crossing to Louisiana of that initial small contingent then became a model followed for the deportation of a far larger group of women chosen from Pancatelin's final list: these prisoners, too, were sent to Louisiana, this time on *La Mutine*.

MANON FONTAINE WAS THE FIRST AMONG THE WOMEN EXILED IN 1719 to have been arrested. In the request made to have her exiled, her police record was misrepresented and the charges against her were wildly distorted. Manon's case is exceptional because so much evidence has survived: of the thousands of trials carried out at the direction of the Parisian Parlement in the years between 1686 and 1701, Manon's 1701 prosecution is among only thirty whose records are now fully extant. Her case is, however, also typical, because the women with whom Manon was exiled received similar treatment.

Documentation survives on nearly all the deported women, and in many cases a complete police file still exists. We know the accusations made against them and do not have to rely on Pancatelin's summaries of their alleged records. Time and again, the dossiers of women labeled "depraved prostitutes" contain mere hearsay, backed up with no evidence. In almost every instance, not a shadow of guilt was uncovered. The police had at most either the testimony of witnesses who clearly bore a grudge against the accused, or only vaguely incriminating evidence that was never linked with certainty to the woman held for questioning.

In such circumstances, women of no consequence in the French social hierarchy—maids, menial workers in the textile trade, shopgirls—refused to sit back and become passive victims of a judicial system in which the deck was stacked against them. Most remained, just as Manon Fontaine did, defiant; they continued to proclaim their innocence and to defend their rights. Time and again, the dossiers of women labeled by Pancatelin "public prostitutes" and "among the most dangerous prostitutes" reveal behavior that was assertive and markedly unconventional in their day.

Some found themselves in prison because they had refused to practice trades that they felt did not suit their talents or because they had refused to continue in abusive workplace environments. They sought instead to live and work on their own terms. In so doing, they challenged the family members with authority over their lives: their fathers, their stepmothers, their brothers. Those family members retaliated by denouncing them to the police. Many of those dismissed as "fit only for the islands" were guilty above all of assertiveness.

Had Manon Fontaine attracted Pancatelin's attention but one year earlier, the warden could never have succeeded with her plan of "ridding" France of women she considered "fit" for an overseas penal colony but not for their homeland. In 1717, a Scottish economic theorist named John Law began to consolidate control over the French economy. Nothing Pancatelin accomplished could have happened before John Law's breakneck rise to power.

Chapter 2

John Law's Louisiana Gold Rush

In Paris, the year 1719 was characterized by what a prominent aristocrat who lived through it all described as "delirium,"
sheer "madness," a veritable carnival of money and speculation. In
an attempt to indicate how widespread that "delirium" became, Voltaire, who experienced the collective madness firsthand, called it "a
contagious disease, an epidemic." As the "contagious disease" of 1719
spread like wildfire through French society, Parisians went mad for
money and windfall profits.[1] And because this sickness was founded
on France's colonial ambitions, money madness sealed the fate of the
women who were deemed "fit for the islands."

The individual who engineered this money madness, Scotsman
John Law, was many things: a speculator, a gambler, a charlatan to
some, a visionary theoretician of money and finance to others. He

lived a life as flamboyant as his theories. In London, Law was convicted of murder after killing his opponent in a duel. He escaped from prison, fled England, and, adopting a series of aliases, flitted through Europe, bouncing from capital to capital, trying to launch various financial schemes, and seeking in particular a prince or a government willing to experiment with the introduction of paper currency and with the use of stock as what Law called "a new type of money, perhaps better than gold and silver."[2] Law had long cherished the dream of using the relatively conservative French economy as a proving ground for his most revolutionary theories, but Louis XIV and his ministers had repeatedly rejected his proposals. Then, after the Sun King's death in 1715, Law at last began amassing influence in France, as it became openly acknowledged that recent wars had saddled the country with a catastrophic public debt, estimated at 750 million *livres.* In an attempt to eliminate that debt, over the course of the next four years Law was given free rein to transform every aspect of French economic life.

The Regent Philippe d'Orléans believed in Law's ideas for reducing the national debt and encouraged his financial experiments. On May 20, 1716, Law was granted permission to establish France's first banking institution, the privately owned Banque Générale or General Bank. On April 10, 1717, its banknotes began to be accepted as currency.[3]

In August 1717, the monopoly on commerce with France's largest overseas colony, Louisiana, was granted to a new trading company also governed by Law, the Compagnie d'Occident or Company of the West. Law vowed to make France for the first time a major power in maritime commerce and the equal of its English and Dutch rivals. He pledged that trade with Louisiana would save the country from looming financial disaster.

---

* Debt and financial transactions were calculated in a money of account for which there was no equivalent coin: the *livre tournois*, called simply the *livre*. *Livre* means "pound"; to avoid confusion with the pound sterling, I'll use *livre*.

On December 4, 1718, at Law's request the General Bank was nationalized and renamed Banque Royale, the Royal Bank. Now a central bank overtly linked to the French monarchy, the Royal Bank was also controlled by John Law. Ten days later, the Company of the West absorbed the Senegal Company, which had enjoyed a monopoly over the slave trade between West Africa and the French West Indies. The following January 10, the Company of the West continued its expansion by incorporating the Ferme du Tabac or Tobacco Farm, the entity that regulated the sale of tobacco in France. Both these mergers were crucial to Law's dream of transforming Louisiana's status as a colony by introducing a new commodity—tobacco—and the slave labor he considered essential for making tobacco profitable.

On March 27, 1719, at the inaugural meeting of the directors of the Company of the West, Law explained that these recent takeovers would assure the success of his grand design for rebuilding the French economy. In 1719, France imported well over six million pounds of tobacco annually from English colonies near the Chesapeake Bay at a cost of roughly 2.5 million *livres*.[4] Law pledged that Louisiana tobacco would be of superior quality and fetch a higher price; the directors were guaranteed a million *livres* a month in profits. The sum Law promised was colossal, fully worthy of his grandiosity. At the very moment when he dangled the possibility of 12 million a year in earnings, Louisiana was being run on the cheap. The colony's chief financial officer had been pleading (until then unsuccessfully) for a meager 14,861 *livres* per annum to clothe all the military personnel stationed there—and for 2,550 *livres*, the paltry sum necessary to provide salt pork for the colony. During the more than dozen years of its stewardship over Louisiana, the Indies Company spent a total of only 20 million *livres*—and the sum covered everything from shipbuilding to salaries, from supplies for the colony's inhabitants to ammunition for its soldiers.[5]

Before Law's tenure, French authorities had refused to develop slavery on the Gulf Coast and in the Lower Mississippi Valley. In early

1719, there were at most a dozen enslaved Africans in the entire expanse of this vast French territory. When Law made tobacco central to his vision for the colony, realizing that enslaved Africans had become an essential part of the labor force in the Chesapeake Bay, he promised to send three thousand enslaved Africans to Louisiana. Law then used his new powers to redirect the French slave trade, and already on June 6, 1719, the first slave ships arrived in Louisiana. This one decision made on John Law's authority had momentous consequences: it ultimately rewrote the destiny of this country's second coast.

Law's pitch to his principal financial backers focused on tobacco. To rope in small investors, he devised a very different marketing strategy: using newspapers to promote the territory as a new land of milk and honey. Because Law counted on the irresistible attraction for these shareholders of what he termed "the craving for profits," he consistently stressed above all the colony's potential for quick returns on every investment.[6] Many prominent European papers were blatantly pro-Law, and none more so than the most widely read French periodical, the Parisian monthly *Le Nouveau Mercure Galant*. The issue for March 1719 featured a letter from a Frenchman newly arrived in Louisiana and sending news home for the first time. The account described the colony as "an enchanted land, where every seed one sows multiplies a hundredfold," "a place laden with gold and silver mines." In July, the *Mercure* announced the discovery of gold mines in the colony. Gazettes also reported that a sample of Louisiana silver had been tested at the Paris Mint and found to have silver content even higher than that of the fabled Potosí lode in Bolivia that had been a foundation of Spanish colonial wealth.[7]

Law's promotion of Louisiana as a new source of fine tobacco and a new El Dorado proved so wildly successful that, within months, he had created the first known modern financial bubble.

In May 1719, an edict merged Law's Company of the West and France's largest trading company by far, the Indies Company. From then on, Law presided over the expanded Indies Company and controlled every aspect of the country's overseas trade. On May 12 at the Royal Bank, shares in Law's Indies Company, the first publicly traded stock in French history, were offered at 500 *livres*. By then, Parisians were willing, even eager, to follow the monarchy's lead and entrust all their assets to John Law. When they rushed to the Royal Bank, in effect Law's Bank, to exchange their gold for banknotes, a contemporary observer remarked that they "threw their money at the cashiers with an impatience that would be difficult to describe."[8] By May 15, the bank had become such a mob scene that royal guards were moved from the Louvre for crowd control.

By May 22, the price of a share had risen to 600, two days later, to 650. By late August, shares had reached 4,100; by October 5, they stood at 5,000. On November 21, their price rose to 9,325. First in December and again in January 1720, shares peaked at just over 10,000.

During the months in 1719 when its stock was surging, Law's Company made some investors extremely wealthy, and it did so virtually overnight. By October, *Le Nouveau Mercure Galant* informed its readers that anyone who had invested 10,000 *livres* in Indies Company stock in May had become "a millionaire." For those who lived through fall 1719 in Paris, this first recorded use of the word "millionaire" conjured up a clear image: that of individuals, often "of humble birth," who in a matter of months had become unimaginably wealthy. Correspondences, diaries, and periodicals chronicled the mind-boggling displays of parvenu wealth that suddenly became part of the Parisian scene.

Brand-new millionaires might be spotted at the opera, "covered all over with diamonds." They might walk into a jeweler's, hand over 100,000 *livres* in newly minted bills, and ask that the shop's entire contents be delivered to their home. In early October, a woman who in only months had amassed 6 million in profits snapped up both a grand Parisian residence (for over 400,000 *livres* in cash) and a fine country estate (640,000, also in cash).[9]

The world's first millionaires were indebted to still another of Law's creations: Paris's first stock exchange. Prior to 1719, Paris had a currency exchange that operated for the benefit of merchants with foreign clients, but stock had never been publicly traded there. In August 1719, just as the price of stock in Law's company was about to surge, "an exchange for the commerce in Indies Company stock" was inaugurated in a house situated at number 65 on the rue Quincampoix.

Number 65 was destroyed in the nineteenth century during Baron Haussmann's redesign of Paris, but the rest of the rue Quincampoix remains much as it was in Law's day. The street is a stone's throw from the Halles market and only minutes from the New City. Still today, the rue Quincampoix is an unprepossessing street, slightly longer than those in surrounding areas such as the New City but, like them, narrow and lined with modest buildings. For a few months in late 1719, it was transformed from an ordinary working-class passageway into the stage for a new kind of urban theater, a freewheeling street market in which stock, rather than apples and bread, was bought and sold.

The contemporary engraving shown in Figure 4 recorded the mob scene that the rue Quincampoix became every day from eight a.m. to nine p.m. The houses along the street were rented out to traders, who sold stock from their offices. Since office space was cramped and the demand ever higher, trading often took place in the street itself. If a trader was willing to purchase stock at a price above its market value, he would ring a bell positioned on a pulley outside his office window and send agents into the street to buy shares from investors. If a trader wanted to sell below market value, he would blow a whistle. All day long, those bells and whistles fueled the perception that those who caught the tide at just the right moment could find instant wealth.

The specter of fast riches transformed well-heeled Parisians into an unruly swarm, and investors rushed in to fill every nook and cranny

Figure 4. Antoine Humblot depicted Parisians frantically buying shares of Indies Company stock during Mississippi mania.

of Law's stock exchange. In Antoine Humblot's depiction, armed guards have been stationed in the foreground to prevent others from forcing their way in. On the rue Quincampoix, new noises became part of the sounds of the city. Traders' bells and whistles and the clamors of the excited crowd begging to become part of Law's investment carnival provided a jarring counterpoint to the timeless cries of Paris's street vendors as the city danced to brand-new calls: the sounds of modern finance.

Two months after the stock exchange began operations, Antoine Louis Le Fèvre de Caumartin de Boissy, among the Crown's most trusted advisers, offered this commentary: "Those who own some Mississippi [stock] can talk only of that. In the beginning, it all seemed like a game; it has become a mania, a madness, a sickness. . . . These people, whose heads are filled only with the idea of profits and calculating their millions, are in the grips of a hot fever." Caumartin de Boissy's description of stock as "some Mississippi"—as well as the term "Mississippian," the name for someone who owned quantities of Indies Company stock, and the phrase "lords and ladies of Mississippi," used to characterize big investors spotted in Paris "completely swathed in diamonds"—shows that everyone realized that the investment mania holding Paris in its thrall was directly linked to the colony being developed along the Mississippi.[10] Mississippi madness also proved essential to the plan to exile women to the banks of the Mississippi itself. While Paris was overwhelmed by the "hot fever" of investment in "some Mississippi," the women singled out for deportation became victims of the collective greed.

IN DECEMBER 1717, WHEN LAW'S TAKEOVER OF THE FRENCH ECON-omy began, Louisiana's population, military personnel included, was likely only 550.[11] Making Louisiana the rival of England's tobacco-rich settlements would require many new colonists, as John Law knew well. Already in September 1717, Law had promised, as the London periodical the *Post Man* revealed, to "transport into the Louisiana 6,000" settlers, but it was only beginning in March 1719 that he at last began to fulfill that pledge.

That month, at the inaugural meeting of Law's Company of the West, its directors were informed that the company's first objective was "to promote the value and the safety of the colony of Louisiana by sending new recruits to live there." That objective immediately became the law of the land when, later the same month, a royal decree announced unprecedented policing policies in Paris: "The need that we have of inhabitants for our colonies has made us regard as a great good for our state . . . the arrest of paupers and the homeless who will be transported to our colonies and put to work there."[12] When patrolling the streets of Paris, the officers of the *guet*, the watch, could and did detain anyone found in the capital who was unable to produce on the spot proof of identity and employment. They were even able to detain those merely denounced by passersby. Parisians shared tales of the imprisonment of "upstanding citizens" and declared that such arrests were often inspired by "the basest jealousy," a claim borne out by the stories of many women who found themselves in the Salpêtrière and selected for deportation.[13]

By May 12, the day that Indies Company stock was initially offered, a new rumor was circulating: the king had given the Indies Company permission to take from Parisian prisons and orphanages "young people of both sexes."[14] Pancatelin's decision to compile a list of women for deportation attests to her realization that, as 1719 unfolded and John Law saw that it was proving far more difficult to find colonists for Louisiana than enslaved Africans, the company's all-powerful director was willing to authorize any means that would help him fulfill his promise to send six thousand French settlers.

The list is marked as having been *"arrêtée,"* or officially approved, on June 27, 1719. On July 9, Pancatelin wrote Lieutenant Général Machault, begging him to "honor her" with a visit to the Salpêtrière so that they could "share a morsel." Explaining that she had already begun preparations for the women's departure and that she hoped to expand her list, she asked him to bring the original copy with the regent's signature when he came to dine. Machault warned her that "because there was opposition, the departure of the women was still not certain."

Pancatelin knew why Machault was likely to be sympathetic to her scheme. Beginning in 1708, he had served as *intendant du commerce*, intendant of commerce, and as a member of the Conseil du Commerce, the Council of Commerce, the regulatory group that advised the Crown on matters of business and trade. After Louis XIV's death, the council focused on trade with France's overseas colonies as a means of dealing with the nation's gigantic debt, and all through 1717 it had debated Law's policies. When Machault took on the administration of the Parisian police in January 1718, he did not relinquish his other administrative posts. The individual in control of the fates of all women arrested in Paris and all women incarcerated in the Parisian prison system had therefore a personal stake in the success of Law's projects.

As soon as stock market fever took hold, all official opposition to the women's deportation disappeared. After Pancatelin got her green light, Machault proved just how valuable an ally he could be. In August and September 1719, officers under Machault's control arrested women at a rate so disproportionally higher than in previous or subsequent years that it seems all but certain that the officers on the beat had been encouraged to lock up women—however and whenever possible.

In August 1717, just prior to Law's consolidation of power, thirty-two women were detained in Paris and confined to the prison administered by the Parisian police, the Grand Châtelet. At all times, many women arrested were released for lack of evidence, and indeed twenty of the women detained in 1717 were soon set free, and only six (18 percent) were sent from the Grand Châtelet to serve terms in Pancatelin's prison. Yet in August 1719, under Machault's watch, those numbers shot up. Fifty-three women were arrested; of those, even though thirty-three were set free, twenty (37 percent) were incarcerated in the Salpêtrière. (In August 1720, the year after the women of *La Mutine* were deported, arrests of women dropped to the pre-Law level, totalling thirty-seven.)

In addition, the women dispatched to the Salpêtrière in August 1719 were dispatched with alacrity. Comparing August 1717 to August 1719, the number of days that elapsed between a woman's arrest and the date on which the order transferring her to the Salpêtrière was issued declined dramatically. During this crucial interval, officers typically interviewed witnesses and neighbors, checked out alibis, and prepared a file to be presented to the presiding official, who then pronounced judgment. In August 1717, in every case over a month was devoted to verifications. In contrast, in one case from August 1719, the entire process, from arrest to verdict, took place in only four days: on August 15, Anne Thérèse Valenciennes was brought to the Châtelet prison by officers of the watch; on August 19, Valenciennes was sent to the Salpêtrière.[15] In the two months between July 29 and September 30, 1719, eleven women detained by officers of the Parisian police were judged as summarily as Valenciennes, and, like her, transferred to the Salpêtrière. All eleven were then deported—with almost dizzying speed. The last woman transferred, Marguerite Letellier, left Paris in chains on October 6, only one week after her initial arrest. Marguerite was never transferred to the Salpêtrière but instead moved directly to the deportation convoy.

Marguerite had worked as a scullery maid in the household of Marguerite Hémart, Dame de Foucaucourt. In November 1712, after Hémart accused the nine-year-old of theft, the girl was imprisoned and ordered to pay a three-*livres* fine. Children worked for food and shelter rather than wages, so Marguerite could never have paid. Hémart next accused Marguerite of "threatening" her, and this time, the child was fined 30 *livres* for "reparations."

Marguerite was mere collateral damage in the matter that truly "threatened" Hémart's peace of mind: her eldest, heir to the family fortune, Adrien Morel de Foucaucourt, had fallen in love with another scullery maid, Françoise Letellier (Marguerite's sister), had had a son by her in 1711, and wanted to marry her. When Adrien's younger brothers had him banished from France in a bid to take control of the family estate, he took Françoise with him.

The seduction of a maid by a young nobleman who promised marriage was a classic tale, but as this story indicates, aristocrats sometimes did intend to keep their word and marry mere servants. In such cases, the servant, considered a menace to the social order, was severely punished. This time, after Adrien put Françoise out of his mother's reach, she took out her rage on another young woman. Five years later, in 1719, Adrien returned to Paris, and the family was once again up in arms. Just at that moment, Adrien's mother lashed out once again at Marguerite, by then sixteen, and had her detained and exiled.[16]

The last women arrested, Valenciennes and Letellier among them, were locked up by officers working in collaboration with the only female administrator in the Parisian prison system, Warden Pancatelin. They were apprehended specifically to be exiled to Louisiana and thereby curry favor with John Law. Even though none of their dossiers had been approved for deportation by the regent, all eleven names were added to the cohort of those set to leave Pancatelin's prison and France forever.

On Friday, September 1, the alliance between Pancatelin and Law that was the foundation of the deportation scheme received official recognition. John Law himself paid a visit to the Salpêtrière, requested more women for his colony, and pledged a donation: 1 million *livres*, a sum worthy of the age of Mississippi millionaires and a windfall that came with no strings attached. Observers added that he promised to return on January 1, 1720, with still another reward for Pancatelin's work on his behalf.[17]

In the fall of 1719, a lawyer for the Parisian Parlement concluded that the dream of instant wealth had thoroughly corroded French society: "There is no longer any honor, any word of honor, any good faith." A Parisian warned his sister living in the provinces that "Paris is no longer the city you once knew." In this world without honor, violence was everywhere, and Paris became a city of mean streets and roaming predators. There were high-profile murders in public and broad daylight—many of them committed on or near the rue Quincampoix, where wealthy investors were knifed to death for their cash. Another prominent lawyer reported that "the police have been fishing out of the river a great quantity of arms, legs, and sawed-off slices of those who have been assassinated and cut into pieces." He added that all Parisians knew why their city had changed: "Everyone blames the violence on the despicable speculation in paper."[18]

NO CONTEMPORARY OBSERVER SUGGESTED THAT YOUNG WOMEN faced any particular threats in those brutal times, but the records of the Parisian police tell a different story. They reveal a pattern common to all moments of sudden and extreme financial upheaval: a sharp uptick in violence against women.

In July and August 1719, when officers were actively rounding up candidates for Pancatelin's deportation scheme, another new type of criminality entered the records of the Parisian police. What officers described as "gangs of young men" roamed Paris, "insulting and mistreating" women. The parents of seventeen-year-old Manon Musquin sent a complaint detailing the manner in which one such gang was threatening their daughter and her friends. They had attacked Manon while she was praying in a church across the street from the Louvre, and after calling her "a whore and a slut who would fuck anyone," they struck her with their canes. Other parents alleged that gangs had knocked on their doors and then forced their way, at knifepoint, into private homes, and even into young women's bedrooms.[19]

Far from the rue Quincampoix, across the Seine in the newer neighborhoods on Paris's Left Bank, the crime wave of 1719 was just as inescapable—and, once again, the women of Paris seem to have been singled out. The enclosure of the abbey of Saint-Germain-des-Prés was known for its elegant high-end shops, many of which were owned and run by women. In 1719, the police were frequently called there to deal with a previously unknown kind of complaint. Women reported that men were rushing in without provocation, screaming insults at them, calling them beggars, whores, and brothel-keepers. Intruders punched them and beat them with their canes.[20]

During the months of financial frenzy, young women in Paris were in danger in their workplaces; they were in danger in public settings such as the Tuileries gardens, and even in churches. They were in danger from the officers of the Paris Watch, who were being encouraged to arrest them; they were in danger from marauding gangs and random hooligans. And they may have been most in danger from their own families. A significant number of those who traveled on *La Mutine* found themselves on board because family members—fathers, mothers, brothers—had asked, indeed even begged, for their exile. Seeking to rid themselves permanently of an unwanted daughter or sister, they willingly put young women into Pancatelin's and Law's hands.

The first record of such a request arrived on Machault's desk on December 17, 1718: it was a milestone in the deportation process, Parisian parents begging that their daughter be taken by force to a colony an ocean away. The couple pleaded extreme poverty—the father described himself as a "poor tailor"—and insisted that they had done everything possible "to correct" the behavior of their twenty-one-year-old daughter. The couple accused their child of "incorrigible" conduct and of "living in debauchery." They asked that Marie Anne Boutin be incarcerated in the Salpêtrière, and then "*la faire partir aux îles*," "have her sent to the islands."

For the Boutins to make such a petition, and at that time, was absolutely extraordinary. Joly de Fleury, Machault, and Pancatelin had after all begun preliminary discussions about Manon Fontaine's "transfer to the islands" not even three weeks before. Confronted for the first time with the idea that parents might willingly collaborate in an effort to rid France of undesirable women, even Machault hesitated. He asked Commissioner Louis Jérôme Daminois to look into the Boutins' unsubstantiated claims. Daminois turned up no proof, but nonetheless quickly confirmed the parents' allegations. Machault then instructed Daminois to bring Marie Anne in for a talk. But instead of complying, Marie Anne "tore up the order and said she had nothing to tell him." Machault could never have suspected that, just like the Boutins' heartlessness, Marie Anne's defiance in the face of parental betrayal was a harbinger.

Marie Anne's noncompliance sealed her fate. That same day, Machault pronounced a categorical verdict: "You could not find a better place than the Salpêtrière for this kind of libertine." The following day, Marie Anne Boutin was arrested "in the presence of her father and her mother."[21]

Five months later, when Pancatelin added Marie Anne Boutin's name to her list of women "fit for the islands," she included accusations found nowhere in her file, calling Marie Anne "a known public prostitute, who had committed debauchery with a married man." With Pancatelin and Machault's help, the Boutins' wish was fulfilled, and Marie Anne left France as passenger 96 on *La Mutine*.

The Boutins' petition ends conditionally—"*si faire se peut*," "if there is a way to do this"—and with good reason. In December 1718, no one, certainly not a "poor tailor," could have imagined that such a request would ever become feasible. In the madness of 1719, as the unthinkable moved ever closer to reality, requests like the Boutins' became familiar to Machault and his officers. March 1719 was the first month during which more than one reached Machault's desk. The earliest petitions concerned predominantly sons. Then, in June and July, as Law's stock began its upswing, the notion of sending a child to Louisiana gained momentum, and appeals increasingly involved daughters.

As the volume of petitions increased, the royal ministers to whom they were addressed became ever more suspicious of parental motivations. One minister remarked: "It's always a good idea to find disinterested persons who can give an account of the situation." For example, on June 14, when the Comte de Chamilly, commander of La Rochelle, received an appeal from a father seeking his son's exile, he asked Machault to search for a financial incentive that could have inspired the request. Machault learned that the son had received an inheritance guaranteeing him an annual income of 900 *livres*, money the father wanted to appropriate. When his son refused to relinquish the funds, the father had him imprisoned and requested exile to Louisiana.

Machault began to share Chamilly's suspicions, and whenever a family's petition to exile a son reached him, he instructed his commissioners to dig more deeply into parental motives.[22] Because of this instinct, numerous young men were spared exile to Louisiana.

Women were not so lucky. Parents' charges against their daughters, no matter how wild, were never closely scrutinized. Not once did anyone—a minister, a police commissioner, Machault—question the motives that might have inspired parents to request exile to Law's colony for their daughters.

By August 4, 1719, when the parents of Marie Chevalier decided to get her out of their lives, the process by which women were deported to Law's colony was a well-oiled machine. Like Marie Anne Boutin's, Marie Chevalier's parents stressed their poverty. Her father was a day laborer who loaded and unloaded ships in the Port de Saint-Paul, a small port at the end of the rue Saint-Paul, across from the Île Saint-Louis. He and his wife had three children, of whom Marie was the eldest. They alleged that for years Marie had stolen anything she could get her hands on. Marie had no police record, and her parents offered no evidence to support their assertion of what the police later termed her "great greed."

Marie worked as a laundress, a profession whose female workforce was particularly vulnerable to accusations of theft. Laundresses were obliged to go in and out of households to collect and deposit laundry. If anything was found missing, everyone seemed instinctively to blame the laundress. Marie was a day worker in the employ of various women who ran services, including a woman named Thomir, who one day hired her to help deliver laundry to the Portuguese embassy. Sometime later, the ambassador's wife accused Thomir of having stolen a diamond-studded cross and furthermore claimed to have "lost" a ribbon, a pair of shoes, and shoe buckles in an earlier theft. Thomir attempted to shift the blame onto Marie, so she arrived at the Chevalier home and threatened her employee. She offered a detail that sealed Marie Chevalier's fate: Thomir *"aurait trouvé,"* "claimed to have found," the diamond-studded cross under Marie's mattress. Marie's parents begged Machault to "put her in the Salpêtrière and to send her as soon as possible to the Mississippi in order to avert the great dishonor that she would inevitably bring on her family."

The Chevaliers got their wish, and very quickly indeed, for Marie was among those whose August 1719 lockup was expedited. No suspicion was ever cast on Thomir or anyone else; no evidence other than the conveniently found cross turned up—not that there was any kind of investigation. Only two days elapsed between Marie's arrest and her incarceration. Already on August 15, Marie was taken to the Salpêtrière; she left there on October 14, part of a chain gang of women bound for Le Havre, a port far larger than the one where her father worked.[23] And when *La Mutine* set sail on December 12, 1719, Marie Chevalier left France forever.

On February 5, 1720, three weeks before *La Mutine* made landfall, a new comedy had its premier in Paris. Alain René Lesage and Jacques d'Orneval's *Arlequin, roi des ogres, Harlequin, King of the Ogres*, premiered at the Foire Saint-Germain, the wildly popular annual fair that attracted huge crowds to the grounds of Paris's Saint-Germain-des-Prés Abbey. Spectators from across the social spectrum were treated to the story of Harlequin's arrest in Paris, along with "200 honest young men and women," all of whom were then shipped off to the Mississippi. The décor shifted to represent "an island inhabited by ogres," the setting for the play's most chilling scene. Harlequin describes the island's ogres preparing to eat a young girl only recently apprehended in Paris. The creatures discuss how they'll cook her up: Should they roast her on a spit? Serve her with a sauce? Or simply poach her?[24] The play's audience surely included spectators who, just months earlier, had begged that their own daughters be banished to the islands of the land they called "the Mississippi."

Chapter 3

"Merchandise" for Louisiana

EVERYTHING ABOUT THE PROCESS IMPLEMENTED TO RID AN overcrowded Parisian women's prison of detainees by shipping them off across an ocean was ill-considered, muddled, and bungled—in every way and at every moment.[1] It was also riddled with corruption: virtually all police officers involved were on the take, willing to do or say anything for the right price.

The entire sorry saga was rooted in one woman's tyrannical rule over the Parisian detention center for women, devised as a punishment for three prisoners whom she considered insufficiently compliant. Deportation was initiated on a tiny scale—just those three women—then grew to include a few more. The process seemed to culminate in the transportation of a small group of prisoners aboard *Les Deux Frères*, but in a second phase, it was vastly expanded—still without forethought and oversight. The second time, deportation led to the crossing of a far larger contingent of women—on *La Mutine*.

The operation epitomized the frenzy, the greed, and the systemic malfeasance that characterized the year 1719.

Marguerite Pancatelin was so eager to take advantage of a window of opportunity that made it possible for her to cast off troublesome inmates that she regularly confused women's names and even entire dossiers. She often referred to one prisoner by another's name; she misidentified and misattributed their alleged crimes. (Her signature was that of someone who possessed only minimal writing skills, and her reading ability may have been limited as well.)

Pancatelin's efforts were consistently aided and abetted by the high government officials responsible for scrutinizing and signing off on the project. All of them accepted without question the notion that any woman Pancatelin singled out was incontrovertibly unworthy of being allowed to remain in France. As a result, officials seldom bothered to verify any of the information Pancatelin passed along, particularly what she alleged were accurate summaries of prisoners' police files. Throughout the French judicial system, Pancatelin's assessments of the women's lives became the absolute truth. On the rare occasions when Lieutenant Général Machault or Procureur Général Joly de Fleury did ask someone to investigate a claim, the officer assigned to the case instantly responded that all was in order.

Because of the carelessness of authorities at every stage in the process, a number of women were deported to Louisiana under incorrect names. The majority of the women were illiterate and thus unable to verify written statements. The spelling of their names indicates that many of them had heavy regional or Parisian working-class accents: their arresting officer had simply inscribed their names as he imagined them, and his error was then recopied again and again. In this way, Marie Baron, an illiterate teenager from a village near Chartres, traveled under the name "Marie Boron." It's easy to imagine a young woman, alone and frightened, who, when questioned about her name, mumbles an answer; an impatient police officer quickly records something that corresponds to what he thinks he heard. In some cases, legal documents from their subsequent lives in Louisiana make it possible to correct the official record and reestablish the women's identities. But we may never know exactly which female prisoners were sent from Paris to John Law's Louisiana in 1719.

This confusion was evident from the start. On November 23, 1718, the day after the alleged uprising in the Salpêtrière, Pancatelin submitted the names of the women she called its instigators to request Machault's approval for their continued solitary confinement: Manon Fontaine, Marguerite Vallet, and a prisoner Pancatelin referred to as "Marie Anne Porcher, *dite* Chevalier." In almost all instances, the identification "*dite*," "known as," was used in police documents to signify that a woman was married; "known as" indicated the name of her husband. Occasionally, "*dite*" designated a nickname by which the person was known, so that someone from the Picardy region might be "known as *la Picarde*," the woman from Picardy. In subsequent correspondence and official documents, "Chevalier" was never again mentioned, and, depending on who was referring to her, the woman's name was written variously: Porcher, Poyer, Proche.

In Pancatelin's version of her police record, Porcher had been convicted of theft; she had also allegedly run a prostitution ring, in which she offered "very young girls" to "*le premier venu*," "the first man who came along." A police file whose cover reads "Marie Anne Porcher" contains little more than the account of her life sent by the woman herself in May 1716 to then Lieutenant Général d'Argenson, begging for his help, an account in which the prisoner spoke of herself as "Marie Anne Poyer." Marie Anne Poyer's explanation of how she ended up in the Salpêtrière had nothing in common with Pancatelin's lurid vision. She described herself instead as still another victim of a family member's financial greed and offered up a tale all too familiar in eighteenth-century France—she portrayed her stepmother as a young second wife seeking to disinherit a child from her deceased husband's first marriage.

Poyer alleged that after her father's death, rather than give her the money due her from his estate, her stepmother had had her confined in the Salpêtrière. D'Argenson asked Pancatelin to look into the matter; she replied that the father of the woman she persisted in calling "Porcher" was very much alive, and that the young woman herself had long ago run away from home and begun to "devote herself to debauchery." The prisoner claimed to have a handicap (her description sounds like epilepsy); Pancatelin said she had venereal disease. In a case riddled with such fundamental contradictions, how is it possible to be certain of the identity of the woman whose name appears on the manifest of the ship that took her from France as "Marie Anne Proche"?[2]

By January 1719, when John Law's economic takeover was gathering steam, Pancatelin's project had gone beyond simple solitary confinement. She was planning to move the three initial detainees to the French port city of Rochefort, from which Indies Company vessels departed for far-flung destinations. The permanent banishment of female prisoners to French transatlantic colonies was then envisioned for the first time.

French authorities set no ground rules; no one considered the exact terms on which female detainees were to be shipped off "to the colonies" or even what the authorities should call the process they were establishing. Instead, throughout 1719, both the nature of the sentence and its name changed constantly. That fundamental instability is still another result of the haste in which this was all done.

BY 1719, ONE POLICY OF FORCED EMIGRATION, KNOWN AS "TRANS-portation," had existed in England for a full century. Transportation was carried out on a large scale—perhaps fifty thousand convicts were sent to colonies in North America alone. It was also broad-based geographically: prisoners were taken from penitentiaries in a number of cities, and they were sent to various settlements along the Eastern Seaboard. But it was above all clearly defined. Convicts transported to English colonies went as indentured servants, and once in the colonies, they almost always remained in servitude until their term was up, at the end of which they were allowed to return to England.[3] Even though in 1719, John Law, someone with direct experience with English practices, was gaining control over France's economy, French officials were apparently uninformed about this precedent.

At least as surprising is the fact that authorities were also seemingly unaware of the only two earlier French policies that could have been seen as related to transportation—most conspicuously the *filles du roi*. In the decade between 1663 and 1673, an official royal program financed the travel of some 750 to 800 Frenchwomen to New France (the eastern part of today's Canada). These women, now known as *filles du roi*, "the King's daughters," for the most part in their early twenties, often came from charitable institutions (orphanages, in particular) in Paris and the surrounding area. All these young women emigrated voluntarily; they traveled in the best possible conditions, with no stigma attached to their journey; above all, they knew exactly why they were being sent across an ocean. At a moment when Louis XIV and his ministers made increasing the population of Canada a clear priority, the King's daughters were sent there for the express purpose of marrying and producing the next generation of colonists.[4]

There was a second, still-ongoing strategy devised soon after John Law began to accumulate power. In late 1717, the French government began to exile to the island colonies in the Caribbean men accused of either of two crimes: desertion from the French Army or smuggling contraband goods. In 1718, the initiative gradually picked up steam, and in 1719 the full-scale deportation of male prisoners to a new destination—Louisiana—began. These men were sent to the colony on Indies Company ships along with families of settlers who were traveling there of their own volition. The Indies Company transported the wives and children of married prisoners at the company's expense. Male prisoners were treated for all intents and purposes like colonists who had freely chosen to emigrate.

Unlike their male counterparts, the women's marital status was never discussed. In the early years of French Louisiana, numerous officials in the colony repeatedly voiced their concern about what one termed "the concubinage among Frenchmen and Native American women" and asked that Frenchwomen be sent there to curb this problem and to create a more stable colony.[5] But unlike "the King's daughters" in the 1660s, the prisoners taken from the Salpêtrière in 1719 were never once described as prospective brides or mothers. In 1719, French authorities only considered how to get rid of these unwanted women. At no time was either their future in the colony or the role they might play in its development envisioned.

At first, the terminology used to characterize this new venture in forced emigration likewise betrayed no knowledge of precedent. Officials discussing Pancatelin's proposals spoke simply of "sending" women outside France. They then switched to a term with legal significance: "to transfer." The women would be "transferred" from the Salpêtrière to the colonies just as prisoners were transferred from one prison to another in France, the authorities decided, suggesting thereby that the country's overseas territories could be seen as the equivalent of a French prison.

Then, in September 1719, these same officials suddenly began to speak of prisoners to be "*déportés*," "deported."[6] They did so seemingly by accident, apparently oblivious to the fact that they were now using a vocabulary without modern precedent. Whereas "deportation" had a clear definition in ancient Roman law, in 1719 the term was nonexistent in French law—and not employed by French speakers without extensive knowledge of Latin and Roman law. Since some of those regulating the new policy, notably Procureur Général Joly de Fleury, did possess this knowledge, they surely realized that under Roman law, deportation was the most extreme form of banishment and that it was originally reserved for the gravest political offenses such as treason. They also realized that Roman deportation took a form remarkably similar to what they were planning: forcible removal, usually to an island—an uninhabited island, if possible—for life. Joly de Fleury initially agreed to the proposal of permanent exile to "the islands" for all the women presented to him as "seditious" at the same time as he refused to banish prisoners for whom Pancatelin sought "admission to the ranks of those who are destined for the islands" who were not characterized as "seditious." At deportation's inception, like the Romans, Joly de Fleury considered a revolt against authority the only justification for deportation.[7]

But while the ancient Romans deported political prisoners to islands in the Mediterranean, places well-known and near at hand, the women's final destination was bandied about vaguely and haphazardly. Although on January 2, 1719, Joly de Fleury suggested that they be sent to the place he called, using an out-of-date spelling, "Loysiane," by February 2, he spoke instead of "the islands of Martinique and Saint-Domingue" (today's Haiti). It was only in September, at the moment when the new policy was first called "deportation," that French authorities agreed that the prisoners were to be sent to the colony they referred to as "*la Louisiane*," "Louisiana," or "the islands of Louisiana."

Nowhere in the discussions was there any attempt to raise what should have seemed fundamental legal questions. Many women, for example, were married, and under French law it was illegal to separate them permanently from their husbands. No official, however, brought this up or wondered what their status would be in the colonies. (The women settled the question themselves when they remarried and made no mention of any previous unions.)

Then, there was the most crucial legal matter of all—the terms of their detention. Joly de Fleury never budged on one key point and insisted that the women would be banished in perpetuity and could never again set foot on French soil. This explains why he initially questioned some of Pancatelin's suggested candidates. It "would not be just," he objected, to transport Marguerite Vallet, sentenced to merely two years in the Salpêtrière. He quickly decided, however, that "because of [her participation in] the uprising" her sentence could be modified. And so it went. One after another, women who had received only relatively light sentences and whose arrest records had been distorted by Pancatelin every bit as much as that of Manon Fontaine found their punishments, in Joly de Fleury's words, "commuted" so that they could be banished in perpetuity. And the Crown's chief legal counselor equivocated in similar fashion on other crucial points as well. Joly de Fleury at first decreed that once the women reached the colonies, they were "to be held in detention for the rest of their lives," yet on February 15, he added a crucial annotation in the margin of Pancatelin's first list: *Liberté aux colonies,*" "freedom in the colonies." From then on, no authority questioned the notion that when they reached their destination, French convict women were to be neither incarcerated nor indentured.

Already on January 3, the exile of the three women Pancatelin had presented as the ringleaders of the violent uprising was approved. Even though all had been in solitary confinement and shackled to the floor of their cells since November, in a letter to Machault, Joly de Fleury repeated Pancatelin's account and alleged that the warden and her assistants remained at risk because "all three were threatening to knife them to death."

A week later, an elaborate organization had been put into place to guarantee that these three dangerous "creatures" could not escape while still on French soil: the woman once known as the Flower Girl, a possible epileptic, and Marguerite Vallet, who, had she, as Pancatelin charged, served as the trusted accomplice of notorious highway robbers and counterfeiters, would surely have been sentenced to more than two years' imprisonment. The mayors and officials of every town on the road from Paris to Rochefort were informed of this terrifying convoy's imminent passing. The Comte de Chamilly, the provincial governor responsible for the port of Rochefort—the traditional home of France's Atlantic fleet and the point of departure for ships bound for its colonies in the Caribbean—was ordered to intern the high-profile convicts in the city's prison until passage could be found for them "on the next ship to set sail for Martinique or Saint-Domingue."[8]

Eighteen days were allowed for their roughly three-hundred-mile journey from Paris to Rochefort. For three women who for six weeks had been kept in solitary confinement and fed solely, in Pancatelin's own words, "bread, water, and a bit of soup," those eighteen days spent traveling through the French countryside in the dead of winter were a fitting beginning to a journey across the Atlantic that took them to their destination more than a year later. Every inch of the way, they were treated in the manner France reserved for its most dangerous criminals.

In the late seventeenth century, France had become the last European power to resort to a singular sentence for hardened lawbreakers repeatedly convicted of capital crimes. Their death sentences were commuted to hard labor rowing in the galleys that departed from the southern port of Marseille. Men destined for the galleys made the journey from Paris on foot and bound to each other to form what were called "*chaines*," "chains." That well-established system was adopted to transfer the three prisoners to Rochefort; thereafter, it was used for every journey made by convict women in 1719.

The three women, and all subsequent female prisoners, traveled in carts or tumbrels rather than on foot, but they left Paris chained to each other at the waist and with armed guards chosen from the ranks of those who escorted male convicts. Police officers loved the trips to Marseille because they were highly profitable—guards were paid by the head and by the day. There was also ample opportunity for graft. Money was budgeted to purchase supplies along the way, but there was no incentive to spend much of it on the prisoners, and a penny saved was a penny in a guard's pocket. The officer initially assigned to accompany the women refused the job, however, because he was offered much less than he would have made accompanying those known as "*galériens*," "galley slaves." Officials were planning to manage this female variant of convict transport on the cheap.[9]

As soon as Pancatelin won approval for the exile of the three alleged ringleaders of the November sedition, she declared that her absolute authority had been challenged once again. This time, the revolt was at least verified by an outside source—although not an objective one. A police report was filed, contending that sixteen inmates had "rebelled" against the conditions of their detention in the Salpêtrière and had very nearly succeeded in breaking free.[10] After Pancatelin requested that these women, too, be sent "to the islands," in early February, a second deportation project was initiated. Pancatelin submitted to Machault a list containing fourteen new names: "A record of several women whom the Salpêtrière could get rid of by sending them to the islands of Martinique or Saint-Domingue." Once again, Pancatelin described the prisoners as "seditious." Once again, she got her way. On February 27, it was announced that the alleged ringleaders of the November revolt were no longer to sail alone but in the company of fourteen women said to have "rebelled" two months later. This document, too, seems hurriedly thrown together—Joly de Fleury simply scribbled comments in the margin next to each woman's name.

Pancatelin drew up a brief profile for every prisoner she was proposing for exile. Each account reveals the same distortions and deceptions found in her portrayal of the first woman singled out for deportation, Manon Fontaine. The full extent of Pancatelin's misrepresentations becomes apparent when her presentations of the crimes of which each woman had been convicted is juxtaposed with a reconstruction of each prisoner's story based on surviving police files and legal proceedings.

1. "Marie Duclos, also known as Geneviève Dudrumay, 22, arrested 1717. Twice flogged and branded for theft."

A woman named "Geneviève Dudrumay" was arrested in 1717, but nothing identifies her with the woman known in police archives as "Marie Duclos." The first entry on Pancatelin's list illustrates clearly the manner in which Pancatelin, whether intentionally or not, conflated the records of different prisoners.

Although accused of breaking and entering, Marie Duclos claimed never to have taken anything of value. Indeed, rather than for theft, as Pancatelin alleged, Duclos was convicted of *"évasion de prison,"* "prison break," an infraction she had pulled off more than once. Unlike Manon Fontaine, Duclos was demonstratively proficient with a blade: she could, by her own admission, "unscrew the hinges on a door with a knife." She could even "bore right through a door with a knife," as she had done to break out of the prison in Bagnolet, a small town on the outskirts of Paris, where her exploits earned her fans, including the village coachman, who had helped arrange her escape.[11]

2. *"Catherine Oudart, also known as Cadiche, 30, arrested 1718. Twice flogged and branded for theft."*

The name "Cadiche" does not appear in the record of the woman named "Catherine Oudart." Pancatelin had once again misrepresented a prison file.

Catherine Oudart was married to a soldier, a key fact that Pancatelin failed to record. Like Duclos, Oudart was accused of breaking and entering, but the offense for which she had been whipped and branded was that all too common violation—that of having returned to Paris while she was officially banished.[12]

3. *"Marie Igonnet, also known as Dauvergne, 26. Incarcerated in perpetuity by the Parisian Parlement in 1710."*

Pancatelin did not mention the charges against Marie Igonnet, and there was good reason for her omission. In 1710, Marie had been convicted by a provincial parliament of a singular offense, *"divine lèse-majesté."* Literally "an affront to the dignity of a ruler," *lèse-majesté* referred to crimes such as treason; an offense called *"divine lèse-majesté"* was not on the books. After Igonnet was sentenced to be burned alive at the stake, her appeal came to the Parisian Parlement, which modified her sentence—she was to be strangled "secretly" before the pyre was lit.

After that verdict, d'Aguesseau, the royal prosecutor responsible for Manon Fontaine's conviction, took it upon himself to visit Igonnet in prison. Igonnet, referred to by police officers as "d'Auvergne" because of her birth in a tiny village in a mountainous area of Auvergne, easily the country's poorest and most isolated region, was the most unsophisticated and ill-educated of all the women on Pancatelin's various lists. After he had interrogated her in her cell, d'Aguesseau reported that the conditions of her long detention in Paris's notorious Conciergerie prison had been so harsh that "she seemed to have lost her mind, so much so that she awakened our pity"—and d'Aguesseau was not given to expressions of compassion for the plight of those incarcerated in Paris's prisons.

Marie Igonnet's father was a weaver. As she testified during her appeal, "she helped him in his work" by looking after the altar cloths in their hamlet's church. If she found damage, she took the cloth home for mending. During one inspection, Marie noticed that the key to the tabernacle had been forgotten on an altar cloth. She used that key, and she paid dearly for her curiosity. Marie noticed that the *ciboire*, the vessel in which consecrated hosts are locked away after Mass, had been damaged: it was, in her words, "all lumpy and smashed up," so she decided that, like that cloth, it needed repair. The seventeen-year-old made the thirteen-mile journey to the nearest town, Saint-Flour, on foot to carry the ciborium to the region's only goldsmith for restoration. The jeweler immediately called the police, who promptly accused Marie Igonnet of theft.

Upon interrogation, Marie explained that it was only once she returned home that she had opened the ciborium and realized that it contained consecrated hosts. Did she panic? Was she so starving that she lost control? When the police asked what happened next, Marie responded simply that she "had eaten them." Her judges chose the term *"divine lèse-majesté"* to justify burning her alive at the stake at the main entrance to her parish church.

In 1710, authorities in Louis XIV's France were on high alert for any whiff of freethinking or blasphemy: religious orthodoxy was an absolute priority for the aging Sun King. But Marie Igonnet's testimony reveals not a trace of radical thought; her gesture had nothing in common with the acts performed by those called "libertines" to challenge the Catholic Church's doctrines. Marie Igonnet "ate" those hosts at the end of a winter so harrowing that it was remembered as the Great Winter of 1709 to 1710.

Beginning in late 1708, temperatures in France were the coldest on record. By the summer of 1709, the price of wheat was over five times what it had been a year before. At the end of 1709, a parish priest in a provincial village left this dire notation: "This year there was no wheat at all."[13] Famine became so widespread that France was overwhelmed by hordes of starving people wandering the countryside in search of food. In the year between January 1709 and January 1710, the country's mortality rate was 40 percent higher than average.[14] Bread was the absolute staple of the French diet, and the average woman consumed a pound and a half of it per day. In late 1709 and in one of the country's poorest and coldest regions, when Marie Igonnet found that key, it had undoubtedly been a long time since she'd seen any bread. The hosts then used in the Catholic liturgy were larger and doughier than modern ones. In a conflict between orthodoxy and starvation, starvation won out.

After d'Aguesseau, in his own words, "chastised the Parlement" for what he considered an incomprehensible verdict, Marie's sentence was changed to life imprisonment in the Salpêtrière. Nine years later, her dossier caught Pancatelin's eye.[15]

4. "Marie Françoise de Jouy de Palsy, 17, royal orders [lettres de cachet], 1718. For debauchery and violence."

The youngest passenger on Pancatelin's list belonged at the other extreme of the social spectrum from Marie Igonnet and Manon

Fontaine. The family name that Pancatelin entered as "de Jouy de Palsy" and that subsequently appeared on the manifest of the ship on which she crossed the Atlantic as "Coutelier de Perty" was actually "Le Coustelier de Jouy de Palsy." Marie Françoise was the youngest member of a venerable noble family, one that possessed numerous châteaux and estates: her mother flaunted "the services rendered by her ancestors to Henri IV and Louis XIV." As far as Marie Françoise was concerned, however, her lineage was worthless.

When her father, Louis Le Coustelier, died, two sons from his first marriage divided the family estate; he also left four children from a second union. Françoise Chopin, his third wife and Marie Françoise's mother, was allowed to reside in a family château, Palsy, during her lifetime; upon her death, her only child would be entirely dependent on her half siblings' generosity and could have expected crumbs at best, perhaps not even lodging, and certainly no dowry. Marie Françoise saw the writing on the wall.

While her mother was briefly absent, the seventeen-year-old made a carefully planned escape. On April 27, 1718, Marie Françoise slipped away, reached the nearest market town on foot, and proceeded to sell her only possessions, the clothes on her back—in her case, the dress that, because of the many yards of fine fabric it required, was the most valuable part of an aristocratic woman's attire. (She would have remained decently garbed in the shift, bodice, and underskirt that noblewomen wore under their dresses. Thus attired, she would have been virtually indistinguishable from working women.) Marie Françoise then continued on to Montereau, a town just over fifty miles from Paris and at the confluence of the Yonne and the Seine rivers, the point of departure for a journey that was the speediest way of reaching the capital.

At Montereau, logs were gathered together into what were called "trains" and floated to Paris. The man her family sent to follow Marie Françoise's trail was on horseback: he explained that he had easily spotted her, perched atop a pile of logs, but that since the "trains" traveled nonstop and on the most direct route, he could not keep up. Marie Françoise reached her destination, and she enjoyed a few days of freedom in Paris before "an acquaintance of her mother" spotted her dressed in a manner hardly in keeping with her rank. Her mother and half siblings joined forces to beg the regent "to lock her up in La Force until they decide that she has changed her ways." On May 29, only a month after her escape, the Salpêtrière's gate slammed shut behind Marie Françoise.

The family had worked relentlessly to obtain the *lettres de cachet* or royal orders that guaranteed her incarceration.[16] Her half brothers stressed that "she had limited monetary resources"—without mentioning that they stood to profit financially from her detention. Her mother made only vague allegations: her daughter had often "behaved badly" and had "a ferocious temper." Their parish priest took it upon himself to add charges mentioned by no family member, contending that Marie Françoise was "addicted to wine and tobacco," "swore," and led "a libertine lifestyle." And when the regent granted the request made by "this family of ancient nobility," he invented still another accusation: "she gave herself over to debauchery." Eight months later, Pancatelin incorporated the regent's allegation into her request to have Marie Françoise sent away forever.[17]

5. *"Geneviève Hurault, 26, thief. Twice flogged and branded. Condemned to life imprisonment in 1715."*

Pancatelin once again failed to mention that a woman she proposed for deportation was married. Geneviève's first arrest, under the name Hurault, was in 1706; her alibi was confirmed and she was discharged. In 1715, under her married name, Champvallon, she was charged with the theft of "two silver forks embossed with a family crest." Even though she was never convicted of that crime, the Parisian police arrested her frequently in the years to come, and those silver forks were always evoked.

Although the official charge in the 1715 case was of having "stolen two silver forks," Geneviève Hurault's trial that year focused instead on the theft of a set of men's clothing. In her defense, Hurault, a laundress, explained that she had many clients, such as soldiers, who were often away from home. These clients left a key outside their door, so that she could go in and remove items to be washed and repaired, neatly wrapped up in her apron. She had not been stealing the clothing found on her at the time of her arrest, merely taking it away for cleaning.

Many of those who found themselves exiled to Louisiana were, like Geneviève Hurault, laundresses. Among the most vulnerable of all Parisian working women, laundresses often lived in dire poverty, barely scraping by. In 1710, in the moment of extreme deprivation brought on by the Great Winter, Commissioner Martin Marier arrested Hurault for the only crime of which she was clearly guilty, having eaten a plate of the rich beef stew called *boeuf à la mode* in a Parisian establishment and then sneaking out without paying since, as she admitted, "she didn't have a cent to her name." Just as happened with Marie Igonnet, and at the same time, starvation won out.

Marier described Geneviève Hurault as "a poor girl, tall, thin, and miserably attired in worn-out grey clothing in a cheap woolen fabric."[18] This was one of only two police accounts of any deported woman to contain details of her physical appearance. Geneviève Hurault was clearly exceptionally tall and, above all, so exceptionally thin and so "miserably" dressed that, even in a time of rampant indigence, she stood out—to such an extent that an officer of the law as hardened to the effects of urban poverty as Commissioner Marier was so powerfully struck by her appearance that he took the time to describe her.

On June 5, 1715, when Geneviève Hurault, still without a single conviction, was at last brought to trial, she was described as "often convicted of theft from people's homes" and sentenced to hanging.

On June 14, this was commuted—to flogging, branding, and a life sentence in La Force.

6. *"Jeanne LeFèvre, also known as Tonton, 28. Twice flogged and branded for theft."*

In LeFèvre's case, "Tonton" seems to have been a true nickname.[19] Beginning in 1716, she had several arrests on her record, always for the same crime and always in conjunction with the woman who was number eight on Pancatelin's list.

8. *"Marie Paris, 31. Royal orders. Debauchery and theft."*

LeFèvre and Paris were *couturières*, dressmakers, another profession that left poor women vulnerable to accusations of theft when fittings and alterations made it necessary for them to be in and out of elite homes. Both women had been arrested in 1716 and charged with having stolen "four diamond-covered buttons worth 10,000 *livres* from the pocket of the Comte de Riom's footman." The two were also accused of "the business of debauchery," though there's not a hint of that in any testimony. Nor was there any proof of the theft, so the women were released. They were banned from Paris but they returned, thus leaving themselves open to rearrest, which happened when Malinoir, their original arresting officer, spotted them again, on the rue de Bussy at eight p.m. on October 25, 1718. He repeated that same, unfounded theft charge and begged Machault for incarceration, alleging that they would strike again if set free, even adding for good measure, "I certify that these women are prostitutes."[20] On November 30, a week after the initial uprising in the Salpêtrière, Machault issued orders for their transfer to La Force.

7. *"Sara de Visme, also known as Beringen, in addition, also known as [autrement dite] Marie Jeanne Daigremont, 19. Dangerous schemer [intrigante]; debauchery. She claimed to be*

a member of the family of M. le Premier." (That would be the family of Van Beringen, long-time *premier écuyer,* or first gentleman to Louis XIV.)

Someone traveled to the colonies as "Marie Jeanne D'Aigremont," but there is no trace of that name in prison archives, nor of "Sara de Visme." In this case, Joly de Fleury gave his approval to the exile of someone officially unknown to the Parisian police. The archives of Paris's prisons do contain, however, a fat dossier on "Sara Misganelle," with a cover marked "de Beringen": it paints the portrait of a true con artist.

On January 4, 1717, the arresting officer wrote Lieutenant Général d'Argenson to describe a woman "who is calling herself de Beringen, and under this cover has swindled [various officers of Louis XIV's court]. At present, she is using the name 'Sara Misganelle' and claiming to be a Protestant refugee from Amsterdam who has come to Paris to renounce her religion. She has even swindled Madame de Beringen herself." D'Argenson's response was immediate, the fastest on record, and the next day the "schemer" with so many aliases was already behind bars in the Salpêtrière.[21]

9. *"Jeanne Vigneron, 33, royal orders from March 1718. Very dangerous due to poison and counterfeiting."*

Vigneron's police file indicates that in 1719 she was in fact fifty-two, rather than thirty-two, and thus the oldest female prisoner deported to the colonies. But it's hard to know what to believe, since what passes for Vigneron's arrest record seems to be a complete fabrication. Rather than the usual reports by arresting officers and witnesses' testimony, her file contains only a story told by Pancatelin without a single source to document the astounding allegations it presents as proven facts. D'Argenson, however, found Pancatelin's claims so convincing that he repeated them verbatim in his verdict: Vigneron, he asserted, was guilty of "prostitution with priests"; she had served as the accomplice of these priests and had worked with them to make counterfeit money and concoct poisons. In March 1718, royal orders were issued to incarcerate in La Force the woman Pancatelin called "a bad creature in every way."[22]

10. "Marie Louise Brunet, also known as Valentin. Royal orders in February 1712 for appalling debauchery."

Pancatelin never explained what she meant by "appalling debauchery," nor did she provide the age of this prisoner. Once again, her omissions were telling. At the time of her arrest in 1712, the inmate Pancatelin pronounced guilty of "appalling debauchery" was only twelve. Marie Louise had been caught up, seemingly by accident, in the last gasp of perhaps the greatest scandal of Louis XIV's long reign.[23]

By 1712, the so-called *Affaire des poisons*, the Affair of the Poisons, should have seemed very old news. It was a wild business, unimaginable today, but in the late 1670s, the glory days of Louis XIV's France, it cast a shadow over his court, and in particular over the king's long-time official mistress and the most influential woman in France, Françoise Athénaïs de Rochechouart, Marquise de Montespan. To ensure her place in the Sun King's affections, Montespan was rumored to have turned to sorcery, poison, and satanic rituals such as black Masses, all under the direction of Catherine Dehayes Monvoisin, usually known as Voisin.[24] At Voisin's extremely prolonged trial, her principal accuser and the government's star witness was her very own daughter, Marguerite Monvoisin. Voisin's public execution—she was burned at the stake in February 1680—was intended to put official closure on the affair, which then lieutenant general of the Parisian police, Nicolas de La Reynie, did his best to cover up. After the execution, Marguerite Monvoisin received a life sentence for her participation in her mother's intrigues.

But suddenly in 1712, there she was again, star witness in another protracted and complex trial, that of a woman accused of just the crimes allegedly committed by Monvoisin's mother more than three decades earlier—sorcery, poisoning, abortions, and impiety. Marguerite was brought from prison to examine the evidence against Marie Guillotin, the illiterate widow of a coachman named Charles Valentin. This time, La Reynie's successor as lieutenant general of the Parisian police, the Comte d'Argenson, was eager to hush up the affair: d'Argenson and d'Aguesseau worked closely together on both police matters and the Council of Commerce, and Valentin had served as d'Aguesseau's coachman. The alleged evidence—many boxes still survive, stuffed with such curious objects as scraps of paper with writing in what the police took to be Hebrew but is actually bastardized Latin, bits of bone, and a strange medal that the police decided was a talisman—was presented to Monvoisin, who pronounced it all the authentic tools of a sorceress's trade. Royal orders were quickly issued to incarcerate "the widow Valentin" for life.

A second person was also locked away: the twelve-year-old who had been found with Guillotin when the police arrived at her home. In his report, d'Aguesseau contended that she had been raised by Guillotin, who had made her an accomplice in her dark deeds and taught her everything there was to know about "all the herbs and ingredients that are used to provoke abortions." He called her "Marie Louise Brunet" and said she was an illegitimate child, "a bastard." If anyone knew the identity of her parents, they didn't reveal a thing.

She was apparently neither the child nor the grandchild of Guillotin/Valentin. In 1717, when the widow's daughter tried to get Marie Louise out of prison by claiming to be her mother, the police investigation concluded that Marie Louise was an orphan, parents unknown. In the long run, the adolescent and her past remained a mystery. Her first name, and her arrest along with Guillotin on February 11, 1712, are the only confirmed facts about the juvenile's life in France.

Guillotin's name alone was on the royal orders that landed her in the Bastille to await trial. But Marie Louise was deposited in the Salpêtrière—without trial and without a police inquiry into her case.

In 1717, Pancatelin, who rarely had anything good to say about her inmates and who never mentioned their appearance, reported to Machault that the accidental prisoner, whom she described as "very pretty," had never given a moment's trouble and was an excellent worker. But out of the blue in 1719, to justify her exile, Pancatelin officially branded the young woman whose early life had been scrubbed from the official record as "debauched." When the "very pretty" prisoner with the mysterious past was deported, officials called her "Marie Louise Brunette, also known as Valentin."

11. *"Catherine Habit, 19. Royal orders on account of public prostitution with soldiers. She is the one who mistreated a woman from the Salpêtrière."*

Habit's troubles began in August 1717, when her own mother, Claude Roger, wrote to Lieutenant Général d'Argenson to denounce her daughter. Describing herself as "an impoverished widow, with six daughters on her hands," Roger begged to have Catherine locked up in the Salpêtrière so that "she would no longer dishonor her family with her dreadful debauchery." Commissioner François de Lajarie, assigned to investigate her claims, reported that Catherine had run away from home and that he had not been able to find her. "Since she has no visible means of supporting herself, it would appear that she is doing so through prostitution."

Just like that, on the basis of simple conjecture, Habit found herself in prison. Since only two weeks later royal orders were issued for her release, the arrest was clearly unfounded. From then on, however, Habit was among the inmates pursued most relentlessly by Pancatelin.[25]

On October 6, 1718, Pancatelin wrote d'Argenson on the subject of her second-in-command and protégée, Mademoiselle Bailly, a woman considered just as despotic as Pancatelin—and even more corrupt. (Bailly was known to provide basic necessities such as blankets in winter only in exchange for bribes.) According to Pancatelin, Bailly had been "mistreated" by an unnamed woman, who had "threatened to slash her face and cut off her nose." She further alleged that all the personnel "are terrified of" this unidentified woman and that several soldiers were helping carry out her threats.[26] Even though she had not been named as Bailly's attacker, Habit was immediately incarcerated again. After this success, Pancatelin accused another prisoner, Marie Denise Beaulieu, of similar behavior. Only weeks later, Pancatelin reported the rebellion led by Manon Fontaine.

Habit's case was the earliest indication of Pancatelin's three major obsessions: her fixation on "seditious" knife-wielding women, her dread of women she perceived as being friendly with soldiers, and her preoccupation with a category on which the attention of the Parisian judicial system was just then focused—the prostitute. Prior to John Law's rise to power, "prostitution" seldom figured in the records of the Parisian police. Relatively few women were prosecuted for sex crimes, and even in those cases, they were charged with far vaguer offences, notably "debauchery" and "*mauvais commerce*," or "bad business." In 1719, for the first time ever, the incarceration of women accused of "prostitution" was becoming frequent, as the Salpêtrière's warden well knew.[27] Catherine Habit was the first woman accused by Pancatelin of "prostitution" rather than "debauchery." Like Pancatelin's subsequent decision to present prisoners she proposed for deportation to Louisiana as prostitutes, this choice was a sign of the times. Catherine Habit's case indicates how, at Pancatelin's initiative, "sedition" and "prostitution" became intertwined in the deportation saga.

12. *"Marie Denise Beaulieu, 22, royal orders. She is an old friend [camarade] of Catherine Habit."*

Beaulieu's arrest warrant is dated November 26, 1718, the day after Machault had approved the way Pancatelin had put down the sedition and given her an early indication that she would be able to act with impunity in her dealings with prisoners. As soon as she was sure of her newfound powers, Pancatelin fixed her sights on Beaulieu. The warrant for her arrest was signed by Inspector Jean Huron, among the officers of the law with whom Pancatelin worked most closely in her plan to rid France of women she deemed undesirable. Huron accused Beaulieu of prostitution, a claim that was never justified and one that was never investigated. On January 3, the very day that Joly de Fleury first evoked permanent banishment to "the islands," the warrant was carried out, and Huron brought Beaulieu to the Salpêtrière. To justify placing her in solitary confinement along with the insurrection's leaders, Pancatelin alleged that Beaulieu was guilty of similar behavior. Accompanied by several soldiers, "in whose company she was frequently spotted," she "had attacked at knifepoint in the streets of Paris an employee of the Salpêtrière," still another baseless claim that she made no attempt to document. Marie Denise Beaulieu's case provides glaring evidence of the absence of legal standards in the deportation process—her exile was finally approved after Pancatelin accused her of nothing more than being the "friend" of a woman she called a knife-wielding prostitute.

On January 3, 1719, Pancatelin was allowed to put Beaulieu in solitary confinement along with the sedition's ringleaders. On January 11, however, Beaulieu was suddenly removed from the ranks of candidates for banishment when Pancatelin declared that "she was riddled with venereal disease" and had "to be sent away for the remedies." (In the early eighteenth century, some still believed the by then widely discredited theory that venereal disease could be "sweated off" in some unspecified manner: inmates were sent to Bicêtre prison in Paris for this "remedy.")[28]

13. "Toinette Genese, 20. The police brought her here in July 1714. A prostitute and a thief."

With Genese—whom she later referred to as "Tiennette Genett/ Genest" but whose real name was "Étiennette Gené"—Pancatelin went all out, adding that she was also "a swindler addicted to all sorts

75

of vices" and alleging that she had claimed to be the niece of a master surgeon from whom she had tried to extort 7,000 *livres*.[29]

14. *"Marie Desmarais, 20. Incarcerated in August 1716 for outrageous debauchery."*

Pancatelin later expanded her case against Desmarais to include charges found nowhere in her file: "having illicit commerce with a married man, by whom she had a child." With no explanation, however, Desmarais was quickly dropped from the list, and she was never mentioned again.

After removing Beaulieu's name, Pancatelin proposed a "replacement": Babet La Fleur, whose profile was almost identical to that of Geneviève Hurault. La Fleur's file includes arrests under two other names: "Elizabeth Delapierre" and "Henriette De La Marche." She was first detained under the name "Delapierre" in November 1713 and charged with the theft of "twelve sheepskins." One month later, this time under the name "De La Marche," someone, perhaps the same woman, was brought in and charged with the theft of those same twelve sheepskins. As happened with Hurault and the silver forks, even though witnesses never connected the woman on trial to any sheepskins, the accused was nonetheless exiled from Paris. Finally, under the name "Babet La Fleur," someone, perhaps the same woman, was arrested in November 1716 and sent to the Salpêtrière for three years for failing to respect the terms of her banishment.[30]

Since the prisoner by then officially known as "Babet La Fleur" was due to be released in late 1719, Joly de Fleury initially rejected Pancatelin's request for her exile as "unjust." On February 24, however, he relented and agreed that she could be "substituted" for Beaulieu, since "she had been branded seven times for theft," information found nowhere in the police record. But when royal orders were issued for "the transfer" of thirteen women out of the Salpêtrière, La Fleur was not on the list. Even though her exile was therefore officially illegal, La Fleur nonetheless crossed the Atlantic as that thirteenth woman.[31]

A MONTH OF HURRIED NEGOTIATIONS HAD PRODUCED A MOTLEY group, unlikely choices to become the first individuals since antiquity to receive a sentence of permanent banishment that was officially referred to as "deportation." One woman was under twenty, six were in their twenties, and six were over thirty. Most had toiled all their lives at menial jobs, the only work poor girls could get, while several had frequented the upper ranks of French society, and one was even a member of its highest echelon.

When the English transported women to their colonies, most had been convicted of theft and crimes of property. In contrast, Pancatelin's choices seem capricious, random. Five women were accused of theft; even though the term "debauchery" was often thrown about, only one was charged with prostitution. The majority were deported because of outlier crimes ranging from impersonation to counterfeiting or familiarity with the techniques of abortion. And nine of the thirteen had first been arrested during the reign of Louis XIV. Their convictions on charges such as *divine lèse-majesté* could have seemed outlandish in the very different climate of Regency France, when the Parisian police less frequently sought to prosecute individuals accused of a lack of religious orthodoxy. An overview of these thirteen cases makes it clear that high government officials proceeded to banish female prisoners in perpetuity without rules and in a completely slapdash manner.

Also striking was the group's geographical diversity. Six of the women were native Parisians, the others from villages and towns all over France—from various parts of Burgundy, the Loire Valley, and central France; from Auvergne, the country's most isolated area even today. This geographical randomness directly affected the women's chances for survival. By the early eighteenth century, the French language as it was spoken in Paris among educated Parisians had been standardized and was relatively close to modern-day French. Outside of Paris and the country's largest cities, however, this standard French was rarely heard. The rural French instead used distinct regional dialects and had varying degrees of familiarity with the national language. To communicate with each other and with the Parisian-born police officers who now controlled their lives, many in the group had to speak a largely foreign tongue.

In their former existences, these women would rarely, perhaps never, have spent time with Frenchwomen from widely separate regions, and rarely, if at all, with women from across the social spectrum. Suddenly, these thirteen Frenchwomen were literally thrown together, becoming members of a second "chain." They ate the same rations, slept on the same straw, lived the same life.

By March 16, the thirteen had been reunited in Rochefort's prison with the three women sent on the initial chain. We know the second convoy of prisoners arrived "exhausted" because of "the poor quality of the vehicles allotted to them"—their guards had found the cheapest transport possible. And they were hungry. Perhaps distracted by the buildup to the initial meeting of the directors of Law's Company of the West, officials in Paris had "neglected" to send orders providing for the women's nourishment during their new confinement. In Rochefort, all authorities—Commander Du Quesne, Navy Administrator de Beauharnois, Provincial Administrator Chamilly—refused to supply the funds necessary for the care and feeding of the sixteen prisoners who arrived from Paris without advance notice.

On March 18, the sixteen women at last encountered someone who saw them as human beings and took pity on their plight. Pierre Thirat, the king's attorney in Rochefort, addressed a scathing denunciation of government policy to the very individual who bore the major responsibility for it—his direct superior, Joly de Fleury. Thirat began by describing the prisoners as "barely clothed," without even what he termed "*le linge absolument nécessaire*," "the most basic undergarments." In the eighteenth century, men and women alike wore a single garment under outer clothing: the "*chemise*" or "shift." Clothes were not changed often, but shifts were. Even individuals of modest means, those who owned but a single set of clothes, had several shifts in order to maintain basic hygiene. The women hadn't had a change of linen for weeks. When they left Paris, guards had refused to return any garments and belongings they had brought with them to the Salpêtrière. With Thirat's help, two women filed a formal complaint and submitted a complete list of "the possessions and money" that had not been restored to them. Thirat demanded that each prisoner be provided at least two additional shifts. "Otherwise," he wrote, "they will soon be covered with lice."[32]

Then, there was the matter of their sustenance. Since Rochefort's prison authorities were months behind in payments to the baker who supplied its inmates with bread, he had discontinued deliveries even before the women's arrival. Indeed, until Thirat took matters into his own hands and personally bore the cost of what he considered a subsistence diet, the women were not being fed at all. Thirat paid out of his own pocket so that each woman could be allotted a daily ration of five to six ounces of vegetables, either a sardine or a herring, and a half-ounce of cheese. Finally, Thirat denounced their sleeping arrangements: all sixteen were forced to share four "small *paillasses* [straw mattresses], old and in bad shape." Not a single blanket had been provided.[33]

In the weeks that followed, the women were in limbo. In early April, it became clear that they wouldn't be going anywhere anytime soon because the next ship scheduled for Martinique had no room for them. On April 6, Thirat addressed a second irate missive to Joly de Fleury, explaining that all local authorities still refused to reimburse him or to contribute toward the women's ongoing care and feeding. He was now concerned that if their detention in Rochefort continued indefinitely, he might not be able to keep them alive.

This time, Joly de Fleury forwarded his letter to several of the officials in Paris who should have overseen the project from the start, notably Louis Alexandre de Bourbon, Comte de Toulouse. A legitimated son of Louis XIV and the Marquise de Montespan, the count served as France's grand admiral and minister of the navy. The correspondence was also forwarded to the Maréchal d'Estrées, co-director of the Indies Company, who on April 26 scribbled in the margin his suggestion that the women be sent instead to another French island colony, Cayenne, now the capital of French Guyana on the northeastern coast of South America. As the Comte de Tou-louse put it, "this is the only place that would be suitable for *pareille marchandise* [such merchandise]." Since, however, the women had just missed a ship bound for Cayenne and the next vessel was due to de-part only in a year's time, this suggestion, too, went nowhere.

At the same moment, all these ministers were exchanging corre-spondence concerning male prisoners who had been sent from Paris and were destined for the colonies. They voiced concern about the conditions of their detention: Did the men have sufficient bedding? Was the cloth chosen for new garments being prepared for them ap-propriate for the climate in which they would live? They also decided on numerous occasions that a young male prisoner destined for "the islands of Louisiana" should be "detached from the chain" and set free.[34] Such questions were never raised with respect to the sixteen female prisoners.

Also included in the correspondence was Law's ally inside the Pari-sian police, Machault. On May 2, Machault brought Law himself into the conversation. Law replied that he was too busy to come discuss the matter in person, as Machault had suggested, as both the merger of his trading companies with the Indies Company and the initial of-fering of Indies Company stock were being finalized. He promised to send instead two Indies Company directors.

Law did, however, quickly realize that these unwanted female convicts could prove useful in the colony he was just then promoting so vigorously. Even though the March 27 meeting of the Company of the West had made it clear that Louisiana was Law's focal point, it was only on May 16, after Law had learned about the women in

Rochefort, that Machault was informed that the regent had issued an order "to send to Louisiana the women who were brought from the Salpêtrière to Rochefort." Machault was instructed "to do everything necessary to make sure that the women were handed over to the Company of the West." When, but five days later, the Company of the West was dissolved and blended into the Indies Company, a new quarrel over responsibility for the women in Rochefort ensued. Once again, no one was willing to cover the cost of their incarceration. In the end, from their arrival in Rochefort on March 16 until their departure in late July, the women remained dependent on one man's charity for their survival.

Finally, on July 8, a decision was reached: the commander of the navy at Rochefort, François de Beauharnois, Baron de Beauville, "alerted the director of the Indies Company that he was turning over to him the 16 women in prison in Rochefort." And on July 25, Roland Michel Barrin, Marquis de la Galissonière, a young naval officer with a big career ahead of him as governor of New France, announced to Indies Company officials that the women were at last on the move toward a final destination, although he likely undercounted their number by two: "The 14 women who were in prison in Rochefort were put in a *yack* and escorted by a detachment of soldiers to La Rochelle, where they are now on board the ship *Les Deux Frères* under the command of Captain Ferret."[35]

The twenty-three miles along France's Atlantic Coast that separated Rochefort from La Rochelle provided the last view of their homeland that the women from the Salpêtrière would ever have. It was surely the first time that any of them had seen beaches or an ocean—or a ship. When did they learn that the vessel on which they had been hastily loaded, *Les Deux Frères*, was bound for John Law's Louisiana and a far distant coast, the Gulf Coast? After months of confused negotiations, their deportation began purely by chance, simply because that happened to be the destination of a ship that happened to have some space in its hold.

Once aboard, the women were chained in the ship's hold, where they probably remained during the entire voyage. While in that hold, they were once again in limbo. For three weeks, *Les Deux Frères* remained stock-still, finally departing La Rochelle only on August 17. From late July to August 17, their last weeks in France, the women's fate was in the hands of a new master, Captain Charles Ferret, an individual hardly above reproach. (When the ship made landfall in Louisiana, Ferret was arrested and deprived of his command by Indies Company officials: he had illegally transported wine that he intended to resell on the black market.[36] Someone so focused on making the voyage as profitable as possible seems hardly likely to have devoted resources to malnourished and lice-covered female convicts.)

In the summer of 1719, three weeks in a ship's hold would have been even more hellish than usual. Throughout the northern half of France, 1719 broke all records for heat. By August, when the wild ride on the rue Quincampoix began, Paris was sweltering, and the death toll from the heat was rising. Just when temperatures were at their peak, sometime during the first half of August, the women of the Salpêtrière were in for a final surprise: twenty additional female convicts suddenly arrived on board *Les Deux Frères*.

These women had all been accused of smuggling either salt or tobacco, two highly taxed commodities. Smugglers traveled to the various sources of salt production in France and to French ports where ships arrived with foreign tobacco. Working in bands, they siphoned off a portion of each shipment and slipped it past customs officials. Smugglers then took these contraband goods to market squares all over France and sold them directly to the many consumers who were eager to acquire salt and tobacco without paying the heavy duties imposed by John Law's Tobacco Farm and the *gabelle* or salt levy, which multiplied the cost of salt by thirty.

Although salt and tobacco fraud was often but a small-time business, the penalties for trafficking were always severe. French authorities were so eager to retain absolute control over major sources of revenue that anyone suspected of having tried to sell even the smallest quantity of salt could be arrested on the spot: possession of just two pounds was enough to guarantee incarceration for smuggling.[37]

In 1718 and 1719, tax fraud, and salt smuggling in particular, were often on the agenda of the King's Council, subjects frequently raised during exchanges among the highest-ranking royal ministers, all of whom were desperate to find a solution not only to the crimes but also to the ever more vehement outpourings of popular support for smugglers. When officers of the law were spotted attempting to arrest smugglers, armed riots had begun to break out spontaneously. Contrabandists had become Robin Hood figures, giving the poor access to commodities otherwise beyond their means, and average Frenchmen were prepared to take up arms to shoot at anyone who tried to put an end to smuggling.[38]

Smuggling, a high-risk and dangerous business, was overwhelmingly a male traffic: female smugglers were few and far between. Indeed, prior to August 1719, while numerous male smugglers had been exiled to overseas French colonies, not a single female smuggler had been deported. The twenty on *Les Deux Frères* were the first and only female contrabandists to be banished to Louisiana.

The female smugglers had been transferred from one prison to another so often that it's not always possible to learn their origins. At least four had trafficked in salt (Marie Claire Annot, Marie Avril, Marie Jeanne Goguet, Anne Namond); at least two had dealt in tobacco (Marie Anne Grise, Jeanne Lenfant). Nearly all were from northern France and one of the country's poorest regions: three came from Doullens, a small town near the cathedral town of Amiens (Annot, Grise, Lenfant), while Françoise Ferret was from Amiens itself; three came from Saint-Quentin, a small city near the Belgian border (Françoise Fresson, Goguet, Namond); two others from Soissons, a small town near Saint-Quentin (Marie Ceinturier, Marie Michel).[39]

Soon after Louisiana became Law's new priority, Indies Company officials ordered these female smugglers to be transferred from provincial prisons to Bicêtre, a Parisian prison primarily reserved for male inmates. Bicêtre was also the penitentiary where the chains of so-called galley slaves were "composed" and from which they departed. On July 9, a chain of male smugglers "bound for Louisiana" was drawn up; the women were added to it.[40] A Parisian, Blanche Vigneron, accused of theft in 1718 and sent to Bicêtre in the company of several men arrested along with her, was somehow included in the ranks of female smugglers.[41]

There was a second outlier: Marie Avril. Avril was the youngest woman deported on *Les Deux Frères*: she turned sixteen on August 5, 1719, shortly before they sailed. Avril was not from northern France but was born instead in a prosperous area in central France, in Turny, a tiny hamlet in Burgundy. Salt smugglers were active in her region, where the Briare Canal provided direct access to both the Loire River and the Seine. Marie, who was literate, was the daughter of the gardener of her village's biggest landowner, the Comte de Chémerault. She was also one of nine children, six of whom were daughters, so she, like Marie Françoise de Jouy, the only other very young woman on board, surely feared there wouldn't be enough money to guarantee her future.

The smugglers rebalanced the group of deported women in significant ways. Their arrival introduced still more geographic and linguistic diversity. Parisians were now a distinct minority—and smuggling overwhelmingly the dominant crime. At first, there were three; then there were sixteen; in the end, *Les Deux Frères* carried thirty-six female prisoners across the Atlantic.

When *Les Deux Frères* finally set sail, it was hurricane season in the seas for which it was bound. The ship was a pinnace, a narrow, shallow, flat-hulled vessel of a type used by the English in North America for scouting coastal waters. Pinnaces were so lightly constructed that they were deemed unfit for long and dangerous voyages. At three hundred tons, the ship was also on the small side for this long crossing. In fact, nine years later, off the coast of Saint-Domingue, *Les Deux Frères* would shatter during a hurricane.[42]

Storms did not concern Indies Company officials, nor were they bothered by sending the ship directly into a danger that was constantly on their minds from July to November 1719, exactly the moment of *Les Deux Frères's* crossing. In 1719, the Gulf of Mexico was an active combat zone. France was at war with Spain for most of the early eighteenth century, most recently beginning in 1718, when Britain and France formed an alliance against the Spanish.

In the summer of 1719, the conflict reached the Gulf Coast. The French captured the Spanish port at Pensacola in May; it was recaptured by Spain in August, only to fall into French hands again before 1719 was out. On July 31, the regent was warned that the viceroy of New Spain had issued orders "to run the French out of Louisiana" and to this end had commanded a force four thousand to five thousand strong to move against the colony. The French commander in Jamaica added that in June he had seen Spanish warships near Puerto Rico, surely bound for Louisiana. He also warned that the war had caused a great scarcity of all provisions and that ships would no longer be able to restock if they ran short near the end of their long voyage. In wartime, prudence dictated that only ships with the requisite tonnage and construction to be well-equipped with cannons be sent into dangerous waters, but the Indies Company had few such ships. On August 17, 1719, they sent instead the totally inadequate *Les Deux Frères*.

Writing from Rochefort on September 12, Beauharnois voiced his concern that the war would interrupt trade with the new colony. In the same letter, he reminded Indies Company directors in Louisiana that upon arrival, Captain Ferret was obliged to hand them a "receipt" for each smuggler on board.[43] For all French officials, the first female convicts exiled to Louisiana remained to the end, in the Comte de Toulouse's pithy phrase, mere "merchandise."

The women who survived the three-month voyage reached John Law's star colony on November 18, 1719. Almost a full year had passed since the alleged uprising in the Salpêtrière, a year during which Manon Fontaine and the other so-called seditious women had had no change of linen and only minimal nourishment. Once Pancatelin realized that it was indeed possible to rid her prison—and France—permanently of women she deemed undesirable, the deportation scheme moved ahead at full tilt. From then on, one thing at least was clear: any woman who left the Salpêtrière as part of a chain was bound for Louisiana.

Chapter 4

The Roundup

B Y THE TIME *LES DEUX FRÈRES* SAILED, DEPORTATION HAD EN-tered its crucial, final phase, and key members of the Parisian police force had become Pancatelin's full, and fully willing, partners. As a result, many women who later found themselves on *La Mutine* shared experiences from their final months in Paris, a moment when the judicial system operated without checks and balances.

The women who crossed the Atlantic on board *Les Deux Frères* had judicial records as varied as their social ranks and their childhoods. Many had first been arrested outside Paris; several had spent years, even decades, in prison. Soon after the first chains of prisoners left the Salpêtrière, Marguerite Pancatelin initiated the next stage of deportation. A selection process then began, in the course of which new guidelines became evident and precise groups were targeted, such as foreign-born women. The pool of candidates was then winnowed down. After all this, a final, far larger chain left the Salpêtrière, bound this time for *La Mutine*, a ship dedicated to the deportation of women to Louisiana. Whereas the departure of female prisoners on *Les Deux Frères* was accidental, *La Mutine*'s voyage was planned from the start as the centerpiece of the deportation project.

The majority of those who sailed on *La Mutine* shared a profile: they were among the poorest Parisians, women whose indigence became glaringly evident at a moment of wild financial excess. Most cleaned or repaired clothing, washed dishes, or in some way helped guarantee the functioning of an upper-class household. Many had, moreover, been arrested only very recently, always in Paris, often by the same law enforcement officers. At all times, poor working women are particularly vulnerable to abusive police practices. In Paris, this was never more true than during the months in mid-1719 when the hunt was on to find human cargo for the ship named *The Mutinous Woman*.

AFTER THE DEPARTURE FROM THE SALPÊTRIÈRE OF THE WOMEN who traveled on *Les Deux Frères*, Pancatelin's next effort at justifying her choices for deportation was the fourteen-page list entitled "Fit for the Islands," a document that stands in sharp contrast to the far more basic earlier records. This time, great care was taken and no expense spared. The paper is of the highest quality, as is the calligraphy, featuring capital letters rendered with grand flourishes. On the final page, Joly de Fleury signed off with his official paraph or mark, leaving no doubt about the document's absolute legality. "Fit for the Islands" appears an exact replica of authoritative royal decrees and seems to signal that, from then on, deportation would unfold in an orderly fashion.

"Fit for the Islands" was thus the Magna Carta of the plan to deport women to Louisiana. It contains the names of 209 women aged three and a half (the toddler, Barbe Reine Alexandre, was the daughter of eighteen-year-old Marie Barbe Laroche, also on the list) to thirty-five. This founding charter also reveals principles that guided the selection process.

The list was designed to prove the assessment Pancatelin offered at its conclusion: these women should be "sent to the islands" to avoid the "great damage" they would inevitably cause if they were allowed to remain in France because "their morals are extraordinarily depraved." In several cases, Pancatelin described a prisoner with a phrase such as "caught begging for the fifth time," as though this were an evident indication of moral depravity. For the most part, however, Pancatelin portrayed candidates for deportation as guilty of sex crimes she referred to as either "debauchery" or "prostitution" and ranked in degrees culminating in "outrageous debauchery" and "*des plus prosti-tuées*," "among the biggest prostitutes of all."

Among those whose depravity Pancatelin considered most evident were women not previously considered for deportation: foreigners attempting to make a life in France. While all the prisoners deported on *Les Deux Frères* were native born, "Fit for the Islands" proposed fourteen foreigners. The woman Pancatelin called "Marie Anne Ellery," "German by nation," identified herself as Marie Anne de Morainville. Morainville explained that she had come to Paris to learn the French way of hairstyling: she hoped to return home to secure a position at the imperial court, where her brother was an officer. "A jealous woman," she further explained, had denounced her to the police. Indeed, in early 1719, the wife of a Parisian financier named Claude Duhamel petitioned Machault for Morainville's arrest, alleging that the younger woman was having an affair with Duhamel. Even though Morainville's prison file contains no proof of any misconduct, her deportation was approved.[1] Since, however, she was clearly fluent in French and since her case seems identical to those of many Frenchwomen brought to the Salpêtrière in 1719, Marie Anne de Morainville in no way seems to have been singled out for deportation solely because she was German. Morainville's case, moreover, was judged separately and on its own terms.

In all other cases of immigrants presented as "fit for the islands," however, the women were never seen as individuals, only as belonging to a dangerously different nationality—undoubtedly because, unlike Morainville, these prisoners had no knowledge of French.

In Paris in April 1719, an officer of the watch arrested "an unidentified Irishwoman who couldn't say her name"—like the many Irishwomen detained in Paris in 1719, she didn't understand a word of French. In such cases, officers made something up. The name of the woman arrested and recorded as "Nozo Zayen"—included on Pancatelin's list as "Nors" or "Noro Rayen"—might well have been "Nora Ryan." It's harder to guess what lay behind "Doyart," the name assigned a girl the police described as English and only ten at the time of her arrest. On her master list, Pancatelin pronounced Doyart Irish and guilty of "scandalous prostitution." She contended, once again providing no proof, that the girl "had been prostituted from the time she was six."

Foreigners like these women were unable to understand the accusations made against them, so they could have offered no defense. The incarceration records of young women identified as Irish indicate that the police arrested them in groups—the five Irishwomen on Pancatelin's list were brought in together on March 9, 1719—and that Irishwomen were always charged with prostitution, as though there were no other possible explanation for their presence in Paris.[2] In fact, had any French authority taken the trouble to find an English speaker to interrogate the young Irishwomen, they would have learned that they were Catholics. At a moment when Protestants were ascendant in Ireland and Catholics were excluded from all positions of influence and had no access to land ownership—or even to education—it seems likely that these young women had fled to a nearby Catholic country in search of religious freedom and better lives.

The remaining foreign-born women were eight prisoners whom Pancatelin called "*Bohémienne*," "Bohemian." These women had also been arrested together, in 1715 near a river in eastern France. They were not given individual police files, and their joint file in no way justified their incarceration. Even Pancatelin alleged nothing more than guilt by association: "Most of these women have husbands who have been sent to the galleys."

Beginning in the sixteenth century, royal decrees had attempted to purge France of those known as *Bohémiens*, individuals defined by a late seventeenth-century dictionary as "wandering beggars, vagabonds and libertines; they live by thievery, sleight of hand, petty crime and above all by fortune telling."[3] By the early eighteenth century, these ancestors of today's Romani people may have been the most unwelcome immigrants of all. To justify their detention, Irishwomen found in Paris were called prostitutes. *Bohémiennes* could be arrested simply for being on French soil.

Other names on Pancatelin's list indicate that, in a city gripped by stock market fever, the native-born poor became as undesirable as *Bohémiens*. The months when the deportation plan took shape—December 1718, January 1719, March 1719—coincided with the publication of a series of royal edicts seeking to criminalize paupers in order to justify their "transportation to our colonies." The December 1718 decree announced a crime wave, the widespread presence in the countryside near Paris of "gangs of armed paupers and vagabonds" threatening the well-being of honest citizens by "forcing people to take them into their homes and feed them." In the months following the March 1719 proclamation describing "the great advantage for our state" of a new policy that allowed judges "to transport to our colonies all vagabonds and those without employment," officers of the law were actively engaged in hunting down the indigent.

In June 1719, an impoverished widow, Catherine Martin, left her hamlet some thirty-five miles from Paris along with her nineteen-year-old daughter, Marie Mercier. The pair wandered from village to village seeking work of any kind. "Overcome by the great heat," Martin explained in an appeal to Lieutenant Général Machault, they "had the misfortune" to sit down on the cool stones in a village courtyard, without noticing that several paupers were begging nearby. Police arrived on horseback to arrest the vagrants, and Marie Mercier was seized along with them. When Martin begged for her daughter's release, the officers beat her. Martin then learned that Marie had been taken to the Salpêtrière. Even though their parish priest joined Marie's mother in protesting that "her daughter was blameless," their plea went unheeded, and Marie Mercier was marked for deportation.[4] And as Paris was transformed under John Law's rule, the city's working women increasingly found themselves as vulnerable to arrest as were unemployed women such as Marie Mercier. In every case, the woman was guilty above all simply of being publicly visible.

In the early eighteenth century, women from across the social spectrum were far more likely to be seen in public in Paris than in capitals such as London, Paris's only rival for the most populous European city.[5] Aristocrats strolled in the Tuileries gardens and joined friends in the city's elegant cafés; handsomely dressed shopgirls waited on customers in high-end boutiques—and working women gathered in far less exclusive establishments. None of this behavior had negative consequences for their reputations, whereas in London, such conduct would have been shocking. Women did not eat and drink in public there; any woman walking in the city's streets risked being labeled a public woman. But when the heat was on to find women for Louisiana, previously accepted activities became—for Paris's working women at least—unacceptable, and Parisian law enforcement officers stepped in to curb their freedom of movement. Suddenly, having a beer with one's friends became an activity that could easily lead to arrest on a charge of prostitution.

Claude Vaudestar was a thirty-three-year-old Parisian who after a day's work dropped by a cabaret near her home in the Saint-Germain-des-Prés neighborhood for "*un demi-sétier*," the small beer of about eight ounces still known in Parisian cafés as a *demi*. A sword fight broke out, and for her protection, an employee helped Vaudestar slip out a side entrance. A man was killed in the skirmish, and another soldier of the watch, Pierre Gaillard, was charged with the crime. Someone had recognized Vaudestar; she was brought in as well, said to be Gaillard's accomplice. Vaudestar was repeatedly interrogated: *Did she earn a living as a prostitute? Was Gaillard her pimp?* She denied everything, as did Gaillard. Gaillard was convicted and sentenced to execution, but the police had nothing on Vaudestar. The charges were dropped, and she was allowed to go free.

Only a week later, however, Vaudestar was arrested again, accused of "debauchery and public prostitution." After but two days between charges and incarceration, she found herself in the Salpêtrière. And there she remained: when Pancatelin drew up her master list, she characterized Vaudestar as "a notorious woman whose prostitution has caused the deaths of several men."[6]

And Vaudestar's story was in no way exceptional. In the early evening, women with strenuous jobs such as laundresses and itinerant street vendors often stopped off, just as Vaudestar did, to enjoy a drink, alone or with others. In an age when water was not safe to drink, wine was the customary beverage, and beer the most common way to quench one's thirst. Working women frequented, just as Vaudestar did, establishments known as cabarets: unlike *tavernes* or taverns, where food was available, cabarets served only wine and beer by the glass. But in the time of economic crisis that followed Louis XIV's death, cabarets became dangerous places for women.

No law enforcement officers were more aggressive in their attempts to regulate the activities of Paris's working women than the officers of the watch. The watch was the most venerable of the companies patrolling Paris, far older than the Parisian police. Although under the jurisdiction of the lieutenant general of police, it operated independently of Paris's police commissioners. Its officers' chief assignment was the task of keeping the city safe at night. In the early eighteenth century, 150 officers, a third of them on horseback, made their nightly rounds. They included stops in cabarets as a regular part of their patrols, and they routinely rounded up all women found there and brought them in for questioning. Officers of the watch as a matter of course portrayed women arrested in cabarets as prostitutes and thieves, there to prey on the establishment's male clientele.

Since the area was known for a particularly high concentration of cabarets, officers of the watch regularly patrolled Passy and Roule, located in the zone on the outskirts of Paris's western limit where Manon Fontaine was said to have been seen drinking with soldiers. In one of those cabarets, officers first spotted Jeanne Pouillot. Pouillot's treatment at their hands illustrates perfectly the tactics used to entrap working-class Parisian women. In late 1715, Jeanne was newly arrested; on November 16, she was taken from the Salpêtrière to police headquarters at the Châtelet to be "confronted" with a number of recently incarcerated "women of ill repute" on the grounds that she had been detained "in the same type of case."[7] Among those women was Babet La Fleur: this was the arrest that eventually led to La Fleur's deportation on *Les Deux Frères*.

In October 1715, when Babet La Fleur and the four others on trial had been found in Roule in a cabaret called the Duc de Bourgogne, the arresting officer claimed that La Fleur and her accomplices had joined officers of the watch at their table, shared a beer with them, and then tried to lure them into sex by touching them, all with the intention of robbing them. But the only theft, and indeed the only crime of which La Fleur was accused during the proceedings, had nothing to do with either soldiers or a cabaret. Instead, for the fourth time since her initial arrest in 1709, La Fleur was charged with the theft of twelve sheepskins. Pouillot, brought in as a witness for the prosecution, had no convictions on her record—but her case could have been seen as "the same type" as La Fleur's because both of them were women and both had been arrested in cabarets in the company of other women. A significant number of working women shared their fate and ultimately found themselves in Louisiana because they had enjoyed a small beer and a bit of female company at the end of a hard day's work.

In the course of four years in Paris, Jeanne Pouillot acquired a long record that in the end proved nothing other than the fact that she had frequented cabarets, where she had often been arrested. Pouillot was a particularly assertive prisoner: she regularly refused to give the police her name; she consistently provided alibis; she was always quickly released because on every occasion, they checked out. But in January 1719, the police somehow made the charges stick: Jeanne was transferred to the Salpêtrière just when Pancatelin began to draw up her master list.[8]

IN EARLY JULY 1719, WHEN THE WOMEN DESTINED TO DEPART ON *Les Deux Frères* were still in limbo in Rochefort, surviving on a daily sardine for which no authority was willing to pay while they waited for a final decision on their transport to an island colony, in Paris, Marguerite Pancatelin had just received official notification that the regent had approved for deportation the much larger group of prisoners she had characterized as "fit for the islands." Until then, Pancatelin had been testing the waters to see what might be possible, but from then on, "Operation Deportation" was an ever greater threat to the women of Paris.

The arrests and incarcerations of Jeanne Pouillot, Babet La Fleur, and numerous other Parisian working women who found themselves tagged for deportation indicate that good relations had long reigned between the Salpêtrière's warden and the Parisian police. Despite this, a bare minimum of procedure had usually been observed. While the women arrested prior to 1719 rarely received anything like the kind of trial that Manon Fontaine had undergone, the charges against them had at least been subjected to some form of scrutiny. But once Pancatelin had carte blanche, the rush was on to collect additional women, and the warden enjoyed the full cooperation of the Parisian police. Officers of the watch, officers on the beat, those who patrolled on foot and on horseback as well, even police inspectors—all rounded up women specifically for deportation to Louisiana. Any woman out in the streets of Paris in the summer and early fall of 1719 was in imminent danger of falling into Pancatelin's clutches.[9]

On July 3, the arresting officer of a young Parisian woman named Marie Villetard received a most unusual order, indicating how quickly the Parisian police hoped to conclude this enterprise: the officer was instructed not to bother bringing Villetard to the Salpêtrière but to take her instead "directly to Bicêtre and to deposit her there in preparation for the departure of the next chain for Louisiana."[10] The police were adopting the method used for the chains of men who were sent from Paris to Marseille to serve as *galériens*, or galley slaves, "depositing" them at Bicêtre until they had accumulated a sufficient number to compose a new chain. This direct-deposit method saved them the trouble and expense of a second prison transfer.

Just over three months would go by before what the Parisian police (having forgotten that the expression had been used before) had begun referring to as "the second chain of those we have to escort to Louisiana" was ready to leave Bicêtre prison to begin the long journey to John Law's colony. Those months, when shares of Indies Company stock were surging and Parisians were burning with investment fever, were among the cruelest and the most dangerous months in history for the women of Paris.

Beginning in mid-1719, the raids carried out by officers of the watch on the cabarets of Roule and Passy became ever more frequent. Officers alleged that particular establishments were known to encourage "bad commerce and commerce of debauchery between loose women and soldiers" and proceeded to arrest all women found on the premises. They often chose to incarcerate them in a convenient nearby prison, Chaillot.[11] Chaillot was a *prison seigneuriale*, a private institution officially outside the jurisdiction of the Parisian police. Upon request, its wardens cooperated with their counterparts in Paris, as they did on August 24, 1719. That day, three women were transferred from Chaillot to the Salpêtrière: Angélique Reffe, Marie Meutrot, and Marie Poton. All three were soon chained together as part of the second chain, in which they were assigned numbers 84, 85, and 86.[12]

Some women under police surveillance became part of the chain even later than these three. During the regency years, Louise Fontenelle had been twice arrested and quickly released for lack of evidence by officers of the watch, who had kept track of her whereabouts. On August 23, 1719, Fontenelle was brought in, allegedly simply for questioning. Instead, on September 2, without having been accused, much less convicted, of a crime Louise found herself in the Salpêtrière. Within weeks, she had become number 146 on the second chain.[13]

And if officers of the watch were able to snare Angélique Reffe and Louise Fontenelle, street-smart Parisians well-versed in the meanderings of their city's back alleys and byways, it's no surprise that numerous young women from the provinces, newly arrived in the capital, easily fell into their clutches. This was the fate of two young women, both from central France, both deported on *La Mutine*. In both cases, their arrest records began and ended when an officer of the watch pinned a charge on them.

Nineteen-year-old Marie Daudin was born in Orléans, a bustling port city. Marie's family lived near the banks of the Loire, and they relied on the river for their survival. Families like the Daudins were the working poor of France's second-largest river port. Marie was the oldest child of Charles Daudin, a *"porteur de sacs,"* a "sack bearer," who unloaded ships, lugging bags of sugar from France's Caribbean colonies that had been sent for processing in one of Orléans's many refineries. Other family members made barrels to contain processed sugar. When they married, Marie's parents were both orphans from small families. In times of crisis, their family had no support network. And 1715, the year of Louis XIV's death, appears to have been such a moment. On April 30, Marie's only sister, Catherine, died. Within months, Marie Daudin had found her way to Paris; she arrived just as newly aggressive policing practices with respect to women were put into place. Exactly a year after her sister's death, Marie was in prison, brought in by an officer of the watch.[14]

Her file is marked "alibi." At the time of the alleged crime, Marie Daudin was somewhere else, and she was able to prove it. But she had been found in the wrong company. Unlike Daudin, the woman arrested along with her, Henriette Mussy, had priors for theft, and at that moment in Paris, a mere association was enough to guarantee that Daudin would remain under surveillance. Indeed, Marie Daudin found herself incarcerated again only three months after her release. From then on, officers of the watch kept tabs on her; when the second chain had to be quickly filled, Marie Daudin from Orléans became number 113, bound for the colony whose new capital had only recently been christened "la Nouvelle Orléans."

Marie Marguerite Grené was born in Villeneuve-le-Roi, a town of about four thousand inhabitants in a lush region of northern Burgundy, the oldest child and only daughter of Jacques Grené. Since Jacques Grené, like all the men on both sides of her family, was a vigneron, Marie grew up hearing talk of nothing but wine. In her early years, Marie witnessed the deaths of her mother, of all her siblings, of both grandmothers and other close female relatives. Her father quickly remarried and had sons. By the time Marie reached adolescence, she lived with a stepmother and in a world of men.

On September 11, 1718, when she was about twenty-six, Marie Grené was arrested in Paris by an officer of the watch named Gasselin who had found her "under the bridge near the Hôtel Dieu just about midnight." Arrested with her was François Duman, who was not ashamed to give his name and his profession, mason and stonecutter. That, plus a detail provided by Officer Gasselin, who noted that he saw them in the same spot on the Île de la Cité "every other day," indicates that the officer was dealing with an upstanding young couple of limited means seeking minimal privacy, rather than a prostitute and her client. Duman was immediately released, whereas in 1719, Marie Grené, charged with "debauchery and prostitution," was incarcerated in the Salpêtrière.[15] Marie became number 141 on the second chain.

One officer provides the most convincing proof of the active collaboration of Parisian law officers in the deportation effort: Jean Bourlon. A significant number of the women whose names appear on Pancatelin's list had been arrested by Officer Bourlon.[16] During the entire deportation process, Bourlon was Pancatelin's right-hand man. He kept careful watch over the places where Parisians gathered—the public gardens for which the French capital was famous, John Law's bank and the stock exchange, theaters, even churches. There, Bourlon carried out just the kind of mass arrests that his colleagues in the watch were conducting in the cabarets of Roule and Passy.

By 1719, Bourlon's close ties to Pancatelin were long-standing. In late 1716, Bourlon arrested a large group of individuals he termed "swindlers": he claimed that they preyed on Parisians strolling in gardens like the Tuileries. The list included Suzanne Bouley, Anne and Marie Maurice, and Marie Antoinette Néron. Bourlon provided no evidence of what their "swindles" might have entailed, and the women were quickly released. In the years ahead, Bourlon repeatedly rearrested the same women; on every occasion, they were released "for lack of proof." But over time, even though their guilt had never been established, these women acquired the reputation Bourlon had hoped to give them, of being, as Pancatelin phrased it when she entered all four names on her list, "famous and dangerous thieves."

In November 1718, when Bourlon brought the four in just prior to the insurrection in the Salpêtrière that set off the deportation process, he freely admitted that he had no proof of any illegal activity. He claimed only that "these vagabonds and thieves are a true public nuisance" and that he had arrested them "in order to guarantee public safety." He threw in prostitution charges as well, although none of the four had ever been arrested on these grounds. Bourlon even noted that "their parents are dependent on them for their survival," as though this were further evidence of wrongdoing.

Bourlon told the truth about one thing: many of the women he brought in came from extreme poverty. Marie Antoinette Néron, for example, was the daughter of a *gagne-denier*, a day laborer. Men like Christophe Néron eked out a living doing odd jobs in Paris's ports. A striking number of women who found themselves on the second chain came from just this background. Another Bourlon capture was Pérette Picard. Pérette's widowed mother had long worked alongside men as a *gagne-denier*, unloading shipments of wheat. She begged Machault not to keep her daughter in prison, because she needed Pérette's help in order to get by, since she was now too old for such hard labor. Marie Anne Benoist was the daughter of a deceased "sack bearer" who had lugged bundles of merchandise in Paris's ports, just as Marie Daudin's father did in Orléans. Thérèse Le Comte's widowed father, Pierre, identified himself as "a poor *gagne-denier*." He asked Machault to incarcerate his only child because he "believed her to be frequenting a young man whose name he had not been able to learn." When Machault convoked her, Thérèse confirmed this report and added that "she was reduced to selling the little clothing she owned just to make ends meet." Even though she pointed out that "she was doing harm to no one," in July 1719 Thérèse was sent to the Salpêtrière. Families like these, living just at or mostly below the poverty line, were Paris's working poor, and in 1719, they were portrayed as "a public menace," as were paupers and the homeless. Along with Marie Antoinette Néron, Thérèse, Pérette, and Marie Anne were taken from Paris in chains.[17]

BY OCTOBER 6, 1719, BOURLON HAD BEEN APPOINTED TO SUPERVISE the journey from Paris to the coast of the women on the new chain, an assignment that recognized the essential role he had played in rounding up so many of those destined to travel under his watch. That day, when he drew up the official manifest or record of the prisoners to be deported, two of the "swindlers" he had so often arrested, Marie Maurice and Marie Antoinette Néron, headed the list.

Whereas the manifest contains 148 names, Bourlon remarked that he was taking *"140 et tant d'autres,"* literally, "140-odd," women from the Salpêtrière, and other police reports refer to "the 150" women on the chain.[18] These diverging tallies indicate something Bourlon knew better than anyone else: the impressive appearance of Pancatelin's master list notwithstanding, the second chain was assembled at least as hastily and as chaotically as the first.

Already on September 25, an official arranging the transfer of women from the Salpêtrière to the new convoy wrote Joly de Fleury to inquire if it might be possible to "relax" normal judicial procedures.[19] Bourlon's offhand lack of precision concerning the number of women destined for deportation covers the fact that, operating under these "relaxed" rules, in the days just prior to departure, he had been allowed to add virtually any prisoner to the convoy—with no due process and, at times, without even bothering to note her name. Because of this disarray, no authority could have known how many women left the Salpêtrière under Bourlon's command. According to my best estimate, at least 152 prisoners were on the new chain.

A comparison of Pancatelin's master list and the manifest provides a clear indication of the chaos that reigned at the Salpêtrière at the moment when Bourlon's chain was being assembled. All 209 women selected by Pancatelin were already in custody, their deportation authorized: they were ready to be shipped off at a moment's notice. But nearly half the women on Bourlon's manifest do not appear on Pancatelin's list of prisoners.[20] With so many inmates already approved for exile, it's hard to understand why only 74 of the original 209 made the final cut. Pancatelin's description of the charges against Marie Fouquet, age twenty-nine and from Saint-Malo, for example, makes her seem a virtual twin of Jeanne Vigneron, who had already been deported on *Les Deux Frères*: "a procuress who prostituted young people to monks and nuns."[21] Why was she not part of the second chain?

Bourlon's October 6 manifest provides an indication of when things went wrong. Whereas the names of virtually all the women in its first half appear on "Fit for the Islands," from number 71 on, almost none of the names are found on Pancatelin's list. For some reason, Bourlon ceased using the master list—he may even have misplaced it. Since he knew that a standard chain was composed of about 150 prisoners, he hastily added over 70 women whose deportation had not been authorized in June. Most of those 70-odd women arrived in the Salpêtrière during the roundup that took place in Paris in the weeks prior to the chain's departure. Some were among the "so many others" whom Bourlon grabbed at the eleventh hour—among them, a young woman whose name Bourlon forgot to add to the manifest: Marie Baron.

Like Marie Igonnet, condemned to be burned at the stake and instead deported on *Les Deux Frères*, Marie Baron endured the worst deprivations of what the Duc de Saint-Simon, among the period's most astute commentators, termed "*les années funestes*," "the deadly years."[22] In France, the end of Louis XIV's reign was marked by disastrous climate events and their consequences: the "Great Winter" of 1709, another extreme cold wave in 1710, and from 1710 to 1714, an unbroken series of disastrous harvests. When the price of grain and all basic foodstuffs soared, famine set in. In 1709 and 1710 in particular, only the wealthiest Frenchmen ate their fill.

Marie Baron was born in Le Mesnil-Thomas, a village of some five hundred inhabitants about twenty miles from the cathedral town of Chartres. Her region in central France, Beauce—flat, virtually treeless, landlocked, and covered with fields of grain—was known as the country's breadbasket. In the deadly years, the area was one of France's hardest-hit regions. Marie Baron's early years were such a relentless cycle of poverty and death that they could hardly be called a childhood. By age seven, she had witnessed the deaths of both parents, her only two siblings, and the two children born from her father's second marriage. Her father, Jacques Baron, an illiterate agricultural worker, died on May 24, 1710, a casualty of the freezing temperatures that once again gripped France that year: the death toll in France in May 1710 was over 121,000, more than twice the mortality of May 1709.[23] His widow was so poor she could not afford a funeral for her husband. Jacques was interred "in the presence of Brothers of Charity from Blemy and Senonches," lay organizations whose members paid the tiny sum necessary so that the truly indigent could receive a Catholic burial.[24]

In the aftermath of the Great Winter, starving people gathered together to roam the French countryside in search of food. Cities all over France, and Paris in particular, were overwhelmed by these wandering hordes. When officials locked city gates, the desperate crowds would try to dig their way under the walls. Those who got in walked the streets begging for help. Some municipalities estimated that 40 percent of their official inhabitants were surviving thanks only to food distributed by civic and religious authorities. All authorities agreed that there was nothing left for outsiders.

Marie surely made her way to Paris as part of one such itinerant throng. At age seven, the child, who had never seen an agglomeration larger than her tiny village, encountered Europe's most populous city. On August 12, 1710, only three and a half months after her father's death, Marie Baron was incarcerated in Paris's Châtelet prison, taken there by an officer of the watch who had swooped down on his prey on horseback. The little girl had been detained in the company of Geneviève Hurault, then about twenty and working as a laundress. Nine years before Hurault was deported on *Les Deux Frères*, this was the second of her arrests for theft, always for that crime for which evidence was never produced, of having stolen "two silver forks." Like Baron, she had been born in the provinces, in Melun, a small town south of Paris. Hurault probably helped Marie find work as a laundress and taught her how to negotiate the big city. Once again, the police failed to document their accusation, but Hurault was condemned nonetheless to a public flogging and to banishment from Paris.

Marie was merely "informed," that is, she was "instructed" about the charges and legal process before being released. The day after her arrest, the girl had been able to prove that she had not been at the scene of the crime: her dossier was closed and marked "alibi." But, just like Marie Daudin, she had been found in bad company. Only months later, on April 16, 1711, ten days after Marie's eighth birthday and not quite a year after her father's death, Jean La Motte, still another officer of the watch, brought Marie to the Châtelet prison for the second time. Once again, Marie was released without being charged, but this time she spent nearly a month behind bars on a technicality: it was not clear that La Motte had had the authority to arrest her, so the king's prosecutor, who had jurisdiction over the watch, had demanded an investigation. All this emphasis on police procedure was unusual, and the girl would have understood little if any of it, as the file on her second arrest closes with "she declared that she could neither read nor write."

Marie Baron had understood one thing: the necessity of living under the radar. Unlike others captured by officers of the watch, her name does not quickly reappear in the records of the Parisian police. But on June 9, 1719, just as Pancatelin was compiling her master list, Baron crossed the threshold of the Châtelet prison for the third time, once again in the company of a friend employed as a laundress and previously arrested for theft, most recently only three months before. That afternoon, Marie, then sixteen, and Anne Gabrielle Crétin, also sixteen, had entered what must have seemed like paradise to an adolescent who had known not a hint of luxury in all her years: an elegant, well-stocked emporium on Paris's premier shopping street, the rue Saint-Honoré, run by a ribbon merchant named Sergé. Alleging that Crétin and Baron had stolen "a piece of ribbon shot through with gold and silver," Sergé called in the police. When nothing was found on them, Sergé added that they had "adroitly" slipped the ribbon to someone not previously mentioned, a third young woman, who had escaped with it.

Realizing that such a flimsy allegation was hardly sufficient to make the charges stick, the arresting officer, Jean Huron—the same man who had delivered Marie Denise Beaulieu to the Salpêtrière at a moment's notice in November 1718—took it upon himself to add that he "personally knew that both of them were completely given over to debauchery and theft; he believed that only a long and severe period of correction would change them." Their release was nonetheless quickly authorized, so on June 21, Huron took things up a notch and appealed directly to Machault. Since Huron was already keeping a close eye on Crétin's father, Jean Milorin (himself an officer of the watch), because of his supposed connections to the best-known theft operation in the capital, he could easily suggest that Milorin's daughter was cut from the same cloth. On "Fit for the Islands," Crétin and Baron appear as numbers 69 and 70, characterized as "public prostitutes and thieves." On June 24, only days before the regent signed off on Pancatelin's master list, Machault concluded that the two "could after all be added to the [chain] of women destined for the islands."[25]

Crétin had an extended family in Paris. When they learned that she was "on the list of women who are to leave for the island of Louzianne [*sic*]," they successfully petitioned Machault for her release. But no one was watching out for Marie Baron, so she remained in prison. Three months later, Marie was swept up in the final rush to complete the second chain—and also in the confusion that reigned.

Bourlon never added her name to the October 6 list, as police procedure required, so no legal proof survives of Baron's "transfer" from the Salpêtrière. On the manifest of *La Mutine*, Baron was the last of the women from the Salpêtrière to be listed. Marie Moule, another young woman from the Beauce and from a village even smaller than Marie Baron's home, was also grabbed by Bourlon at the eleventh hour, arriving at the Salpêtrière only on October 14, perhaps the very day that the chain at last left Paris. Three days later, when Elisabeth Le Brun was transferred to the Salpêtrière with instructions "to keep her there until the departure of the next chain for Louisiana," the second and ultimate convoy of women had just departed, so Le Brun never left French soil.[26]

The episode that led to the deportation of Marie Moule, the final prisoner to make the chain, began in July 1719, when Machault received a complaint from Jacqueline Elizabeth Regnauls, wife of Charles Croiset, a *marchand d'essences* or fragrance merchant. Regnauls alleged that the minute she "had had the misfortune of hiring Marie as a domestic," the new maid had set about seducing her husband. Even after she dismissed Marie, the servant continued "to pursue" her husband, who then began to mistreat his wife and their six children. Regnauls's account was confirmed by none other than Officer Bourlon.

Upon investigation, it transpired that Croiset was doing all the pursuing. After he learned that Regnauls had denounced Marie to the police, Croiset left home. He refused to give Marie Moule up and begged to be allowed to visit her in prison. On September 29, a great aristocrat also intervened on Marie's behalf: Charlotte Elisabeth de Cochefilet, wife of the Prince de Guéméné, wrote from the couple's château in Rochefort-en-Beauce near Marie's home village to plead for her release, describing her as "from a very good family and the sister of a young man who helps out in our kitchens." On October 20, when the chain had already left, the princess wrote again, explaining that, having learned that Marie "is to be sent to the Mississippi," she felt obliged to reveal that the case was based on nothing more than "the jealousy of Croiset's wife." On October 26, Machault justified his refusal in a long letter: "Croiset was moving heaven and earth to obtain [Marie's] freedom," and Machault could not agree to a request that would break up a family.

As the convoy traveled, Marie Moule may have learned the story of a twenty-two-year-old born in still another tiny village in central France, one very near Moule's home, who had also been in service in a wealthy household and had known a virtually identical fate. Marie Chartier had worked for a nobleman, the Sieur Roberdeau, the *seigneur* or lord of Marcilly-en-Beauce, a hamlet about three miles from the town of Vendôme, serving as governess to his two children by his first wife. After Roberdeau remarried, his new wife, Claude

Gautier, addressed a complaint to Machault, alleging that she had arrived in Marcilly after her marriage, only to find her husband engaged in a "*mauvais commerce*," "bad commerce," with the governess, whose "scandalous behavior," she further asserted, was "known to all." Gautier contended that she had dismissed Marie Chartier, who had then moved to Paris. Once there, or so Gautier claimed to have recently learned, Roberdeau had set her up in an apartment near the Palais-Royal, "and this is causing the complete ruin of his family." While the village priest backed up Gautier's story, their testimony was undercut by that of the lieutenant general of the Vendôme police, who "certified" that the priest was "lying."

Despite this, the Parisian police accepted the wife's allegations, and Chartier was sent to the Salpêtrière. Marie Chartier, among the best-educated of the deported women, then wrote Machault directly, testifying that she had left the Roberdeau household of her own free will and that Roberdeau had found her a position in Paris, where his wife had arranged for her arrest. When Machault turned to Pancatelin for an account of the prisoner's behavior, she repeated the wife's story of Marie Chartier's "prostitution" with a married man. She also alleged something confirmed by no other report, not even Gautier's denunciation, and contended that at the time of Chartier's arrest, she was pregnant with Roberdeau's child and had since given birth. Because of Pancatelin's unverified allegation, Marie Chartier remained in prison.

When Machault refused to release Marie Chartier, at three a.m. on a winter morning Roberdeau turned his wife out of their home "in a fury" and proceeded to sell all her clothing and possessions. It's not clear if the nobleman was motivated by a wild passion or if he simply considered Chartier, as he claimed, "a judicious and trustworthy servant," but it does appear that the lord of Marcilly truly and palpably cared about his employee.[27]

Just when the roundup was on, in cases that defy belief, two women actually volunteered for the voyage. After an eighteen-year-old

Parisian named Marie Anne Giard decided "*de bonne volonté*," "of her own free will," "to ask to be sent to the islands," she became a last-minute addition to the chain.[28]

Next, in early August 1719, Machault received a request to have seventeen-year-old Jeanne Mahou confined to the Salpêtrière "for bad behavior." The petition came from Mahou's older sister Anne and her husband, Guillaume Acquart, who described himself as "the servant of M. Francine, the King's maître d'hôtel." (The Francine family, creator of the complex hydraulic system that still provides water for the château's celebrated fountains, was prominent at Versailles.) Acquart was excessively proud of his very tiny connection to the French court, and he complained of Jeanne's alleged misconduct with great self-righteousness.

Two years earlier, he and his wife had brought his sister-in-law, then fifteen, to Paris from the family's home in Saint-Dizier, a town of some five thousand inhabitants in northeastern France, Acquart explained, and found her employment as a domestic servant. But Jeanne, who had come to Paris with the dream of working in its fashion industry, had not taken to life in service. She began apprenticeships first in wigmaking, later in dressmaking, and found her calling as a seamstress. When Jeanne complained, as apprentices often did, about the conditions in the atelier where she was training to become a *couturière*, her sister and brother-in-law decided that they had had enough. They denounced her to the police as a "libertine" with "a penchant for debauchery." At their request, the parish priest in their neighborhood near the Louvre pronounced Jeanne "on the road to ruin"—although he did admit that he had never even met her. On August 13, Machault asked Officer Bourlon to bring "the libertine" in to see him.

By August 19, Machault had already written his report on their conversation, and it's a striking one, perhaps the only time that this hard-liner neither simply agreed to a family's request nor exhibited any desire to punish a young woman, who was, by her own admission, wayward. Jeanne frankly confessed, in Machault's words, that she "was unlikely to change her behavior," which, she explained, was "in her blood." It's evident that Machault liked Mahou. Normally such audacity on the part of a woman brought out his most repressive instincts, whereas in this case he chose minimal punishment and merely ordered Mahou to leave Paris and return home.

But Jeanne would have none of it. She remained in Paris, where on September 10, Bourlon tracked her down. When Julien Divot, the commissioner in charge of her case, tried to convince her to leave the capital, Jeanne's reply stunned them all: "She replied that she would never return to Saint-Dizier . . . ; she asked me to implore you to put her instead on the first manifest for transport to the Mississippi, hoping that since she was going willingly she would not be treated like the others and shackled during the voyage." Divot concluded that "since she was quite pretty" and "*d'une grande bienfaite*," "really shapely," she would surely "be agreeably received in the colony."[29] This was one of only two instances in which an officer of the law commented on a deported woman's appearance and the only time when anyone paid one of them a compliment. Jeanne Mahou's comeliness must have been striking indeed.

Jeanne Mahou failed to explain that her refusal to return to her birthplace was based on more than what she described as her bad blood: in 1719, there was little left for her in Saint-Dizier. Jeanne's family background was unlike that of other provincial women who found themselves in the Salpêtrière and on the chain. For generations, the men and women alike had been exceptionally well-educated and were all highly literate. Men on both sides of the family occupied positions in the royal administration: her father as a bailiff, a maternal uncle as a notary. But education, upward mobility, and social status made no difference when the Great Winter struck. Even more than Marie Baron's, Jeanne's once large family was decimated. In just seventeen months in 1710–1711, Jeanne, then but eight, had lost both her parents, as well as her older brother Claude, the sibling closest to her in age. After her sister Anne's departure for Paris, Jeanne was the youngest surviving child. She had two older sisters who required dowries, with no parent to provide them. Jeanne left for Paris, counting on her sister Anne's help, and hoping to create her own future. After Anne turned against her, Jeanne Mahou once again set off into the unknown, this time the complete unknown, the place she called "the Mississippi."

Jeanne's request arrived just in time to help Bourlon fill out the second chain. On Bourlon's October 6 manifest, Jeanne Mahou appears as number 76: like all the others, the free spirit traveled in shackles.

As the terms of Jeanne's request indicate, by the time of the roundup, Parisians were well-informed about the deportation process. As that knowledge spread through the city, more and more parents proposed that their daughters be shipped off to Louisiana—and by then, they could be sure that their proposals would be accepted.

In this way, Charles and Pierre Fourchet begged Lieutenant Général Machault to incarcerate their sister Marie Anne "for as long as [he] liked." The brothers claimed to have been "penniless" when they arrived in Paris from their home in Épernay, the capital of the champagne trade, and to have made their way in the world as wine merchants. Just as self-righteously as Jeanne Mahou's brother-in-law, they explained that they had brought their younger sister to Paris and arranged a position for her in service. Rather than show gratitude, however, Marie Anne had "seduced the man of the household in which she served as a maid, had had two children by him and was pregnant with a third." They "prayed to heaven" that Machault would "put an end to this bad commerce [*mauvais commerce*], because of which their reputation was suffering."

When Commissioner François de Lajarie had their sister brought in to defend herself, Marie Anne had a very different tale to tell. She "had been seduced and abused by M. Masson, the married man in whose home she had long been a servant; she had borne him two children, both of whom had died." Although Lajarie seems to have found Marie Anne's account credible, he nonetheless concluded that she should be sent to the Salpêtrière because "this disorder was disturbing M. Masson's household." Machault approved the incarceration of "this 29-year-old who had cultivated a criminal commerce with a married man, a relationship that is bringing dishonor upon her brothers," and royal orders were issued for the incarceration of "Marie Anne Fourchet, a known public prostitute."

After Marie Anne Fourchet reached the Salpêtrière as the roundup was in full swing, she was assigned number 108 on the chain. Late that summer in the Hôtel Dieu, a public institution near Notre-Dame Cathedral, she had given birth to a third child by Masson. The infant had surely died as quickly as Marie Anne's first two children. The babies of women declared prostitutes were taken from them and handed over to wet nurses, who gave them such minimal care that 90 percent perished in their first months, usually during the month that followed their birth.[30]

IN EARLY OCTOBER, SHORTLY AFTER MARIE ANNE FOURCHET'S roundup and shortly before that of Marie Moule, two names were added to the chain: Marie Louise Balivet and Geneviève Bettemont. On the chain, Balivet and Bettemont were assigned consecutive numbers, 125 and 126. They remained shackled together during the trip to the coast. Balivet was of modest extraction, the daughter of an illiterate mason. But she was raised in Saint-Germain-en-Laye, an exclusive enclave on the outskirts of Paris. Louis XIV was born in Saint-Germain-en-Laye's royal château, which remained the principal residence of the French court until its move to Versailles. In Saint-Germain-en-Laye, the opposite ends of the social spectrum often met, even in families as humble as Balivet's. The godmother at the baptism of her sister Françoise was named "de Bourbon."

No information survives on the arrest of prisoners 125 and 126. We can't know either the nature of the incident that landed them spots on Bourlon's chain or what Balivet was doing in Paris and in the company of Geneviève Bettemont, a Parisian of modest extraction, although one who had most decidedly never crossed paths with anyone of royal blood. But one thing is clear. Geneviève Bettemont's fate was determined once again by urban indigence—in her case, by a type of genteel poverty that became unbearable when stock market madness set in.

Whereas the misery of the men who toiled in Paris's ports was so plainly visible that these workers were often confused with beggars, that of Geneviève Bettemont's family might well have remained largely inconspicuous to the outside world. Bettemont's parents, Pierre Bettemont and Charlotte Delormel, did everything in their power to conceal the family's financial plight and concomitant loss of social status.

Whenever he was asked to identify himself, Pierre, a mere dyer who did not even have his own shop, claimed to have attained the more lucrative and prestigious rank of master dyer. This exaggeration betrayed a basic insecurity about his place in the city's social hierarchy. And Pierre Bettemont had serious cause for concern.

In addition, whenever identification was requested, Pierre never provided an address. This, too, he did for a reason: the family moved so often that they were surely on the run, fleeing from creditors and skipping out without paying overdue rent. The one street address Pierre ever volunteered, rue Darnetal, was an excellent choice for a family seeking to avoid detection. Darnetal was a tiny street that gave into the rue Saint-Denis, by far the longest artery in the bustling working-class neighborhood just north of the Halles market. In the early eighteenth century, over 60 percent of Paris's population was concentrated on the Right Bank, and no Right Bank neighborhood was more teeming than the area smack in the capital's center, the so-called "belly" of Paris, the Halles. Merchants, customers, itinerant vendors in search of wares—all invaded the area every day. On the rue Saint-Denis in particular, the hubbub of the nearby market, as well as the commotion generated by the profusion of shops and merchants located on the street itself, guaranteed that a family could easily go unnoticed.

The family of four children—a boy named Pierre and three girls, of whom Geneviève was the oldest—lived decidedly below the poverty line. From January 1708 (when Geneviève was three) on, the family seems to have survived solely or nearly so on 320 *livres* a year, the interest on a *rente* or annuity offered by Paris's Hôtel de Ville (City Hall). Such annuities, a conservative investment, had been particularly popular among Parisians before John Law turned them into frenzied speculators. This particular annuity dated from the late seventeenth century and was a so-called perpetual pension that paid interest on a quarterly basis during the investor's lifetime and could be passed on to the investor's heirs. The tidy sum that constituted its principal—7,200 *livres*—represented the carefully accumulated life savings of Marie Madeleine Damiette, Charlotte Delormel's aunt.

On May 25, 1705, shortly after Geneviève Bettemont's birth, Damiette drew up a particularly well-considered will, of which the annuity was the centerpiece. Upon Damiette's death and during her own lifetime, her niece Delormel was allowed to use the interest "for her food and personal expenses." She could not, however, touch the principal, since the annuity itself was bequeathed to Delormel's children, Pierre and Geneviève Bettemont, and to any future offspring.

By the time of Damiette's death in 1708, Pierre Bettemont and Charlotte Delormel had four small children and a mountain of debt. They owed back rent; they had mounting grocery bills; they had never repaid a sizeable sum borrowed from Damiette in 1704. And there was no one to whom the couple could have turned for help. Bettemont was the only son of a poor family in Sarcelles, about ten miles from Paris, while Damiette was Delormel's last close relative. The couple's few friends were all illiterate and worked at low-paying jobs. Charlotte Delormel inherited Damiette's very modest possessions, virtually worthless at a total of 74 *livres*, and the interest on the annuity: 80 *livres* every quarter, a sum that from then on became the family's principal source of revenue—and this at a time when even the cheapest single rooms in Paris rented for 45 *livres* a year.[31] Damiette had paid them far more than that each year to provide her meals.

Nothing suggests that Bettemont had any income to speak of from his trade. Geneviève, though born to parents who both wrote well, was herself illiterate, so there had been no money for her education. Her two younger sisters never reappear in family documents and probably became casualties of malnutrition and the Great Winter that struck not long after Damiette's death. Pierre Bettemont had died before December 1713, when destitution beset his family.

The interest on the annuities offered by City Hall was not fixed: that month, it was reduced from 5 percent to 4, the lowest rate ever offered during Louis XIV's long reign. According to the rationale behind such reductions, those dependent on the interest from annuities represented only a small percentage of the population and were usually well-off. No one considered households like the Bettemont's, a poor family with no other visible means of support. And on August 27, 1719, when the roundup to fill out the deportation chain was in full force, financial disaster struck the Bettemonts once more.

That day, a decree from the Royal Council officially lowered the rate on annuities still again, this time, from 4 percent to 3. In addition, all interest payments on existing annuities were suspended. The news was in print within days and would have spread like wildfire along the rue Saint-Denis. By the first days of September at the latest, Delormel realized she could expect neither her July payment (they were always late) nor October's.[32] From then on, she would be forced to get by on little more than half of the sum on which she could rely in 1708.

At the same moment, stock in John Law's Indies Company passed the four thousand mark and began its definitive surge. By reducing the rate of return on annuities while Parisians of means were obsessed with the stock market's vertiginous rise, the government definitively discouraged the old, conservative investment. Prices for basic commodities began to soar, just at the time when those without access to ready cash could least afford the rise.

At age fourteen, Geneviève Bettemont became a casualty of declining interest rates. Her entire life in France had been blighted by the annuity that her great-aunt had hoped would guarantee her a fine future. Instead, she became number 126 on the deportation chain and the second-youngest passenger on *La Mutine*.

At no other moment are the arrest records of the Parisian police more jumbled than during the final frenzied weeks before the October 6 manifest was drawn up. Bettemont entered the system sometime between August 19, when passenger 121, Anne Thérèse Valenciennes, received her sentence with lightning speed, and the October 14 transfer of Marie Moule and Jeanne Mahou, who became Geneviève Bettemont's lifelong friend.

Shortly before that, another case of genteel poverty led to the deportation of Anne Françoise Rolland. Once again, her parents had hidden their financial situation well. Because Parisian authorities could not have known the indigence that defined her family's daily life, Anne Françoise's arrest might have appeared to them a case much like Jeanne Mahou's, that of a free spirit deported because she had refused to conform to the norms that governed French society in her day.

Anne Françoise Rolland was born into a Parisian family that to an outside observer might have seemed what would now be termed solidly middle class—that at least was her father's dearest wish. Anne's father, Amboise Jean Baptiste Rolland, was a very insignificant employee of a Parisian merchant guild, but, like Pierre Bettemont, he sought to inflate his status. In 1686, when Rolland married Jeanne Catherine Lucas, the daughter of a master writer who drew up documents for the illiterate, the groom called himself a "*bourgeois de Paris*," a phrase that in the parlance of the day designated those now known as "financiers." But Rolland was a financier only in his dreams. He lived in a single room; since he had no money and his bride had but the most minimal dowry, she moved in with him. Even when they had three daughters—Anne Françoise, the second, was born in 1697—all five family members continued to share the same room and its only bed.

Also like Pierre Bettemont, Rolland sought to hide his address. He lived on the rue Saint-Honoré near the Louvre, but unlike the working-class neighbors who witnessed his marriage contract and other important documents, he did not declare as his parish church Saint-Eustache, located north of Saint-Honoré and serving those who resided near the Halles. Rolland pronounced himself instead a parishioner of Saint-Germain-l'Auxerrois, south of the rue Saint-Honoré and directly across from what was then the Louvre's main entrance—and the parish church of the kings of France.

With this switch, Rolland sought to cover up his extreme downward mobility—a free fall from the upper middle class all the way down to the poverty line. His father, a true financier, lived in the aristocratic elegance of Saint-Germain-en-Laye with his second wife. Neither he nor Amboise Rolland's only brother, François, also an authentic financier and the man for whom Anne Françoise was named, ever lifted a finger to help the son who was clearly considered the black sheep of the family.

At the time of Lucas's death in 1703, Rolland's bed was virtually all the couple owned. The family of five possessed but four chairs, in the cheapest wood of all, pine, and only one tablecloth, with not a single frill or decoration to brighten the room they called home. They were in deep financial trouble: they owed money for food; they were far behind on their rent. Lucas was buried in her only outfit.[33]

Rolland remarried just three months later, rather quickly, even for a widower with daughters aged thirteen, six, and four to care for. More surprising is the fact that he chose a woman at least as old as his deceased wife to raise them. Amboise, however, was seeking above all the best financial match possible; since he brought absolutely nothing to the table, it's a wonder that Barbe Dumontel accepted his hand.

Barbe had no money and a limited claim to social status. She did have one thing going for her, a potential source of revenue from her deceased father's modest position at Versailles. Guillaume Dumontel had served as *garde-vaisselle*, watching over the tableware at the small court of Louis XIV's sister-in-law, the Princesse Palatine, a position he had purchased in 1673.

Upon his death, his only child, who could never have assumed his functions since she was a woman, technically had no right to claim compensation. But Barbe Dumontel seemed sure enough of her entitlement to drive a very hard bargain with Rolland. In particular, she had written into their marriage contract an exceptional clause: the couple would feed and house Rolland's three daughters "only until age 15." Contracts normally never mention a cutoff point since it was understood that daughters could remain at home at least until twenty-five, the age of majority, but the financial power was all Dumontel's, and she was not about to pay for someone else's children any longer than absolutely necessary. Indeed, life seems to have changed immediately for the girls: while the two older daughters had clearly been carefully educated and wrote skillfully, the third daughter, only four when their mother died, had a very primitive hand.

It took two years of nonstop litigation, but amazingly, in June 1705, the Orléans family—the Princesse Palatine was the mother of the future regent, Philippe d'Orléans—finally agreed to pay 3,000 *livres*, half of the original price of Dumontel's father's position. The couple invested it just as most Parisians still did in 1705, in an annuity that paid them 5 percent interest, or 37.50 *livres* on a quarterly basis. That year, Dumontel gave birth to her only child, a son they named Jean Baptiste.

Also that same year, Anne's older sister Marie Françoise turned fifteen, the age at which she would be cast out. She cut a deal with her father and agreed to forfeit all claims on her mother's inheritance in return for a small lump sum. She soon left home and began to live with a maternal uncle. With no dowry, Marie could hardly have hoped to find a husband; twenty years later, she was still sharing her uncle's apartment, probably assisting him in his trade as a pewterer.

Anne Françoise never accepted any kind of buyout. Instead, in 1712, when she herself turned fifteen, her father sent her off to a convent for nearly three years, "in order to repress her bad habits," or so he alleged. She was away in 1713, when interest rates were cut and the family's finances became even more precarious. When Anne returned to Paris, she had no hope of a dowry and no future prospects. On February 2, 1719, Anne Françoise, then twenty-two, left that cramped single room on the rue Saint-Honoré to attend a dance, apparently without asking permission from Barbe Dumontel. Anne returned at eleven p.m. in the company of a young man who, in her stepmother's words, "spoke to her [Dumontel] so rudely that she was forced to take to her bed for two days." Her father, identifying himself to the authorities as "Amboise Jean Baptiste Rolland, employee in the agency of the fresh [as opposed to salt] fish merchants of Paris," quickly denounced his daughter's "debauchery" to the police and requested her incarceration in the Salpêtrière.[34]

By the night when Anne Françoise went dancing, her father was desperate.

It's not clear exactly what Rolland's work for the Fresh Fish Merchants' Guild entailed, because he sometimes described himself as their bookkeeper, but more often as a mere clerk. What is clear is that he brought in little income from this employment, making his second wife's annuity key to the family's survival. Months before City Hall's annuities were affected, smaller entities offering these investments had already begun to reduce their interest rates, as Rolland was well aware. On April 1, 1719, he represented a wealthy cousin from Rheims and accepted in her name a reduced rate on an annuity subscribed with the Fish Merchants. Dumontel's investment soon suffered the same fate.

It could hardly have been an accident that on February 29, 1719, as the interest rate reductions were beginning, Amboise Jean Baptiste Rolland decided to rid himself permanently of the daughter who refused to go away quietly, thereby freeing her stepmother of the expense of her care. The case he made to Machault about the "bad inclinations" that Anne Françoise had allegedly demonstrated since the age of fifteen is easily the lengthiest of all the complaints written about a woman deported in 1719.[35]

Other than the example of the dance and another February evening when Anne Françoise stayed out "until 10 p.m.," Rolland offered no precise information about the young woman's "shocking and scandalous life" and "the debauchery and libertine behavior" to which, he alleged, "she had abandoned herself," behavior that was "dishonoring her family." He did, however, make a pledge that he knew would be key to the quick acceptance of his proposal to lock her away. In the upper left margin, Rolland's appeal was annotated, perhaps by Machault: "He promises to pay 100 *livres* for her board and lodging." That note functioned as a stamp of approval for Anne Françoise's incarceration. At a time when the authorities estimated that 60 *livres* was more than enough to cover a year's upkeep for a woman in the Salpêtrière, 100 was an enticement that could not be refused.[36]

As indeed it wasn't.

At regular intervals in Anne Françoise's police file, everyone from Police Commissioner De La Vergée to the regent evokes Rolland's pledge: the refrain "100 *livres*" punctuates the final chapter of her life in Paris. Anne Françoise had refused to acquiesce to her stepmother's demand that she renounce any claim to her mother's inheritance and leave her father's home, as her elder sister had done. Her father took his revenge by offering to pay for her lodgings in the Salpêtrière.

While his daughter's fate was being decided, Rolland was busy dealing with the new interest rate reduction, an affair that was finally settled two weeks after the regent had approved Anne Françoise's deportation. Dumontel could have hoped that the first payment of 22.50 *livres*, not even half the 50 the couple owed in rent every quarter, would arrive in September—the month before her stepdaughter left Paris forever on Bourlon's chain.

On February 29, when the regent authorized Anne Françoise's incarceration, and still on March 7, when Officer Ponce arrested her, none of the authorities had yet realized that they would never see a penny of a sum that was wildly beyond Rolland's means. By the time reality set in, project "Fit for the Islands" was underway: when Pancatelin added Anne Françoise's name, she pronounced her guilty of "debauchery and public prostitution." Anne Françoise Rolland left the city of her birth as number 52 on the second chain, shackled to Marie Chartier, the governess deported because her aristocratic employer had fallen madly in love with her. The two shared an age, twenty-two.

Five days before *La Mutine*, with Anne Françoise on board, made landfall in John Law's Louisiana, on February 22, 1720, a general Assembly of the Indies Company took place, with Law and the regent presiding. The directors announced that the Crown had decided to reduce still further the rate of interest on the City Hall annuities on which the Bettemonts and the Rollands depended, from 3 to 2 percent.[37] Barely a month later, on April 1, 1720, Amboise Jean Baptiste Rolland was dead.

He died in the same tiny apartment in which he and Dumontel had raised four children. There was still only one large bed, undoubtedly the same one, plus a small cot for his son with Dumontel. A straw mattress and a blanket were tucked into a corner so that the last daughter, twenty-year-old Geneviève, could sleep on the floor. There was little furniture, all of it old and battered and worthless. The family of a man with distinct social pretentions had lived well below the poverty line. Rolland was buried in the only suit of clothes he owned; his widow paid a mere 40 *livres*, the minimum necessary to avoid a pauper's grave, for his interment.

At the time of Rolland's death, the estate, such as it was, could not be settled, for one of his heirs—Anne Françoise, newly arrived on the Gulf Coast—could not be located. It was only on September 18, 1723, that a notary was able to make an inventory of the family's meager possessions, as French law stipulated. Nearly three and a half years had been required for information to be exchanged between Paris and the recently founded capital of Louisiana, New Orleans. Once it had been determined that Anne Françoise was still alive, a lawyer, substituting for the king's counsel, had to be appointed to represent her at the settlement—she was not allowed to return from her permanent banishment.[38] Things were tied up quickly, since there was nothing to fight over. His widow was over a year behind on rent; she had borrowed heavily to pay for food and owed a baker named Mouchy a hefty sum. In the years since Rolland's death, things had not gone well for his family in Paris.

ROLLAND'S FATE MIRRORED THAT OF HIS COUNTRY.

On November 30 and December 1, 1719, initial runs on the Royal Bank took place. Thirteen days later, Indies Company stock plummeted to just under 7,500 *livres* per share. Law intervened to reassure investors, and before the month was out, shares rose to 10,000, twenty times their initial value. In January 1720, inflation soared to 23 percent, and by February, panic-stricken withdrawals of money from the Royal Bank became a common sight. On February 22, to put an end to the public spectacle of the loss of investor confidence, the Royal Bank was shuttered without warning.[39]

From then on, Indies Company stock continued its downturn: within three days in May alone, stock declined by 44 percent. On that second day, May 29, Law was removed from his position as royal finance minister. By July, six thousand soldiers were positioned around the Royal Bank in an attempt to contain the riots that broke out on a daily basis. By New Year's Eve 1720, both banknotes and shares in Law's company were virtually worthless.

Due to the collapse of Law's system, the window of time during which Pancatelin and Law were able to operate with impunity did not last long. "Ridding" France of undesirable women became conceivable in December 1718, within weeks of the uprising in the Salpêtrière.

121

A year later, that window began to close definitively, sometime near December 12, 1719, the day *La Mutine* left France.

Just as Law's policies were beginning to unravel, on March 10, 1720, a royal declaration against paupers and vagrants for the first time explicitly mentioned women: homeless persons "of both sexes" found in Paris were given a week to find homes and jobs; otherwise they would be arrested and, "if of an appropriate age," sent "to the colonies." About a month later, Law once again took advantage of the economic turmoil agitating the French capital to launch a campaign to arrest women specifically for deportation to Louisiana. A special branch of the Parisian police was formed under the direction of Machault's successor as lieutenant general, Marc Pierre de Voyer de Paulmy, Comte d'Argenson. Its officers were known as *bandouliers* because of the blue-and-white bandoliers worn across their chests as a sign of their status, and Parisians called them "*bandouliers du Mississippi*," "Mississippi bandoliers," since by then everyone knew the fate that awaited those they brought in. The new officers were armed with swords and pistols and given the authority to roam the streets of Paris and arrest on the spot any young person who could be considered a vagrant. We don't know if the officers who brought in women during the roundup of 1719 received a financial incentive, but we know that the Mississippi bandoliers were promised a bonus of ten *livres* for every new colonist arrested.

This time, however, all did not go according to plan. At a moment of rapidly falling stock prices, Parisians were no longer willing to go along with practices to which they had turned a blind eye and perhaps even endorsed during market mania. Rumors circulated about false arrests and honest workers accused of vagrancy and quickly spirited away. Soon, whenever Mississippi bandoliers were spotted, an angry mob quickly formed to attack the bounty hunters and prevent further arrests: one such uprising apparently left eight officers dead.

On May 9, 1720—less than two months after the final decree criminalizing the homeless—a royal ordinance banned the arrests of "vagabonds, vagrants, smugglers, and criminals" and put an end to their exile "to Louisiana." The measure was being taken, the edict specified, to avoid transporting individuals who "would corrupt the colony's French settlers and Native Americans."[40] In 1720, d'Argenson received a few stray petitions from parents seeking to exile their daughters "to the islands" or "to the Mississippi," but after Law's stock crashed that May and Law himself was removed from his position at the head of the country's finances, never again was such a request successful.[41] Deportation madness had ended as quickly as it began.

Despite considerable support from numerous authorities in high places, frequent royal decrees, and the police frenzy of the summer of 1719, Pancatelin was ultimately unable to "rid" the Salpêtrière of anywhere near the total of several hundred women she had classified as undesirable. The departure of a handful of prisoners on *Les Deux Frères* initiated an operation that culminated four months later in the sailing of *La Mutine* with some 96 women taken from the Salpêtrière on board. Despite the readiness of those who controlled every aspect of the French judicial system to bend all the rules, in the end barely 130 female prisoners were deported to John Law's signature colony. Never again would women be transported to Louisiana permanently and against their will.

By the time of Amboise Rolland's death in April 1720, those with shares in John Law's company were cashing in: a new French verb was created in March 1720, "*réaliser*," "profit taking." From then on, nothing the government did could restore investor confidence. A year after the deportation of women ended, John Law fled France, leaving behind a mountain of debt. Six months after he bolted, Law's personal debt to the Indies Company was evaluated at 16,254,709 *livres*, 3 *sols*, and 6 *deniers*—far more than the Indies Company under Law's control ever spent on Louisiana.[42] That colossal deficit depressed the French economy for years to come.

A few days before that debt evaluation, an Amsterdam periodical, *Lettres historiques*, *Historical Letters*, declared, "No one can see how France will ever emerge from the labyrinth of misery into which the entire country has been plunged." No part of France was plunged into deeper misery by the debt with which John Law saddled the nation than the country's newest colony, Louisiana.

Chapter 5

Chains and Shackles

Two months after *Les Deux Frères* set sail for Louisiana with the first group of prisoners from Pancatelin's La Force, the "140-odd" women rounded up by Lieutenant Bourlon were paraded through the streets of Paris like criminals on their way to the gallows. On October 14 or 15, 1719, they departed from the Salpêtrière's location beside the Seine in what is now Paris's thirteenth arrondissement, crossed the river via the Pont Neuf near Anne Françoise Rolland's home, and traversed the neighborhood where Geneviève Bettemont had grown up. Some were surely spotted by former neighbors as they traveled in the most ignominious conditions possible: in straw-filled tumbrils, clad only in shifts, and chained to each other at the waist. Along the way, the women saw Notre-Dame Cathedral, the Louvre, and the Seine for the last time, before exiting the city via the Saint-Honoré gate, scene of the murder that had led to Manon Fontaine's deportation.

The women's final sights of Paris, where many had been born and where all had been dragged from pillar to post by police officers seeking to lock them away for good, would have been the streets of Chaillot, where Angélique Reffe and Marie Meutrot had been imprisoned, and Roule, in whose numerous cabarets many of those deported had fallen prey to the schemes of corrupt officers of the watch. Some of them had been torn from their former lives in Paris only days before and, with dizzying speed, become part of this public display of "depraved" women rejected by their homeland. Others had been confined inside the Salpêtrière's high walls for many years, trapped with their fellow inmates in the squalor of a crumbling prison. And yet here they all were, moving through the City of Light and past its fabled monuments, surrounded by urban crowds and street life, hearing the cries of Paris, a city in the throes of stock market madness. All of them knew they were being sent on a voyage from which there was no return. Indeed, only one of the women who sailed on *La Mutine* ever saw Paris again. Only two of their numerous children ever visited their mother's homeland—or met their grandparents, or knew any of their cousins.

With Lieutenant Bourlon leading the way and numerous officers guarding the convoy, the women set out on the 125-mile journey to the port of Le Havre and the same coast where prisoner number 28, Madeleine Benoist, had been born. Early on, the carts passed near Versailles, birthplace of nineteen-year-old Justine Henoch, number 57 on the chain. The women then traveled close to Poissy, which was the hometown of number 32, Jeanne Pouillot. Midway, the convoy traversed Rouen, home to Marie Madeleine Bidault, prisoner 45, and Marie Boucher, still another woman whose deportation was illegal since Bourlon had neglected to add her name to his list. They passed through villages that would have reminded many of them of the hamlets in which they had been born, particularly those who had fled the hunger and poverty in central France, hoping to find a better life in Paris—and finding instead a quick lockup in the Salpêtrière. As they moved through landscapes familiar and unfamiliar, the women crossed a countryside blighted by drought.

Already in the summer of 1718, France had begun to heat up. There was no appreciable rainfall that winter. Spring 1719 was totally dry, and conditions continued to worsen. That summer, Parisians were complaining that "everything was burning" and "the heat was like fire." Most French homes were built of wood, and by July, officials were so terrified at the prospect of a great urban conflagration that they ordered residents to water the streets to cool them down. In late summer, one contemporary observer remarked that "the earth looks like ashes." The harvests were desiccated; famine set in. Hay was so scarce that its price that fall was five times higher than normal; there was little fodder for animals. By September, wells all over the country had run dry, and river water was polluted. That pollution, combined with unrelenting heat and drought, unleashed epidemics of dysentery, smallpox, and other infectious diseases that were called simply "fevers."

There were under 700,000 deaths in France in 1718. In 1719, the death count was well over 1.1 million, higher still than in that memorably lethal year, 1709. The epidemics took their highest toll between August and November, just as the stock market was soaring: fully half the year's fatalities were recorded during those four months. The women on the second chain had spent August and September in the Salpêtrière, where the blistering heat, the dearth of water, and complete lack of ventilation would have rendered the prison's normally squalid conditions vastly more insalubrious. When the prisoners left that hellhole, they traveled through parts of France where conditions were most dire and the death toll from dysentery highest. In October 1719, as the convoy was on the move, mortality in France was 70 percent greater than the year before.

To feed prisoners, convoys always counted on buying supplies along the way, but in the fall of 1719, that policy was doomed to failure. Farmers lacked food for their own families and grain for their livestock.[1] Prisoners already undernourished in the Salpêtrière would have been fed next to nothing while on the road. And their guards acted with barbarity and complete inhumanity. A particularly well-connected and powerful aristocrat, the Duc de Saint-Simon, was so moved by the plight of those forced to traverse the country in chains that he denounced the manner in which prisoners were treated when the day's journey was done: "At night, [the prisoners] were either locked up in barns without being fed or, if the property had ditches deep enough so they couldn't escape on their own, they were tossed into them. All night long, they let out cries that awakened pity and indignation."[2]

TIME SPENT TRAVELING IN SUCH DIRE CONDITIONS GAVE THE WOMEN abundant opportunity to compare notes on how they had ended up on Bourlon's chain. They would soon have realized that a handful of police officers whose corruption was well-known had been responsible for a disproportionate number of their arrests. When the dots among the various women's stories are connected, a conspiracy among those bent officers and high-ranking government officials seems brutally evident.

In fact, well before the convoy set off, a number of their arresting officers had found themselves among the defendants in one of the century's highest-profile inquiries into police corruption, the Procès des Inspecteurs de Police, the Trial of the Police Inspectors. The name of at least one of those officers is found on the dossier of virtually every deported woman; many of their dossiers were the products of collaborations among two or more of the inspectors tried for malfeasance.

There was Inspector Jean Huron, who had taken it upon himself to pronounce Marie Baron "an incorrigible prostitute," thereby guaranteeing her incarceration. Earlier that same year, Huron provided a sign of the kind of cooperation between the Parisian police and officials with oversight over the Royal Bank and the Indies Company that made the women's deportation not only possible but inevitable.

On March 21, 1719, acting under orders from Lieutenant Général Machault, Huron apprehended thirty-year-old Marie Tenon and her widowed mother, Elizabeth Jumeau. The women were charged only with having been found in Paris despite the fact that they had been banished to their native Orléans. But just four days after their arrest, authorization for their incarceration was granted by none other than the minister with the final say on questions regarding the policing of Paris, head of the Royal Household Maurepas himself.

Mother-daughter arrests were usually cases of begging resulting from extreme poverty, but Tenon's name appears on Pancatelin's list as still another "inveterate prostitute," even though she, just like Marie Baron, had never been so charged. The timing of her arrest is also impossible to overlook. Tenon and Jumeau were apprehended just the day after the promulgation of the edict declaring that any homeless person found in Paris was subject to immediate detention and deportation to Louisiana, and only days before, at the inaugural meeting of the directors of Law's Indies Company, the company's first published directive expressed the urgent need for "recruits" for Law's colony. Marie Tenon's exceptionally fast lockup was possible because Machault and Maurepas, both of whom were heavily invested in the success of Law's colony, knew they could count on Inspector Huron to bring in more "volunteers."[3]

In August 1719, that same collaboration allowed Huron to hasten the incarcerations of others who soon found themselves on the chain. On August 12, twenty-three-year-old Nicole de Cercueille entered the Salpêtrière when Huron was allowed to present anonymous accusations as evidence justifying her incarceration. It seems that the vicar of Andrésy, population one thousand and some twenty miles north of Paris, had warned his young parishioner that the village's officer of the peace had designs on her and discouraged de Cercueille from seeing him. That, at any rate, was the explanation the vicar gave Huron when he was interrogated about the anonymous letters that had arrived on Machault's desk, alleging that de Cercueille had been obliged to flee her village after her "criminal debauchery" with the vicar had come to light: the vicar attributed the rumors to the local officer's desire for revenge. Huron ignored the vicar's testimony and locked up "this woman whose depravity was scandalizing her entire neighborhood."[4] Three days later, Marie Chevalier, the laundress accused of theft by the woman who ran the service in which she was employed, became Huron's catch of the day.

Among Huron's collaborators was Jean Chantepie, lieutenant of the watch, the officer responsible for Jeanne Pouillot's arrest in 1718. Already in 1706, Louis II Phélypeaux, Comte de Pontchartrain, the longtime chancellor of France and the grandfather of Maurepas, had been notified that accusations against Chantepie were mounting up. Among them were allegations that, for a fee, the lieutenant would willingly incarcerate women on false pretenses. By the time of Pouillot's arrest, Chantepie's corruption had been thoroughly documented. Jeanne Pouillot's warrant was signed "Sieur *de* Chantepie," because the lieutenant had used his ill-gotten gains to purchase a title of nobility and the right to refer to himself as an *écuyer* or noble. By then, Chantepie was also among the eight high-ranking officials of the Parisian police who were the principal suspects in the Trial of the Police Inspectors.[5]

Because so many Parisians were eager to testify to police misconduct, extortion, and fraud, the trial, which began in 1716, went on until 1720. Thousands of witnesses, huge numbers of them women, came forward with accusations of flagrant miscarriages of justice. Investigations turned up abundant evidence supporting their assertions. Commissioners and inspectors of the Parisian police were shown to have hired master forgers to produce fraudulent arrest records and allegations, even fake accounts of interrogations. Officers routinely carried with them forged royal orders, blank forms that they could fill in with the name of any suspect they wanted to put away for a long time, without bothering to obtain an arrest warrant.[6]

The lawyers for the Parisian Parlement who were in charge of the inquiry further concluded that officers had practiced extortion on a massive scale. Policemen demanded a monthly sum for protection from those who rented out furnished rooms or tended bar in cabarets—and even from laundresses or women who sold used linen in makeshift stalls on the Pont Neuf bridge or day-old fruit from baskets, as Manon Fontaine did. Anyone who couldn't pay up was charged with an offense subject to a fine. Those who couldn't or wouldn't pay the fine were charged instead with theft or prostitution so that they could be incarcerated, and evidence was planted to make the charges stick. Huron thus conveniently "found" in Marie Chevalier's room the very objects that her employer had accused her of stealing. Officers would send someone—often a small child—to a poor woman's rented room to tell her that a commissioner wanted to see her. She would follow the child and, as they passed a prison, a guard would leap out and lock her up. The police would then demand money (72 *livres* in one case) from the prisoner's friends and relatives. Many victims testified that Inspector Huron had boasted to them about his considerable profits from this scam alone.

Whereas officers were required to incarcerate suspects in the nearest prison within twenty-four hours of their arrest, inspectors on trial had locked up arrestees in their own homes, in those of other officers, or even in the apartments of Parisian artisans. They constructed "makeshift prisons" by dividing rooms, a practice that allowed even the lieutenant general to slip in under cover of darkness and interrogate prisoners illegally—and without leaving a trace of his presence. Chantepie had detained one woman in his own residence for three months.[7]

No inspector was more often accused of wrongdoing than Étienne Simonnet. Between November 1716 and August 1717, 286 witnesses for the prosecution, for the most part working-class Parisians, came forward to testify against him. Numerous victims attested that Simonnet had used informants to put them in compromising positions so that he could step in and take them into custody. Others testified that he had burst into their homes in the middle of the night, claiming to have received a complaint about noise, and proceeded to arrest them on a trumped-up charge. Simonnet signed off on the incarcerations of twelve of the women on the second chain, from Marie Anne Fourchet to Marie Anne Boutin.[8]

In every case, Simonnet guaranteed that their side of the story would never be heard. After Claude Heuret, an eighteen-year-old servant, came forward to testify, under oath, that her employer, a Parisian apothecary or pharmacist, had slipped her "a drug that rendered her unconscious [*comme morte*] for two hours," during which time, she contended, he had "brutally abused her," the pharmacist put the blame on Heuret, claiming that her accusation was an attempt to extort money from him. But Simonnet charged Heuret as "a loose woman" and Pancatelin informed Machault that she had been convicted of prostitution—and Claude Heuret became number 137 on the chain.[9]

Then there was Catherine Boyard. In 1717, then inspector general of the Parisian police d'Argenson had relied on Simonnet, one of his right-hand men, to wrap up Boyard's case expeditiously. On her master list, Pancatelin declared that Boyard's family had "begged that she be sent to the islands," but there is no trace of any such petition in her file. In fact, Boyard landed in the Salpêtrière at the request of Catherine LeFebvre, wife of Parisian merchant Jean Bapiste Digeon. Digeon was a dyer, and Boyard had found part-time employ in his workshop, reweaving damaged textiles. LeFebvre dismissively described Boyard as "the daughter of a woman who sells tripe." She claimed that Boyard was "only after Digeon's money," that Boyard had enjoyed "complete control over her husband for more than eight years" and had "forced" him to abandon his wife and family and leave Paris, "taking with him everything of value that they owned." She begged d'Argenson to put "this creature" behind bars in order to prevent "the ruin" of Digeon's family.

The only detail of LeFebvre's story confirmed by Boyard's file is the fact that her widowed mother, Marie Le Clerc, did indeed sell tripe. Le Clerc contacted the police at the same moment as LeFebvre: her complaint, however, regarded not her daughter's behavior but that of Digeon, whom she considered the guilty party. Catherine, she explained, had tried to escape Digeon's control. She had found work in a household outside Paris, but Digeon had tracked her down and "coaxed" her into leaving the city in his company. Now, even though Le Clerc knew that Digeon was back in Paris, there was no sign of her daughter, so she begged the police for their help.

The investigation launched after these two complaints turned up an uncommon story. Catherine Boyard had given birth to two sons by her employer; she had them christened, with friends from her neighborhood as their godparents. On their baptismal certificates, she listed her profession and her address, an apartment in the home of a merchant named Gondar. On the second certificate, Catherine even had it noted that the boy was "the son of Jean Digeon." All this indicates that Boyard was attempting something unheard of in eighteenth-century Paris: she refused to accept her status as an unwed mother as scandalous and had decided instead to raise two children openly as a single parent.

Simonnet saw to it that the case's complexities disappeared. A mother's concern for her child's safety was described as "the widow Boyard's testimony against her daughter," and royal orders were issued authorizing Simonnet to incarcerate "Catherine Boyard, a loose woman who has corrupted Digeon, a married man."[10]

Even more unscrupulous was the officer given full rein over the second chain, Jean Bourlon. Bourlon's first position was in a division of the Parisian police known for its corruption, the unit created to keep the city's homeless population in check.[11] Next, during the years when the ranks of police inspectors were depleted because so many inspectors were on trial, Bourlon acquired a position in this more prominent division. All appointments in the Parisian police were purchased at considerable expense, and officers like Huron and Bourlon considered the outlay a smart investment. When Inspector Bourlon arrested women on false pretenses in Paris's public gardens, he then immediately facilitated their release—for a fee. Bourlon also sometimes played a long game.

On March 2, 1718, in the Franciscan church of the Cordeliers near Saint-Germain-des-Prés, Bourlon apprehended Marguerite Denise Langro and Marguerite Salot. It was their third arrest for theft, always by Bourlon. That day, as on previous occasions, Bourlon had no proof against them and thus, as he himself admitted, no hope of a conviction. In Salot's case, he presented the only "evidence" of her guilt that came to mind: orphaned at a young age, Salot had spent her early years in the Salpêtrière. The girl left when Michèle Bazire, a much older woman also frequently detained by Bourlon, promised to care for her. All the care Bazire had taken, Bourlon alleged, was to "train Salot to become a pickpocket."[12] Bourlon requested that Langro and Salot be sent to the Salpêtrière "for the public good," and, as usual, Bourlon got his wish.

Bourlon kept tabs on women like Langro and Salot, information that he exploited as soon as the Royal Bank was founded and he was put in charge of the patrols intended to protect investors who walked about the premises carrying large sums. It was then that Bourlon devised his own get-rich-quick scheme, one that was fully worthy of 1719, the year in which it was carried out. Bourlon organized a complex operation in which he obliged women to work as pickpockets under his orders. As the officer charged with security, he was informed in advance of the arrival of important shipments of bills. He knew that on those days, the bank would be packed with Parisians eager to convert coin into newly minted paper. Officer Bourlon would quickly assemble a team of women, point out investors who had converted particularly hefty sums, and order the women to relieve them of their wallets. Bourlon's pickpockets then disappeared into the crowd—after turning over the billfolds to the officer, who kept the lion's share of their contents.[13] As soon as Bourlon was put in charge of the October convoy to Le Havre, he made certain that some of those in on his secret would leave France forever. Marie Maurice and Marie Antoinette Néron, whose reputations as "swindlers" he had painstakingly invented, were first on his list.

But Bourlon underestimated the criminals he had created. As the deportation convoy crossed the French countryside in the blistering heat, his web of entrapment began to unravel, and women began to outwit their captors.

THE DESERTIONS BEGAN SOON AFTER THEY STARTED OUT. BY THE time the chain reached a village named Guoy, some twenty-five miles from Paris, Pérette Picard, daughter of a widowed day worker who lifted sacks of wheat from ships arriving in the capital, became the sixth woman to escape. Bourlon alleged that she had called out to anyone they met along the way, begging for help, and in Guoy a number of men joined forces to free her from her chains.[14]

Next, as the convoy neared her home city of Rouen, it was twenty-year-old Marie Françoise Boucher's turn. Boucher's deportation was blatantly illegal since she was a married woman whose husband, André Seroin, had emphatically opposed her departure. In fact, a few days before the women left Paris, Seroin sent Machault proof of the legitimacy of their marriage and begged for her release. Machault made inquiries and learned that Boucher was indeed part of the convoy, even though Bourlon had "forgotten" to add her name. Bourlon hastily assigned Boucher number 149, but Machault ordered her released upon arrival in Le Havre. Well before then, however, her liberation had been accomplished—with help from Seroin, a lieutenant in the Royal Guards, and his fellow soldiers.[15]

Then there was Marie Anne Gachot. Gachot was part of the last-minute flurry of arrests, brought in on accusations made by Françoise de Launay, who claimed that Gachot had ruined her daughter's marriage to Pierre Petit. At the time of Gachot's arrest,

Petit "pledged that only death would ever separate them." The minute the convoy departed, he enlisted in a cavalry regiment and soon yet another woman had been set free.[16]

As they neared their destination, five more prisoners made a break for it, among them, one more woman whose name does not appear on Bourlon's official list, Louise Magoulet, whose father had had her incarcerated in order to retain control over an inheritance rightfully hers. The rescue of twenty-five-year-old Marie Madeleine Bidault was surely arranged by Jacques Bidel, the married man whose wife had denounced Bidault to the police as her husband's "concubine." When convoked after her arrest, Bidel promised Lieutenant Général Machault that "he would get Bidault out, even if he lost his life in the process and that no power on earth could keep her from him."[17]

The convoy was but fifteen miles from Le Havre when two women chained together, numbers 44 and 45, Suzanne Lavergne from Gascony and Madeleine Benoist from Dieppe, also "escaped," or so goes the official record. But no dashing cavalry officers had come to their aid—instead, these women had bought their way out. They enjoyed only a few weeks of freedom before Bourlon tracked them down and returned them to the Salpêtrière. He also arrested a fellow officer, one of the convoy's guards, Le Comte, for "malfeasance," explaining that Suzanne Lavergne had revealed that "Le Comte had facilitated their escape in exchange for money paid by Benoist." Le Comte had demanded 100 *livres* a head and insisted on payment in gold—by the fall of 1719, confidence in John Law's paper money was waning, and even extortion payments had to be made in coin.[18] Because of mad love and mad greed, by the time the convoy reached its destination, ten of the women who had left Paris together were no longer part of it.

And when the remaining women finally arrived in Le Havre, their ship was not ready for departure, so Bourlon "deposited" the prisoners at the Salpêtrière's sister institution. The official record indicates that six more women escaped from that lockup. Three of them were

Parisians incarcerated by Bourlon on theft charges: Marie Antoinette Néron, by then nineteen; an eighteen-year-old orphan, Françoise Gavelle, who had earned a living as Manon Fontaine did, reselling used goods at the Halles; Elizabeth Portelaitte, twenty and described as "young, pretty, and well-dressed," who had peddled oranges to wealthy visitors taking the air on Paris's fashionable promenade, the Cours-la-Reine. The parents of a fourth Parisian, Françoise Lebel, had been among the first to request that their daughter be sent "to the islands." Also among the escapees were two women from the provinces, including a thirty-year-old from a remote village in central France identified by Pancatelin with the improbable name "Aubin Aubin" and accused of "throwing consecrated hosts into a toilet."[19]

In the final tally, seventeen of the women who left the Salpêtrière under Bourlon's command were officially classified as having "deserted" from the deportation chain. But this total was also erroneous, because one of those listed as having deserted, passenger 202, Marie Baron, the penniless orphan accused of stealing a ribbon, did indeed sail. Finally, in addition to the women who bought or fought their way out, other prisoners were delivered through official channels, to begin with, six women described on the manifest as *sortie*," or "released." In these instances, in the days just before their ship departed, their parents' long-running campaigns for their deliverance had at last proved successful. Every one of these cases offers conclusive proof that, well before *La Mutine* left France, the highest French authorities—the commander of Le Havre, Machault, and even the regent himself—were well aware of numerous grave miscarriages of justice involving women about to be exiled to Louisiana.

Geneviève Marie's story illustrates the lengths to which Pancatelin had gone to prevent women from being reunited with their families. Geneviève was incarcerated in 1716, after her father accused her of taking "a small sum of money." Jacques Marie almost immediately changed his mind and asked that she be set free. When Machault "investigated" as he most often did, by requesting Pancatelin's opinion, the warden replied that it would be unwise to release "a prostitute" and a notorious thief who had murdered one of her accomplices, accusations nowhere in Geneviève's file. Jacques Marie went repeatedly to the Salpêtrière, but Pancatelin refused to let him see his daughter. For three years, Marie badgered Machault, who never replied. At the eleventh hour, a father's three-year-long struggle finally prevailed— but only after Jacques Marie went straight to the top and appealed directly to the regent. On November 11, 1719, La Grange, Le Havre's commander, was informed that Geneviève Marie was "to be returned to her parents."[20]

Marie Madeleine Monvoisin's plight further indicates the kind of persistence necessary to have a deportation order revoked. After the death of her Catholic mother, the seventeen-year-old was raised by her father and stepmother, both Protestants, who refused to allow her to practice her Catholic faith. Although Protestants were officially denied freedom of religious expression in France, her father and stepmother nonetheless forced Marie Madeleine to attend underground services at the home of a Protestant ambassador. Marie Madeleine was determined to remain a Catholic, so she denounced the couple to her parish priest, Father Goy, who found her a temporary home with Charles de La Barre, director of the Royal Mirrorworks. After Father Goy turned to the police for help, Commissioner François de Lajarie contacted Pancatelin, requesting that Monvoisin be given work as a laundress at the Salpêtrière. Pancatelin agreed "and promised that she would be well treated." But on October 25, 1719, La Barre learned that, on the pretext that she had disobeyed an order, Marie Madeleine had instead been sent away on the second chain. For a full month, both he and Father Goy repeatedly contacted Machault, urging him to have her released, until he at last relented.[21]

The men who organized these successful appeals occupied positions of some influence. They were also literate and fully aware of the workings of the French judicial system. How many other women might have been released from their captivity had their family members been able to do as much? From Le Havre, passenger 110, Justine Henoch, sent her family a desperate, final appeal for help. Because Justine's widowed mother and all her relatives were illiterate, it was only on December 22, ten days after Justine had sailed, that they managed to find someone able to write Machault, pleading for her release.[22]

Other families failed in their attempts because they did not learn of the deportation scheme until there was no longer time to mount a prolonged campaign. Only in early December 1719 did Marie Raflon's family learn that she was "about to leave for the Mississippi." Her brother wrote the Duc de Saint-Aignan, governor of Le Havre, to explain that the family had sent her to the Salpêtrière merely "to punish her just a bit." They had never imagined that she would be banished permanently from French soil and now wanted "to care for her themselves." But on December 9, when Saint-Aignan contacted the regent, it was too late to change Marie Raflon's fate—not that the regent and Machault were keeping a close eye on *La Mutine*'s schedule. In fact, they jointly approved the final order releasing "one of the 150 girls [*filles*] destined for Louisiana" on December 29. No one had bothered to inform the men running the kingdom that the ship carrying those "girls" away had sailed a full seventeen days earlier.[23]

In the midst of this last-minute flurry of activity—requests approved or denied, parents arriving to take their daughters away—a decision was reached that called into question the legality of the precise police practices that had led to the arrests of the vast majority of the women on the chain. When *La Mutine* sailed, thirty-two women "remained in Le Havre's General Hospital." These women were left behind because someone high-placed in the judicial system had vetoed their deportation at the last possible moment. The determination that so many women would remain in France was in fact an implicit recognition of the fact that every type of arrest, every charge accepted as justification for deportation—all were miscarriages of justice.

The deportation of paupers? Marie Mercier, the poor village girl who sat down with her mother in a cool courtyard for a bit of respite on a steaming summer afternoon only to find herself caught up in a mass arrest intended to purge the country of beggars, remained in Le Havre. Ridding France of foreigners? Two of the foreign-born women—Elizabeth Makranel, Irish, and the German hairdresser, Marie Anne de Morainville—were allowed to stay on French soil. The wholesale arrests of women in the taverns of Paris during the roundup? Anne Berthault, locked up by Simonnet in June; Anne Véri also in June; Marguerite Vasseur in August; Louise Lanneau brought in on September 28; Jeanne Colin, arrested in mid-September—all of them remained in Le Havre.[24]

Blaming every act of violence committed against women in 1719 on the victim? Barbe Lambert, fifteen, had worked as a servant to the gardener of Paris's Saint-Martin-des-Champs priory. On August 2, 1719, she made a formal complaint to the priory's lawyer concerning a young man named Fanot, an apprentice to the priory's carpenter. On Saturday, July 29 at eleven p.m., Lambert alleged, she was crossing the courtyard to reach the building's communal toilet when she ran into Fanot. She said only, "Good evening," but Fanot grabbed her and started kissing her. She attempted to run away; he threw her to the ground and began touching her. Barbe tried to scream; Fanot covered her mouth, beat her, and broke her tooth. When Barbe was finally able to attract attention, Fanot was found with his pants down and Lambert with her skirt pulled up. After Fanot claimed that the encounter was consensual, Lambert was classified as a "loose woman" and grabbed by Bourlon.[25] But in the end Barbe Lambert did not leave France.

Inventing a tale of sexual misconduct or "bad commerce" as a pretext for deportation? Bourlon alleged that Marie Pasquier had left her husband for another man, with whom she had had a child. After Pasquier's husband, Louis Descoins, protested that the story was a complete fabrication, and Claude Rigaud, director of the Royal Printing

Press, for whom they both worked, assured Machault that Marie was a valued employee, Pasquier remained in Le Havre.[26]

Allowing family members to denounce a woman as debauched and to have her deported so that they could claim funds rightfully hers? Catherine Blanchet's parish priest explained that her mother and stepfather had requested that Catherine be incarcerated because of her "outrageous debauchery," denouncing her as "worthy of Louisiana"—but only because they wanted her out of the way in order to keep the considerable inheritance due her from her father's estate.[27] Catherine remained in France, as did Marie Anne Olivier. Olivier's arresting officers repeated endlessly that she was the mastermind behind "the biggest school of prostitution in the capital," while Olivier denounced those who had "tarnished" her reputation so that they could have her sent away and claim her inheritance.[28]

The deportation of women found on no list of those officially approved for banishment and simply grabbed by Bourlon at the last minute? Toinette Luce, a sixteen-year-old Parisian accused by Pancatelin of helping foment the November 1718 "rebellion," and Marie Thérèse Perronnet, accused by her husband of "debauchery" after she alleged that he had mismanaged their affairs, were both "discharged" in Le Havre. Neither woman's name is found on the list of those who left Paris in October.[29]

The deportation of someone accused of a crime and imprisoned despite a complete lack of evidence? After her husband was charged with theft, Marie De La Cour spent six years in the Salpêtrière, even though officers freely admitted that they had no proof of her alleged complicity. Marie De La Cour did not sail.[30]

Sixteen escaped, six returned to their parents, two "discharged," and thirty-two left behind in Le Havre. When all was said and done, at least 56 of the approximately 152 women who departed from Paris in chains never left French soil. That tally offers a sobering commentary on the process French authorities named "deportation." The case files of women "discharged" in Le Havre are strikingly similar to those of many women who found themselves aboard *La Mutine*—but no official stepped forward to denounce the entire deportation project.

For the women who did sail, those who had found no means of fighting for their release and no one to plead their cause, life from then on was dominated by the utter incompetence of the individuals with power over their fates. It is impossible to determine the precise number of women taken from Paris in October because of the "relaxed" rules under which Bourlon was allowed to operate. The fact that it is impossible to determine the precise number of women taken from France on December 12, 1719 is a direct result of the negligence that characterizes the record-keeping of the Indies Company officials who supervised their deportation.

Two manifests have survived, each purporting to contain a list of those who traveled to the colony that month. One of them concludes, "*98 filles en tout*," "98 women in all," whereas it in fact lists only ninety-six names—those of ninety-four of the prisoners who traveled on the second chain, and those of two women taken at the last minute without explanation from Le Havre's General Hospital: Suzanne Chevalier and Marie Deschamps. The other lists ninety-five names, including the two women from Le Havre. This manifest does not record several of the last-minute desertions, so it was presumably drawn up first. That fact alone, however, cannot account for the numerous discrepancies between the two manifests.[31]

The women who did leave France were loaded like so much deadweight onto a ship with the improbable name *La Mutine*. "*Mutine*"—the feminine form of "*mutin*," "seditious," "rebellious." "*Une mutine*," "a seditious or mutinous woman," and "*la Mutine*" a feminine variant of "the *Mutineer*."[32] To those who chose the names for the French Navy's vessels, the idea of a female mutineer likely seemed ludicrous, a complete joke. No one could have imagined that one day a ship named *La Mutine* would prove essential to a scheme to rid France of "seditious" women.

The profile of the women on board *La Mutine* was very different from that of those who sailed on *Les Deux Frères*. To begin with, the passengers on the second voyage were distinctly younger. Only Françoise Deveaux, forty-two, Marie Louise Balivet, forty, and Jeanne Pouillot, thirty-two, were over thirty; five women, including Françoise Vaudetart and Catherine Boyard, were thirty; and most were in their twenties. Twenty-one women deported were under eighteen: Marie Madeleine Doyart, thirteen, Geneviève Bettemont, fourteen, and Marie Anne Dinan, fifteen, were the youngest. In addition, while the first group was dominated by women from the French provinces, the second was far more urban: 57 percent of the women were Parisians.

By far the most striking distinction concerned the justification for their deportation. Only three women on *Les Deux Frères* stood accused of "debauchery"; most were allegedly guilty of a wide range of offenses—from sedition to smuggling, from counterfeiting to sorcery and even murder. The women on the second voyage largely found themselves there for one reason alone: at some point in the deportation process, fully 73 percent of them were charged with prostitution.[33] And that focus on a single crime—"prostitution," used to characterize everything from having been seduced by one's employer to being a victim of rape, as well as completely unrelated charges such as theft—determined the manner in which the women who survived the voyage to French Louisiana have been remembered.

In both the historical record and popular memory, all the deported women, including those accused of offenses of a radically different nature, have been inscribed as prostitutes, as though they had been legally convicted of engaging in the exchange of sexual acts for money. Because of the efforts of Pancatelin and officers of the Parisian police whose criminal activity was, unlike that of virtually every woman they deported, incontrovertible, and with the approval of major government officials with a vested interest in the success of John Law's ventures, a legend that has endured through the centuries was born.

Like the groups of women, the ships chosen to transport them were quite distinct. Indeed, *La Mutine* and *Les Deux Frères* shared only one important characteristic: both had been shoddily built. In 1726, after an anonymous report circulated among high officials in France, denouncing "the poor construction of Indies Company ships built in France," *La Mutine* was immediately and definitively removed from service.[34]

French authorities knew full well, moreover, that both vessels were unsuitable for this difficult voyage. A month before *Les Deux Frères* sailed, two ships were outfitted for the crossing to Louisiana on a high-profile scientific expedition led by astronomer Father Antoine Laval. Before their departure, Laval recorded the lengthy, intricate process by which these vessels were given "as carefully as possible" a thick new lining, as a result of which "not a drop of water got in" during the long crossing. The process, Laval explained, was also necessary to stabilize vessels so that they did not toss about as violently in storms.[35] Neither of the ships on which the women sailed was outfitted in any manner.

La Mutine belonged to a class of rapid and easily maneuverable vessels known as frigates. In its early years in service for another French trading company, carrying 276 men and forty cannons, it had often done battle with English ships along the Guinea coast. Whereas the average size of vessels typically used for a crossing lasting at least six weeks and often far longer was 300 to 400 tons, in comparison *La Mutine*, with a capacity of only 180 tons, was minuscule.[36]

La Mutine was, furthermore, inadequately provisioned. Governor Beauharnois in Rochefort repeatedly alerted those at company headquarters in Paris that supply-chain management was completely dysfunctional. Even though orders for supplies for a ship due to depart for Martinique in December 1719 had been issued in August, in mid-November nothing had as yet been done.[37] And it's certain that whatever provisions were loaded were substandard. In the summer of 1719, Indies Company representatives in Louisiana complained loudly about the quality of commodities being purchased in France—most notably, flour. Although authorities in Louisiana begged for more-refined flour, with all bran eliminated, bakers in France conspired to cheat the Indies Company by preparing for shipment to Louisiana barrels of cheaper, coarser flour. Time and again, that coarser flour spoiled during the crossing. By February 1720, when a decree was finally issued banning this practice and imposing fines upon those found guilty, *La Mutine* was about to make landfall.[38] *La Mutine* had thus transported the very same flour—and far too little of it at that, for the stock that did not spoil ran out well before they made landfall.

On December 12, 1719, the poorly stocked vessel left Le Havre. After a brief pause in the nearby port of Lorient, the base of operations for Law's Indies Company, *La Mutine* set sail across the Atlantic. It stopped again in the French colony of Saint-Domingue, before the final leg of the voyage. The women finally reached Louisiana on February 27, 1720.

Rather than the typical six- to eight-week crossing, their journey had lasted more than ten and a half weeks. The Atlantic in January is often rough, and frigates had a pronounced tendency to veer off course in bad weather. Charles Franquet de Chaville, an engineer sent to help design New Orleans, made the identical voyage a year later in a vessel twice the size of *La Mutine*: he described several weeks of seasickness so severe that he "had no memory left of that time" and reported that most passengers suffered equally. "Nothing is comparable to the pain one experiences on such waters."[39] After crossing the blighted French countryside and spending months at the mercy of Bourlon and his cronies, the women had endured many weeks in a small ship fighting heavy weather.

They had done so, moreover, without any covering to shield them from the frigid temperatures and the intense humidity that would have seeped through the vessel's inadequately built and lined hull. For every crossing of an Indies Company vessel, funds were budgeted for heavy clothing and blankets for crew members and for soldiers being transported to the colony. Not so for the women aboard *La Mutine*, who were treated like mere freight; no provision was made for their protection.

In the immediate aftermath of the propaganda campaign for John Law's Louisiana, hundreds of Frenchmen volunteered to work there on the land grants or "concessions" made by the Indies Company to major investors who promised to develop the land. On the manifests of ships carrying them to the colony, these men were often identified as "*engagés*," "enrolled" or "indentured," to indicate that they had traveled of their own volition. The name "*engagé*" set them in direct opposition to individuals like the women brought there "*de force*," forcibly and against their will. In the years ahead, the distinction between those who came voluntarily and those transported "*de force*" remained a basic one in French Louisiana.[40]

Upon arrival, *engagés* regularly lodged complaints against the captains of the Indies Company ships on which they had traveled, accusing them of "brutality," alleging that captains had "refused to distribute food," even when the death toll on a crossing was mounting. After his journey, Franquet de Chaville left a detailed account of the captain's cruelty and confirmed that even the most important passengers on board had been denied food. Captains cared only, he contended, about maximum profit—for themselves and for the Indies Company.[41] The passengers Chaville was describing were men who could take care of themselves and who were hardly desperate: they were in full possession of their forces, rather than half-starved prisoners when the voyage began.

In addition, all these men had employment waiting for them and a clear role to play in the new colony. The deported women had been pronounced unsuitable for France but "fit for the islands," yet no authority had bothered to establish what exactly that meant and to determine the place reserved for them once they got there. The women's lack of status in the New World meant that *La Mutine*'s Captain de

Martonne knew that upon arrival no one would be concerned about the condition of *La Mutine*'s human cargo.

In addition to the female prisoners, *Les Deux Frères* carried 197 passengers, the vast majority of whom traveled voluntarily. At a moment when the Indies Company was trying to launch John Law's Louisiana, they were a standard mix. Thirty-four were bound for new concessions: three noblemen who had received land grants were journeying to Louisiana; their wives and children traveled with them, as did a few servants, male and female. Two men had been hired by the Indies Company to ply their trades in the colony: a tailor and a carpenter, each accompanied by family members. Thirty-eight officers and soldiers were destined to help build and defend fortifications.

Les Deux Frères also carried other passengers traveling *de force*: there were six paupers rounded up in the city of Orléans and seven more from Lyon, including one woman; there were two army deserters, eight male tobacco smugglers, and fifty-five men who had trafficked in salt, as well as two of their wives. The professions of many male smugglers were listed—wigmaker, baker, papermaker, weaver—indicating that they might prove useful in the colony.

The thirty-six women who traveled *de force* on *Les Deux Frères* were therefore hardly an anomaly. There were many other women on board, as well as numerous contrabandists. All of this could have provided a sense of community, some sympathy, and a degree of security for the female prisoners.[42] Their crossing was far closer to an average voyage than that of *La Mutine*, which, in the annals of French commerce with Louisiana, was in every way a one-off.

To begin with, there was the passenger list for *La Mutine*'s December 1719 crossing. Captain de Martonne commanded a crew of fifty, including two carpenters, a sailmaker, a cook, twenty sailors ranging in age from sixteen to fifty-five, and four cabin boys, all age eight. Everything about each crew member was carefully noted: age, height, place of birth, even their wages. (De Martonne received 200 *livres* for the voyage, the sailors 20.) Only three "ordinary" travelers

were on board, all of them men. Above deck, fifty-four men, all able
to circulate freely.

Below deck, nearly a hundred women. The manifest noted no particulars concerning these hidden passengers, not their age, not their
place of birth. In *La Mutine*'s leaky hold, the women experienced a
rough and humid crossing in the dead of winter, clad in rags, without
blankets. With no woman on board but their fellow prisoners, all of
whom traveled in chains, the women were defenseless, at the mercy
of those with the keys to their irons, dependent on strangers who had
no interest in getting them to the colony alive.

And *La Mutine* had one final distinguishing characteristic: it was
a seafaring death trap, and it had been since well before this voyage.
In late 1704, on an island in the Gambia River, Captain Du Dresnay
purchased enslaved Africans for the ship's first Atlantic crossing, to
the French colony of Martinique. For this mission, *La Mutine* was
outfitted as what the French called a *négrier*, a slave ship, even though
the vessel was hardly ideal for such retrofitting. Because quarters below deck were so constricted, *La Mutine* transported many fewer enslaved Africans than hoped for. The ship left the Guinea coast with
196 enslaved Africans. They had been sailing for only two days when
the first death was recorded: that of "a tall Negress." The next day,
"a tall Negro" died, as did a second on day six. The following day,
three additional captives expired. Only a week into the journey, six
enslaved Africans were already dead. Ten days out, the first suicide
was recorded, that of a man; a second took his life soon after. On
and on it went: in the course of a middle passage that lasted not quite
eight weeks, 46 of the 196 enslaved Africans—nearly a quarter of
those acquired on an island in Africa—died before they reached the
island of Martinique.[43]

Captains considered the voyage from the Guinea coast to Louisiana far more hazardous than that to Martinique: as ships neared
the Mississippi, the winds often died down, adding days to the journey. A longer journey meant increased time without fresh food and

water. As a result, cases of dysentery and scurvy were exceptionally frequent on this crossing. Captains on slave ships reported notably higher death tolls on the voyage to New Orleans: on one 1723 passage, 155 enslaved Africans were boarded in Senegal, but only 90 reached Louisiana. On another, 20 percent of the deaths occurred on the journey's last leg.[44]

In 1719 and 1720, John Law sent German colonists to his personal concession in Louisiana: over 40 percent died during the voyage. The Indies Company knew well how important these settlers were to Law, so their deaths were carefully recorded. The next time *Les Deux Frères* sailed for Louisiana, for example, it carried 213 Germans. There was disease, perhaps pestilence, on board: 173 died before it landed in early 1721.[45]

And yet only one passenger was reported as having died on the women's crossing, during which they were shackled in the hold of a crowded slave ship: passenger 209, Marguerite Denise Langro.

In early 1718, Langro's husband, shoemaker Alexis Philippe, had denounced her to Machault in a fit of jealous rage.[46] When Bourlon added Langro to the second chain without bothering to include her name on the list, he surely felt certain that her husband would never come looking for her. But at the very last moment, when there was no longer time to beg for Langro's release, Philippe decided that he could not be parted from her and chose to become passenger 208 on *La Mutine*. Because Philippe was on board, the captain was obliged to note that Marguerite Denise Langro had died during the crossing, in January 1720.

Not one additional death was reported, and no other bodies were buried at sea, but then no one was keeping track of merchandise considered, just like the flour on board, substandard in every way, "fit" only for Louisiana.

Nearly a quarter of the enslaved Africans transported on *La Mutine* in 1704 and 42 percent of those transported in 1723 died during the middle passage. Forty percent of German colonists expired on their way to Louisiana. In light of these statistics, how likely is it that only one of the women on the 1719 voyage succumbed to the rigors of the journey? Yet when *La Mutine* at last reached Louisiana, and Marc Antoine Hubert, Indies Company *ordonnateur* or finance officer, drew up an official tally of its passengers, Hubert reported that all the women had survived.

However, one other contemporary estimate survives, in the memoirs of an early inhabitant of the French colony on the Gulf Coast. That individual contended that sixty of the women transported on *Les Deux Frères* and *La Mutine* survived the crossings.[47] Sixty-one is the number of deportees whose survival can be proven on the basis of the official censuses mandated by the French government in the early 1720s and the earliest records of marriages and baptisms found in the archives of the archdioceses of Mobile and New Orleans. These records prove that at least sixty-one women were able to begin new lives in the colony.

Roughly 132 women were transported to Louisiana on two ships that departed France in 1719; perhaps 61 were still alive in 1720. If correct, these tallies signify a nearly 54 percent mortality rate, which, given the particularly horrific conditions that the women endured, seems remarkably low. A 46 percent survival rate stands as proof of astounding resilience. It also testifies to unbreakable bonds forged during their horrendous journey across the ocean.

The administrator who reported that all passengers on *La Mutine* had survived, Finance Officer Hubert, was working under duress. On February 27, 1720, the Indies Company director in Louisiana, Charles Le Gac, noted with astonishment that the sails of five ships traveling together had suddenly appeared on the horizon. This was an astounding apparition in a colony largely forgotten by its home country—in all of 1718, only two ships had reached Louisiana from France. The hundreds of unexpected passengers from those five vessels, including the women who traveled on *La Mutine*, were brought to shore pell-mell and lists of survivors drawn up in great haste.[48]

Thus for the women who did reach "the islands," their new lives began exactly as their old ones had ended: in complete bureaucratic mayhem.

Their new lives were identical to their old ones in a second way as well. Hubert's tally and Le Gac's account of the sighting of five sets of sails were but details in a lengthy, panicked report to the directors of the Indies Company in France. Le Gac sent that report because he was terrified by the sudden arrival of so many new mouths to feed in a land where food shortages were already well beyond critical. Rather than bringing the aid that Louisiana so badly needed, the five inadequately provisioned ships full of starving passengers placed a massive and unexpected new burden on the struggling colony. Le Gac reserved his most stinging criticism for those who had sent *La Mutine* off with "96 female prisoners and only 200 *quarts* of flour for the entire journey."

A *quart* was a measure fixed by the Indies Company at 160 pounds. In 1722, at a time when the population of New Orleans was not even twice that of *La Mutine*, the city required five thousand to six thousand *quarts* of flour a year. The ship's allotment, a mere two hundred *quarts* of the commodity most basic to the French diet, was insufficient even for the captain and crew—and allocated nothing for the women.[49]

In fact, funds for provisions were allotted only for voyages that French officials considered prestigious. Before Laval's scientific expedition left France for Louisiana in February 1720, the Council of the Navy had the vessels stocked with "a massive quantity of rations," such a stock, in fact, that passengers had enough for the crossing, their stay in the colony, and the return voyage—with plenty to spare.[50] On Indies Company ships sent to Louisiana, however, critical undersupply was standard operating procedure. Franquet de Chaville recounted that the day before they sailed in 1720, the captain warned the team of French engineers about to travel to New Orleans that he had on board only "provisions barely adequate for the crew." The men rushed out and used their own money to purchase food for their crossing.[51]

Faced with such blatant disregard for those being transported to the colony and for those already there, the Indies Company's chief representative in Louisiana was incredulous. How was it, Le Gac admonished, that the company had transported "troops and colonists and others without sending at the same time food and supplies"? "The situation has to be remedied without delay," the director warned, "if general famine is to be avoided."

The Salpêtrière women who reached this strange new land had been surviving on next to nothing for months. And it would be a long time before the women would be satiated.

ONLY THREE DAYS AFTER *LA MUTINE* SET SAIL FROM LE HAVRE, AT eight a.m. on December 15, 1719, Inspector Jean Huron, age thirty-one and accused of falsifying and planting evidence, became one of the last inspectors to stand trial in Paris. Witnesses testified that Huron would "stop at nothing" to prevent those he had falsely accused from denouncing his practices. In his only defense, Huron simply repeated incessantly that he had done it all "to please Commissioner Cailly," that he had merely recorded whatever Cailly told him to note and had no idea if it was true or not, and that "he had never profited personally from anything." His trial lasted until March 1720. By then, numerous witnesses had made it clear just how much payback there had been for Huron.[52]

Like most inspectors, Huron got off lightly. But soon after his release from the prison where he had been in custody during his trial, the career of one of the most corrupt officers in the Parisian police force came to an abrupt end. Huron was knifed to death in a Parisian public garden in the fall of 1720.

It took longer, but finally in 1722, the jig was up for Lieutenant Bourlon as well. He spent that summer in Paris's Concièrgerie Prison, on trial for malfeasance and abuse of power. It's not clear whether any of the women on the list of those Bourlon led to Le Havre were hardened criminals before he arrested them, but it is clear that Bourlon's cynical corruption made criminals of some of them. In that way, the lieutenant had helped dig his own grave.

In Le Havre, when the remaining prisoners were most desperate, Bourlon extorted exorbitant bribes and, in exchange, facilitated the escapes of the six women he later described as having "deserted" there. Upon their return to Paris, four of them, having become expert pickpockets under Bourlon's careful instruction, joined forces with the most famous outlaw in French history, Louis Dominique Garthausen, a.k.a. Cartouche, and became members of his gang. In 1720, during the months that witnessed John Law's downfall and the collapse of the Royal Bank and of Indies Company shares, and at a moment when rumors of corruption and insider trading were the order of the day, Cartouche and his band were legendary, heroes to many: all over Paris, it was reported that they stole only from those who had become millionaires thanks to their investments, and that Cartouche repeatedly came to the aid of ordinary Parisians facing ruin in the financial meltdown. It was also said that Cartouche was responsible for the murder of Inspector Huron. In the warrant for his arrest, Cartouche was referred to as "Huron's assassin."[53]

Only days after *La Mutine* landed, a marriage contract was signed in Paris: Marie Antoinette Néron became Cartouche's wife.[54] Néron was already active in his gang, as were three fellow escapees from the chain, Geneviève Bara, Madeleine Benoist, and Françoise Gavelle.

Lieutenant Bourlon made his big mistake in early 1721, when he rearrested these four women, whom he had personally allowed to go free.[55] On February 13, 1721, Bourlon cornered Néron in the company of Cartouche's sister Charlotte in a cabaret named Le Sabot, or the Wooden Shoe, on the rue Saint-Germain l'Auxerrois adjacent to the Louvre. He charged Néron with having participated in "a commerce of debauchery and theft with the man named Cartouche" and called Néron "an accomplice in Huron's murder."[56] A year later, Charlotte was freed, but Néron's luck, such as it was, had run out.

Cartouche himself landed in prison for the last time in October 1721. On November 28, he was publicly tortured and executed. In the months that followed, over 350 of his alleged accomplices went on trial, and many were sentenced to death.

One of the victims was Cartouche's wife. On July 10, 1722, Marie Antoinette Néron, then twenty-two, was executed in Paris's Place de Grève (today the Place de l'Hôtel de Ville), for criminal activity for which Bourlon seems to have been in large part responsible. Just prior to her public hanging, Néron made an extended deposition to the police. Of Bourlon, she declared, "With him, all that mattered was that you had money and that you gave him some." From the gallows, Néron revealed the fee Bourlon had demanded for her release in Le Havre.[57]

While in prison awaiting execution, after being subjected to torture, many made similar revelations about the gang's activities. In their testimony, dozens explained how some of Cartouche's exploits had been accomplished with Bourlon's help.[58] Bourlon had maintained an intricate network of informants (*mouches*, or flies), who answered only to him and kept a close watch over the pickpockets of Paris. Relying on an equally intricate network of members of the Paris watch and under the protection of police commissioners and other high-placed officers of the law, Bourlon arranged first for arrests and incarcerations of pickpockets, and then for their release from prison, always for a fee—up to 11,000 *livres*.

On the day of Néron's execution, Bourlon was "confronted" with several members of Cartouche's gang, who denounced him for extortion and false arrests and laid bare the elaborate network of informants and protectors on whom his operations' success had depended. Before her execution, one "escapee" from Bourlon's chain, Françoise Gavelle, turned on Bourlon and divulged the details of thefts in the Royal Bank. While Bourlon was making his rounds on one side of the bank, on the other, pickpockets following his orders fleeced the bank's clients, she revealed. Another witness testified that Bourlon had consistently "escorted to the islands" every woman he "feared might testify against him."[59]

The sole defense Bourlon offered was identical to Huron's. Bourlon contended he had only followed orders, and laid all blame at the feet of three police commissioners: Louis Jérôme Daminois—the very official who had presided over Manon Fontaine's trial way back in 1701, as well as Marie Anne Boutin's arrest in late 1718 at the inception of the deportation scheme—Pierre Regnard, and François Le Trouyt Deslandes.[60] On September 26, after a guilty verdict was handed down, Bourlon asked to be removed from his duties in exchange for having his record scrubbed. The Parisian Parlement chose instead merely to "admonish" him and required someone who had demanded at least 1,000 *livres* for a woman's freedom to contribute a token 3 *livres* for bread for his fellow prisoners in the Concièrgerie.[61]

It's not clear if or when the women whose lives in Louisiana had been determined by the malfeasance of Bourlon and Huron would have learned of their comeuppance. During their early years in Louisiana, communications between the colony and their homeland remained spotty. All the women would immediately have felt, however, the repercussions of John Law's downfall, which began during *La Mutine's* crossing. When the French economy abruptly crashed, the colony whose riches and bounty Law had so ceaselessly promoted quickly became a living hell for the settlers Law had enticed there, and in particular for the women who had arrived in shackles.

Part II

~

The Second Coast

Chapter 6

"The Islands" of Louisiana

WHEN THEY WERE BANISHED FROM THEIR HOMELAND, THE women were sent straight into completely uncharted territory. In France during the year of the women's deportation, although the names "Mississippi" and "Louisiana" were inescapable, freely used by everyone from government ministers to working-class Parisians, few of those who did so knew anything about the region. In *Description of the Mississippi, the Cities and the Colonies Established There by the French*, the Chevalier de Bonrepos evoked the curiosity about France's territory in the Lower Mississippi Valley that invaded Paris in 1720: suddenly, people could talk of nothing else. Yet they were woefully ignorant about this newly fashionable place. Was "the Mississippi" a continent, Parisians were wondering? Was it an island? Or was it a river? Readers gained no new information from Bonrepos, who served up still more propaganda about the "immense profits" that France would derive from "the Mississippi," while offering no verifiable particulars about the region or life there.[1]

Like those who churned out copy for John Law's propaganda machine, Bonrepos was able to publish fantasies about the utopian existence found in the happy colony, because even in 1720, little legitimate information about the territory was available. Accurate maps of the Lower Mississippi Valley were not yet in circulation. Published travel accounts, such as Father Louis Hennepin's 1683 *Description of Louisiana*, concerned only the Upper Mississippi Valley.[2]

As both Bonrepos's and Hennepin's titles indicate, even the territory's name was still in flux. When Indies Company officials sent orders to transport the women "to Louisiana," they were referring to the Gulf Coast. Whereas "Louisiana" had previously designated only French territory in the Upper Mississippi Valley, at some point during the deportation process, it was decreed that the colony now in John Law's hands would be renamed. Henceforth, all French possessions on the Gulf Coast and the Lower Mississippi Valley would officially be known as "Louisiana." In 1720, however, Europeans who lived in the Lower Mississippi Valley still called the land where they resided "Mississippi," or "the Mississippi country."[3] As the women disembarked, local authorities might have announced that *La Mutine* had arrived "in Louisiana," whereas inhabitants would have told them that they were "in Mississippi."

In January 1720, when the women were about to reach their destination, the *Nouveau Mercure Galant* featured still another glowing portrayal of the prosperity that awaited those fortunate enough to settle in Law's colony. The Indies Company, it proclaimed, had promised to grant each family 220 *arpents* of land (roughly 187 acres). In addition, settlers would "be given free of charge all implements needed to establish a household, as well as all tools required for farming, and even a full year's worth of provisions." Soon, the periodical guaranteed, the new territory would be covered with villages, two miles apart and each inhabited by twenty families, whose homes would be built around a central residence, that of the village's *seigneur* or lord.

In no time at all, the paper predicted, a new and improved slice of France would take shape an ocean away, Burgundy on the Mississippi. And unlike villagers on French soil, where famine still raged because of the disastrous harvests of 1719, the inhabitants of these perfect hamlets would never know hunger: "In just a few years, all these farms will be hugely profitable."[4]

In reality, over two decades of colonization had not yet begun to transform Louisiana into anything remotely resembling a successful colony. In January 1720, many Europeans who lived there believed that the territory should simply be abandoned.

THE HISTORY OF FRENCH SETTLEMENT ALONG AND NEAR THE GULF Coast began in 1699, with the founding of Biloxi by Pierre Le Moyne d'Iberville.[5] In early 1699, Iberville explored both the Bay of Mobile and the Bay of Biloxi. He chose to establish the first construction in the colony, the primitive fort that became Louisiana's cornerstone, at the entrance to Biloxi Bay because of the surrounding area, which he thought promising for farming, and the easy access for large vessels provided by the nearby Île aux Vaisseaux, Ship Island. In early 1702, when Iberville decided that Mobile offered more fertile soil as well as a better harbor, the capital was moved there.

At the start, French settlement of the Lower Mississippi Valley was conceived in both strategic and economic terms. The region was seen above all as essential to protect French interests, and it was developed in order to create a geopolitical buffer between English colonies along the Eastern Seaboard and Spanish possessions to the west and the south. If the French did not occupy this land, Louis XIV and his ministers believed, one of France's two great rivals would lay claim to the area.

Settlement of the Lower Mississippi Valley was also viewed as a logical extension of French colonization in the Upper Mississippi

Valley and New France, the French possessions in what is now eastern Canada. Territorial expansion would give France a giant trade route down the Mississippi, thereby facilitating export of New France's most valuable commodity, beaver.

In addition, the region's proximity to land under Spanish control, particularly in what is now Mexico, seemed a guarantee of great mineral wealth. Louis XIV pronounced the search for precious metal "*la grande affaire*," "the major business," and gave Iberville detailed instructions in this regard.[6] It was also hoped that new commodities from the Lower Mississippi Valley itself would provide additional sources of revenue at a time when French coffers were badly depleted. From this perspective, "the Mississippi" quickly began to disappoint. After the first sample products Iberville brought back to France, such as hides of wild cattle, generated little enthusiasm, the monarchy decided against any major investment.

The initial settlers from 1699, roughly eighty men in all, were a mix of colonists from New France, French soldiers and navy officers, and French artisans. The men from New France were well accustomed to life in the difficult conditions of brand-new settlements. But they were unprepared for the intense heat along the Gulf Coast, and many quickly succumbed to tropical diseases, as did many of those newly arrived from France. Because of high mortality, by 1703 there were still well under 200 European inhabitants in all, and during the entire first decade of its existence, the colony knew only very limited growth. By 1708, the European population was but 379.[7]

These few inhabitants occupied minute parcels of cleared land surrounded by vast expanses of dense forest and vegetation. They were also vastly outnumbered by Indigenous peoples, roughly 70,000 of whom inhabited the Lower Mississippi Valley in 1700. In 1700, the inhabitants of the Mobilian villages north of Mobile alone numbered 500, and theirs was but a small nation. The total population of all Choctaw villages has been estimated at 17,500.[8] Such presences were a constant and powerful reminder to those newly arrived from France that they were encroaching on long-settled lands.

The early colonists were able to produce very little food and were almost totally dependent on supplies from France. Iberville imported plants from Caribbean islands, but the climate and the sandy soil on the coast killed nearly all basic crops, and the winters were too cold for sugar cane from Saint-Domingue.[9] Determined to shake their dependence on flour sent from France and to ensure a regular supply of the basic staple of the French diet—bread—colonists repeatedly tried to grow wheat. The relentless heat and humidity destroyed every harvest before it reached maturity.

As for meat, a few cows and pigs were brought in from nearby island colonies but never enough for the colony's needs. In 1701, the total livestock stood at about thirty, and in 1704, there were only fourteen cows at Fort Louis in Mobile.[10] There was so little poultry that the cost of a chicken or even an egg was prohibitive for almost all inhabitants. In the early years, so few ships arrived from France with supplies that without the aid of their Indigenous neighbors, colonists would have died from famine.

In 1702, some fifty settlers gave up and returned to Canada and France. This pattern remained consistent during the territory's early decades, when an inability to grow crops locally, dependence on supplies from France and on food obtained from Indigenous peoples, and the constant threat of famine combined to drive many settlers away.

With the outbreak of the War of the Spanish Succession (1701–1714), in which England, the Dutch Republic, Austria, and German states joined forces in an anti-French alliance, the already fragile colony entered a truly desperate new age. During the war years, the king and his ministers dealt with issues they considered far more urgent and paid no attention to Louisiana.[11] The French Navy in particular was in grave financial crisis. All French overseas territories were neglected, but Louisiana, almost totally dependent on ships from

France for all essential commodities, suffered most when it was abandoned to its own devices.

In 1703 and 1704, a few vessels still made the crossing, but in 1705 came the announcement that the colony could now expect but one arrival every other year. When the long-awaited *L'Aigle* reached Louisiana in the spring of 1706, colonial authorities learned that crew members had left onshore in France the flour and other basic necessities that settlers desperately required and had brought on board instead merchandise that they hoped to sell in the colony for personal profit. The same thing happened in 1708, when a missionary denounced the "greed for making money" displayed by the ship's master of *La Renomée*.[12] Then followed three long years during which the colony experienced complete isolation. As one colonist remarked about those years: "Nothing happened."[13]

When *La Renomée* finally returned in 1711, bringing clothing for soldiers stationed in Mobile, the garments had for some inconceivable reason been transported in barrels containing nails, so they arrived in tatters.[14] On and on it went, with an eerily similar tale of negligence and fraud on every voyage. French government ministers, ships' captains and masters, officers and crew members, merchants in French port cities: all of them were apparently in on it together, trying to make a quick illegal profit off the back of a barely surviving colony. Fraud was so widespread and so flagrant that numerous officials were indicted on corruption charges; the trials went on until the early 1730s. The convictions—and there were many—resulted in the recovery of important sums of money for the royal treasury.[15] None of this, of course, could do anything to make up for all that had been lost to the colony and its inhabitants. Indeed, the years between 1708 and 1711 were among the most dire in Louisiana's early history in terms of famine and shortages of all basic commodities.

By 1707, after France had experienced a series of crushing military setbacks, Louis XIV, increasingly displeased with what he considered the excessive funds being poured into a colony whose "usefulness" seemed to him ever more doubtful, threatened to abandon Louisiana "without getting further involved."[16] Ministers in France initiated what became in the years ahead a seemingly instinctive reflex: laying the blame for the colony's shortcomings on its European inhabitants, whom they consistently claimed were unwilling to perform the hard labor necessary to stabilize Louisiana's economy.

No one ever mentioned that the few remaining residents would have been hard pressed to accomplish much of anything. How could they have cleared away the dense vegetation that covered the landscape near the Gulf without proper tools? How could they have cultivated land without so much as a single plow? In addition, since the first horse reached the colony only in 1704, and by 1708 there were still but four on the entire Gulf Coast, how would farmers have pulled a plow anyway? French officials had at least equipped the very first colonists with basic implements, but from 1703 on, no new tools arrived, and by 1707 any farming was accomplished with the few remaining pickaxes.

Inhabitants were similarly without any means of preserving or processing comestibles. At no point in the early years was the colony equipped with a mill for grinding any corn grown or obtained through trade with Native Americans; only mortars and pestles were available. Colonists had no salt with which to preserve pork or beef and no fishing equipment. They survived on wild game, when it was available, and when they could obtain it from their Indigenous neighbors, since few settlers had guns and ammunition was in short supply. Soldiers often subsisted on crushed and boiled corn.[17]

Inhabitants were also virtually without transportation. Iberville left behind a few small boats built in France, but there was no means of upkeep in the colony, and hurricanes soon destroyed those still serviceable. Settlers thus could not do business with or obtain supplies from French possessions in the Caribbean. And even if they had reached one of those islands, how would they have acquired commodities? They had no trade goods and no means of purchasing anything. Even more so than in France, during the War of the Spanish Succession, coin became ever scarcer in Louisiana. Since no ships arrived to bring a new supply, no one, not even the highest officials in the colony, was being paid.

There was almost no immigration during the lean war years. In 1704, twenty-two or twenty-three unmarried women did arrive on *Le Pélican*, as did twelve others in 1713 on *Le Baron de la Fauche*. These women, who traveled freely rather than by force, were the last groups of women to reach the colony before *Les Deux Frères* arrived.[18] But *Le Pélican* also brought disease to Louisiana, killing many, including some of the newly arrived women. By 1708, when there were 196 men in the colony, there were still only twenty-eight women.[19]

Members of the tiny garrison of roughly ninety soldiers stationed at Mobile in 1704 were among those dead from *Le Pélican*'s epidemic. During the war years, the size of the garrison grew only minimally, to perhaps 120 in 1711. And even by the end of the war, no fortifications had been built to protect the Gulf Coast from invasion. From 1699 to 1711, in wartime, the colony was defenseless.

Fort Louis in Mobile provides a particularly flagrant example of this negligence. Authorities had long realized that the location initially chosen flooded easily and had extremely poor drainage. By 1704, the small fort, built almost entirely of the only readily available material—wood—was already rotting. By 1706, it was completely disintegrating, decaying from the excessive humidity. The fort's cannons could not have been fired since the bastions supporting them would have collapsed. Jean Baptiste Le Moyne de Bienville, who had succeeded his elder brother Iberville and who governed Louisiana during its leanest years, knew well that brick and stone were essential for the construction of solid defenses, but he was equally aware that the colony had no artisan trained in stone cutting and no one to make bricks.

It was only after alarmingly bad inundations in March and June of 1711 that the fort was moved to a site near Mobile Bay.[20] But at first even the new Fort Louis was so poorly defended that it was hardly worthy of being called a fort. There weren't enough workers to accomplish much. There was a shortage of all building supplies, even nails. Over a decade after its founding, the colony's principal stronghold could never have withstood a minimally serious attack.[21]

The military crisis went well beyond the wretched physical structures. The few soldiers in Fort Louis's garrison still lived in primitive conditions. They had no barracks and slept in tents without mattresses or blankets; they had no uniforms and wore makeshift garments made from squirrel skins. Very few weapons had ever been shipped over; soldiers were rarely paid.[22]

On June 20, 1711, Bienville sent French authorities an urgent plea for help, explaining that the colony "can no longer hold out against its own misery."[23] In 1710 and again in 1712, the navy commissioner in Louisiana, Jean Baptiste Martin d'Artaguiette, wrote evaluations that confirmed Bienville's assessment: conditions of life in the colony were "pitiful," with "a degree of misery that breaks one's heart."[24]

Small wonder that, as the bruising War of the Spanish Succession at last concluded, Louis XIV decided to end his government's exclusive financial responsibility for a colony long considered by many of his key advisers an encumbrance weighing on the French economy. In September 1712, a new era began for the Lower Mississippi Valley.

The turning point came when Antoine Crozat, a financier who had risen from modest origins to become perhaps the wealthiest man in France—widely known simply as "Crozat the rich"—was convinced to devote large amounts of his vast private fortune to the colony's upkeep in exchange for a monopoly on trade with Louisiana. The articles of incorporation, published on September 14, 1712, indicate that French authorities had but a vague idea of the territory they were conceding to Crozat for a twelve-year period, possessions that had yet to be thoroughly explored or charted. In return, these *Letters Patent* demanded remarkably little of the financier. He was obliged above all to send two ships a year to the colony, carrying provisions and munitions, and to transport French officers at his own expense. (Soldiers' passage would be paid for by the Crown.) Crozat agreed to only a minimal role in the colony's settlement, pledging that each ship would carry ten "young men" or "young women"—"at his choice."

In exchange, the government dangled the promise of substantial riches guaranteed to flow into Crozat's coffers. "A considerable commerce" between France and Louisiana would be easy to develop, it was said, since the colony was sure to produce valuable "merchandise" of all kinds. Its mineral wealth was stressed above all. Crozat was given the right to "prospect and develop every kind of mine": gold and silver were emphasized. He was also allowed to control trade in "precious stones and pearls" from Louisiana, as well as trade in all furs but beaver, which remained the domain of New France.[25]

At first, Crozat did resume sending badly needed supplies to the long-deprived colony, everything from metal fittings for windows and doors to simple farming equipment (still no plows, though) and guns for the soldiers stationed in Mobile. Just as the *Letters Patent* specified, two ships outfitted by the financier left for the colony in 1713.

Already in 1714, however, the contract was broken, and only one vessel sailed. In addition, like the Royal Navy before him, Crozat used small vessels for the voyage, ships without sufficient capacity to transport the volume of merchandise he had agreed to send. The goods that did arrive, offered for sale at exorbitant prices, were out of reach for nearly all inhabitants. Even when "M. Crozat's warehouses were full," long-time resident and early historian Le Page du Pratz explained, "it wasn't easy to obtain merchandise." Since no wages were being paid, "who could pay for anything, for where would anyone have found any coin?" Crozat's clerks "wouldn't issue credit, no matter how solid the guarantee."[26] The colony still produced almost nothing that could be sold in France for meaningful sums, so Crozat's ships brought no exports back.

In the course of the four and a half years of Crozat's monopoly on trade with Louisiana, famine remained a constant threat, and the colony's economy never stabilized. Beginning in 1713, even settlers who had spent years in the Lower Mississippi Valley decided that they could take no more. Some moved north to the Upper Mississippi Valley; others returned to France. In 1714–1715, soldiers at Fort Louis, paid irregularly and very late, when they were paid at all, remained as poorly clothed as in the past, still housed in rudimentary conditions. The colony's sole port was virtually without defenses, protected by only ten cannons. Sailors and soldiers began deserting to colonies with more flourishing economies: the Spanish settlement in Pensacola and the English possessions in the Carolinas.[27]

Crozat still controlled Louisiana when Louis XIV died on September 1, 1715, and the longest reign in French history came to an end. After his death, Louisiana was governed by councils, above all, the Council of the Navy. The Sun King left France poised on the edge of utter economic collapse. Public debt was staggering, credit ruined, the treasury bankrupt. Unemployment was massive, manufacturing at a standstill, commerce barely functioning, agriculture in crisis. With the nation itself in dire straits, Louisiana was hardly a priority. Only one ship reached the colony in 1716, and it was a tiny one, merely ninety tons, with room for little cargo. During the early years of Philippe d'Orléans's regency, the situation did not improve—in fact, 1717–1718, the prelude to the women's deportation, witnessed perhaps the most severe economic downturn yet in the Mississippi.[28]

From 1715 on, the navy's budget remained unfunded, and in 1718, the council was still begging for what was owed from years past. Authorities in Louisiana had been promised money for additional troops and to complete the fortifications in Mobile, but it never arrived. By early 1717, Crozat had had enough. He sent no more ships; he invested no additional funds; he didn't pay salaries promised for 1716.

Under Crozat's rule, the colony's European population barely rose, to perhaps 550.[29] At the end of his regime, there was still no agriculture to speak of, virtually no export, little coin in circulation. In March 1717, an edict to strike copper coins for the colony was proclaimed, but after an error in the minting process was discovered, the money was never sent.[30]

In a report from May 1717, the administrators of the most successful nearby French settlement, Saint-Domingue, offered a grim assessment of the neighboring colony's economic prospects: "Louisiana is not a place merchants want to do business with. There are few inhabitants, no commodities, and you see no coin there." Later that year, Hubert, the finance officer who subsequently tallied up the passengers arriving on *La Mutine*, was equally bleak: "No one can see any progress in the colony since it was founded." One early traveler and chronicler of the Lower Mississippi Valley, Father Pierre François Xavier de Charlevoix, even contended that Crozat, "far from having accelerated Louisiana's development, had instead a detrimental effect on the colony."[31]

In discussions of Louisiana's future during the months after his decision to abandon the colony had been announced, Crozat offered "advice" to the Council of the Navy. He declared, most importantly, that Louisiana was too great a burden for a single individual and recommended that a trading company on the model of the Indies Company be created to share the expense of the colony with the king. Despite his own glaring failure to make the territory profitable in any way, the financier extolled Louisiana precisely as it had been promoted to him five years earlier: the colony had the potential to become as successful as Virginia agriculturally, Crozat declared, and its mines were sure to prove as rich as Mexico's.[32] Those often repeated but still baseless claims had lost none of their power to seduce. No authority wanted to risk putting such riches in English hands, so the French chose once again not to pull out of Louisiana.

THE MOMENT IN MID-1717 WHEN CROZAT RELINQUISHED THE COLony but convinced the regent's government to continue to invest in it determined the women's fate, for it was then that Louisiana first became crucial to John Law's vision for the French economy. By August

1717, Law had already founded the Company of the West, the trading company whose necessity Crozat had proclaimed. The transfer of power was seamless, and within months Law controlled Louisiana.

In 1717, new *Letters Patent* gave the Company of the West a monopoly on commerce with Louisiana that was even more complete than that enjoyed by Crozat, since the lucrative trade in beaver denied Crozat was granted to Law. The monopoly's duration was similarly enlarged, from twelve to twenty-five years, extending until December 31, 1742. Like the *Letters Patent* from 1712, everything about the 1717 edict assumes that trade between the colony and its homeland would be vast as well as vastly profitable: financial benefits, customs duties to be paid on various types of merchandise, and the price of shares in the new venture were laid out in great detail. In exchange for all these guaranteed returns, Law was required to make only one notable pledge: to transport during those twenty-five years six thousand European settlers and three thousand enslaved Africans to Louisiana.[33]

In December 1717, the Company of the West began to acquire ships for trade with Louisiana and to initiate construction on new vessels. Soon after, for the first time in its history, Louisiana experienced regular commerce with France: two ships arrived in early 1718, and three more in late summer, making 1718 the busiest year for maritime contact with the homeland since the colony's founding.[34]

In the summer of 1718, France found itself once again at war with Spain, in the War of the Quadruple Alliance. News of the conflict reached Louisiana in late 1718 via a ship sent by the Company of the West. In 1719, when the French in France were obsessed with speculation and the price of Indies Company stock, life for the French in Louisiana was focused instead on the hostilities and their consequences for the Gulf Coast. In May 1719, Bienville captured the Spanish fort at Pensacola; in August, the French were forced to surrender it to the Spanish; in September, the French retook the fort.[35]

171

The Company of the West did not cease sending ships with the war's outbreak, as three vessels arrived just prior to Bienville's move on Pensacola. Indeed, more vessels reached Louisiana during the first sixteen months of Law's rule than during all of Crozat's mandate. One thing did change because of the war: in the second half of 1719, when six additional ships were sent, they traveled with the protection of a ship from the Royal Navy. *Les Deux Frères* was the last of these six vessels, as well as the first vessel dispatched by Law's recently expanded company, known as of May 1719 as the Indies Company. By the time the initial contingent of deported women arrived, the greatest danger from the War of the Quadruple Alliance was over.

The war ended in 1720. Throughout that year, travel between France and the colony continued to increase. The Indies Company landed *La Mutine* and another vessel in Louisiana early in the year, three more in July, five additional vessels in August and September, as well as six ships in November and December.

Beginning in the summer of 1720, Indies Company ships carried significant numbers of settlers to the colony, individuals who had freely chosen to make the voyage to find employment on the enormous tracts of land along the Mississippi granted to powerful financiers and major investors in Law's company. The deported women thus arrived immediately prior to a most exceptional moment for Louisiana, the only time in the colony's early history when it knew significant, rapid population growth. The families many of the women soon founded in Louisiana played an essential role in that expansion.

One quota established for Law's company in 1717 was very quickly surpassed. In 1721, the Indies Company reported that between October 1717 and May 1721 alone, some 7,020 Europeans had been transported to the colony, significantly more than the 6,000 specified in the *Letters Patent*.

Prior to the moment in 1719 when the women from the Salpêtrière were deported, however, Law's company had never made female settlers a priority. In 1718 and early 1719, only a handful of women traveled to the colony: married workers coming to find employment on land grants brought their wives and daughters along; a few female servants accompanied elite French families sailing to the colony to take possession of concessions there. Before the policies that led to the women's arrests and deportations were put into place, no more than perhaps sixty to seventy-five women, most of them already married, had been transported by the Company of the West. During the crucial early years when the still-new territory was taking on a fresh identity and becoming definitively known as "Louisiana," the deported women constituted therefore a particularly noteworthy proportion of the emerging colony's female population.

Beginning with the fusion in January 1719 between the Senegal Company and the Company of the West, Law's companies also actively worked to fulfill another significant requirement in the *Letters Patent*, the pledge to transport three thousand enslaved Africans. The Indies Company quickly equipped some of its vessels as slave ships, and the first vessels transporting only enslaved Africans arrived in Louisiana in mid-1719. Then, at the moment in 1720 when significant numbers of ships carrying settlers from France reached Louisiana, there was a parallel uptick in voyages from Africa to the colony. Once again, the deported women reached Louisiana just before a major milestone in its history: the emergence of slavery in the colony.

Slavery reached Virginia in 1619, and a century later, it was developing rapidly in English colonies. Although Iberville had considered introducing slavery at the colony's inception in 1699, the 1708 census shows that there was still not a single enslaved African in the Mississippi Valley. Bienville brought the first enslaved Africans to Louisiana in 1709 as his personal property. In 1712, when Crozat's mandate began, there were still only ten enslaved Africans in the Lower Mississippi Valley. Since Crozat opposed the reliance on the labor of enslaved Africans in the colony, just as Louis XIV had, the situation remained unchanged during his mandate.[36] Had John Law not been given responsibility for Louisiana, the Lower Mississippi Valley might have remained closer to Canada, where the trade in enslaved Africans was never actively developed, than to Martinique or Saint-Domingue, each of which already had some thirty thousand enslaved Africans by 1715.[37] Instead, during Law's tenure, approximately two thousand enslaved Africans were brought to Louisiana.[38]

The increase in various populations was Law's sole significant contribution to Louisiana's growth. In other areas, virtually nothing changed under the governance of Law's two companies. A few small boats built in France to be used for navigation along the Gulf Coast were sent by the Indies Company in late 1720, making transport among the various tiny communities possible.[39] Since this meager gesture was accompanied by no agricultural policy, however, the colony was never able to provide even basic subsistence for its inhabitants.

How could it have been otherwise? By the moment in late 1720 when the tide at long last seemed to be turning for Louisiana, it was already too late.

BACK IN PARIS, AS LAW'S FINANCIAL EMPIRE BEGAN TO UNRAVEL IN early 1720, the Parisian press treated the French public to accounts of wild economic swings—as well as to a last attempt to frame Louisiana as a real-life utopia.[40] But twenty-one years after its founding, Louisiana was not even close to becoming a successful enterprise. In July 1720, when the high-profile scientific expedition led by Father Laval reached the colony in ships that, unlike *La Mutine*, had been properly kitted out for the transatlantic voyage, Laval confronted a still-floundering territory that produced little of its own food and remained dependent on supplies from France. Many years would pass before local pork and beef were produced in significant quantities; rice was first cultivated near New Orleans only in 1728.[41] Laval concluded his assessment by remarking that "this land may be worth something one day, but the colony is just beginning."[42]

In 1720 in the "just beginning" colony, there was never enough food, and disaster was sometimes only narrowly averted. For example, Father Laval's final gesture upon leaving the colony was what he termed "a work of charity." The abundantly stocked ships on which his expedition had traveled had so much more than they needed for the return voyage that they were able "to give food to the hungry, five months of supplies that we won't be able to use, while the people of this colony have nothing, because [*La Mutine*] failed to bring over what was needed. Without our food, famine would have broken out, since it's been so long since Indies Company vessels brought them anything."[43]

Meanwhile, what went back—rather than what was brought over—revealed the colony's poverty in another way. Even still in 1726, the captains of ships returning to France from Louisiana carried back as exports only what was termed "bad wood," a bit of tobacco, also considered of inferior quality, and squirrel skins, most of which deteriorated during the long voyage and were worthless upon arrival. Average total for a ship's cargo: under 50,000 *livres*. That same year, ships returning from Martinique typically had cargos worth 2 million *livres*, while vessels returning from Puducherry carried merchandise whose value in France was estimated at 8 million *livres*.[44] Who would have chosen to invest in any way in a colony that, twenty-seven years after its founding, was not yet commercially viable? Indeed, ships returning from Louisiana in 1726 transported back to France still more long-time residents of the colony who had given up.

The ones who returned to France may have been the lucky ones. Due to famine, disease, and the colony's dire economic situation, perhaps as many as seven thousand of the roughly nine thousand individuals transported to Louisiana on Indies Company vessels during Law's tenure died soon after arrival. In May 1721, the total population in all settlements, including enslaved Africans and enslaved Native Americans, was under three thousand. That figure comprises all Europeans already in the colony prior to the population surge, as well as a considerable number of enslaved Native Americans.[45] As the May 1721 tally indicates, of the nine thousand transported, many fewer than three thousand had survived.

The high point in population in Louisiana's early history is thus also a reminder of an extraordinary loss of human life and of what might have been, had the Gulf Coast been made even remotely ready to receive all those shipped off to its shores. By 1721, when census takers tallied up the colony's population, Law's takeover of France had ended, and the French economy was once more on the verge of collapse. The deported women had arrived in Louisiana at one of the worst possible moments for survival.

But at the same time, Louisiana was at last becoming a reality for the French in France. Thanks to the "Mississippi madness" fomented by John Law, Louisiana finally found a place on the map. After widespread curiosity about the colony was first awakened because of the stock market boom, newspapers and publishers took note. Alongside the last of Law's wild propaganda, increasingly accurate information about the Lower Mississippi Valley and the Gulf Coast began to circulate. The first reports of extensive travel to the places where the women settled were composed in the early 1720s; they were sent back to France and went into limited circulation there in manuscript copies. These covered everything from engineering reports to explorations of the strange and often inhospitable new terrain.[46]

Increasingly accurate maps of the region also became for the first time readily available. Some of the most widely circulated images sprinkled actual place names over an imaginary landscape, while others offered ever more precise depictions of the Gulf Coast and French outposts in the Lower Mississippi Valley. All these maps, fantastic and accurate alike, had one thing in common: they made plain basic realities of life in the colony. They showed, for example, that the various settlements, far from being situated only two miles apart, as propaganda for Law's company had proclaimed, were both few and far between and scattered over large expanses. Since transportation

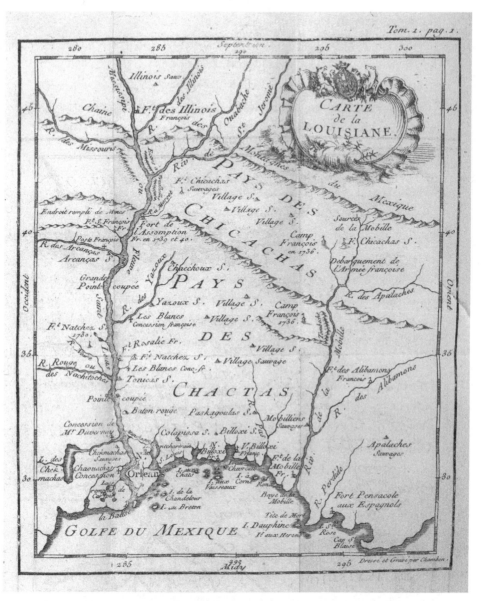

Figure 5. The map of Louisiana included in Dumont's 1753 history of the French territory in the Lower Mississippi Valley.

remained extremely limited and difficult, each outpost would have functioned largely in isolation. All maps highlighted above all the fact that French forts and land grants were most clearly situated in relation not to the estates of various European *seigneurs* or lords, as Indies Company promotions alleged, but rather to the ancestral lands of Native Americans—the *"pays"* or "land of the Choctaws," "the village of the Mobilians," and so forth.

The first authoritative histories of the colony were published only in mid-century. The one often considered definitive, *History of Louisiana*, by Antoine Le Page du Pratz, a long-time resident of the colony, appeared in 1758. Just as had been done in early maps of French Louisiana, Le Page du Pratz gave pride of place to the Indigenous. His account of the colony refers to it still as "a new land," in the sense that the French did not yet have a long history there, and devotes two volumes of three to the peoples, the flora, and the fauna native to the sites on which the French had built their settlements. In a related gesture, when Le Page du Pratz speaks of Europeans who, like him, lived in Louisiana, he uses the French term *habitants*, inhabitants or residents, a word that, unlike "settler" or "colonizer," reflects an awareness of local cultures and high regard for the Indigenous. French *habitants*, Le Page du Pratz's history indicates, had chosen to move to and to reside on land already populated by those native to it. But in his otherwise inclusive chronicle of Louisiana's early years, Le Page du Pratz found no place for the deported women, whom he does not mention.

The earliest authoritative history appeared somewhat before Le Page du Pratz's, in 1753: the *Historical Memoirs on Louisiana*, narrated from the perspective of Jean François Dumont, an officer in the French Navy who had served in Louisiana and become a long-time inhabitant, and based on his memoirs. Near the beginning of his version of the colony's history, Dumont features in early 1720 "the arrival of a ship loaded with women," as well as something still now generally overlooked in histories of French Louisiana, the fact that "most of the women were soon married."[47] Dumont's account of their arrival is the only time that a French historian of Louisiana included the deported women in the colony's official record. He speaks of them as women and future wives, without a trace of pejorative language and with no negative comments about their alleged pasts.[48] For Dumont, they were simply women starting a new life.

Financial Officer Hubert did not accurately tally up survivors from *La Mutine*'s crossing; French government reports made no mention of what happened to the ship's passengers upon their arrival. For this information, we can rely only on Dumont. Without Dumont, we would be oblivious to the first chapter of the women's lives in Louisiana. More horrific than the Salpêtrière, more nightmarish still than their crossing on *La Mutine* was the fate French authorities had reserved for the deported women when they reached at last "the islands of Louisiana."

Chapter 7

The Desert Islands of
Alabama and Mississippi

B Y THE TIME THE WOMEN WHO TRAVELED ON *LA MUTINE* FI-
nally reached their destination, they had spent four and a half
months in chains. It's not known if new irons were attached when
they were released from the shackles they had worn during the voyage, but one thing is clear: even if they were allowed to walk unfet-
tered, they were definitely not fit for the islands on which they now
found themselves.

What must the first sight of their new home have been like for
them? They'd spent so long in a ship's hold with perhaps an occasional glimpse of an endless vista of empty water as their only dis-
traction. And then they arrived—and became strangers in a truly
strange land. *La Mutine* dropped anchor in the colony's only port,
situated on Dauphin Island, thirty miles offshore from Mobile. Since

all those deported were from landlocked regions, the only islands on which they had set foot until then were Paris's islands in the Seine, such as the Île de la Cité, on which Notre-Dame Cathedral stands. When they first heard talk of "the islands" to which they were being transported, those islands surely came to mind.

But the Parisian isles would hardly have prepared them for the place where the women first disembarked. The Île de la Cité and the Île Saint-Louis were urban islands, built up right to the water's edge and covered with some of the most splendid and notable architecture in Paris. On Dauphin Island in 1720, the women found instead a scene unimaginable to them—sand-covered beachfront on which only scattered pine trees grew. A few rough-hewn, uninhabited structures were the sole sign that humans had ever lived there. The seashore culminated in high dunes that obscured from view both the island's interior and the mainland beyond. The women had never encountered white sand or long stretches of beach—they had never even seen a pine tree before. The women had crossed France and the Atlantic Ocean just to face a ghostly wilderness.

There was also the vastness of the alien landmass that confronted them. Even the largest island in Paris, the Île de la Cité, is barely a mile long and only about eight hundred feet wide. Like all Paris's islands, it is also well connected to the cityscape with bridges that the women had often walked, and it functions as an integral part of the city. Dauphin Island today is fourteen miles long and one and three-quarters miles wide at its widest point. In 1720, it was significantly larger: numerous hurricanes have battered it, sweeping away bits and pieces. Today, a bridge connects Dauphin Island to the coast, but in the eighteenth century the island's isolation was total. Upon arrival, the women would have believed that the island's desolate coastline was the colony to which their parents and their country had been so eager to exile them.

Even the island's name was straight out of Europeans' worst nightmares. Well before 1720, the Gulf Coast's largest island had been officially rechristened "Île Dauphine" in honor of the Duchesse de Bourgogne, the Dauphine, mother of Louis XIV's great-grandson and heir, destined to reign as Louis XV. (In English, the name was later shortened to "Dauphin.") But Nicolas de Fer's map of the coast, published only months before the women landed there, nevertheless retained the island's original name: "*Île Massacre, aujourd'hui Île Dauphine*," "Massacre Island, today Dauphine Island." When the women reached Louisiana, the name "Massacre" was still used by all, and they would have been told that they were standing on "Massacre Island." They would then have learned that the name had been chosen because of the extensive human remains found on the island when the French first arrived there and which they believed to be the result of battles and cannibalism among Indigenous nations.[1] And this precise image of a desert island was very much on Europeans' minds in 1720.

Within months of the women's deportation, still another publication tapped into the intense interest in "the islands" that gripped Paris in 1720. That August, Parisians got a preview of the first French translation of *Robinson Crusoe*, Daniel Defoe's legendary depiction of a shipwrecked European that introduced Europeans to the concept of a desert island. The novel was presented as the true story of a man's experience "on a desert island off the coast of America," and the preview featured a scene depicting "savages" tearing their enemies to pieces and preparing to roast a European prisoner over an open fire.[2] Massacre Island indeed.

Upon arrival, for the first time since they had been torn from the bustle of Paris's streets, the women were at least no longer completely cut off from their fellow human beings. When the prisoners were taken from *La Mutine*'s unseaworthy hold, they were immediately loaded onto still another boat. Since Massacre Island's small, elliptical harbor was extremely shallow—often a mere twelve to fifteen feet deep—even a relatively tiny seafaring vessel like *La Mutine* was obliged to remain well outside. *Chaloupes*, small rowboats or lifeboats, were used to transfer passengers to the shore. The day *La Mutine* made landfall, Massacre Island's normally sleepy small harbor was bursting at the seams with the hundreds who had suddenly arrived in a convoy of five vessels and were landing on the beach in what must have been a veritable flotilla of rowboats. In the midst of all this hubbub, the harried finance officer hastily jotted down whatever each captain told him with no regard for those in front of him. Skeletal, caked with filth and salt, covered with vermin, clad in tattered rags, and surely characterized by their ship's captain as notorious prostitutes, the women would hardly have been welcomed.

Many—if not most—of them were undoubtedly seriously ill. On one ship in the convoy with which they had traveled to Louisiana, every crew member had contracted scurvy and required immediate assistance. Bienville wrote Indies Company directors to complain that virtually all sailors who reached Louisiana during the numerous crossings in 1720 were so weak from illness by the time they arrived that they were fit for no duties whatsoever during their time on the Gulf Coast—and these men had been better nourished than the deported women and had traveled above deck.[3] If the swollen, bleeding gums and skin lesions typical of scurvy were also part of the women's appearance, some who saw them debark would hardly have appreciated that rarest of sights in the colony: a large group of women, in fact, the largest group of women that had yet reached Louisiana.

Their off-putting appearance, as well as the iniquitous reputation that preceded them, may explain why almost all the original chroniclers of Louisiana's early years omit the arrival of the deported women from their accounts of 1720. Nothing, however, can justify the fact that, in a colony desperate for colonists—and for female colonists in particular—when the deported women finally reached the land on the other side of the globe to which their country had exiled them, Indies Company authorities wanted nothing to do with them.

In late 1719, in the immediate aftermath of the hostilities with Spain, authorities decided that Mobile's proximity to the Spanish port at Pensacola had become a dangerous liability and that it was urgent to displace the colony's principal base of operations. Already in 1718, the construction of a new capital, New Orleans, had been mandated, but the project had quickly broken down, turned into still another Louisiana debacle. The propaganda organ *Le Nouveau Mercure Galant* announced in January 1720 that six hundred houses had already been built in New Orleans, whereas in reality, as Bienville admitted, "work had barely begun on perhaps four constructions."[4] With New Orleans so far behind schedule, an interim solution was considered essential.

Biloxi had been pronounced the first capital in 1699, but it had quickly proven to be a poor choice. Nevertheless, on January 30, 1720, not a month before *La Mutine* landed, the colony's seat of government was moved right back to the same site. Since there was virtually nothing there, construction began from scratch and in great haste to provide lodgings for soldiers. This plan had barely begun to be implemented when a nearby site was also proposed, named "New Biloxi" to distinguish it from the original capital, now termed "Old Biloxi." Workers were desperately needed to turn either location into a new seat of government, so the inhabitants of Massacre Island were immediately moved to the mainland.[5] When *La Mutine* dropped anchor, the only built environment that greeted the women was the baleful view of the former islanders' hastily abandoned dwellings.

The twenty-three women who reached the colony in 1704 had been given the best possible accommodations, and this could easily have happened once again in 1720. But Massacre Island's deserted shacks were used as housing for the sailors and soldiers who had arrived at the same time as the women, while the women were not allowed to remain on the island. Though the barracks being hurriedly thrown up at Biloxi were primitive, mere shanties made of stakes driven into the ground with a "roof" of bulrushes, even this would have seemed palatial to the deported women after prison cells and a ship's hold.[6] These shelters, however, were reserved instead for the soldiers assigned construction duty on the new capital, and the women were not authorized to set foot on the mainland.

After denying the women access to both the mainland and then Massacre Island, officials finally selected a spot where they were permitted to live: an island truly remote and completely uninhabited. The Île aux Vaisseaux, Ship Island, was a barrier island then so uncharted that it remained unexplored and did not yet figure on published maps. Ship Island is now about eight miles long, a quarter mile wide at its widest point and five hundred yards wide at its narrowest.[7] Ship Island in 1720 was somewhat larger than it is today—over time, like Massacre, hurricanes have whittled it down; one twentieth-century storm even split off a tiny independent island. Barely a year later, the women could have traveled there directly on *La Mutine*. But in 1720, Ship Island was hardly worthy of its name, since it did not yet have a port that could accommodate seafaring vessels.[8] Did the man who had defined deportation, Royal Attorney Joly de Fleury, ever learn that the women he had banished had been deposited on the perfect equivalent of the places to which the ancient Romans exiled their most dangerous political prisoners, a completely barren speck of land? On Ship Island, they were hidden away, forgotten by all. Indeed, without the testimony provided in Dumont's history, one of the most horrific chapters in their story would never have come to light.[9]

Even in a large vessel, the transfer between the two islands took a full day. Covering the sixty-five miles that separated them, as the women did, in far smaller rowboats, was a substantial enterprise. Several tiny barrier islands edge that part of the Gulf Coast. To move the women from Massacre to Ship Island necessitated several days and a series of displacements from island to island, additional days of travel on the heels of the ocean crossing, this time fully exposed to the February cold. Along the way, survivors might have had their first glimpses of the mainland. If so, they found an unvarying scene

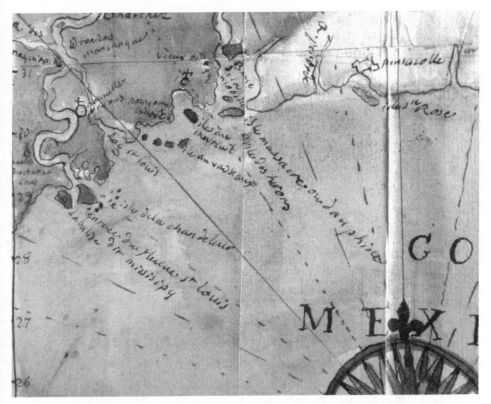

Figure 6. A manuscript map by Dumont depicts the Gulf Coast shortly after the women landed there. The "Île aux Vaisseaux," Ship Island, is offshore from New Biloxi, "Nouveau Biloxi." Old Biloxi, "Vieux Biloxi," is inland and to the right, nearer "Île Massacre ou Dauphine," Massacre Island or Dauphine Island. New Orleans, "Nouvelle Orléans," is to the left of New Biloxi.

of beachfront and marshlands, native wildlife and grasses, against a backdrop of still more pine trees—all of it completely uninhabited.

And then the women saw Ship Island. Twelve miles separated Ship Island from the mainland and the spot referred to as "New Biloxi"; the original capital, "Old Biloxi," was situated considerably farther inland. On Ship Island, the women were thus once again completely on their own and thoroughly isolated, true pariahs. Any contact with the mainland would have necessitated a full day's journey. And for women condemned to remain there indefinitely, Ship Island would have been hell on earth, surely even more miserable than solitary confinement in the Salpêtrière—perhaps even more terrible than an ocean crossing in *La Mutine*'s hold.

When, after months of travel, the women at last came to their assigned abode, nothing had been prepared for their arrival. Nothing, moreover, would be done for them. While administrators were focused on planning yet another new capital, no one gave a thought to a shipload of unwanted women officially deemed prostitutes.

In 1720, protection from the elements was on officials' minds—but only with respect to the soldiers assigned to the Gulf Coast. Local authorities were concerned for their well-being and compared notes on the shelter necessary in winter and what was appropriate "in more clement weather."[10] No official considered the shelter required for the women deposited on Ship Island.

Since tents alone were considered inadequate protection in colder months, even the most poorly outfitted soldiers wore some type of heavy clothing. The women—clad only in whatever bits of linen had survived a voyage in conditions that destroyed most fabric sent to Louisiana from France—had no blankets, and it's not known if they were allotted tents. Furthermore, since soldiers in Mobile's garrison didn't have proper footwear because the Indies Company had refused to supply any, we can be sure that the women arrived on the island without shoes.

Cold there would have been. While a barrier island protects the coastline from erosion and storms, nothing protects a barrier island such as Ship Island. French settlers who stopped there on their way to the coast stressed the absence of trees on the island. There were none on either end and in the middle only scrub oaks and marsh pines, small trees that grow in a saltwater environment, shrubs that bend with the winds and acquire a wild, twisted look. What such small vegetation cannot do is break the gales. Louisiana's early inhabitants emphasized the fact that, "morning, evening, and night," there was no escape from the wind. Rangers from the National Park Service assigned to Ship Island today feel just as the first French residents did and describe themselves as "cold-soaked" from the winds that rip across the sands when fronts come through. One ranger characterized the months he spent on Ship Island as the coldest he'd ever known.[11] While February technically brings winter on Ship Island to an end, in early March, the moment when the women were sent there, the winds are still harsh. Dumont, a hardened soldier, called those that tore across the Gulf "particularly bitter and penetrating." There were few places, he added, where their effects were felt as keenly as on Ship Island.

And then there was the air itself. The rainy season on the Gulf Coast lasts through winter and spring, and on the barrier islands at all times of year, soldiers found the humidity at night so bone-chilling that they chopped down branches and formed a thick layer to protect themselves from the damp below. The air was also heavy with salt—salt that corroded and rotted everything very quickly.

The land is so low-lying that it is barely above sea level. Whenever winds buffeted its shores, the island flooded, as French authorities well knew. When the women moved even a short distance inland, the water level would have been so high that they could not have walked easily or far—and any walking would have been further impeded by the sharp grasses that would have cut their legs and arms.

In this unforgiving environment, the women were left to fend for themselves for sustenance. After a 1701 hurricane filled its freshwater ponds with salt water, there was no longer drinking water on the island, and as for the soil, an official report from 1720 characterized Ship Island as "barren terrain." No one had ever tried to cultivate it, nor had supplies ever been brought to the island—there was not even a storehouse to protect provisions. Officials had intended to build one but had never gotten around to it.[12] During a brief stopover shortly after the women left the island, the party of royal engineers who finally mapped Ship Island was "reduced to eating wild cats and oysters." Whereas these men at least had the wherewithal to kill and skin those cats and the knives necessary to open oysters, the women

had not a single tool. They could have caught crabs running along
the beach or fish trapped in tide pools along the shore and eaten
them raw. One thing was certain: anything they did not immediately consume would have been lost to the island's only abundant
native life form. Every early visitor commented on this phenome-
non, but none evoked it more graphically than historian Le Page
du Pratz, who described Ship Island as "inhabited only by rats, who
swarm all over it."[13]

The coast is not visible from Ship Island. All around their rat-
infested salt marsh of a home, the women saw stretching out in every
direction and as far as the eye could see only the waters of the Gulf.
And water was most emphatically not their element.

The main thing these women from landlocked regions knew about
the substance that had come to define their lives was that water could
be deadly. Immediately upon their arrival in the colony, on February 29, 1720, a sailor from *La Mutine* drowned off Massacre Island:
twenty-year-old Philippe Baudu, born on the Atlantic Coast in Le
Havre. In early eighteenth-century France, virtually no one knew
how to swim, not even those who lived and worked by and on the sea.
And the idea that women would or should learn to swim would have
been completely foreign to the French. A contemporary introduction
to "the art of swimming" was designed exclusively for French men
and contained not one mention of female swimmers.[14]

The fate of the women of *Les Deux Frères* during their first months
in the colony remains unknown. Thanks to Dumont's history, however, it's clear that they rejoined the women of *La Mutine* in their
confinement on Ship Island. Dumont refers to "the two ships of the
Company of the Indies" that arrived in Louisiana at about the same
moment transporting women from France, and indicates that all
these women were taken to Ship Island together. The passengers from
La Mutine thus had company in their misery. The women arrested
during the roundup had reached the Salpêtrière too late to meet the
prisoners deported on *Les Deux Frères*. But any woman imprisoned

before 1719—the single mother Catherine Boyard and the Irish girl, Marie Madeleine Doyart, among them—would have crossed paths with Manon Fontaine before her solitary confinement and would have frequented Marie Brunet, who, like Doyart, had been incarcerated at a tender age, and also Catherine Oudart, locked up without evidence on theft charges but banished from France because she had refused to leave her husband and her life in Paris. On Ship Island, all the deported women at last had a chance to learn from its alleged ringleaders the story of the so-called sedition in the Salpêtrière that had set off the chain reaction that had led them all to a desert island in the Gulf of Mexico.

IT'S IMPOSSIBLE TO SAY HOW LONG THE WOMEN WERE INTERNED ON Ship Island: Dumont writes only that they were there "for some time." When they were allowed to leave, they spent another very long day being rowed to their next destination. It was then that the women got their first glimpse of the land in which they would spend the rest of their lives.

Even the poorest village in the most remote French province was imposing next to what awaited them when they were finally permitted to leave the desolation of Ship Island and set foot on the mainland. Two women from Burgundy, for example, survived the voyage on *Les Deux Frères*: Étiennette Gené and Marie Avril. Gené was from Sens, population roughly ten thousand, a municipality with significant monuments, notably a twelfth-century Gothic cathedral. Avril was born twenty-five miles away in Turny, a hamlet that was only six hundred strong, but that nonetheless featured a château with extensive gardens. When Jeanne Mahou, passenger 129 on *La Mutine*, the aspiring designer who came to Paris hoping to find work in the fashion industry, volunteered for the voyage to "the Mississippi," she declared that she "would never go back to Saint-Dizier." But Saint-Dizier, the hometown she considered so provincial, was founded in the thirteenth century and in 1720 boasted a château and numerous churches, as well as some five thousand inhabitants, more than the entire population of the Lower Mississippi Valley.

Compared with their homeland's rich architectural heritage, when survivors first encountered Biloxi, they found nothing that could be called a built environment, not a single house or structure of any solidity. They were greeted instead by still more sand-covered wilderness and, beyond the shoreline, by an unbroken, impenetrable wall of vegetation, a tangle of trees and grasses and rushes and vines unimaginable in France, vegetation so dense that it could only have been produced by a kind of climate unknown in Europe. There were even trees dripping with a plant that gave a ghostly aspect to it all: now called "Spanish moss," it was dubbed by French colonists "Capuchin's beard" in honor of the friars who served as missionaries. For those who had only ever seen the comparatively gentle Le Havre shore, this was nature run dangerously wild.

On the mainland, however, for the first time in at least two years—and, in the case of Manon Fontaine, for the first time in nearly two decades—they were authorized to live among the free, among individuals who had come to Louisiana of their own volition rather than *de force*. Freedom was all that was necessary for many of them to begin to transform what had been a long chronicle of injustice and suffering into a tale of survival, and even triumph.

Soon after the women reached the mainland, the world that John Law had created imploded, and both France and the French economy went into free fall. But the total chaos that reigned at this moment of financial collapse created a window of opportunity for the women. In mid-1719, their arrests and deportations had been facilitated by the feverish obsession with a surging stock market. In 1720, the implosion that soon became known as the Mississippi Bubble similarly distracted all colonial authorities, in France and in Louisiana.

Also in 1720, an Indies Company officer in Louisiana addressed a "Memoir on the State of Louisiana" to company directors in Paris. He enumerated the various groups newly arrived in the colony and assembled in Biloxi while waiting for settlement, among them, "500 people transported *de force*," a number that included the women, before explaining that authorities had "resolved to keep all the useful ones to help build the new capital."[15] No mention was made of any plans for those "not useful" for construction.

The women surely guessed that they were in effect free to do as they liked and began to slip away from Biloxi. Within months, they could be found all over the colony: some were in nearby Mobile, while others had traveled up the Mississippi to New Orleans—and some had reached the outer limits of the immense French territory in the Lower Mississippi Valley and gotten at least as far as today's Arkansas. Some married soldiers, others wed employees of the Indies Company. These survivors continued to travel far and wide in Louisiana's vastness when their husbands were posted to different settlements. In almost all cases, the deported women's new lives in the colony were clearly documented. Considering the very openness of their participation in the life of the colony, it's difficult to understand how and why, from the very start, their presence in Louisiana has been almost completely ignored.

This blindness began immediately. In January 1721, an engineer involved in planning New Orleans reported that "very few" women had found husbands and that the situation was unlikely to change. Because of their "ugliness" and their "wild behavior," "no one is in a hurry to marry any of them."[16] Time and again over the centuries, this assessment has been validated: even a notoriously scrupulous twentieth-century researcher concluded that but twenty-eight women had survived and that "only a tiny minority of them contracted legitimate marriages."[17]

The reality of their lives was altogether different, as the one eyewitness who from the start noticed the women's presence, Dumont, then a soldier, pointed out. In his history of Louisiana, Dumont noted that after survivors reached the mainland, "most of them were married." His assertion has been disputed by those who believe instead colonial administrators' assertion that no one cared to marry the deported women. Dumont, of course, was right.

La Mutine survivor Marie Anne Fourchet was among the first to wed in Mobile: her marriage with a soldier named Jean La Case took place soon after the women were allowed to leave Ship Island. On January 19, 1721, the couple's first son was christened in Mobile and named, in the time-honored French manner, "Jean" for his father and "Pierre" for Fourchet's father.[18]

The priest who officiated at that January baptism described the baby as "born of legitimate marriage," a phrase that recognized the difficulty faced by anyone who sought to marry when Fourchet did. In some areas, there were no priests. Dumont reported that in Natchez in the early years, "French inhabitants married in front of witnesses, because there was no missionary there."[19] Such ceremonies naturally left no archival trace. Still in 1721 and in established outposts such as Mobile, priests lacked the means to record any ceremonies they were able to perform, and officials were pleading for "large note books, paper of any kind, as well as the ingredients needed to make ink" to be sent from France.[20] In Paris, every false arrest and reams of fraudulent testimony against these women had been recorded, but in Louisiana paper was not available to document their marriages in the manner theoretically obligatory under French law.

Even officially registered marriages would hardly have seemed official by French standards. At the moment when the deported women arrived and were beginning new lives in Louisiana, there was no European construction dedicated to religion anywhere in the colony. In New Orleans in 1720, Mass was celebrated in what was then the capital's grandest public edifice: the warehouse that sheltered provisions from the elements. In such circumstances, couples were obliged to marry however and wherever possible.[21]

Nonetheless, marry they did. These women had been pronounced dissolute and without morals. They had been sent across the ocean to a dysfunctional colony the blame for whose problems colonial administrators laid at the feet of those who had settled there. But survivors refused to give in to the reigning atmosphere of seemingly preordained failure. Instead, they fought hard for official recognition of their respectability because they cared deeply that their marriages be acknowledged as lawful. By June 1721, when a new census of the Mobile garrison was drawn up, at least nine survivors—Manon Fontaine, the oldest woman on *Les Deux Frères* to survive, among them—were already listed as officially married. And this was the tally in Mobile alone.

Survivors cared just as deeply that their children's legitimacy be protected.

In Paris, three babies born to Marie Anne Fourchet as a result of what she had denounced as "seduction and abuse" at the hands of her employer were taken from her at birth. For Fourchet, the words "born of legitimate marriage" pronounced in January 1721 at the baptism of the first baby born to her in her new home were no empty formula. They were instead proof that, from then on, her children were legally hers and would not bear the stigma of illegitimacy.

On July 1, 1720, the official recording of marriages performed in Biloxi and New Orleans began. The second marriage celebrated in New Orleans took place on July 29; the first of three banns, or required public announcements of a forthcoming marriage, had been published on July 21. Marie Jeanne Goguet, deported on *Les Deux Frères* for smuggling salt, married Pierre Texier from La Rochelle, a seaport four hundred miles from her home in Arras. Texier had come to work on a land grant just north of New Orleans and was among the lucky few to have escaped Biloxi and quickly traveled on, and he had taken Goguet with him.

In the summer of 1720, New Orleans was still emerging from the brush and hardly a true city. It was also a considerable distance from Biloxi, a distance that was not easily or quickly traveled. Nonetheless, already by July, survivors had found their way to New Orleans and were beginning new lives there. On August 8, the fourth and fifth marriages in the city's history were celebrated, including that of Marie Brunet, arrested by accident at age twelve, forced to grow up in the Salpêtrière, and then accused by Pancatelin of "outrageous debauchery" so that she could have her deported.

On August 19, it was the turn of Marie Grenet, born in a tiny village in Burgundy and arrested in Paris for cuddling with a young stonemason, to marry Étienne Majardon from Bordeaux. And on September 9, Marguerite Salot, among those on whom Inspector . Bourlon had worked diligently to pin theft charges, married Jean Roset from Lausanne, a member of the regiment of Swiss soldiers serving in the colony.

Of the first ten marriages performed in New Orleans, five of the brides were deported women. And it didn't stop there. In addition, not only did most of the women marry, but they married exceptionally well. Some chose husbands with the kind of useful professions whose appeal seems evident: shoemaker, tailor, carpenter. Those who had been for so long without a roof over their heads or shoes on their feet and almost without clothing ended such deprivations on the spot. Others elected never to go hungry again.

Some, like Geneviève Bettemont, had grown up ill-nourished because of their family's poor investment choices and then endured the caloric deprivation of the deportation process. Bettemont, the second-youngest survivor, quickly exchanged the Gulf Coast and the never-ending struggle for basic necessities that defined life there for what soon became the most prosperous area in the colony, the rich farmland along the Mississippi north of New Orleans. She and her husband, Jacques Antoine Le Borne, grew food crops and owned livestock, so that Bettemont and her eight children wanted for nothing.

In Paris, Anne Françoise Rolland had wanted for everything because the man who denounced her to the police, her own father, so badly mismanaged his family's affairs. In Louisiana, she immediately chose status, money, and security. Rolland went right to the top and married the man with the keys to the only store in the colony, the storehouse where all provisions sent by the Indies Company were kept under lock and key. In Louisiana, Anne Françoise Rolland, by then twenty-three, instantly acquired the kind of status her father had longed for all his adult life.

Nicolas Sarazin was *garde-magasin*, storehouse guard, first in Mobile and then in New Orleans. His was a privileged position, among the best paid in Louisiana, with a key proviso: it came "with provisions," guaranteeing that Sarazin and his family would be the best nourished of the early settlers. In a colony where all commodities had from the start been desperately lacking, storehouse guard was a position with real status. On the 1721 Mobile census, Sarazin is among the few to be granted the honorific "*sieur*," "lord."[22] During the thirty-eight years she spent in the colony, Anne Françoise outlived her first two husbands, married a third, and raised nine children—and the woman brought up in genteel poverty always had everything she needed, and more. Indeed, in 1723, the Sarazins were even accused of living too "magnificently," with lodgings, furniture, and a table so fine that they attracted undue attention.[23] The woman who had spent the first twenty-two years of her life sharing a single bed with four others and had never been sure of finding even a miserable chair in which to sit now had more chairs than she knew what to do with and could enjoy a pleasure always denied her own mother—putting on a display for guests.

Several of the women—Marie Grenet, Marie Bordeau, and Marguerite Salot among them—survived all the horrors of prison and the crossing only to succumb soon after they married to the combination of climate, disease, and malnutrition that wreaked destruction in every settlement in the colony. Most survivors, however, had life spans that far exceeded expectations in France. At a moment when the average life expectancy in France for a woman was but twenty-seven, they lived into their forties and fifties.[24] A number of women even demonstrated a longevity truly exceptional for the age. In July 1738, having outlived her first three husbands, Angélique Reffe married for the fourth time in New Orleans. Life along the Mississippi was also kind to Geneviève Bettemont. Whereas only one other of her siblings in Paris survived infancy and her father died young, when Geneviève was barely eight, Bettemont herself was seventy-nine at the time of her death. She had outlived her longest-surviving sibling in Paris by twenty-one years.

In such cases, the women lived a far greater part of their lives in French territory across the ocean than they had in the country of their birth. In all the years they spent in Louisiana, the only unlawful activity of which any survivors were accused seems readily comprehensible: "seditious" conspiracy to desert the colony.

These facts make it difficult to understand the manner in which survivors' lives in Louisiana have consistently been presented. Soon after their arrival, local authorities began to complain that the deported women had returned to their old ways. Already in 1720, one asked rhetorically, "What can one expect from criminals who find themselves in a country where it's more difficult than in Europe to repress licentiousness?" In 1722, an army officer wrote that "men of any stature cannot agree to marry [such women] because of the bad reputation that they bring from France." In September 1724, Indies Company representative Gilles Raguet petitioned Louisiana's Superior Council: characterizing survivors as "good for nothing," "libertines" who had "continued their bad conduct," and alleging that many were working as prostitutes and "debauching others," he begged that they be "rounded up and transported to the most distant outposts of the colony." In a 1725 petition to Indies Company directors, Commissioner La Chaise went him one better: since "many of these women have not found husbands and are ruining the colony," he asked permission to return them to France and thereby "purge the colony of women of ill-repute who are entirely lost."[25] "Purging" Louisiana of women no one wanted—it might have been Pancatelin all over again.

Even though the name of a survivor was never attached to any such accusation, through the centuries the myth created amidst the financial delirium of 1719 by parents seeking money that rightfully belonged to their daughters and by a prison warden and police officials seeking to curry favor with John Law has taken on a life of its own. For this reason, the notion that women "convicted" of prostitution in Paris had returned to their old ways when they reached the colony has gone unchallenged.[26]

In the years immediately following the women's arrival, Louisiana at last took on the contours of an established colony. The building of New Orleans advanced, and a recognizable, if miniature, capital emerged. For the first time, the belief took hold that, now that it had a significant population, Louisiana required "a new form of government," a more developed administrative structure located in the colony itself. (One justification given was the need "to keep all those exiled there under tight surveillance.")[27] Censuses included for the first time a significant number of families, in New Orleans and in Mobile and Biloxi and even in small settlements along the Mississippi. Also for the first time, Louisiana knew an important birth rate.

That normally scrupulous researcher, Marcel Giraud, concluded that, of all those who arrived on *Les Deux Frères* and *La Mutine*, only seventeen married in Louisiana. In fact, of the sixty-one survivors, at least fifty-two married. In a colony that in 1712, just seven years before their arrival, had counted only twenty-eight families, not only along the Gulf Coast but in its entire vast territory, these marriages played a significant role in the settlement of the Lower Mississippi Valley. Whereas it was alleged that none of the women deported on *Les Deux Frères* "recorded any descendants," in reality, several founded dynasties that flourish still today. The November 1721 census of the Lower Mississippi Valley listed 140 Frenchwomen in the greater New Orleans area and 95 more in Mobile. A quarter of these 235 Frenchwomen were survivors.[28]

Survivors were among the original property owners in New Orleans. There, and in all early settlements from Natchez to

Natchitoches, they were among the founding inhabitants, present at the start. They helped clear the land, making way for the first constructions, which they often helped build. These allegedly worthless women played a crucial role in shaping French Louisiana and in giving this country's second coast a French identity.

Survivors and their husbands were highly visible when the colony developed religious and civic structures. As their children contracted ever more prominent marriages, their families rose in status. By the time of their deaths, many women who had left France in disgrace and had been treated as subhuman upon their arrival in Louisiana had become notables, pillars of their communities.

Chapter 8

Biloxi's Deadly Sands

A T THE PRECISE MOMENT WHEN THE WOMEN WERE ABANDONED on Ship Island, all authorities were at last reaching the conclusion that the site at Biloxi where work on a new capital had already begun was unacceptable. Shortly thereafter, building started, once again in haste, on still another interim seat of government, this time, one situated on the coast rather than inland. When the women were at last authorized to leave Ship Island and to set foot on the mainland, they were taken directly there. They found a place still under construction and still officially nameless. The new seat of government definitively began to be called "New Biloxi" only some months after their arrival.[1] For the first time in all their travails, the women were truly nowhere, off the grid. Only five of them chose to stay in New Biloxi and to get a fresh start in life there. Numerous factors explain why so few remained, but it was first and foremost the complete disorganization that surrounded the establishment of the latest outpost intended to serve as the capital of the colony that was just then the talk of the town in Paris.

In his history, Dumont describes in detail the five weeks he and sixty other soldiers spent trying to help Louisiana's new capital take shape. They felled trees, using them to construct crude, bark-roofed housing intended for thirty-two soldiers. In the end, they cleared just enough land for an encampment consisting of nothing more than those rudimentary barracks, a pavilion for officers, quarters for the commander, a guardhouse, and storehouses to protect food and supplies from the elements.[2]

French authorities then proceeded to articulate still another confoundingly wrongheaded policy. As 1720 unfolded, vessel after vessel deposited on Massacre Island new residents of various kinds, in particular *habitants* arriving from France to develop land grant holdings. A few managed to leave the island quickly and traveled on to their inland destinations. Then, as soon as the decision came to make New Biloxi the capital, all remaining recent immigrants were sent there. Since the boats that the Indies Company had guaranteed to transport new arrivals to their final destinations had never been built, would-be inhabitants—hundreds and then thousands of them as the months went by—found themselves trapped at New Biloxi with no way out. Because the recently completed encampment was intended only for military personnel, prospective inhabitants were simply discarded on the waterfront and abandoned to their fate. When they were taken from Ship Island, the women were dropped off on New Biloxi's beachfront and left to become part of an ever larger mass of underfed and unwashed humanity.

By the time the situation in New Biloxi became critical, authorities in France were trying to recover for the French state what they were now presenting as ill-gotten gains, the fortunes made by the biggest investors in Indies Company stock. Because a number of those with the largest profits were individuals who had received major land grants in the colony, by the end of the recovery process, their concessions were bankrupt. Among the insolvent concessions was what had been intended to become the largest of them all, the one owned by Law himself—that grand project to develop a chunk of Louisiana fell apart the minute the financier left France. Although the news of Law's downfall would not reach them until June 1721, most of those stranded on the sands of Biloxi no longer had a future in the colony.

By January 1721, the Indies Company was on the verge of bankruptcy and was selling assets, including ships used for trade with Louisiana, in order to raise cash. During the year that followed, month after month decrees were published abolishing privileges granted the Royal Bank and the Indies Company in 1719, when Law was consolidating his power. On January 23, one edict even announced that "all bank accounts have been eliminated." At the same time, cost-cutting measures revealed the government's desperation. In May, the month that witnessed the devaluation of all coin, even copper, a dramatic cutback of the French Army was proclaimed, and every battalion was reduced in size. It would be a long time before any additional troops were shipped off to defend an overseas colony. It would also be a long time before anyone made new investments in Louisiana's development. Indeed, from 1721 to 1723, nothing could be budgeted for Louisiana's subsistence. In May 1721, Bienville believed that the colony was unlikely to survive the latest crisis.[3]

Those who had come to work on Indies Company concessions had arrived with a stock of supplies that had been intended to tide them over until their first harvest. Officials decided that all stocks should be used immediately. Because provisions had been allocated only for small groups, while the horde on the seafront grew ever larger, supplies quickly ran out. A colonial administrator bemoaned the fact that prices for any available comestibles were sky-high. And even then, "almost no food was to be had. People are staying alive only with the greatest difficulty."[4]

By late 1720, Indies Company officials openly recognized that the situation was untenable. They estimated that over twenty-five

hundred prospective residents had been abandoned on the beachfront. In early 1721, they estimated that five hundred to six hundred
had died in New Biloxi in the course of the second half of 1720 alone;
by April, the estimate had risen to nine hundred.[5]

They died from overcrowding; they died from eating food that
had spoiled in the heat—and from not eating at all. They died from
dehydration and the relentless summer temperatures on the Gulf
Coast. Above all, they died from disease, especially scurvy and dysentery. When a land grant holder named Pellerin found himself
stranded on the beach along with countless other new inhabitants,
he wrote his family in France, detailing the horrors of New Biloxi.
The eyewitness chronicle that Pellerin, who spent three months
watching the deaths mount up, sent home on October 16, 1720,
makes plain that the official toll was surely a wild underestimation
of the loss of human life. In August, Pellerin noted, 45 out of some
240 in his party were already ill; by October the number had risen
to 112, and 13 had died; he judged that another 20 would likely not
survive—and Pellerin observed only the most fortunate, those who
had traveled with their own supplies. "A ship from Dunkirk arrived
two days before we did with 300 on board," he concluded, but "only
ten remain alive. You can imagine the rest. It seems that death is an
offering that this land demands."[6]

On the beach, record-keeping was spotty at best. A note later ap-
pended to Biloxi's sacramental register explained that missionaries at
the site had often had no time to document deaths "because priests
had all they could do taking care of the sick."[7] Even though there
were quite likely others, only one death of a deported woman was
recorded. On December 16, 1720, Marguerite Dupuys, passenger
number 45 on *La Mutine*, was buried at Old Fort Biloxi.[8]

FIVE SURVIVORS BEGAN NEW LIVES EVEN AS THE WORLD AROUND
them was disintegrating. To marry, they had to travel the twelve miles
between the coast and the site of French Louisiana's first capital, now

officially dubbed "Old Biloxi." For anyone newly arrived from France, even Old Biloxi, a long-standing French outpost, would have been risible. In the words of one French official who first saw Old Biloxi in November 1720, the month when two survivors married there, "There is one hut that perhaps could be called a house; the administrators live there. Everything else is just a few sticks in the ground, holding up a covering of bulrushes."[9] A proper settlement? Hardly. To the Frenchwomen who wed there, the agglomeration of sand and shoddy construction must have seemed a shantytown.

Marriages took place in Old Biloxi's sole construction of any substance—the fort, in a makeshift chapel wedged inside a corner of one of its bastions.[10] Fort Maurepas was named for the Maurepas dynasty of royal ministers. Many names the survivors heard around them in the New World—such as Biloxi (in French, most often written "Bilocci," a transliteration of the name of nearby Native Americans)—would have had no resonance for them. Not so "Maurepas." From the turn of the century, when the fort was founded and Manon Fontaine arrested, until the women's deportation, one of three successive Comtes de Maurepas had signed off on the decisions that sealed their fates.

For Catherine Boyard in particular, the shadow of Fort Maurepas would have served as a reminder of all that France had taken from her. On November 5, 1720, when Parisian Catherine Boyard stood before Father Jean Mathieu, parish priest of Old Biloxi, and became the first survivor of *La Mutine* to marry there, she declared as her parish church Saint-Jacques-de-la-Boucherie, where she had been baptized, rather than the nearby Saint-Jean-en-Grève, where she had had her two out-of-wedlock children christened.[11] Boyard raised her sons as a single mother, only to lose them forever upon her incarceration on charges of having "debauched" a married man. At age thirty-two, when Boyard wed Augustin Dupart in a French capital hardly likely to recall to her the city of her birth, she got a second chance. Dupart, a native of Saint-Malo, was a ship's pilot, knowledgeable in the ways of maneuvering vessels through difficult passages, skills invaluable in a colony with many treacherous waterways, including the Mississippi itself.

In his brief account of the ceremony, Father Mathieu used a most unusual formula repeatedly found in records of the earliest marriages of survivors in Biloxi. When he "certified that he had married them *juridiquement en face de l'église*"—"lawfully in front of the church"—the priest pronounced their unions valid both *juridiquement*, according to the terms of French law, and *en face de l'église*, according to the regulations of the Catholic Church. Priests thereby stressed something essential to survivors, the fact that, although these unions between Frenchmen and Frenchwomen were being performed in conditions unthinkable in France, notably not in a church, the marriages were both legal and sacramental, legitimate in every way.

On November 25, a woman added late to the chain of deportees, Marie Louise Balivet, married Jacques Duval. Balivet, by then forty-one, was the second-oldest survivor from *La Mutine*. Balivet and her new husband had lived but twenty-six miles apart in France, he just southeast of Paris, in Vitry-sur-Seine, she just west of the capital, in Saint-Germain-en-Laye. Not long before they wed, they met across an ocean on Biloxi beach. Seaman Duval had reached the colony only on September 22, after a voyage during which seven of twenty sailors died.[12] The ceremony was unusual, even by local standards. The officiating priest was not the fort's chaplain but that of the ship on which Duval had sailed, *L'Alexandre*. The priest did not require the couple to wait for the usually obligatory publication of three banns. They grabbed two witnesses—one of whom would soon marry another *La Mutine* survivor—and the formalities were over. There was good reason for the hurry, since *L'Alexandre* was armed for its return voyage the very next day. The chaplain was on board, and perhaps the new husband as well.[13]

By the time Boyard and Balivet married, New Biloxi had just been named, the crowding along the coast had reached its maximum, and the death toll was mounting inexorably.

The situation in late 1720 was already grim, but in early 1721 it deteriorated still further. At the moment when France's latest financial crisis began to blight the colony's future, all supplies were running out, and no more were on the way. Local resources could not make up for the shortages, for there was no meat other than wild game, hunting season was soon ending, and there was still no mill to grind corn. Perhaps because they lacked the equipment to catch any, few appear to have eaten fish. The would-be inhabitant Pellerin made the one known reference to consuming fish, their only readily available source of protein.[14]

On January 22, 1721, New Biloxi was officially proclaimed the colony's *"endroit capital,"* its "capital place."[15] On February 17, 1721, one of the first marriages following that proclamation was celebrated. Officially, the bride, Marie Vibert, was not even in the colony, since her name was not approved for deportation and she was not listed on *La Mutine*'s manifest. Vibert married an even more recently arrived inhabitant. Claude Fontaine—described by army recruiters as age thirty-seven, five feet tall, and with auburn hair—had been among the last soldiers conscripted during John Law's regime. The couple's chief witness, Jacques Dureau, was still another future husband of a survivor.

On March 12, it was the turn of Pierre Fugere and Étiennette Gené. Fugere, born in La Croix, a tiny village fifty miles from Gené's native Sens now called La-Forêt-Sainte-Croix, was known to his fellow soldiers as "La Croix." As his regiment's fifer and drummer, Fugere was a figure of some importance. La Croix's tunes were a rare reminder of discipline in a colony where chaos was rampant, and he was called upon for public ceremonies of all kinds.[16]

By June 1721, most of the deported women had fled the crisis-stricken settlement, and the censuses drawn up that month in Mobile and New Orleans show that many had moved there. Bienville's report on the state of Biloxi from May 24, 1721, concluded on a dire assessment. "We lack every means of health care," he explained. "The sick are sleeping on the ground: we don't even have cloth to cover them or to make straw mattresses." (Bienville didn't say that the only remaining cloth had been devoured by rats.) "The best workers are already dead," he continued, "and those who are left can't work because there is no fabric to make clothing for them, no hats, no shoes. . . . In a word, we have nothing."[17]

And yet, on June 3, four couples were jointly wed. The group ceremony was surely necessitated by another critical shortage: priests. As the death toll mounted, the demands on missionaries' time grew.

These June brides were not deported women; they belonged instead to a contingent of Frenchwomen who had traveled to Louisiana under very different circumstances. On January 5, 1721, eighty-one female passengers landed in the colony on La Baleine, the Whale. Their arrival was duly noted by the early historians who made no mention of the deported women, surely because these women quickly won the reputation of being, in Dumont's words, "more distinguished than those who had arrived before them."[18]

The women on La Baleine were the "casket girls" still remembered on the Gulf Coast today and about whom a narrative was soon constructed. While these women had also come from the Salpêtrière, they had all been taken, or so it was said, not from the dreaded La Force, where the deported women were imprisoned, but from the section where girls and women from impoverished families were housed. They had all allegedly traveled not "by force" but voluntarily. They did not travel in chains, and they did not travel alone but in the company of nuns sent to protect them. But the reality was sometimes more complicated. Survivors from La Mutine surely recognized, for example, Catherine Blanchard, who had arrived on La Baleine and who married in Mobile on April 5, 1721, since Catherine had been imprisoned in the Salpêtrière's Maison de Force along with them. Her record was also identical to that of many deported women, and Catherine appears as number 182 on Pancatelin's list of women "Fit for the Islands," identified as "from Paris, 25, libertine and prostitute."[19]

The last marriage in Biloxi of a passenger on *La Mutine* was celebrated on June 9, 1721, when Marguerite Letellier, only sixteen when she sailed, wed Maurice Pigny. Letellier had worked from age eight as a scullery maid in an aristocratic Parisian household, only to be arrested because of theft charges trumped up by the lady of the house, as soon as her eldest son sought to marry Marguerite's older sister.

In Biloxi, Marguerite attempted to earn a living as she always had: in service. She worked as a maid for the settlement's principal medical man, Surgeon Lasonde. In February 1726, Marguerite was still attempting to collect wages due her. She was owed pay for the period from November 1720 to May 1721, seven months at ten *livres* a month, plus the additional ten *livres* she requested as a penalty on money long overdue.[20] There is no record that she ever received a penny. Letellier's husband found work in a much-needed field, as a wagonmaker; he earned an honest wage, 250 *livres* a year, but in an economy like Louisiana's, that was hardly enough to get by.

THE FIRST HALF OF 1721 WAS DEVASTATING TO THE COLONY, BUT THE months of July and August were the most disastrous of all. Authorities discovered that their last resource, the hardtack or biscuit sent over with land grant settlers, hadn't been properly baked and had all spoiled—as had the corned beef and lard included in their provisions. They learned about the meat only when inhabitants fell gravely ill after eating some.

This famine was so devastating that life came to a standstill. Sailors weren't strong enough to sail. Workers didn't have the strength to clear land for New Biloxi, so construction of the settlement ceased, before even the completion of the most basic structure: a storehouse to protect supplies. One of the rare boats in the colony was requisitioned to function as a temporary warehouse. Bienville offered this grim assessment: "What can be undertaken without sustenance?"[21]

And then the rains came. On August 10, 1721, authorities in Biloxi informed their counterparts in France that "it's been raining heavily here for more than 40 days." All over the Gulf Coast, flooding was massive. Crops had already been planted, and the harvest was washed out. Native Americans were just as badly hit, so colonists could not expect their help. "Famine will continue," their report warned.[22]

This prediction proved correct. Even in a colony by then well accustomed to lethal shortages, the two years that followed, the moment when survivors were beginning new lives, were one of the worst periods of scarcity and want in the colony's history.

In the midst of such havoc and desolation, little work on the new capital was accomplished. Fifteen months after its founding, in April 1722, the colony's "capital place" consisted of two constructions: a storehouse and a hospital. Both were elementary structures, mere wood frames clad in shingles. New Biloxi's fort had been planned but not built, and a palisade, still incomplete, indicated its outline. Then, in May 1722, word arrived that the seat of government was being moved to New Orleans.[23]

When viewed against the backdrop of the reality of Louisiana's "capital place," the image shown in Figure 7, advertising itself as a view of "John Law's concession at 'New Biloxi,'" is astounding. The scene is idyllic. Inhabitants are impeccably outfitted; not only do they have hats and shoes, but some even sport periwigs, as though ready to set off for an evening in a Parisian salon. A large quantity of land has been thoroughly cleared, so that workers have room to use the readily available, appropriate tools to fell trees and build fences. The lodgings are tentlike structures, but they are solid, clearly professionally built. In the background, there is even a sizeable construction, easily as fine as or finer than any in the colony at that time. The foreground depicts the preparation and the serving of food—these happy colonists know only abundance.

Figure 7. The last propaganda for the perfect colony that John Law's Indies Company used to attract investors and inhabitants.

The image is dated December 10, 1720. Barely three weeks before John Law fled France in disgrace, his propaganda machine had churned out this final attempt to convince Europeans that, in John Law's Louisiana, inhabitants lived an idyllic life in the finest colony on earth. The depiction is also signed, by Jean Baptiste Le Bouteux, who would have served as director of Law's concession in Louisiana, had it not been a casualty of Law's bankruptcy. At a moment when "New Biloxi" was virtually nonexistent and had barely been named, when the thousands crammed onto Biloxi's sands were competing for limited resources and the death toll was soaring, Le Bouteux dared allege that this view depicted the reality of life at "New Biloxi" for the residents sent there by John Law's Indies Company.

During the particularly lethal period following the move to New Biloxi, at least one of the women who had been among the first to wed in Biloxi, Marie Vibert, died, in 1723. After her death, her husband, Claude Fontaine, proved his own rebellious blood when he successfully fled the miseries of Louisiana and went over "to the foreigners"—probably to an English colony. Already in June 1722, desertion had become a household word, as a French traveler to the region remarked: "These days, everyone is talking about desertion plots." In mid-June, when New Orleans became army headquarters, many soldiers refused to move there. Instead, led by their captain, they stole a boat and sailed to Carolina, where "they were very well-received."[24] They got out just in time.

Soon after came natural disaster in the form of the first tropical storm system whose devastation along the Gulf Coast was documented in print, the *"ouragan,"* the "hurricane," that brutalized the colony from ten p.m. on September 12, 1722, to noon on September 13. Mobile and New Orleans were disaster zones, but Biloxi was hardest hit of all. The entirety of its limited built environment was pulverized by the monster storm. The gulf overflowed, and massive flooding ensued. Crops were once again water-soaked, and famine continued unabated. The hurricane destroyed most small boats and dugout canoes on the coast—and also some larger vessels.[25]

By then, authorities were so overwhelmed that once again many deaths, including perhaps those of deported women, went unrecorded. The Biloxi death toll received formal recognition only nearly three centuries after the fact, in the aftermath of more recent monster hurricanes.

When Hurricane Camille struck in August 1969, a burial ground was partially revealed, situated just off the Gulf Coast in Biloxi. That burial ground, the earliest known French Colonial cemetery in the United States, was fully uncovered in August 2005, after Hurricane Katrina made landfall. It is today perhaps the most poignant reminder of the time when this country's second coast was French.

Known as the Moran Burial Site, the cemetery made it possible for archeologists to study remains that were, in their words, "relatively complete." These were individuals whose interments had taken place, they concluded, principally in 1720–1721, at the moment when many survivors remained in Biloxi. Their sample was small—twenty males, three females, two undetermined—a ratio of male to female that reflects the imbalance of the time. The average height among men was five feet four inches, rather tall for the day; for women, just under five feet. The remains show signs of what the archeologists termed "frequent growth disruptions during childhood," hardly surprising in individuals who had grown up in late seventeenth-century France.

Of the roughly twenty-five buried at the site, only two had been interred in coffins. The boards and the oh-so-precious nails used in these biers were the only trace of "luxury" the site contained. Few artifacts were found. How many on Biloxi beach would have had any left? A button or two were the only indications of clothing. Shrouds may have been used in three cases, even though the scarcity of cloth makes that difficult to imagine. The poverty of Louisiana followed these inhabitants into the grave.[26]

In 1721 and 1722, censuses that charted the colony's recent increase in residents were drawn up in other settlements. No census was taken at Biloxi, since the transient population and the chaos that reigned on the beach rendered bureaucracy futile. By the time a census was drawn up, in 1726, the multitude had moved on. That year, Biloxi had only eight residents—two men, two women, four children—protected by seven soldiers. Not a single deported woman remained there.[27]

Chapter 9

Putting Down Roots in Mobile

IN ONE CRUCIAL WAY, SETTLEMENT OF FRENCH LOUISIANA CAN BE
said to have begun on September 6, 1704, when, five years after
the colony's founding, a first baptism was recorded by the priest who
administered the sacrament. On September 3, 1720, at Mobile, baptism number 287 was documented. Anne Beaulieu's christening provides the earliest indication of one crucial way in which survivors of
John Law's and Pancatelin's schemes would shape the future of the
Gulf Coast and the Lower Mississippi Valley—through their descendants and the families they founded.

Baby Anne Beaulieu was "weak," so she was baptized at home.
Her parents had married so soon after *Les Deux Frères* landed on November 18, 1719 that no record of their union, the first for a survivor,
exists. Anne's father, Sergeant Beaulieu, first name unknown, served
in Mobile's garrison. Beaulieu had reached Louisiana in late June
1719 and had spotted the woman who would become Anne's mother,

Catherine Oudart—by then at least thirty-four—immediately upon her arrival. He saved Catherine from the ordeal most survivors endured in their first months in the colony.

In Paris in 1713, Parisian Catherine Oudart received a life sentence to the Salpêtrière because, like Manon Fontaine, she had remained in Paris when banished and because, like so many of those with whom she crossed the Atlantic, she had been arraigned by a corrupt police officer, Charles Bizoton. Oudart was singled out by Pancatelin for deportation because of Pancatelin's dread of women with military connections. At the time of her arrest, Catherine Oudart was twice a widow and married for the third time. All three of her husbands were soldiers. The fleur-de-lys branded onto both Oudart's shoulders as punishment for having refused to leave Paris did not deter Sergeant Beaulieu from becoming husband number four.[1]

Catherine Oudart may have been pronounced undesirable in France, but she married well in Louisiana. By April 1722, Beaulieu had been put in charge of the sale of alcoholic beverages at Mobile's fort. Someone entrusted with money and commodities that soldiers would not do without clearly enjoyed the confidence of his superiors.[2]

In France, the women's files were filled with arrests, testimony—often fraudulent—against them, incarcerations, and transfers from one prison to another. In Louisiana, they immediately began to acquire a very different kind of record: that of their marriages and the births of their children. Nowhere was this more visible than in Mobile, where women "unfit" for France began families and helped transform a garrison town into a community. It was in Mobile that survivors became aware that two key paths to influence were now open to them. They could establish families and ensure their children's upward mobility. And they could acquire a crucial marker of status: land.

The first marriage of a survivor from *La Mutine* to take place in Mobile was celebrated on March 12, 1720, when Jeanne Mahou married Laurent Laurent, a Breton nine years her elder who had reached Louisiana in late 1718, traveling in the party of Indies Company director Charles Le Gac. In late February 1720, as company officials were trying to manage the sudden arrival of five ships, Laurent spotted Jeanne Mahou emerging from *La Mutine*. In Paris, Mahou's arresting officer had described her as "quite attractive," and predicted that she would be "agreeably received in the colony."[3] Even caked in filth and vermin, Jeanne Mahou retained her charm. Her appeal was so evident that Laurent immediately took her away from the chaos on Massacre Island to Mobile, and Jeanne was spared the horrors of Ship Island and New Biloxi.

Their marriage appears in no official register, but Jeanne Mahou herself made sure that its date can be verified. On August 17, 1737, when Mahou was putting her affairs in order after Laurent's death, she produced copies of essential legal documents, including proof of their marriage, that she had safeguarded through the years. Importantly, Jeanne Mahou was literate. When she reached Louisiana, she realized that there was not always an official record of events like her marriage that were essential to her respectability and the legitimacy of her children. From the start, she had maintained her own records, signing each document with a firm and distinctive hand.

Two decades after the colony's founding, when Mahou and Laurent married in the settlement that had until recently served as its

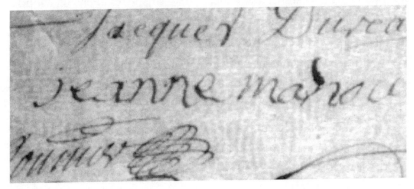

Figure 8. Jeanne Mahou's signature, confident—and with a flamboyant *b* that provided an individual touch.

capital, Mobile's perpetually decaying Fort Louis was not up to the standards of Jeanne Mahou's home, Saint-Dizier, or any other garrison town in France. In May 1721, the citadel was pronounced "in truly terrible shape. If we are to command any respect," the official concluded, "we'll have to build a new one."[4] In Mobile, survivors were married in a setting that was a far cry from the great cathedrals and centuries-old churches found in every city, town, and village in France. Fort Louis had no construction designed as a church. Instead, services took place in a room inside a house, a space so small that barely twenty could be shoehorned in.[5]

And then there were Mobile's environs. While many French villages, such as those in central France where so many survivors were born, were surrounded by neatly planted fields, Mobile was encircled instead by marshy bogs and swamps, canebrakes, muddy streams, and bayous. In France, it was possible to walk about and enjoy the countryside, but near Mobile even soldiers on horseback found the going rough.

Mobile was, notwithstanding these drawbacks, by far the most propitious place in the Lower Mississippi Valley in which to make one's home. Survivors like Oudart and Mahou who married quickly and lived there chose to build their new lives in the colony's only relatively substantial outpost. In early 1721, an engineer sent from France to help design New Orleans left this assessment of Mobile: "This community is the most established of all. There are properly framed and solidly constructed houses; there are three or four streets of dwellings."[6] During that crucial moment in the founding of Louisiana, the early 1720s, that "established community" attracted more survivors than any other outpost.

The influx of survivors quickly helped make Mobile the most populous settlement in the colony. The census compiled on June 28, 1721, listed sixty-six Frenchmen, seventy Frenchwomen, and sixty-three children. When outlying outposts were included, those totals climbed to one hundred, ninety-one, and ninety-six, and fully accurate tallies would certainly have been a good deal higher. Although twelve deported women were counted that June, their recently born children were not recorded. Seven women who show up only on the next census, in 1726, were almost certainly there in 1721, as well as several survivors who were included on neither census. In contrast, the November 1721 census of New Orleans, where construction was advancing at a glacial pace, listed only fifty-eight Frenchwomen and thirty-nine children. The women who lived in Mobile could count on the support of a far larger community, and their children grew up with a wider choice of playmates. Finally, Mobile also had many cattle (384), giving its inhabitants access to meat and dairy products, and horses (42), guaranteeing work for its principal blacksmith, Jean Melin, newly married to Manon Fontaine.[7]

In the tiny outpost that greeted survivors in 1720, there was no sense of history or of an architectural heritage. There were no monuments, either secular or religious, other than the fort. But Mobile was in other respects up to the standards of a reasonably prosperous French village, something that could hardly have been said of any other French settlement. Inhabitants could have been proud to call Mobile home.

The rules of contemporary French urban planning were carried out to the letter in Mobile. The fort fronted on the Mobile River, and the settlement's streets were lined up behind it with military precision. Following the example of Paris, Mobile was what Louis XIV termed an "open" city. It was not surrounded by walls designed to protect it from invasion, as medieval towns had been and as many European cities and towns—and even some in North America as well—still were. Mobile's streets were not the meandering alleys found in the older Parisian neighborhoods where some survivors had grown up, but instead resolutely modern, straight and regularly laid out, running parallel and perpendicular to the river and intersecting each other at right angles. Like Parisian neighborhoods built from scratch in the seventeenth century, such as the Île Saint-Louis, the Mobile that survivors found was a vision of straight lines and right angles.

Streets changed name at every intersection. This was customary in Paris before street numbering was introduced, since it was easier to locate residents on these shorter stretches. A few street names evoked the Bourbon monarchy—the rue de Conti, named for princes of the blood—while most commemorated men who had been crucial in Louisiana's history: Iberville, Pontchartrain.

Lots were large and well-spaced, with ample room for private gardens. Some lots were roughly 150 feet square. Some were 180 feet wide by 150 feet deep, while others, in the manner traditional in Paris, reversed those proportions and were deeper than they were wide. This variation lent variety to the appearance of Mobile's streets. Houses were single story, mostly eighteen to twenty-five feet high. Their dimensions—up to sixty feet long—were imposing for Louisiana and by the standards of the day. In the early years, construction in Mobile had been crude, but by 1720 the standards were considerably higher. Homes followed simple designs, but most were competently and solidly built—unlike the shacks the women found on Massacre Island and at Biloxi. Rather than bulrushes, their sloping roofs featured shingles, and some were even edged with tiles. Bricks, made in a brickworks on the edge of town, were available for use in construction in Mobile.

Also situated on the edge of town because of the fire hazard they represented were two blacksmiths' shops. And there were taverns—indeed some private homes seemed to have doubled as taverns—making it possible to share food or a drink in public.[8] Parisians would have felt right at home. Women who had grown up in dire poverty would also have been lodged more spaciously than they ever had been in their lives in France, in newer constructions and with more green spaces around their homes.

As a result, in Mobile, the numerous survivors who chose to live there found it possible to lead a life unlike any other in the colony. To begin with, they interacted every day with women with whom they had shared formative experiences—in the Salpêtrière, during deportation, on Ship Island. In rural outposts such as Pointe Coupée, inhabitants were isolated on separate farms, and New Orleans soon developed a population density that guaranteed some degree of separation, but in Mobile, survivors lived in near proximity along Mobile's "three or four streets." Their lives unfolded together. They were godmothers at the baptisms of each other's children, witnesses at each other's marriages, and later at their children's marriages. Their continued participation in the colony's religious life helped give Mobile an identity beyond what it had been until then, a mere military outpost designed for the defense of the Gulf Coast.

In 1721, two survivors were unmarried and living alone. One had been passenger 164 on *La Mutine*, Marianne Brossard, who after a false arrest found herself in the Salpêtrière at the worst moment, just when Pancatelin went on her rampage. Angélique Reffe similarly ended up on *La Mutine* after a false arrest; she was also single in June 1721. From then on, however, over the course of decades, Angélique was never single for long.

Angélique Reffe was the quintessential Parisian, with a characteristic working-class accent so thick you could cut it with a knife.[9] She was born in the heart of the French capital and baptized at Saint-Merry Church, on the Right Bank immediately across the Seine from Notre-Dame Cathedral. In a tiny capital city across the Atlantic, Angélique became one of the quintessential early Mobilians.

Her first three marriages, all to soldiers, took place in Mobile: to begin with, Nicolas Mirodot, whom she married by early 1722 at the latest; then on January 17, 1726, Pierre Bertin. Théodore Robin, Reffe's third husband, died before July 1738, when she married still again. Another recent addition to Mobile's population, Louis Bourbon, whom Angélique described as "an old friend," stood up for her on two of those occasions. Former neighbors in Paris thus helped their new community coalesce.

It was in Mobile that Angélique Reffe's two sets of twin daughters with Mirodot were baptized: Jeanne and Angélique Claude on

October 20, 1723; Antoinette and Andrée on September 13, 1725. On September 25, 1725, Mirodot was buried, also in Mobile.[10] Angélique's three unions with members of Mobile's garrison brought her a degree of prosperity rarely attained by working women in the city of her birth. By the time of her fourth marriage, she had accumulated personal property worth 300 *livres*. And during all her years in Mobile, the woman arrested on prostitution charges without proof was a model resident. She was repeatedly chosen, even by the garrison's most prominent officers, as godmother for babies named "Angélique" in her honor.

Marie Meutrot, the shoemaker's daughter from central France with whom Angélique Reffe had entered the Salpêtrière and to whom Angélique had remained chained on the long journey from Paris to the colony, appeared on the 1721 census as the wife of army officer Gabriel Menadet. Meutrot was soon widowed; she then married soldier Louis Pajot. Because of the scarcity of priests, a girl born from Pajot's first marriage in September 1721 wasn't baptized until March 12, 1722. The baby's godmother was one of only two deported Irishwomen to survive. In Mobile, when the woman arrested in Paris as "Nozo Zayen" and listed on *La Mutine*'s manifest as "Noro Rayen" was free to choose her own name, she gave it French flair: "Honoré Rayenne."

The Pajot-Meutrot wedding at Mobile on June 6, 1726, was a gathering of the clans. Witnesses included a woman Pancatelin had identified as "Claude Vivier." Due to Bourlon's carelessness, Vivier had traveled on *La Mutine* under the name "Marguerite Du Vivier." In Mobile, Vivier married Pierre Le Roy, a close ally of some of the most important men in Louisiana's longtime capital. Their marriage was a perfect example of the ties that soon bound deported women and the Gulf Coast's notable residents. Vivier often served as a witness or godmother, using her preferred names "Claudine" and "Claudette." Only two weeks after Meutrot's wedding, she was dead.[11] The announcement of her burial in Mobile's cemetery is the last trace of Claudine Vivier's life.

Also a witness for Meutrot was Barthélemy Delamare, husband of another survivor not counted in the 1721 census. The woman who traveled as "Françoise Vaudetard," in actuality "Claude Françoise Vaudestar," was married to a soldier in Paris. She was arrested by accident, when a murder took place just outside the cabaret where she had stopped off for a beer at the end of a hot day. Her new husband in the colony had been a merchant in Paris, with a grocery shop near Les Halles "on the corner of the rue Neuve Saint-Martin," near the scene of Vaudestar's arrest.

In 1721, three survivors—Marie Anne Fourchet, Jeanne Pouillot, and Françoise Deveaux—were identified as "wives of soldiers" to indicate that their husbands were deployed elsewhere, and they were living at the fort alone. Françoise Deveaux, forty-two when they sailed, was the oldest prisoner on *La Mutine* and the oldest survivor. Françoise was married in Paris, to Antoine Chignard, likewise a soldier, who was arrested while trying to sell a silver plate. After the jeweler noticed an engraved coat of arms and alerted the police, they decided the plate must have been stolen, charged Chignard with theft, and sentenced him to the galleys. When Chignard took the silver into the shop, he mentioned that "his wife was getting rid of [the plate], so he thought he should get some money for it." This remark was Deveaux's only connection to the case, but without so much as a formal accusation, she nonetheless landed in the Salpêtrière. In Mobile, Françoise Deveaux married another soldier.[12]

On the 1721 census, just before the name "Angélique Reffe" appears "Gabriel Prévost, *dit* La Chaume," "known as La Chaume." While the formula "known as" often designated the nicknames that soldiers used among themselves, the story behind "La Chaume" was no ordinary one. Gabriel was the younger son of Charles Prévost, *seigneur* or lord of La Chaume, a hamlet in Charente in western France. His older brother Jacques was heir to the estate, so in 1706, sixteen-year-old Gabriel left to seek his fortune in Louisiana. Even though he had no claim whatsoever to the actual townlet, for Prévost, "La

223

Chaume" functioned as a reminder of his noble status.[13] In 1721, the thirty-one-year-old lived in Mobile with his new wife, Marie Françoise Le Coustelier de Jouy de Palsy, the only aristocrat among the deported women. Amidst the chaos that reigned in November 1719 when *Les Deux Frères* made landfall, these two intrepid younger children of provincial nobility had somehow found each other. Marie Françoise had grown up in a vast château and on the fiefdom of her father's family, Palsy les Pilloneaux. She may have been the only deported woman who found in Mobile lodgings far less spacious than the home she had known in France.

Several survivors not counted on the census were surely also in Mobile at that time, among them *La Mutine* passenger 113, Marie Anne Bourguenet. At seventeen, Marie Anne fell prey to the kind of mass arrest favored by officers such as Bourlon when, along with five other women and four soldiers, she was apprehended at the request of Lieutenant Général d'Argenson—no charges, just a quick lockup. In Mobile, Marie Anne Bourguenet married Jacques Bray, a soldier, and had a daughter, also named Marie Anne.[14]

Absent from the 1721 census as well was another "Marie Anne"— Marie Anne Tabouret, who arrived in the Salpêtrière during the roundup of summer 1719 and soon became passenger 176 on *La Mutine*. Like numerous fellow survivors, Marie Anne Tabouret married a soldier, Joseph Gardon; by 1730, they had a son, Jean Joseph. On November 28, 1735, Marie Anne Tabouret was buried in Mobile. We know nothing else about her life in Louisiana.

A similarly stark record is all that remains of the new life of still another deported woman not counted in the census, Claude Sarazin, passenger 115 on *La Mutine*. In Mobile, she married a fellow Parisian, Gilbert Dumas. On April 2, 1731, when Dumas remarried, he called himself "the widower of Claudine Sarazin, who died in Mobile."

Marie Raflon is also absent from the 1721 census. Marie became passenger 158 because her brother waited until December 8, four days before *La Mutine* sailed, to have a change of heart and beg that his sister not "leave for the Mississippi." On May 19, 1722, when Marie married Jean François Hérissé in Mobile, she mentioned her parish church in Paris, Saint-Eustache near Les Halles, and added a street address, "rue Saint-Denis," a precious reminder of the life she'd left behind. Hérissé had come to the colony to serve as a drummer, a profession in such demand that drummers received far better pay than mere soldiers.[15]

The survivors who made the best matches did not marry soldiers but chose instead men with more prestigious professions. In a colony with few buildings and even fewer truly solid ones, for example, no workers were more ardently desired than those with experience in construction. Only two carpenters are listed on the 1721 census. Étienne Fièvre, a master carpenter and a specialist of what the colony most required, large-scale constructions, had come to Louisiana in April 1719 voluntarily, as an *engagé*. Fièvre was well-paid: over two *livres* a day, plus a benefit more attractive than money in 1721, "food and provisions."[16] In Mobile, Fièvre married Marie Anne Grise, deported on *Les Deux Frères* for trafficking in a commodity as prized in France as it was in Louisiana, tobacco.

Marie Delisle, passenger 189 on *La Mutine*, was not counted for the 1721 census, but in Mobile Delisle made one of the best matches—to Philippe Olivier. Olivier was someone with real influence. Like Fièvre, Olivier was a builder, and with more status still. As *"entrepreneur des batîments et fortifications du roi,"* "the king's contractor for buildings and fortifications," he served as engineer and contractor for both civil and military constructions. In 1732, Olivier entered into a partnership with the garrison's commander. And in 1737, Olivier signed a massive contract to supervise the reconstruction of the frame, masonry, and foundations of Fort Condé, the citadel that had succeeded Mobile's original fortress, Fort Louis.[17]

But no match was more impressive than that made by Anne Françoise Rolland. In Paris, Anne Françoise had lived in a nondescript neighborhood, sharing a single room with four family members. In Mobile, she resided in one of the post's most impressive homes, in a prime central location. On the 1721 census, her new husband's name figured in sixth position, immediately after Bienville, the commander of the garrison, and its three highest-ranking officers: "le Sieur Sarazin, *garde-magasin des vivres*," "keeper of the storehouse for provisions." Sarazin was one of only five men in Mobile to be awarded the honorific "*sieur*," "sir" or "lord"—and his wife may well have been known as "*dame*," or "lady." In a colony always on the brink of famine, those with access to comestibles outranked petty nobility, such as Gabriel Prévost, would-be lord of La Chaume.

Even though she and her husband first appear only on the 1726 census, one of the youngest survivors, Marie Avril, just sixteen when she was transported on *Les Deux Frères*, was almost certainly at Mobile in 1721. Avril, deported for trafficking in contraband salt, married a man from Tarascon, a small city just south of Avignon. Often called "Tarascon," Avril's husband Jacques signed his family name "Lorreins," and he was referred to as everything from "Lorins" to "Lorense," from "Laurens" to "Lorinze," from "Lorrain" to "Lorin" and even "Laurenson." Tarascon arrived in the colony only two months before Avril, on a ship transporting numerous male deportees. Tarascon, age twenty, was exiled for desertion from the Royal Army. Marie Avril lived her entire life in the colony near Massacre Island, where it had begun. Marie Avril and Jacques Lorreins were never major landowners, nor were they farmers. Theirs was an elusive life, leaving relatively few traces in the colony's archives. This was probably true mainly because the two were such a perfect match.

Marie Avril had moved contraband salt up and down the rivers and canals of central France; she was an expert at negotiating interconnected waterways in small craft and at remaining under the radar. In Louisiana, Tarascon acquired just these skills—and others. He became a *voyageur*, a significant player in a domain essential to the colony's economy. *Voyageurs* (literally "travelers") were more or less officially sanctioned fur traders. These traders maintained a complex and far-flung system for the exchange of merchandise between settlers and Native Americans—exchanging French-made goods such as textiles for meat and bear oil, for example, or for the skins of beavers and other peltries, destined for export to France. Tarascon was among the *voyageurs*—only twenty in early New Orleans according to one estimate—who plied the colony's southernmost rivers and bayous.

In his pirogue or dugout canoe, sometimes working independently, sometimes on behalf of French authorities, sometimes in collaboration with a network of partners in settlements from Natchez to Fort Toulouse, Tarascon traded with everyone from the Choctaw to the Spanish in Pensacola. He moved all kinds of goods, imported and local, from soap and rum to deerskins, and at times he cut deals involving significant sums. While the dugouts used by the army in coastal waters to ferry people between the barrier islands and the mainland were often thirty to thirty-five feet long, *voyageurs* like Tarascon used instead much smaller pirogues, which were more practical when navigating inland marshes and bayous.[18] Tarascon traveled great distances and was far from Mobile much of the time. "Travelers" got essential supplies to the most distant and least accessible settlements. Since they performed a vital function of which French authorities seemed incapable, *voyageurs* in many ways kept Louisiana's economy functioning.[19] Tarascon's professional life, while complex and unusual by modern standards, left so many legal traces that it seems like an open book next to his personal life.

The 1726 census of Mobile included Tarascon, Avril, and two children, Jacques and Elisabeth. Three additional children were subsequently baptized in Mobile: on June 29, 1727, Pierre Charles; on April 13, 1729, Marie Pélagie; on November 12, 1734, François. While Marie Avril regularly appeared in parish archives because she was so often called upon to serve as godmother, Tarascon was as much a stealth presence in Mobile as his wife had been in France.

On June 23, 1738, Marie Avril was buried in Mobile at age thirty-five. In contrast, all her children but François lived exceptionally long lives. All but one married more than once, and they were survived by many children of their own. In Louisiana, the smuggler from Burgundy founded a dynasty.

Tarascon, characteristically, did not have an inventory of Avril's belongings drawn up. Her children were still pleading for one in 1745. When a reckoning was finally available, it became clear that the estate was sizeable and that her family had been among the most prosperous of all the survivors' families. By 1745, Tarascon and their children had long since left Mobile for New Orleans and the surrounding area. Some had acquired property, even significant tracts.

Unlike Marie Avril, Jeanne Mahou quickly moved far from the place where she married. Jeanne spent the first eighteen years of her life in Louisiana on an isolated farm situated near Fort Toulouse, the minuscule outpost some two hundred miles northeast of Mobile that marked the eastern limit of French Louisiana. Fort Toulouse was founded in 1717 to maintain French influence in a region not far from English colonies and to attempt to limit English encroachment onto French territory. Overland, at least a week was necessary to travel between Mobile and Fort Toulouse; by river, at certain times of year, the trip required many weeks.

Fort Toulouse, its garrison of fewer than twenty men, a dozen wives and children of soldiers, and the Laurents' home were near a Native American village referred to by the French as "*les Alibamons*," the French name for the Alibama or Alibamu people.[20] Mahou and Laurent lived in the midst of the Muscogee Creek Confederacy, an informal coalition of Native American towns and villages along the rivers of today's Georgia and Alabama.[21] There, they farmed, raising the crops basic to the region—maize or corn, beans, sweet potatoes, rice, a bit of tobacco, as well as local produce such as *giraumons*, pumpkin-like squashes. This guaranteed that during the famines of the early 1720s, their family would have been self-sustaining. Laurent also made a living as an unofficial trader. Traders purchased on credit from merchants in France goods that they used to acquire deerskins from Native Americans; they paid the merchants in deerskins.

At the village called *"Alibamons,"* the couple created the kind of independent existence that would have suited Laurent, a Breton from one of the most fiercely separatist regions in France, the Finistère. Mahou, the young woman so desperate for excitement and a life on her own terms that she refused to return to her home near the eastern limit of France, found at the eastern limit of French Louisiana a reality unlike anything she could have known in France. Had she been allowed to remain in Paris, Jeanne would undoubtedly have made her way as a dressmaker—perhaps even rising to status in the powerful guild of Parisian *couturières*. In Louisiana, Jeanne found status by using her talents and knowledge to fashion a truly exceptional home for her family and to preserve all her family's records, thereby guaranteeing that their status would always be recognized.

Her family was so thoroughly on its own that it took all Jeanne Mahou's fierce determination to make sure that her children's legitimacy could never be questioned. When Joseph Laurent was born on January 2, 1729, there was no priest at Fort Toulouse, so the baby received a provisional baptism until June 17, when the parish priest of Mobile, Capuchin Father Mathias, could finally administer the sacrament. Marie Jeanne, born on January 16, 1732, was baptized the following day and buried on April 30, 1733. On January 22, 1736, a second daughter named Marie Jeanne was born. The baby's godfather, Henry Kolb (Gallicized as "Colque"), was among the Swiss soldiers garrisoned at Fort Condé and Fort Toulouse. The baby's godmother was her older sister, Marie Laurent, whose age can't be determined since, in her case alone, no record of her birth survives.

Two weeks later, on February 7, 1736, Marie Laurent and Henry Kolb were married in Mobile. A young woman calling herself "Elisabeth Tarascon" served as Marie's witness: Marie Avril's and Jeanne Mahou's daughters had bonded.

Laurent Laurent knew he was seriously ill and unlikely to survive, so he and Jeanne Mahou had made the long journey to Mobile. There, on March 6, documents were drawn up naming Mahou guardian to their underage children—Simon, age twelve, Joseph, age nine, and Marie Jeanne, twenty months old. Kolb was named substitute guardian, in effect, the surrogate male head of the household. On August 14, 1737, Laurent Laurent, age forty-four, was buried in Mobile.

The management of his death is testimony to Jeanne Mahou's exceptional skills at navigating French bureaucracy. Only three days after the funeral of her husband of some seventeen years, in a colony governed by chaos and in which all bureaucracy unfolded at a glacial pace, by eight a.m. on August 17, Jeanne Mahou had had all the couple's worldly goods legally evaluated.[22] No family in France could have managed a speedier or more efficient handling of the settlement of an estate.

Mahou and Laurent had lived on their own; they had also lived well. The house in which they had raised their family had a design typical of French homes in the colony. Surrounded by a picket fence and with a bark roof, their home stood forty-two feet long and eighteen wide. It contained only two rooms, with wood flooring, an unfinished space above, and a lean-to on one end, but for the colony this was a structure to inspire pride in its owners—after all, the largest among the buildings constructed in early Mobile measured sixty-eight feet by sixteen.[23] Value of their home and land: 600 *livres*, far more than the price of many properties in New Orleans.

The couple owned 450 *livres* worth of livestock: eight milk cows branded with a double "L," five calves, three bulls, and two bull calves. Their house was well furnished, including a wardrobe armoire and a sideboard for dishes, large pieces not often found in the colony and, due to the difficulty of transporting them, never so far from a major port.

Their possessions were notable in many ways. Jeanne Mahou had maintained an exceptionally well-equipped kitchen, with many implements, often sophisticated, such as copper pots and pans of all sorts, even a special pan for *tourtes*, the meat pies that are a specialty of eastern France. While Jeanne's wardrobe was not inventoried, the listing of Laurent's clothing reveals that, two decades after her apprenticeship to a Parisian dressmaker, Jeanne Mahou had not lost her touch. Her husband owned several complete suits and multiple changes of linen. The fabrics, while ordinary, mostly inexpensive French wool cloth, were identified with extraordinary precision—Jeanne, after all, knew textiles well, and she was proud of all the fabrics that she'd been able to obtain in a place so far from major trading centers. Those prized textiles were also extraordinarily colorful. Laurent had favored blue, with grey and yellow accents; he even owned striped pants. In an obscure outpost far from Paris, the epicenter of French fashion, Laurent Laurent had been stylishly and distinctively dressed.

The inventory of their possessions totaled 1,581 *livres*. Master artisans in Paris often raised families at least as large as the Laurents' in two-room apartments; the value of the Laurents' estate was fully up to totals amassed by such artisans.[24] The couple had maintained Parisian standards in a backwoods existence. If living well is indeed revenge, Jeanne Mahou had taken hers.

After Laurent's death, Jeanne quickly remarried, as widows with families to support typically did. On January 27, 1737, she wed Jacques Dureau, a carpenter from Poissy, a small town some twenty miles west of Paris. Dureau had a prior connection to the community of *La Mutine* survivors, having served as a witness at the marriage of Marie Vibert. Jeanne soon moved with her family to the capital, where her children had opportunities impossible near Fort Toulouse.

The realities of military life often determined the unfolding of the lives of the survivors who remained in Mobile. When Jeanne Pouillot was arrested in 1714 on the basis of "evidence" presented by one of the most corrupt officers in Paris, Chantepie, she was already a widow. Pouillot shared a birthplace, Poissy, with the man she married in Mobile, soldier Jean Marchand, called La Croix. On October 8,

1721, their daughter was christened and named "Marie Anne" for her godmother, Marie Anne Fourchet, another survivor and soldier's wife. Jeanne Pouillot's choice of godmother for her daughter testified to the bond forged when the two survivors, both recently arrived and newly married, remained with the garrison when their husbands were needed elsewhere. It may also have been a sign that Jeanne realized that Marie Anne Fourchet was beginning to become a person of note in Mobile.

Jeanne Pouillot and her second husband did not have much time together. Only a year after his daughter's birth, Marchand was deployed on a mission to the French post at Natchez. On October 29, 1722, when a fight between a Native American and a sergeant in the garrison escalated, soldiers killed the son of a leader of the Natchez nation. In the ensuing battle, seven French soldiers were killed, among them Marchand.[25] Such skirmishes were frequent in the area near the Natchez garrison in the 1720s. On those occasions, French soldiers left Mobile for what they assumed would be a quick deployment intended as a display of French military might. Some, like Marchand, never returned, leaving their widows back at Mobile's fort to face an uncertain future.

In the early 1720s, Marie Anne Grise and Étienne Fièvre moved briefly to New Orleans, where the services of a master carpenter were desperately required to help build a new capital. By 1724, the couple was back in Mobile, where they remained. In Mobile, Fièvre's skill was also urgently required—for example, in August 1724, when pigs escaped from someone's garden and damaged Fort Condé's fortifications, and the citadel was in need of extensive repairs. Devin, the fort's engineer, reported the damages and lamented in particular the fact that the fine new storehouse that Fièvre was to construct would be roofed with bark because, in 1724, there was no money to cover the cost of shingles.[26]

When she returned to Mobile from New Orleans, Marie Anne Grise set about creating the kind of life she could never have had in France. With their deportation, the women lost their families and their family life in France: their connection to their family's history, the futures they had imagined in the company of their siblings and their cousins. In many cases, family members—even their own parents—had actively worked to exclude them from their ranks and to deny them the chance to take their place in their family's line. In Louisiana, survivors founded new families. Some also fashioned the kind of family they would never have known, had they remained in their homeland. In the process, they rewrote their family story and reinvented their lineage. Their fathers—farmers, winemakers, cobblers, and dyers—became the grandfathers and the great-grandfathers of individuals of real note. In France, survivors' families worked land that belonged to the aristocracy, while in Louisiana, their descendants became the landed gentry. Few survivors accomplished this feat more spectacularly than Marie Anne Grise. In Mobile, Grise did her family in Amiens one better. And her children sometimes even did the French monarchy one better.

It was in Mobile that eight Fièvre children were born and baptized, in Mobile that Fièvre and Grise became people of influence in their community, very frequently called upon to serve as witnesses at weddings and as godparents. The names of those who stood as sponsors at their own children's baptisms are sure indicators of the couple's standing in the colony: a member of the Superior Council, Louisiana's governing body; each successive commander of Fort Condé; the garrison's highest officers and their wives. In Mobile, the trafficker in contraband tobacco and the carpenter were on an upwardly mobile trajectory, and this revealed itself in many ways.

While Fièvre wrote well, Grise was illiterate. Although their children wrote far less fluently than their father, they at least managed signatures rather than the simple x so often found on documents in a colony where any form of literacy was hardly the norm, and where still well into the 1730s, virtually no formal education was available for most children.[27]

On April 27, 1745, when the couple's oldest daughter, Marguerite, married Claude Belluc, a soldier from Auvergne, she signed "Margritte fievre." In January 1759, at the wedding of Marguerite's younger sister

Marthe to Valentin Dubroca, who had come from Bordeaux to be employed at the naval office in Mobile, Marthe signed "Martehe." In 1760, the youngest Fièvre daughter, Louise, got her name right.

As well she should have. Louise's marriage on March 20, 1760 to Louis Augustin Rochon sealed her family's rise in the social order. Louis Augustin was the son of Charles Rochon, among the handful of men who in the very first years of the eighteenth century traveled from New France to become Mobile's original residents.[28] The marriage of Marie Anne Grise's daughter and Charles Rochon's son united the children of two founding generations. It also linked the bride's family to the most historic property and architecture in the Mobile area.

The structure now considered the oldest construction in Mississippi as well as the best-preserved example of French colonial architecture on the Gulf Coast stands outside today's Pascagoula, Mississippi. Known as the La Pointe–Krebs house, the residence now visible was built c. 1770 on the site of a home from c. 1720. Even that 1770 incarnation of the La Pointe–Krebs house is only a larger, slightly more sophisticated version of Jeanne Mahou's early 1720s *habitation* and gives a good idea of the appearance of the best homes in Mobile at the moment when survivors arrived there. The dwelling consists of three rooms with wood flooring, unfinished space above, and a lean-to on one side. The structure is what is called post-in-sill construction: simply hewn posts set close together in a timber sill form the walls, with the spaces between the posts filled with bousillage (silty soil with Spanish moss added as a binding agent) or tabby (a type of concrete for which oyster shells were burned to form lime, which was mixed with ash and broken oyster shells). The exterior walls were coated with lime-based stucco plaster.[29]

The home sits on terrain originally part of a land grant made late in the Crozat regime to Joseph Simon de La Pointe. One of La Pointe's daughters became Augustin Rochon's first wife and moved to his property on Mobile Bay; the other married Hugo Krebs, who took over La Pointe's concession near Pascagoula upon his death. In 1760,

Louise Fièvre became Augustin Rochon's second wife and joined this land-rich clan.

Rochon, a significant figure in Mobile's establishment and a major property owner, had six children with Louise, including an eldest son, Louis Augustin, who had six children of his own. Until Rochon's death in 1780, the family resided at Rochon's home, situated directly on Mobile Bay, and one of the area's most imposing residences. After the British and their Choctaw allies burned it to the ground on October 1, 1780, the home was never rebuilt.

Marie Anne Grise, buried in Mobile on July 30, 1767, lived to see Louise Fièvre, her youngest daughter, marry Rochon, but she did not witness Louise's most remarkable achievement, an accomplishment possible in Mobile alone. Other settlements in the Lower Mississippi Valley had no architectural heritage to speak of, but in Mobile, the colony's most established community, truly historic property—and the status that came with it—could be acquired. After Rochon's death, in the 1790s Louise Fièvre continued to amass property on her own, and she favored land whose links to the history of French Louisiana were clear—notably a significant tract on the Mobile River that is now a National Historical Landmark. With this acquisition, Louise Fièvre brought into her domain many square miles, even an entire island. Included in this substantial parcel was the site of the original Fort Louis de la Louisiane, the capital of French Louisiana between 1702 and 1711.[30] Whenever Louise Fièvre put her cattle out to pasture, she could enjoy watching them trample on what were by then the ruins of the empire that had ordered her mother's deportation. The daughter of a woman so poor that she was forced to smuggle bundles of tobacco across France in order to survive was wealthy enough to buy the place where France's military history on the Gulf Coast began. It's hard to imagine a more spectacular rewriting of family history.

All the vast properties near Mobile such as those acquired by Louise Fièvre also participated in a crucial way in the story of French

Louisiana as it was dictated by John Law's policies. In 1724, the future chronicler of Louisiana, Dumont, then a simple soldier, visited the La Pointe concession and enumerated La Pointe's possessions: buildings, livestock, and "slaves," before adding that "the latter were Indians at that time, but some time later, he had Africans."[31] One of Louisiana's earliest historians thus provided a succinct overview of the history of slavery on the Gulf Coast.

Prior to 1719, when the women were deported and the first slave ships reached the colony, slavery in Louisiana was limited almost exclusively to a system familiar to Native Americans such as the Natchez and the Choctaw, for whom slaves were cast out of society but never purchased and sold. Prior to 1719, numerous Native Americans were held in slavery at every French outpost in the Lower Mississippi Valley. After 1719, as historian Dumont noted, the number of enslaved Native Americans declined quickly and steadily, at the same time as chattel slavery, in which enslaved Africans were considered property and a financial investment, became dominant, principally on and because of landholdings such as La Pointe's concession. Chattel slavery arrived in Mobile in April 1719, when ships reached Massacre Island with enslaved Africans aboard.[32] Four months later, *Les Deux Frères* landed there, following by *La Mutine* six months after that. The deported women who settled in Mobile watched as enslaved Africans became in various ways a significant part of its population.

After listing Frenchmen, Frenchwomen, and their children, the censuses of the various settlements drawn up in 1721 added three categories: French indentured servants, enslaved Africans, and enslaved Native Americans. Whereas in 1712, there had been but 10 enslaved Africans in the entire colony, by 1721, in Mobile alone, there were 241 enslaved Africans.[33] In Mobile in 1721, solely the households of the highest-ranking officials included individuals in any of those three categories: Bienville (one indentured servant, six enslaved Africans), the post's commander Delatour (one indentured servant, fourteen enslaved Africans, four enslaved Native Americans), and storehouse keeper Sarazin (two enslaved Africans, three enslaved Native Americans). Barely a year after her deportation, along with status and a fine home, a prominent marriage had already made Anne Françoise Rolland a slave owner.

During the women's early years in Mobile, their lives became personally implicated in those of enslaved Africans in various ways. A few became slave owners. Many became godmothers to the children of enslaved parents. Virtually a year to the day after *La Mutine* made landfall, Anne Françoise Rolland acted as godmother to a five-year-old African boy, one of many of those newly arrived whom the missionaries who served as priests in Louisiana baptized soon after they reached French territory. In the Catholic faith, godparents promise to ensure that the child is raised a Catholic if his parents are unable to fulfill that obligation. What might Anne Françoise have seen as the definition of her duties? And when in 1727 Angélique Reffe became godmother to a nineteen-year-old enslaved African woman who was the property of a high-ranking officer in Mobile's garrison, might she have reflected on the fact that they had both been brought to Louisiana at virtually the same age, and that they had both traveled in shackles—and perhaps even on the same ship, since after the women's crossing *La Mutine* was quickly returned to duty in the African slave trade with Louisiana?[34] Unlike Angélique Reffe, the young woman who was given her godmother's name and called "Angélique" was destined to live her life in slavery.

In agricultural areas surrounding Mobile, inhabitants who farmed completely on their own, as Jeanne Mahou and Laurent did, were soon the exception. The 1721 census reveals that substantial landowners such as Pierre Rochon already relied on the labor of enslaved Africans (ten, in his case). Over time, as descendants of survivors acquired significant amounts of land, their households increasingly turned to the labor of enslaved Africans. As Anne Françoise Rolland learned at the very start, in Louisiana as it had been shaped by John Law, status and wealth were almost invariably linked to slavery.

AMONG THE FORMER HUBS OF THE FRENCH COLONIAL EMPIRE IN the Lower Mississippi Valley, today Mobile seems the least visibly marked by its French past. In the area surrounding the modern city, however, one aspect of Mobile's French past, the presence of the families of two deported women, is inescapable. The family legacy created by Marie Anne Grise, transported on *Les Deux Frères*, is rivaled only by that of Marie Anne Fourchet, passenger number 161 on *La Mutine*. Every bit as much as Marie Anne Grise, Marie Anne Fourchet understood that she could realign her family legacy in the still-new country of Louisiana. Thanks to Marie Anne, in Mobile, the Fourchet dynasty of champagne merchants from Épernay began a radically new chapter in its history. Fourchet's children married in Mobile, and they married well. Soon, descendants of the woman accused in Paris of "public prostitution" were members of early Mobile's important families. Her children then made their mother proud when they acquired, just as did Marie Anne Grise's daughter Louise Fièvre, historic property. Significant sites in the Mobile area not the property of Grise's descendants were almost certainly in the hands of Fourchet's.

Fourchet, perhaps the first survivor to marry after the women were allowed to leave Ship Island, gave birth to two children in Mobile before she moved with her first husband, Jean La Case, to New Orleans.[35] Soldiers from Mobile had been requisitioned for the construction of the capital, where La Case worked on projects directed by Marie Anne Grise's husband, Étienne Fièvre. After a year, both families were back in Mobile, where Marie Anne Fourchet's life soon changed course—suddenly and dramatically. Given the future unfolding of the two women's lives, it's tempting to believe that during the time they shared in New Orleans, Marie Anne Grise and Marie Anne Fourchet considered their options carefully, and that they did so together. Also during the time they spent in the new capital, they watched New Orleans taking shape, and, as part of that process, they saw firsthand how the possession of property had begun to transform the status of their fellow survivors who had chosen to be among New Orleans's original inhabitants.

On March 20, 1726, Marie Anne Fourchet's last child with La Case, Marie Jeanne, was baptized. Only three months later, on June 22, the baby's father was buried, leaving Fourchet with two young children to provide for. In such circumstances, widows traditionally felt obliged to move on quickly, but Fourchet's remarriage must have been among the fastest on record. Only four days after La Case's death, Marie Anne Fourchet and Pierre Lorandini, an Italian from Florence and a corporal in the Mobile garrison, were wed. Lorandini and La Case had served in the same regiment, and the three had surely been friends before La Case's death. In her moment of need, Lorandini married his friend's widow. That gesture of friendship was the foundation of a decades-long union. Marie Anne Fourchet's marriage with Pierre Lorandini provides a second, textbook example of the manner in which deported women founded dynasties whose impact on the Gulf Coast remains visible today.

Lorandini was himself newly widowed, with an eight-month-old daughter. In March 1732, when their first child together was baptized, she was named "Marie Louise" in honor of her godmother, fellow survivor Marie Louise Balivet, who had come from New Orleans for the christening. In February 1736, a son, Jean Baptiste, was baptized; by then, his mother was forty-seven. Those four children—two from Fourchet's first marriage and two from the second—secured Marie Anne Fourchet's legacy. All of them rose to distinction.

Fourchet's children from her first marriage both founded dynasties of their own. Her daughter, Marie Jeanne La Case, had nine children from her marriage to Joseph Guillory. They settled far and wide across the Gulf South. Fourchet's son, Jacques La Case, followed in the footsteps of his father and stepfather and became a military man. He was active at Fort Toulouse until 1763, when, after its defeat in the Seven Years' War, France ceded the eastern part of its territory in the Lower Mississippi Valley to the English. His marriage to Marie

Anne Colon produced many children who put down roots all over what is now the state of Louisiana.

Following France's defeat in 1763 at the hands of England, Mobile's fort was christened "Fort Charlotte" in honor of the wife of England's George III. On October 2, 1764, members of some of Mobile's leading French families pledged their allegiance to George III. Of the ninety-eight French families in Mobile, only forty chose to remain and take that pledge. The others left Mobile for New Orleans and other settlements not under English rule. Marie Anne Grise took the oath, one of only two women to do so, as did Pierre Lorandini and Marie Anne Fourchet's son with Lorandini, Jean Baptiste.[36] A month later, Fourchet was still alive for Jean Baptiste's marriage. Pierre Lorandini died in 1778, but it's not known when Marie Anne Fourchet died—or if she lived to watch her son Jean Baptiste demonstrate his outstanding business acumen.

Jean Baptiste Lorandini prospered under English rule and, from 1780 on, under the Spanish regime, acquiring significant property in Mobile and the surrounding area. In 1807, the year of his death, Marie Anne Fourchet's last child obtained his greatest prize—a vast concession originally granted by Bienville in 1733 that had since passed through various hands. Known as the Saint-Louis tract, it stretched between what are now called Chickasabogue and Three-Mile Creeks and is today a truly enormous city park, Chickasabogue Park. Chickasabogue Park's 1,100 acres far surpass the mere 840 acres occupied by New York's Central Park.[37] Those who swim in the park's sandy-bottomed creek, or bike or walk its seventeen miles of trails, or spend time in its campground can appreciate the very striking mark left by the son of a survivor of deportation on the modern Gulf Coast.

In 1749, Jean Baptiste's sister, Fourchet's daughter from her second marriage, Marie Louise Lorandini (by then, the name was written "Lorandine" or "Laurendine"), married Louis François Baudin, heir to Nicolas Baudin, holder of a land grant to a tract that extends over many square miles on the coast south of Mobile. (Lawsuits subsequently debated whether Massacre Island was included in the concession as well. A second site that played an essential role in the women's deportation saga may thus also once have been owned by a survivor's daughter.) The entire parcel is still known as Mon Louis Island in honor of Marie Louise Lorandini's husband, Louis Baudin, and is now considered "a coastal area of particular significance" because it contains thousands of acres of largely unspoiled coastal pine savanna and salt marsh. Mon Louis Island, still another historic property once owned by the child of a survivor of deportation, may well be as close as we can get today to the Gulf Coast that the deported women found after their long and harrowing voyage.

Marie Louise Lorandini had four children with Louis Baudin, three of whom were officially married on July 30, 1778. The couples had previously exchanged vows, but they took advantage of a moment when a priest was present at Mobile to receive the sacrament. Daughter Pélagie Baudin, Marie Anne Fourchet's granddaughter, made a particularly auspicious match. She married Jacques de La Saussaye, a captain in the Royal Navy and the son of a naval captain as well. La Saussaye was born in the Royal Navy stronghold Rochefort, the port where, a half century earlier, the Royal Navy had refused to feed the first sixteen women marked for deportation.

It was in Mobile, "the most established" of all communities in the Lower Mississippi Valley, that two deported women understood that their new lives could take them in directions outside the realm of the possible in France for women of their rank. Among the deported women, only Marie Françoise Le Coustelier de Jouy de Palsy belonged to the landed aristocracy, and even she would never have become a landowner in France. But in Louisiana significant residential architecture and significant property were no longer the preserve of the aristocracy but were available instead to any inhabitant, even a deported woman. In Mobile, two survivors propelled their families into a new kind of prominence. Descendants of women deemed unfit for France became notables, leaders of the establishment. Land and status: that was the formula for success that Marie Anne Grise and Marie Anne Fourchet passed on to their descendants.

Between the sizeable chunks of Alabama real estate owned by Marie Anne Fourchet's two Lorandini children and just off today's main route to Dauphin Island lies Laurendine Road. That 3.5-mile-long thoroughfare is perhaps the most telling geographic reminder of the time when Mobile was French and of the massive influence over Mobile's European settlement exercised by the women who arrived there on *Les Deux Frères* and *La Mutine*.

IN PARIS, *LE NOUVEAU MERCURE GALANT* INCLUDED IN ITS AUGUST 1722 issue what was destined to be the last puffery for the colony once promoted as an overseas paradise. It published a letter from Mobile by Jean de Pradel, a young officer who had just returned for a second stint at Fort Louis. What he called "this charming colony" had become, he claimed, "infinitely more refined" in the two years between his postings.[38] Merely a month later, Mobile's "charms" were obliterated.

At ten p.m. on September 12, 1722, the full force of that devastating hurricane hit Fort Louis. The storehouse was overturned, and precious supplies, guns, and ammunition were all washed away.[39] This time, authorities decided not to repair the aging fort. They built instead a new one, named Fort Condé, in honor of one of the families that had profited most spectacularly from insider trading on John Law's stock. The monster storm tipped the scales for Mobile, which would never again be considered a major French colonial settlement. Rebuilding efforts were concentrated instead on New Orleans.

By 1726, the shift in the balance of powers had become evident. For the first time, the population along the Gulf Coast had declined, while that of New Orleans continued to increase.[40] A new capital had taken shape.

Chapter 10

Building a Capital
in New Orleans

F OR THE FIRST SURVIVORS WHO SETTLED THERE, NEW ORLEANS
had a big advantage. Where better to go if you wanted to shake
your past than a place without one? Later, as New Orleans created
a story for itself, deported women were able to come into their own
there as nowhere else. Some built lives unimaginable anyplace else
in the world, for themselves or for any European women of their day.
They did so, moreover, despite the fact that, at the start, nothing about
life in the place now often called "the Big Easy" was easy.

New Orleans's founding is usually dated 1718. In February of that
year, Bienville selected a site for a future capital, as yet unnamed,
and assigned some fifty men to clear land. They accomplished almost
nothing.

In April 1718, when Indies Company directors first spoke of "la Nouvelle Orléans," they were not convinced that the proposed location on the Mississippi was well chosen and were still considering a spot on the nearby Bayou Manchac that they believed would provide easier communication with the Gulf Coast. As late as September 1720, Law and other company directors remained uncertain about the site, and even about the capital's name. That same month, when Bienville referred to the projected city as "New Orleans or Manchac," he was indicating that Louisiana's capital might be moved elsewhere and called something else. Over two years after its founding, the place where many survivors were already living had an uncertain future. It barely had a name.[1]

Years would pass before New Orleans would amount to much. On October 25, 1719, Indies Company directors appointed Louis Pierre Le Blond de La Tour "chief engineer in charge of their interests in Louisiana" and gave him two main tasks: to evaluate the site chosen for the city and to determine whether it was possible to navigate the Mississippi from its mouth to New Orleans. It was only on July 7, 1722, that the city's chief engineer reached the capital. The interval between October 1719 and July 1722 was, even by Louisiana's standards, a lawless time in the would-be town. Little was accomplished: a few streets were delimited, some primitive constructions erected.

During that interval, John Law's stock market boomed and crashed, the deportation scheme was executed, and the city's original inhabitants reached New Orleans.[2] The first marriages of survivors were recorded in the summer of 1720, when the future town was largely brush-covered terrain unprotected from storm surges. For half the year, flooding turned it into a marshy bog. It was also wide-open space, where residents' pigs roamed freely, damaging what little had been built. Next to Paris, their new home was not even Podunk.

In one essential way, however, New Orleans was a true French metropolis. During the crucial first years of the city's existence, at least thirty-six survivors of *Les Deux Frères* and *La Mutine* resided there.

Because of them, from the start diverse customs and experiences from the four corners of France were woven into the urban fabric of the new capital.

It was only in 1721 that Le Blond de La Tour began actual planning. To help design the city he chose his student, Charles Franquet de Chaville, as well as Adrien de Pauger. Both were, like him, royal military engineers who had gained experience in the construction of fortifications while defending France's frontiers during the last of Louis XIV's wars. In March 1721, Le Blond de La Tour put Pauger in charge of planning New Orleans.

In January 1720, *Le Nouveau Mercure Galant* had assured Parisians that there were already six hundred houses in New Orleans. In reality, as Pauger discovered when he arrived there on March 29, 1721, the would-be capital consisted of "several shanties surrounded by brush and trees." Among the few "official" buildings was a "pitiful" temporary storehouse in which, as in Mobile, religious ceremonies such as marriages took place.[3] This was the environment in which numerous survivors started their new lives.

With a handful of workers, Pauger began clearing enough space so that street layout could begin. And the work was no simple matter since there were huge cypress trees to be uprooted and felled and thick masses of cane and river reeds to be hacked away.[4] With Le Blond de La Tour's consent, Pauger next set about "assigning lots along these streets to residents." A few spaces were earmarked for public edifices, but otherwise land was virtually up for grabs. Pauger drafted an informal map of projected streets, using letters to reserve spots for specific individuals.[5] With this understanding, New Orleans's original inhabitants then pitched in. They cleared their own land and did their own construction. They even, as Pauger admitted, helped fell trees "to build this city."

Some quickly succumbed to the rigors of such a life. After their August 12, 1720 marriage, there is no further sign of Marie Grené and her husband.

Manon Fontaine and other survivors who outlasted the early days of the place destined to become New Orleans lived on land they had cleared themselves, in homes of their own construction. In Paris, most of the women had been no strangers to hard labor. Laundresses lugged hefty parcels through the city and then pounded clothes clean. Street vendors like Manon Fontaine walked the cobblestones of Paris all day long with heavy loads attached to their bodies. In New Orleans, these women were fully able to work alongside their husbands. Manon and two other survivors married blacksmiths, and those farriers' hands, hands strong enough to pound metal for hours on end, proved essential to carving homes out of canebrake. When the nowhere of New Orleans became somewhere, Manon and other founding inhabitants were part and parcel of the city's first built environment, with the mud from which New Orleans was shaped embedded under their fingernails.

It was only in May 1722 that authorities in New Biloxi learned that New Orleans had become the colony's administrative center. And it was only in November 1722 that Louisiana's Superior Council began issuing decisions in New Orleans. Well over two years after the first marriages of survivors had taken place there, the law had finally come to France's latest outpost on the Mississippi.

In July 1722, Le Blond de La Tour reached the capital with a number of craftsmen. They were just in time to watch the monster hurricane take down the majority of all completed buildings: over thirty structures were wiped off the map and all others badly damaged.[6] The city, such as it was, in effect no longer existed. The thirty-seven French artisans chosen by Le Blond de La Tour were the first highly trained craftsmen to work on New Orleans's construction. In a colony virtually without master artisans, Le Blond de La Tour saw these men as vital to his plan for building a successful capital, and in the hurricane's aftermath, they came through for him.[7] Engineer Franquet de Chaville marveled at all they accomplished, with the help of inhabitants, in the months after the hurricane hit. Four master carpenters, foremost among them Marie Anne Grise's husband, Étienne Fièvre, were responsible for the original governmental edifices near the Place d'Armes. At a moment when blame-laying was ubiquitous, Fièvre won universal praise for his technical expertise. He was key to the construction of monuments that provided the earliest indication that New Orleans might one day resemble a European-style capital city.

Rebuilding took place so quickly that by January 1723, the first accurate maps of New Orleans were available. Both attempted to represent simultaneously work already done and construction planned; both were color coded. The earliest, signed by Le Blond de La Tour, shows in white the small area near a central square (the Place d'Armes

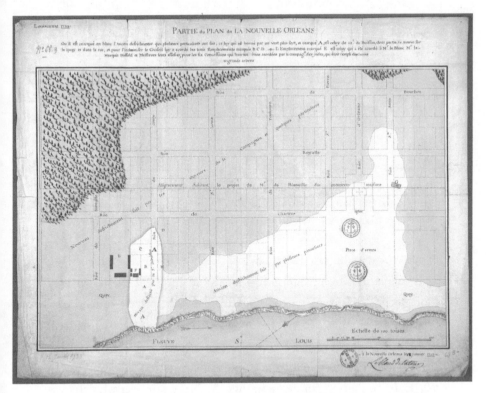

Figure 9. City planner Le Blond de La Tour's 1723 map of New Orleans introduces the city's first street names and juxtaposes the earliest area to be cleared, land more recently cleared—and wilderness beyond.

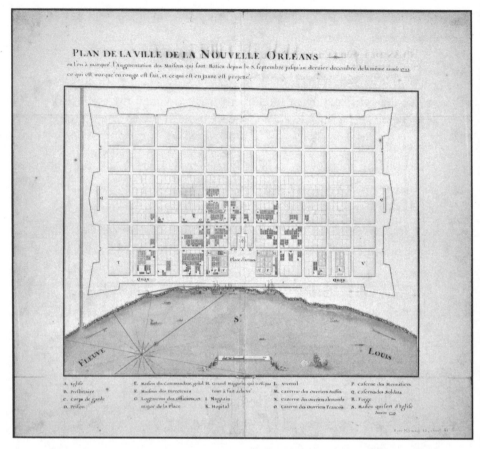

Figure 10. A second map from 1723, the original depiction of the Vieux Carré, or French Quarter, indicates constructions already completed, others merely planned for, and the city's port on the river that residents called "the Saint-Louis River."

or military parade ground, today's Jackson Square) cleared early on, as he explains, "by private individuals" and in green the larger area more recently cleared "by company workers and private individuals" (see Figure 9). This was the first map to feature the street names still in use today, many of which (Bourbon, Orléans, Conti) honored the royal family responsible for the women's deportation. There was even a "rue de Toulouse," commemorating the Navy minister who charac- terized the deported women waiting in Rochefort as "merchandise." When those names were finally made public in early 1723, New

Orleans became only the second place in the colony to boast streets with names—and survivors learned that they would be reminded of the Bourbon monarchy every day of their lives.[8]

Beyond those clearings, the map depicts the vast wilderness that surrounded the minuscule capital. In 1723, when a reorganized Indies Company emerged from John Law's shadow, New Orleans barely existed.

The second, more idealized map, shown in Figure 10, is the earliest depiction of what came to be known as the Vieux Carré, or French Quarter. The city's existing constructions figure on the map next to those not yet completed (H, the storehouse) and others planned for but not begun (A, the church). Structures either built or rebuilt in the final months of 1722 are indicated in red, those not yet built but planned in yellow. Official buildings (officers' quarters, blacksmith's forge) are marked with letters; private homes are small, unmarked squares or triangles. A significant number of those were inhabited by survivors.

But even after the rebuilding effort, another major hurdle remained. In March 1723, Pauger left to address that problem, one that made authorities still hesitant to invest in New Orleans: no one had yet successfully navigated the lower Mississippi. When that feat was accomplished, two men proved essential, one of them also married to a survivor.

Marie Daudin, the nineteen-year-old daughter of a dockworker in Orléans, France, a city defined by its river and river trade, incarcerated despite having an airtight alibi and then deported, found herself in New Orleans, also defined by its river and hoping to be defined by river trade. She soon married Antoine Michel Caron, an Indies Company employee who had traveled to the colony voluntarily as a land grant settler. Caron was the ship's captain considered by Pauger singularly capable of guiding boats in a river that had bested many others and the person on whom he counted to make New Orleans a true port.[9]

It's not clear if Daudin and Caron lived in New Orleans in November 1721, when the town's first census was drawn up. Numerous survivors not counted were almost certainly already there. Given the chaos that reigned, the tally can hardly be considered systematic. Even so, it provides a snapshot of a city in the making. In 1721, when New Orleans was nothing by European standards, by the colony's it was already a distinct kind of place, with aspirations that went beyond its size.

A comparison of its population and that of Mobile makes this clear. Numerous inhabitants of Mobile were early immigrants: some had come from France in the colony's first years, including several women in 1704, others from New France, today's Canada. By 1721, they had well-established lives in Mobile. In New Orleans, almost everyone was a recent arrival, clueless about life in the colony and how things worked—or didn't.

Mobile's population was predominantly military, and the city was centered around its fort and defined by a defensive spirit. There were fewer soldiers in New Orleans but far more seamen of all stripes: the captain of an Indies Company ship, fourteen sailors, and, above all, twenty captains of boats, the kind of small craft best suited to navigating the Mississippi and the Gulf Coast. Well before large vessels docked there, New Orleans was open to travel and to the world outside.

It was also acquiring the urban fabric particular to French cities. Even though there was as yet little work for them, New Orleans immediately attracted artisans skilled in luxury trades: a *patissier*, a wigmaker (also married to a survivor), three tailors (even a master tailor, also married to a deported woman), a *sommelier* (someone employed in a great home to care for linen, china, and wine). Already in 1721, New Orleans aspired to a grand, French style.

That same census of November 1721 concluded on a category making its unique appearance in such a tally: individuals, both male and female, considered unequal to the city's other inhabitants by virtue of the fact that they had come to the colony *de force*. Included among these outcasts were two deported women: Anne Namond, a salt smuggler from the tiny village of Marchelpau in northern France, and Louise Fontenelle, a young woman from Rouen who was caught in the roundup of 1719. Only months later, neither would have found herself on that list.

Namond soon married Claude Baguerois, known as "La France," a fellow exile (for desertion from the Royal Army). On September 25, 1725, when Namond died at age twenty-nine, both were described as "residents" of New Orleans: four years on, the outcasts had been assimilated. Fontenelle's story is similar. On June 2, 1722, she married Pierre Bel from La Rochelle, an employee of the Indies Company with a most desirable trade, ship's caulker. On December 23, 1726, Fontenelle, by then another established New Orleanian, was buried there.

In 1721, only one survivor's child was counted. Marie Chartier, the highly educated governess for the children of a nobleman who was denounced to the police by her employer's jealous second wife, married quickly in the New World. Her husband, Pierre Antoine Duflot, a wigmaker and a voluntary immigrant, reached Massacre Island in February 1720 in the same convoy with *La Mutine*; the pair had soon moved on to New Orleans.[10]

By September 1724, Marie Chartier had lost her husband and their second child. She was also remarried to Manu de Tronquidi. He was not only a nobleman, at least as noble as her employer in Paris, but also the captain of the Indies Company vessel *La Loire*. Marie Chartier's natural distinction had won the heart of a second aristocrat. In 1726, Chartier and Tronquidi and her first child from her marriage to Duflot, Marie Thérèse, lived on Bourbon Street, at the corner with Saint Louis Street, and the couple soon had a child of their own. Another deported woman had acquired status in the colony.

THE JUNE 1721 CENSUS OF MOBILE INCLUDED "JEAN MALAN, *FORgeron*," "blacksmith," and his wife. The blacksmith's name was actually "Jean Melin," and he was known to all as "Bourguignon" because of his birth in the tiny Burgundian village of Prunoy. Melin, thirty-two, sailed to the colony voluntarily to work on a concession. He reached Massacre Island shortly after the woman he soon met and married: Manon Fontaine, by then probably thirty-nine. They spent about a year in Mobile before leaving Louisiana's old capital for its new one.

Even though the November 1721 census of New Orleans did not count the couple, they were surely already there. On January 1, 1722, authorization for a half lot was granted to "Manon Fontaine, *femme Bourguignon*," "Bourguignon's wife." That grant, renewed at regular intervals, gave Manon the right, always in her own name, to a plot clearly marked on a 1731 map of New Orleans: today it is number 819 Bourbon Street. The grant was the earliest sign of Manon's drive to possess key bits of the Bourbon monarchy's new capital. A woman repeatedly exiled from the city of her birth was determined to have a firm foothold in her new home.

In New Orleans's early years, property rights were as muddled as most legal questions, and each governing body proposed a different means of attributing land. Manon immediately understood that in early 1722, local authorities were desperate to have the city built and built fast. If you filed a petition requesting a lot, pledged to clear the land and build on it, followed through on your promise, and later renewed your petition as specified, the land and the home on it were yours to live in or sell. Manon observed procedure meticulously, and she and Bourguignon were soon land- and homeowners on Bourbon Street. They had felled the trees, hacked back the cane, and constructed the dwelling themselves. A blacksmith and a woman accused of murdering sixteen men thereby earned a place among Bourbon Street's original residents.[11]

Only one other street in the city counted as many survivors among its first inhabitants as did storied Bourbon Street. Survivors who were among Bourbon Street's initial residents surely experienced as nowhere else in the new capital the same sense of a tight-knit community that they had known in such Parisian neighborhoods as the New City and the Halles. In New Orleans's original incarnation, you couldn't have gone two or three blocks in any direction without encountering the home of a woman who had arrived there *de force*. And on Bourbon Street, every second or third house was home to a deported woman.

As a result, on Bourbon Street, Manon Fontaine and Marie Chartier crossed paths every day with many familiar neighbors. Catherine Oudart, Manon's fellow passenger on *Les Deux Frères*, moved to Bourbon Street after the deaths of Sergeant Beaulieu and their daughter Anne, the first deported woman's baby whose baptism was recorded in Mobile. Another survivor was married to Bourbon Street's drummer, Jean Bastien, known to all as "Baguette," or "Drumstick," the official drummer of the city's garrison. The musician who first made Bourbon Street pulse with rhythm was so closely identified with his profession that "Baguette" came to replace his family name, and the couple's daughter, named "Marie Anne" after her mother, even used "Baguette" as a surname. Baguette's wife was the outlier in Pancatelin's scheme, for although she left France in chains, she traveled voluntarily.

In May 1719, Pancatelin eagerly reported that Marie Anne Giard, eighteen and born in the heart of Paris near the rue Saint-Denis, "*de bonne volonté demande d'aller aux îles*," "of her own free will asks to go to the islands." Even though she had knowingly put herself in Pancatelin's hands, Giard got no special treatment. She became part of Bourlon's convoy of deported women; she traveled as passenger 78 on *La Mutine*. Her fellow passengers never let Marie Anne Giard forget how she'd come to share in their fate. In his history, Dumont reports that Giard was known to all as "*la demoiselle de bonne volonté*," "the young woman who volunteered."[12] Her neighbors may well have used just this phrase when they ran into the drummer's wife on Bourbon Street.

A number of Bourbon Street's original residents had occupations that were essential at the moment when New Orleans was taking shape. Just as they did in Paris, in New Orleans artisans from similar trades tended to live near each other, and Bourbon Street had a cluster of craftsmen involved in construction: roofers, masons, carpenters.[13] One of Bourbon Street's carpenters, Pierre Evrard, married passenger 85 from *La Mutine*, Marie Jeanne Philbert.

In Paris, Philbert had been arrested, released on grounds of insufficient proof, then rearrested just when Pancatelin was on the prowl for colonists for John Law.[14] Marie Jeanne Philbert was a widow; when she was deported, she was forced to leave behind in France a daughter from her marriage to Pierre Beauregard. From New Orleans, she pulled off the truly remarkable feat of locating her daughter in France and bringing her to the colony. On May 24, 1728, in New Orleans, Marie Jeanne Philbert watched as her daughter, Marie Anne Beauregard, married François Pintureau from Poitiers. The husband of survivor Marie Daudin, ship's captain Michel Caron, was their witness.

The second large concentration of deported women took shape along the street named rue Royale, Royal Street. Many were also married to craftsmen. Françoise Dinan, passenger 64 on *La Mutine*, lived there with her husband, Louis Brouet, a fellow Parisian and master wheelwright—and a second old friend of still another *La Mutine* survivor, Angélique Reffe, who may well have introduced the couple. Among their neighbors was passenger 62, Marie Simone Martin, married to mason Pierre Caillou.[15] Marie Simone had worked as a laundress in Paris and had been deported after a corrupt police officer pinned a theft charge on her, just what had happened to another of their neighbors on Royal Street, Marie Chevalier.

Also a resident of Royal Street was Marie Paris, accused in France so repeatedly of the theft of diamond-studded earrings that, even without evidence, the charge finally stuck. In New Orleans, Marie married Antoine Jobelin, one of the *voyageurs* or traders who, traveling in their dugout canoes, helped keep goods circulating up and down the Mississippi.

Marie Paris was deported on *Les Deux Frères* along with Étien-nette Gené, who at first settled in Biloxi with her husband, La Croix, regimental drummer and fifer. When New Orleans became the new capital, La Croix was named the official drummer of the Indies Company, and the couple moved to Royal Street. On November 28, 1726, their unnamed infant was buried, and on August 23, 1727, Étien-nette herself was interred. Étiennette's burial notice concludes with a most uncommon phrase: "She came to this colony *de force*." La Croix wanted the violence that had brought Étiennette to New Orleans in-scribed in the official record. Seven years on, the phrase *de force* was no longer a social stigma for survivors—but almost a badge of honor.

Among their neighbors on Royal Street was passenger number 155, Parisian Marie Angélique Dimanche, who on June 7, 1721, married Julien Binard, a Breton blacksmith employed by the Indies Company and known as "La Forge," or "The Forge." The couple had just arrived from Mobile, where Binard and Bourguignon had earlier shared the work of maintaining the forty-two horses in or near the settlement. Both farriers made the mistake of moving to New Orleans, undoubt-edly after Indies Company officials encouraged them to do so. As a result, in 1721, when there was only one horse in the capital, the city had three blacksmiths. In 1722, when the Indies Company decreed that farriers had to diversify, Binard shifted to making edge tools.

By 1723, desperate to earn a living, Binard sold a parcel of land (surely one he'd received from Pauger in exchange for clearing it) and agreed to build a house on it for 450 *livres*. That contract devolved into the kind of fiasco commonplace in a city where few had access to currency. Binard built the house, and when the new owner moved in without paying up, Binard had notice served on him. In Decem-ber 1725, the house was found locked and empty, and was put up for auction.[16]

The couple faced the unhappy consequences of those years of crisis in their domestic life as well. In July 1727, Dimanche and Binard had just had their first child. And in the following months of what became known as a notably deadly year, Marie Angélique Dimanche proved her generosity. She did so in the immediate aftermath of September 16, 1727, when a burial took place, that of a Parisian supposedly named Geneviève Grenier, "who came to this colony *de force*." This information fits none of the deported women, but the burial records for 1727, like those of *La Mutine*, are more than usually confused. On October 14, when the woman's newborn child was buried as well, the death notice stated that the baby had been "*en nourrice* with the woman called La Forge"—Marie Angélique Dimanche. One deported woman had nursed another's orphaned infant daughter, hoping to keep her alive.

A third passenger from *Les Deux Frères* was also among Royal Street's original residents. Marie Louise Brunet was the fourth survivor to get married in New Orleans, to Gilles Lemire, and the couple settled on Royal Street. Upon Lemire's death, Brunet married fellow Parisian Jean Baptiste Montard, who had traveled to the colony along with the man Manon Fontaine married, Bourguignon. Unlike Bourguignon, however, Montard, age thirty-one and five feet two inches, with skin so fair that it was noted on the ship's manifest, did not sail willingly. In Paris, Montard was still in training, gaining experience in the workshop of a master *menuisier* (joiner), when he was arrested for theft, condemned first to flogging and banishment, then to deportation.[17]

Montard's marriage with Brunet was a rare example of a union between fellow deportees. It was also the only time that exiles not only put their allegedly criminal pasts behind them by winning respect and newfound status, thereby reassuming an identity taken from them by Law and Pancatelin, but also took advantage of the colony's isolation from France to reimagine their personal histories. In New Orleans, Montard inflated his status. When they married on June 29, 1729, he identified himself as a "master joiner," as though he had completed his apprenticeship in Paris and had become the professional equal of his father, an authentic master *menuisier*.

Brunet likewise used the announcement of their marriage to conclude her reinvention and settle once and for all the question of her identity. Arrested at age twelve along with an alleged poisoner and abortionist to whom she was not related but who claimed to have raised her from early childhood, pronounced after a police investigation an "orphan" and a "bastard," characterized by Pancatelin as "completely debauched," Brunet had grown up with these competing versions of her life story. The thick file that contains the record of her long incarceration in the Salpêtrière refers to her by several family names and speaks of three different women as her mother. When she found herself in a city that, like her, had had trouble finding a definitive name, she took matters into her own hands and resolved the inscrutability of her past.

At the time of her marriage to Lemire in 1721, Brunet identified herself as "Marie Louise Brunet, daughter of Philippe de Montfrein and Marie Françoise Brunet." By the time of her second marriage in 1729, she had perfected her story, calling herself "Marie Montfrein, *dite* [known as] Brunet, daughter of the deceased Félix de Montfrein and Marie Brunet." Did Marie have memories from a time before she had been taken in by the alleged abortionist whom the police called "the widow Valentin"? Had someone given her proof of her ancestry, particularly the fact that her father was deceased and a nobleman, "de Montfrein"? Or had she simply invented an identity for herself by choosing a definitive name and parentage?[18]

From then on, Brunet remained "Marie de Montfrein." The couple continued to reside on Royal Street, and on February 8, 1730, they had a son, Jean Baptiste. A daughter, Marie Jeanne, known as "Jeannette," was a newborn infant in January 1732, when the Montard family was still among the inhabitants of Royal Street.

On September 16, 1752, Jeannette married Pierre Charpentier in a small settlement on the Mississippi, Saint Jacques de Cabahannoce, much of which has now been engulfed by the river whose voraciousness caused the Indies Company to doubt the wisdom of creating a capital on its banks. Jeannette declared herself the daughter of "Marie de Montfrein"; "Marie Brunet" was no more.[19] Through Jeannette, the woman deported under the name "Marie Louise Brunette, known as Valentin" founded a dynasty. Across the decades, families bearing the names "Charpentier," "Duplantis," and "Thibodeaux" have claimed descent from "Marie de Montfrein."

FOR SOME REASON, SURVIVORS NEVER CLUSTERED ON THE STREETS that run perpendicular to Bourbon and Royal. At first, those cross streets counted only one deported woman per street. On the rue Saint-Pierre that lone survivor was Thérèse Valenciennes, arrested and sentenced in a flash in August 1719 without so much as an accusation. When she was widowed, Thérèse remained on Saint Peter with her child.[20] The rue Saint-Philippe also had a sole deported women among its original residents, Marie Anne Bouru, passenger 181 on *La Mutine*. Even as the situation became desperate for New Orleans's two original blacksmiths, a third farrier, Étienne Barrasson, set up shop on St. Philip. On April 7, 1723, Barrasson and Marie Anne Bouru wed. The couple and their child resided on St. Philip until Barrasson's death on November 28, 1728.

Once New Orleans had expanded a bit, a brand-new street at what was then the city's eastern limit, the rue de l'Arsenal, Arsenal Street, today's Ursuline Avenue, similarly counted a single survivor. Marie Madeleine Doyart was only ten when she was arrested in Paris and accused of "public prostitution" along with three other Irish girls and young women, and only twelve when she traveled in *La Mutine*'s hold.[21] At her tender age, the youngest prisoner of all would have learned French more readily than did other foreign deportees. She could thus have easily bonded with the older Frenchwomen with whom she was shackled. Because she would have reminded them of the little sisters they were forced to leave behind in France, they would have adopted her and helped ensure that the Irish girl became the youngest prisoner to survive. In New Orleans, Marie Madeleine Doyart resided on Arsenal Street along with her husband, soldier René Malain, known as "Sans Chagrin," "Carefree," and their children.

One deported woman, Marie Louise Balivet, lived at another newly traced city limit, the southern one. Balivet was among the first to wed in Biloxi, where she married sailor Jacques Duval. After Duval died in a shipwreck, Balivet moved to New Orleans, where on April 24, 1726, at age forty-five, she married Joseph Lazou, captain of *L'Abeille, The Bee*, a boat in the service of the Indies Company. Lazou received many commendations for his work; his annual salary of 1,200 *livres*, among the highest in the colony, reflects his employer's appreciation. Lazou may or may not have been born an aristocrat, but in any event, because of his exceptional service, he became a nobleman in Louisiana, where his name was often written "Joseph *de* Lazou." In the aristocratic enclave near Paris where Balivet was born, her family of artisans had brushed shoulders with noble families on a daily basis, and that familiarity with the ways of the aristocratic world may have helped ensure that still another deported woman rose to the top of Louisiana's society. Balivet and Lazou did not have children of their own, but they raised one of many orphaned in a colony where disease and famine continued to take a heavy toll. They owned a home on the Quai, today's Decatur Street, the elevated walkway that, following a model recently introduced in Paris, created pedestrian space beside the river while offering some minimal protection from flooding. Today Balivet and Lazou's property sits opposite a modern New Orleans landmark, Café du Monde.

Marie Louise Balivet lost a second husband to the sea. On September 22, 1733, Lazou was buried in Mobile cemetery, having died while piloting his boat. Governor Bienville pronounced his death "a loss for this colony, where there are very few people of his caliber."[22]

After Lazou's death, Marie Louise Balivet moved to Mobile, surely because of her enduring friendship with Marie Anne Fourchet. She put the New Orleans property on the market, and when her home sold on November 10, 1736, it fetched a fine price—1,250 *livres*—but it was too late to help Balivet, who died penniless on April 28, just shy of her fifty-seventh birthday. In France, her father, stonemason Jacques Balivet, had been only fifty at the time of his death. Jeanne Boissinet testified that she had housed and fed Balivet for three and a half months and that Balivet had promised to reimburse her from the proceeds on the sale of her house. Honorable to the last, Balivet kept impeccable records of every penny she owed: for lodging and laundry, to her butcher. She also claimed a debt to another old friend—"Madame Tarascon," Marie Avril—"for cheese." Women who had arrived in a new land as outcasts only to become persons of note there had come through for each other to the end. Balivet was buried in her only remaining possessions, clothing made from fabric imported from the country that had exiled her: "an old, cinnamon-colored dress of French cloth and a worn-out skirt, in a blue and white striped print."[23]

There was one indication that Marie Louise Balivet's second husband may not always have been a loyal servant of the Indies Company. In the summer of 1723, fifteen inhabitants of Biloxi were arrested and charged with plotting to escape the failing colony in two boats. At a time when Louisiana was under threat from all sides, any such attempt—and especially those involving military personnel—was always considered a significant menace to the colony's security and officially labeled "mutiny" or "sedition." Even though, under interrogation, the conspirators did not implicate Captain Lazou in their plot, one of those boats was his.[24] That 1723 desertion attempt was a sign of the times.

IN 1723, RAINFALL IN THE COLONY WAS NEARLY TWICE AS HEAVY AS usual, and after massive floods, still another famine ensued. Despite Bienville's repeated pleas, no help came from France, which, in the years following Law's downfall, was in perpetual crisis mode. After flooding and famine, a third horseman soon arrived: epidemics. Dysentery, fevers of all kinds, including perhaps malaria, all took a toll.

In the summer of 1723, New Orleans's first hospital was completed. It was forty feet by twenty and intended for eighty. Nine hundred patients rushed there all at once.[25] It was at this moment that Bienville first warned that mutinies and desertions were becoming ever more frequent.[26] Anyone who could was trying to get out.

The years 1723 to 1728 were among the most lethal in the history of a colony well accustomed to such episodes. Françoise Dinan, Louise Fontenelle, Étiennette Gené, and Anne Namond were but four of numerous survivors residing in New Orleans who did not make it through. Other deported women lost those nearest and dearest to them.

On February 10, 1724, Parisian Marie Anne Automne, passenger 108 on *La Mutine*, buried Mathurin, her son with Joseph Quevedo. In January 1725, Marguerite Salot, age twenty-five, among the first survivors to marry in New Orleans and twice widowed there, became still another casualty of those deadly times. On February 1, the Superior Council voted to "grant her orphan son the ration formerly given his mother," but that help was not enough, for on September 21, Louis, aged nine months, was buried.[27] Françoise Ferret, deported on *Les Deux Frères* for smuggling, was interred on November 28, 1724. When asked to identify her, her husband, Charles Gaigné, said she was forty-five and had been baptized at the Church of Saint-Jacques, in the center of the northern French city of Amiens.[28]

Parisian Marie Anne Le Fort had spent fifteen years in the Salpêtrière, jailed by the notoriously corrupt Inspector Simonnet on particularly outlandish sorcery charges, and then transported on *La Mutine* as passenger 107.[29] In New Orleans, Marie Anne married a fisherman named Claude Imbert. After her death in early 1725, in July of that year, with his wedding to passenger 143, fellow Parisian Thérèse Le Comte, Imbert became the only man to marry two survivors from *La Mutine*.

Thérèse, daughter of an impoverished Parisian day laborer, had spent her first years in the colony in Natchitoches, where she had cleaned house for a prominent landowner, labor for which she was never paid. In New Orleans on November 17, 1727, Le Comte and Imbert began legal proceedings to recover wages due her.[30] Imbert died soon after they filed suit. Thérèse remarried quickly, but on October 12, 1728, a burial took place in New Orleans: "Gillette Thérèse Le Comte, wife of Saint-Laurent, a native of Paris and the parish of Saint-Nicolas-des-Champs," was interred. The previous day, in New Orleans's hospital, after only months together, both Thérèse, then thirty-five, and her second husband had succumbed to the same illness.

The hospital in which Thérèse and so many others spent their last moments was, by all accounts, a miserable place. In December 1724, a member of the Superior Council governing Louisiana denounced its inadequacies and included a lengthy "memorandum" of all the "merchandise, effects, and utensils" desperately needed, stressing that there were no sheets left, no towels, indeed no linen at all, and no syringes, neither pans nor spoons.[31]

On August 14, 1727, passenger 96 on *La Mutine*, Marie Boutin, was among those who died in New Orleans's hospital. With her last breath, Marie, by then twenty-seven, confirmed the names of her parents, the "poor tailor" and his wife who, on December 17, 1718, had become the first family in Paris to request expressly that their daughter be sent "to the islands."[32]

So many were dying so quickly that year that missionaries were overwhelmed. They found the time to record some deaths only long after the fact, when they could no longer remember precise dates. The vagueness of one entry in the burial register testifies to their impossible task: "The year 1727. Vincent's child died in this city."

During those lethal years, two new censuses were published, in January 1726 and July 1727. Even such dry documents could not mask the reality of the troubled times. Two families living on Bourbon Street were identified solely as "*passent en France*," "returning to France." They were among the lucky few to have been granted permission to flee the misery of life in New Orleans in the late 1720s.

BY THE END OF THAT DEADLY PERIOD IN NEW ORLEANS'S EARLY HIS-
tory, in 1728, Manon Fontaine and Bourguignon lived on one of the
first streets that did not feature a royal name, the rue Sainte-Anne.
Once again, they had cleared the land and built their own home; once
again, Manon had secured their rights to the property. But by then,
the long years of suffering for all New Orleanians had taken a severe
economic toll on the city's working people. Bourguignon, a blacksmith in a city without need for one, much less three, was deeply in
debt and unable to find work. He had also turned to drink.

On May 21, 1728, Bourguignon walked into one of the unlicensed
establishments where inhabitants practiced the kind of activity that
had gotten some of them deported: selling contraband goods, no longer tobacco and salt in New Orleans, but usually alcohol and meat
instead—in this case, pork obtained directly from local farmers and
sold without official markup.[33] Bourguignon had come to pay the
four *livres* he owed the proprietor, then stayed on to drink. This establishment, near the corner of Bourbon and St. Ann, where Manon
and Bourguignon now lived, functioned just like the cabarets of
Paris. People dropped in for the local equivalent of a *demi*, crafted by
the Alix brothers, the brewers of New Orleans. When Bourguignon
spotted some illegal bacon, in his version of the events, he took out
his knife, cut himself a chunk, pronounced it delicious, and asked to
buy some. Vincent, the town's *huissier* or bailiff, was there as well. He
accused Bourguignon of stealing the lard and punched him in the
face. But Bourguignon's knife was still out, and he attacked Vincent
and wounded him.

In the accusations, interrogations, and confrontations that ensued,
Bourguignon was described as "a poor guy who has often engaged in
drunken brawls," a description with which his wife by then clearly
agreed. On May 24, Manon appealed to Louisiana's Superior Council, reminding them that, two years previously, she had requested that
her husband be sent back to France. Manon's petition contains none
of the boilerplate usual to such documents. It is instead beautifully

phrased, eloquent, moving, authentic. The woman it reveals seems both real and admirable. Her words give the lie to Pancatelin's nonsense about her.

Her husband, Manon explained, had acted "under the influence of drink and of madness well-known to all, madness either congenital [*causée par naissance*] or triggered by the operation with a scalpel that he endured in France." The *"opération du trépan"* to which Manon referred, a procedure during which a *trépan* or very crude surgical saw was used to remove part of a patient's skull, was widely considered "dangerous and difficult." Manon begged "on her knees" that the council now honor her request and send Bourguignon back to France. She even offered to pay "not only his passage but the cost of his food and dressings for his wounds." She explained that she had been taking in sewing and embroidery to support them, but she was concerned that she wouldn't continue to find work and would be reduced "to misery." Bourguignon was convicted of assault and condemned, in a verdict that would have been familiar to Manon, to a public flogging and banishment.[34] In this case, banishment meant that Manon's wish was granted; Bourguignon would soon return to France.

The man assaulted by Bourguignon in May 1728 was the same "Vincent" whose baby's death in the course of that particularly lethal year 1727 was never properly reported. He was in fact "Jacques Talmont, known as Vincent," the law's most public face in New Orleans. Vincent carried out arrests, delivered summonses and verdicts. Vincent's wife, Jeanne Coroy, was no stranger to the kind of massive mortality that claimed their only child.

The tiny French village, now called Saint-Martin-sur-la-Renne, in which Jeanne Coroy, passenger 75 on *La Mutine*, was born was particularly hard hit by the famine and disease brought on by the Great Winter of 1709–1710, the moment that had also determined the lives of Marie Baron and Jeanne Mahou. The priest who recorded the death of Jeanne Coroy's father in 1710 began that year's entries by evoking the misery that 1709 had brought to the village. Since there

had been "no wheat, almost no fruit, and no wine at all," he was pow-
erless "to ease the suffering" of his parishioners. Jeanne, then fourteen, saw her family of vignerons brought low when they could no
longer make wine. After her father, a surgeon, succumbed to the pestilence he had been struggling to combat, like Baron, Jeanne Coroy
fled her devastated village for Paris, where, like Baron, she was soon
arrested for theft.[35]

In New Orleans, after Jeanne Coroy saw her firstborn become a
victim of a new incarnation of the deadly years that had scarred her
adolescence, she demonstrated that same desire for flight. And by
1728, she was not the only survivor to have had enough. Her friend
Manon Fontaine had, too. Coroy and Fontaine had remained close in
the decade since their deportation. At the exact moment when their
husbands had an altercation, they were in frequent contact with regard to a very different matter.

In November 1719 in Paris, Manon was accused of fomenting a
"seditious rebellion." A decade later in New Orleans, along with several fellow survivors, Coroy first among them, Manon was accused
of instigating "a seditious desertion plot"—in fact, of having plotted
to flee Louisiana for an English colony. This time, the mutiny was
no fabrication. This time, the deported women's involvement was established in a court of law. Indeed, it was even established that they
were the plot's chief organizers. The numerous conspirators whom
Fontaine and Coroy gathered together had a variety of reasons for
deserting Louisiana: to escape the disease that ravaged New Orleans;
to make a fresh start in a more prosperous economic climate; in some
cases, to break free from enslavement.

Whereas in Paris, the women were accused of using violence to
achieve their ends, of wielding knives and bashing in heads, in New
Orleans, nothing they did involved violence. This "sedition" was carried out with stealth. And, unlike violence, stealth was something of
which Manon Fontaine was entirely capable. The Flower Girl always
knew her city's streets well, and she knew how to use that knowledge to

avoid detection—and to contact others without being noticed. The two mutinous women were in fact such successful stealth presences that they organized and very nearly pulled off one of the largest desertion plots in the early history of New Orleans—and they did it all right under the authorities' noses.

For this "rebellion," the women were hardly alone. In particular, survivors worked alongside a large and varied group of men, including, most notably, numerous high-ranking military men. This was a mutiny in every sense of the term.

On May 30, 1728, the day after Bourguignon was sentenced, a key meeting took place. It was a Sunday, at the time always chosen for covert activities—during high Mass, when law-abiding New Orleanians were attending services in their first real church, then but a few months old. Along with Bonaventure Langlois, a fellow Parisian and fellow passenger on *Les Deux Frères*, upon which he had traveled as an army cadet, Manon Fontaine went for a drink at the home of an Englishman they called "Pierre Schmit" or "Smit." Schmit revealed that their co-conspirators in the military had already obtained the guns, gunpowder, and ammunition that might prove essential after they left Louisiana and that all was now ready for them to begin the journey "beyond the land of the Choctaw to the English colony [Carolina]." The next day, their plot was no longer secret: someone had grassed up the would-be defectors.

Numerous arrests were made; interrogations lasted from May 31 until June 14. A coalition of at least forty conspirators was exposed— male and female, multinational, mixed race, covering the entire social spectrum, and based in both New Orleans and Mobile. Information seems to have been shared among them mainly by *voyageurs*, who were difficult to track since they were constantly on the move, and by those to whom authorities never paid much attention, deported women, in particular someone whose status as wife of the city's chief law enforcement officer provided the best cover possible, Jeanne Coroy.

Those interrogated first, on May 31 and June 1, were the most vulnerable, three members of the colony's enslaved population. A fifteen-year-old enslaved African known as "Guillory" explained that he was on the run, "fleeing continual ill-treatment at the hands of his master," and that he had been "enticed by Bontemps to join a party of fugitives." "Bontemps," "Good Times," was an eighteen-year-old enslaved Native American. Baptiste, a fifteen-year-old enslaved Native American and a servant of the Capuchin fathers, was a third suspect.

Also quickly brought in for questioning were another deported woman, Marie Marguerite Moule, thirty-two, and her husband, Jacques Joseph Catherine, known as "Capitaine," or "Captain," a voluntary emigrant. Moule was interrogated mainly about commodities such as textiles that the conspirators planned to take along as trade goods.[36] The foreigners, two Englishmen, were up next.

On June 2, authorities finally brought in the consummate insider whose cooperation would have been essential to any successful plot: Baron Jean-Ferdinand d'Hombourg, thirty-six, Swiss, long a captain in the employ of the Indies Company, and from 1722 the commander of a company of Swiss soldiers, a regiment that was still another failed Indies Company initiative. From 145 in 1721, the company's numbers soon dwindled to 40, and this was before soldiers' pay and rations were cut and desertions began. Since they were Protestants, Swiss soldiers always attempted to desert to Carolina rather than Spanish outposts.[37] A significant number of them admitted to having collaborated on the escape plot, including a sizeable contingent of the regiment's officers.

Under questioning, the baron denied any knowledge of the conspiracy. Curiously, the first thing d'Hombourg denied was having spoken with Jeanne Coroy or offered to help her leave the colony— and at this point Coroy had not yet been interrogated.

She was up next. The very first question Jeanne was asked was how she had come to the colony, to which she replied that she had come "*de force*, on *La Mutine*, in 1720." When asked if she had planned to leave the colony with the baron d'Hombourg, Coroy explained "that the Baron had offered to help her return to France" and added that he had warned her that "a woman could never stand the fatigue of a trip like this one." Jeanne was questioned about numerous Swiss soldiers; she denied knowing them. Jeanne had, however, discussed the matter with a soldier's wife, for Angélique Reffe, married to a member of the Swiss regiment, had been Coroy's eyes and ears in Mobile. The last question put to Jeanne was if her husband had planned to leave with the baron. Jeanne explained that he had never agreed to do so and that she would have left only if her husband had.

When interrogated about the conspiracy, Vincent himself, the bailiff of the Superior Council, the very organization leading the hearings, said only that "he would accuse no one." Vincent did admit that, years earlier when he was unable to find work, the baron had proposed finding passage out of the colony on a ship under his command.

Bonaventure Langlois provided the most damning testimony of all—not against d'Hombourg, but against Jeanne Coroy, whom he portrayed as the intermediary who linked everyone. It was Jeanne who had informed him about the conspiracy and encouraged him to participate, Jeanne who had told Pierre Schmit that d'Hombourg was in on it. Langlois also described his drink with Manon Fontaine.

Weeks of interrogations failed to produce a result likely to deter future conspiracies. D'Hombourg and the other men were cleared of blame in the "seditious desertion plot" and released from prison. The only two conspirators found guilty, Bontemps and Guillory, were convicted of crimes against their owners rather than crimes against the state.[38] In fact, when the verdict came down in the desertion plot, a single judgment was issued, and only Bontemps, Good Times, a member of the Natchez nation and considered the property of concession holder Pellerin, was sentenced. On June 14, 1728, Bontemps was condemned to public execution on the grounds that he had "persuaded" the other enslaved persons to join the conspiracy to flee Louisiana.[39]

The way the proceedings were conducted would have been familiar to those like Manon Fontaine who had been on trial in Paris. There was, however, one big difference. Manon Fontaine, a woman deported for allegedly having fomented a "sedition" in a Parisian prison, was never even called in for questioning about the "seditious plot." Not a single woman was mentioned in the verdict; even Jeanne Coroy, who freely admitted having come to New Orleans *de force*, got off scot-free. In New Orleans, the women had acquired status, and they could no longer be used as universal scapegoats.

Authorities in Louisiana sent back to France numerous reports alluding to the destabilizing effect that women sent there *de force* were having on the colony. But the 1728 desertion plot in which Manon Fontaine, Jeanne Coroy, Marie Marguerite Moule, and Angélique Reffe were among the conspirators was the only crime of which any deported women was ever accused. The offense was a serious one, but it seems easy to understand why, after nearly a decade on the Gulf Coast during which they had watched husbands and children and dear friends die of starvation and disease, these four at last became truly mutinous women—ready to give up forever on the country that had caused them so much suffering, to throw in their lot with Swiss soldiers, and to join forces with the English.

Even during years when the death toll was surging and the word "desertion" was on everyone's lips, New Orleans continued to harbor aspirations to a stylishness otherwise sorely lacking in the colony. In 1726, a goldsmith worked just off the Place d'Armes, a wigmaker on Royal Street, and on St. Louis Street, Toinette Isambert had set up shop as a *couturière*, a woman working independently, just as many did in Paris.[40] The liquor trade already flourished on Bourbon Street, where François Alix, called La Rose, brewed beer from corn.

By 1727, urban modernity was making timid strides. The first public mill in the colony went into service in New Orleans—no longer would residents have to rely solely on mortars and pestles to crush corn. Still in 1726, flour had been so scarce that bakers were often unable to practice their trade. By April 1727, the city's first church, dedicated to Saint Louis, was completed; the church was consecrated that December. It was far from a proper church—there was as yet no altar, no tabernacle—but religion at last had an official home in New Orleans. Until then, Mass and marriages, including those of all survivors who wed in New Orleans, had been celebrated, as Capuchin Father Raphael explained, in a building built as a barracks, where "the entire decoration of the altar consists of a picture that I pasted as neatly as possible and had put into a frame."[41]

Much, however, remained unchanged. In December 1727, Jacques de La Chaise, the colony's finance officer, begged Indies Company directors to send panes of glass "and a diamond to cut them," since windows were covered only with linen cloths, which did not last long because of the extreme humidity.[42]

Through all the city's trials and tribulations, one street had a special cachet: Chartres Street, named for Louis d'Orléans, duc de Chartres, son of Philippe d'Orléans for whom the city itself was named. Chartres ran directly behind New Orleans's central square and largest public space, the Place d'Armes, and was the place to indulge in that particularly Parisian pastime—showing off any finery one possessed. The two survivors whose status in the colony was most evident lived on Chartres Street: Anne Françoise Rolland and Marie Anne Dinan.

Anne Françoise Rolland had married up when she wed warehouse keeper Nicolas Sarazin. Sarazin and Rolland had lived only briefly in Mobile before moving to New Orleans, where Sarazin was put in charge of the "large storehouse" newly constructed by Étienne Fièvre that was the first significant magazine in the colony's history. The couple took up residence on the north side of Chartres Street, just three blocks east of that grand storehouse.

Another survivor also settled on Chartres Street, among the youngest of all those deported: Marie Anne Dinan, only fifteen when

La Mutine sailed. On Chartres, Marie Anne lived just one street over from her older sister Françoise, a Royal Street resident. In New Orleans on August 4, 1720, Marie Anne, daughter of a master *fripier* from a dynasty of Parisian artisans, married Jean Cariton, a master tailor from Paris who had come to Louisiana to work on the land grant of financier Étienne Demeuves. The Demeuves people were among the lucky few able quickly to leave Biloxi; Cariton managed to get out, and he took Marie Anne away with him.

Fripiers dealt in secondhand clothing, but masters were hardly rag merchants. They restyled the clothing of aristocrats, reshaping fine fabrics according to the latest fashions. The Dinan-Cariton union would have been considered ideal by Parisian luxury goods artisans. Tailors were in high demand because there were but three in New Orleans, and Cariton was the only master.

Like her neighbor on Chartres Street, Anne Françoise Rolland, Marie Anne surely expected a fine future. But during the deadly mid-1720s, even their households, among the grandest in the city, could not escape the financial crisis that destabilized working-class New Orleanians like Manon Fontaine's husband Bourguignon. Death also touched them as well.

In the early years of her marriage, Anne Françoise Rolland profited from her husband's status in various ways. Had she not been married to a powerful official, for example, she would never have been so quickly informed of her father's death in Paris and never have so quickly gotten representation at the settlement of his estate. But by 1726 the man who on the first Mobile census was identified as "*Sieur* Sarazin" had been taken down a few notches. That year, the census identified him merely as "formerly the storehouse keeper." In fact, Sarazin's troubles had begun already in 1722. By September 1723, Commissioner La Chaise, his most virulent enemy, passed on to Indies Company directors in Paris scathing complaints that made Sarazin seem a poster child for what was by all accounts a moment of rampant corruption in the colony. He accused Sarazin of watering down the brandy for sale

271

in the company's store, and alleged that he was among those trying only to "*faire leur main*," "maximize their profits."

The extent to which those allegations had merit isn't clear. Even though Bienville vigorously defended him, Sarazin was arrested and detained in a jail, or what passed for one in the era's typical makeshift style, "*chez les Capucins*," "at the residence of the Capuchin friars." There were interrogations, confrontations, a full inquiry. In the end, although Sarazin lost his high-status position, the family did retain the allegedly "magnificent" lodgings and accouterments that were the envy of many.[43]

By 1726, the couple had three sons: Antoine, François, and Michel. In 1727, Sarazin became one of the many casualties of that famously lethal year. That November, part of his estate was settled. The bulk of that estate, however, was not accounted for, and in 1752, the two surviving sons, Antoine and François, were obliged to begin a suit to claim their inheritance.[44] Sarazin seems to have left his widow with three young children and muddled finances. The years immediately following his death were surely among the most difficult in Anne Françoise's life. They include its only grey area.

On January 15, 1730, a baby was baptized. The entry in the register of the still-recent Saint-Louis Church is nothing short of extraordinary: "*Nicolas, fils d'Anne Rolland, le père est inconnu*"—"Nicolas, son of Anne Rolland, the father is unknown." The use of that formula, "the father is unknown," while not unheard of in New Orleans, was nonetheless shocking, even scandalous. Not long before, in November 1727, Louisiana's governor had condemned all women who refused "to declare the names of the fathers" of their children as "*femmes de mauvaise vie*," or "loose women."[45] New Orleans was a tiny town, where everyone knew every detail of every ceremony performed in its only church. Anne Françoise could hardly have forgotten that her father and stepmother had had her deported for conduct that was far less scandalous than this. The widow of someone addressed as "*sieur*," or "lord," who publicly declared that her baby's father was "unknown" was choosing to risk her reputation rather than deprive her child of the sacrament of baptism.

Two events quickly followed that baptism. On February 5, Nicolas Rolland, "about 15 days old," was buried. Exactly fifteen days after that, a ceremony of a very different kind took place, also in Saint-Louis Church, where on Monday, February 20, Anne Rolland married a second Indies Company employee, Laurent Bordelon. The first bann announcing their upcoming union was published on Sunday, February 5, the very day baby Nicolas was buried. Those bare facts are all that can be recovered concerning this moment in Anne Françoise Rolland's life. We'll never know the name of her baby's father, a fact she was determined not to make public, nor will we ever know why Rolland and Bordelon waited until the day Nicolas was buried to announce their marriage.

While Rolland's first husband had enjoyed temporary status, Bordelon's ironclad connections made him virtually untouchable. His father, Jean Baptiste Thomas Bordelon, was a prominent career administrator for the French Navy. As the commissioner in charge of supplies and sustenance at the port of Rochefort, Jean Baptiste Thomas Bordelon bore the ultimate responsibility for the navy's refusal to feed the women deported on *Les Deux Frères*. The groom's mother belonged to the powerful Rochechouart family, as did the mother of the navy minister who had called the women "merchandise."

In France, because of her family's indigence, in all likelihood Anne Françoise would have shared her sisters' fate and remained unmarried. In New Orleans, she made a match so fine that it awarded her a level of distinction guaranteed to impress anyone in France.

When they married in February 1730, Bordelon was a man of the hour. He was assigned to the fort at Natchez, where he had the task of accounting for Indies Company supplies in its storehouse and where he proved as hard-nosed an administrator as his father had been in Rochefort. All eyes were then focused on Natchez because three months before their wedding, Native Americans had again attacked its fort. And this offensive was no mere skirmish, as had been the case in 1722 when Jeanne Pouillot's husband died there, but a full-blown uprising against the French military presence. Many were killed, and Frenchwomen—including a woman who had been deported with Anne Françoise—were taken hostage. The very day Rolland married Bordelon, French forces laid siege to those holding the Frenchwomen captive. Fighting broke out up and down the river; many feared that New Orleans would come under attack. Plans were drawn up, though never carried out, to surround the city with fortifications.

Their wedding day would hardly have been carefree, nor would the years of their marriage. In 1731, a new outbreak of pestilence carried off Rolland's last son with Sarazin, Pierre, born in 1728. Her first Bordelon child, a second boy called "Nicolas," was born before January 1732. That December, a second child died before it was named. A last Bordelon son, Antoine, was born in 1733. All that time, Rolland and her family remained on Chartres Street.

It was also on Chartres Street, two doors nearer the church, that the household of Marie Anne Dinan and master tailor Jean Cariton went through a similarly troubled time. Master artisans in Paris hoping to attract a well-heeled clientele chose addresses where the elite were sure to walk—near the Louvre, for example—and the strategy seems to have worked for Cariton in New Orleans. He was soon copying French fashions in local materials, such as the "breeches and stockings in black leather" that he agreed to confect in 1724.[46]

In Paris, master artisans in the luxury trade presented themselves on an equal footing with their preferred clientele, and the Caritons adopted this strategy as well, by acting as notable New Orleans families did. Even before Saint-Louis Church was completed, for example, pews were available for pre-rental. Securing a prominent seat for Mass guaranteed visibility—and the display of one's outfits. Marie Anne Dinan immediately signed up for one; in May 1726, she was paying six *livres* a month in rental fees. Cariton was already behind with payments, an early indication of the debt problem that later compromised their marriage.[47]

On July 15, 1726, a most unusual burial was recorded: "the body of a child about a year old who died at the home of Sir Cariton, the tailor." When asked to identify the body, Cariton *"n'a pas voulu dire son nom,"* "didn't want to give its name," refusing to reveal the identity of either of the child's parents. Interestingly, Cariton's reaction, seemingly indicating that he had something to hide, did not affect the couple's status. The 1727 census described Cariton as *"sieur,"* and Dinan as *"la Dame, son épouse,"* or "the Lady, his wife." This time around, she was the only survivor thus singled out.

That status did not signify financial stability, for Cariton seems to have faced continuous cash-flow problems. On the one hand, the fancy trimmings a master tailor required to make his creations stand out had to be imported from France at great cost. Cariton borrowed heavily for these purchases, and while he sometimes paid up, his creditors were often forced to take him to court to extract payment. On the other, his clients frequently failed to settle their accounts. In 1743, for example, Cariton was suing to receive payment for elegant outfits delivered three years earlier: a cinnamon-colored suit in a fine cotton cloth, a black waistcoat and trousers—on and on the list went.[48] Frequent lawsuits put Cariton's liquidity difficulties on public display.

The tipping point occurred in 1742. That year, like numerous Parisian wives facing similar situations, Marie Anne Dinan requested a *séparation de biens*, a legal division of property. Since a husband's creditors could not touch possessions officially defined as belonging to a wife alone, a separation offered a form of asset protection. In Paris, the contract that specified what each brought into the marriage would have guided the process, but in 1720, when Dinan became the first survivor from *La Mutine* to wed in New Orleans, no one bothered with legal niceties such as contracts. Dinan's suit dragged on until 1747, and in the process, a more complex family story emerged.

Cariton was clearly a genial fellow, well-liked by all. Few residents were so often asked to serve as a witness at weddings, or as a godfather at baptisms. And he indulged in a form of sociability that surely brought as many men together in New Orleans as it did in Paris: gambling. Cariton, however, had far less card sense than fashion sense.

On September 3, 1747, "Dame Marie Anne Dinan" was obliged to make a private drama public. Her husband, she explained, "has for many years been addicted to gambling; his losses consume all the profits from his business." He had often promised to stop, but in the last four years alone, "he has lost 40,000 *livres*"; just that week, he'd dropped "600 *livres* at cards." Dinan's fear of being reduced "to indigence" had "forced her to divide their property."

Her lawsuit also revealed that Marie Anne had become the first deported woman to accomplish something that many surely dreamed of but only two achieved: she had obliged the family that had allowed a fifteen-year-old to become passenger 118 on *La Mutine*, banished for "public prostitution," to recognize her legal rights and award her a share of an inheritance—only to watch her husband squander it. As part of the settlement, Cariton admitted having spent 5,000 *livres* of his wife's money, money "that had arrived from France on August 16, 1739."[49]

When Cariton died in 1752, Marie Anne inherited a mountain of debt. To maintain the illusion of status, the couple had lived well beyond their means. Their flour came from France; only recently, a ship's captain had delivered wine from Bordeaux.[50]

Right to the end, the first *La Mutine* survivor to wed in New Orleans had been the only one whose marriage followed familiar French models. Marie Anne Dinan and Jean Cariton could well have met in Paris; their families would have encouraged the match. They would have lived much as they did in New Orleans, and, like so many artisans in the luxury goods trade, they would have known significant financial difficulties in the years following the collapse of Law's system, when few managed to get ahead—and many died insolvent.

New Orleans's burgeoning high-fashion trade did bring abundance to a second survivor. In 1726, Marie Daudin and ship's captain Michel Caron were living on Bourbon Street. Their daughter Marie Anne was buried three months before the census was taken. A son, Michel Georges, was born shortly after the 1727 census. Then, in November 1729, the family's life was upended.

That November 26, Caron, "captain of the [Indies] Company's boat," reached Natchez to drop off supplies and collect tobacco for shipment to France. Two days later, when Native Americans began the major uprising against the French military presence that destabilized the colony, Caron was among the first of those killed.

On July 5, 1730, Marie Daudin married widower Pierre La Roche, a master carpenter from Auvergne who had been her next-door neighbor on Bourbon Street since 1727. On October 22, 1731, their daughter was born and named "Catherine" after Daudin's younger sister, who had died long before her time in Orléans, France.

Daudin's new family lived frugally. On December 22, 1736, the inventory drawn up after La Roche's death indicates how they had combined their neighboring properties: a small lot with a "badly built hut" that Daudin and Caron had cleared and constructed together, and a larger lot with a house professionally framed by master carpenter La Roche. In sharp contrast to Jeanne Mahou's beautifully furnished and equipped household, they had owned but 29 *livres* of possessions. All La Roche's clothing totaled a mere three *livres*.

The inventory was required because of a significant debt incurred only two months before La Roche's death. On October 8, he had assumed joint responsibility with Daudin for the 1,642 *livres* owed by her first husband, ship's captain Caron, to his former employer, the Indies Company. The couple promised to repay the sum within four years and offered their property as collateral. The Indies Company's representatives in the colony were obliging the heirs of all its employees killed at Natchez to repay every penny owed at the time of their death. Seven years after Caron was killed in the company's service, its agents continued to pursue his widow, Marie Daudin, and her second husband—thereby impoverishing the heirs of a long-serving and exemplary employee.[51]

In 1737, the woman who had worn rags for years because of her late husband's debt to the same implacable company that had deported her after a mistaken arrest planned for a child's future: that May 7, Daudin signed an apprenticeship for her son by Caron, Michel Georges, with tailor Étienne Chabuit. Soon, Daudin's third marriage, with merchant Jacques Massicot, solidified her connections to the garment trade. It also turned her life around.

Massicot served as go-between among merchants in New Orleans and their counterparts in France, importing, for example, goods for Cariton and advancing funds to him. When Pierre Bourdet of Rochefort, a major exporter to the French colonies, decided to begin trade with New Orleans, he partnered with Massicot. Massicot took on a younger associate, Pierre Revoil, and together they invested significant sums and imported high-end French textiles.

The saga had come full cycle. In Rochefort, the first deportees had been considered inferior "merchandise." Twenty-five years later, a deported woman's husband was calling the shots with tradesmen from the same French port.[52]

In New Orleans in 1747, Marie Daudin's daughter from her second marriage, Marie Catherine La Roche, wed at sixteen, the age at which her mother had been arrested in Paris. On September 9, a detailed contract was drawn up in preparation for Marie Catherine's marriage to Pierre Revoil, the junior partner of her stepfather, Jacques Massicot. The agreement reveals that trade with her homeland had dramatically improved Daudin's finances. With those profits, Marie Daudin was able to realize in particularly spectacular fashion a goal shared by her fellow deportees. In New Orleans, a city built right before their eyes and constantly expanding during their lifetimes, women were able to create better lives for their children, to make sure they enjoyed experiences and opportunities that they themselves had never known.

The marriage contracts that were obligatory under French law were usually purely business arrangements, designed to protect each family's investment in the union. Rarely does a touch of the personal creep in. This exceptional document, however, provides ample evidence of a close, loving family. Massicot, the agreement makes plain, could not have cherished Marie Catherine more deeply had she been his biological daughter. In addition to a dowry of over 2,000 *livres*, the bride received a well-considered trousseau—everything from bed and bedding to cutlery and dishes—and a wardrobe that would have been the envy of Parisiennes: dresses, skirts, many yards of lace, two pairs of gold earrings. The icing on the cake? Marie Catherine was given money "so that she can make whatever outfits she likes." The woman who had spent her young years wearing only tatters had guaranteed that her daughter would never know what that was like.

The bridegroom, a dry-goods and fabric merchant, understood this obsession with clothing. Revoil put 3,000 *livres* cash and all his stock into community property—suits and buttons, stockings, and dozens of combs. When all involved signed the contract, Marie Catherine's signature closely resembled her mother's, for Marie Daudin had taught her daughter to write.[53]

A few months later, when the house built by Marie Catherine's father, master carpenter Pierre La Roche, was sold at auction, Marie Catherine's new husband purchased it for 3,000 *livres*, the sum to be divided between his wife and her mother.[54] This was further proof of his generosity—and the first sign of the young couple's passion for real estate.

From then on, Marie Catherine La Roche and Pierre Revoil bought and sold land enthusiastically. On February 9, 1761, they closed their most memorable deal, when from cabinetmaker Jean Baptiste Laporte they purchased a property 60 by 120 feet, its house facing St. Philip Street. The brick and half-timbered structure had front and rear galleries, hardwood floors throughout, doors and

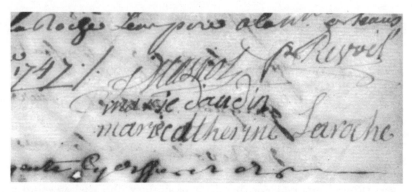

Figure 11. The signatures of survivor Marie Daudin and her daughter, Marie Catherine La Roche.

windows that locked. They acquired the property, on the corner of Bourbon Street and only two lots over from the house in which Marie Catherine was born, for 13,800 *livres*. The land had been cleared in 1722 and sold twice before passing into their hands. Today, Marie Catherine and Pierre's property is home to another French Quarter institution, the bar known as Lafitte's Blacksmith Shop.[55] In Mobile, the children of survivors acquired historic property, sites meaningful in Louisiana's history. In New Orleans, a town without a past, the daughter of a survivor purchased land destined to become historically significant in a way characteristic of the Big Easy.

Revoil had such confidence in Marie Catherine's business acumen that he soon gave her power of attorney to handle all transactions on her own. From then on, the signature "Marie Catherine La Roche Revoil" appeared on numerous deeds of sale, including that of the handsome house thirty feet wide that she acquired in her own name in 1773.[56] Today, that property, number 621 St. Louis Street, is the site of the Omni Royal Orleans Hotel.

As Marie Catherine scooped up prime New Orleans property, her mother, Marie Daudin, the daughter of a penniless dockworker in old Orléans, was there to watch her do it. In 1759, Marie Daudin saw her only child from her third marriage with Jacques Massicot, also named "Jacques," marry Geneviève Grevenberg, who had moved to the capital from the far reaches of French Louisiana, in Arkansas. Daudin even lived to see four of their six children born.

She was still alive on November 21, 1767, when three generations gathered in Pierre and Marie Catherine's home. Marie Angélique, the eldest daughter of the nine children born to Marie Catherine La Roche and Pierre Revoil, was marrying Jean Joseph Duforest, a wine merchant from a long line of Bordeaux vintners, and another intricate contract was signed. Angélique, at sixteen, her mother's age when she had married, received an even more magnificent dowry than the one her grandmother had been able to give her mother: a large lot fronting on Royal Street, and a home whose construction, design, and amenities, up to Parisian standards, were far more sophisticated than anything New Orleanians had previously known.[57]

Marie Daudin died in 1768 at age sixty-eight, after nearly a half century in the colony. On April 22, 1770, her estate was divided between her surviving children, Marie Catherine La Roche and Jacques Massicot. And quite an estate it was.

Her final years had been spent with her third husband on their land on the Mississippi. At the end of her life, Marie Daudin dressed in the same Asian textiles fashionable in Paris. The couple ate off silver plates and enjoyed the four hundred books in their library. They also owned two houses in New Orleans. At the time of her death, Marie Daudin left not a single debt. Total value of the estate: 50,593 livres, enough to give each grandchild a significant start in life.[58] In France, even great noble families rarely passed on anything like this to their children.

IN DECEMBER 1731, AN ARCHITECT'S DRAFTSMAN NAMED GONI-chon created a map considered the most accurate representation of New Orleans a decade after the engineer Pauger began clearing brush to build a capital.[59] The map depicted new streets and recent construction. It showed along its northern edge what inhabitants already called Dauphine Street, even though the actual street did not

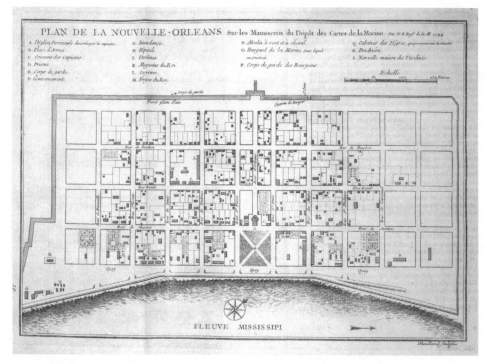

Figure 12. A map of New Orleans in 1731, with both public buildings and the homes of inhabitants indicated, as well as the city's port on "the Mississipi [sic] River."*

yet exist—New Orleans's original residents continued to observe their city as it was made. The map also revealed that the houses situated on that officially unnamed street looked out at untamed wilderness and swampland. It did not reveal that all New Orleans's streets, Bourbon and Royal as much as Dauphine, were still dirt roads—which, in such a flood-prone location, meant that for nearly half the year, they became a mire of slippery muck. Street paving, already the norm in Paris in the 1670s, finally reached New Orleans in early 1821, a full century after the city's founding.[60]

---

* The engraving of Gonichon's map in Figure 12 does not include one feature of the original map, the numbering of property belonging to private individuals. A digital version of the map with lot numbers visible can be found at mutinouswomen.sas .upenn.edu.

On Gonichon's map, lots were numbered, and an accompanying chart listed their owners.[61] In many cases, the map and the chart combined make it possible to determine precisely who lived where. In 1731, colonial administrators continued to deplore the destabilizing effects on the colony of women sent *de force* and were still considering shipping them off to a far-flung outpost for the well-being of New Orleans. The map uncovers the reality behind such fantasies. Even though, by then, a number of survivors had been obliged to sell their original allotments and others had arrived too late to be granted land, the map demonstrates how solidly implanted numerous survivors had become.

There, right on the quay on lot 36, were Captain Lazou and Marie Louise Balivet. Laurent Bordelon and Anne Françoise Rolland lived on lot 53 on Chartres Street. (Nearby number 55 was lost to Cariton and Marie Anne Dinan in a crisis of debt.) Françoise Dinan's widower occupied their home, lot 168 on Royal Street, while two blocks away on lot 47 at the corner of Royal and Orléans, Marie Louise Brunet lived with her second husband, joiner Jean Baptiste Montard, and their first child. On lot 119 on Bourbon Street, Captain Troquidi and Marie Chartier inhabited a spacious property. Two blocks down near the corner of Bourbon and Toulouse, Marie Anne Giard and children from both her marriages lived with her second husband, soldier Pierre Faucheur, on the very modest lot (number 200) and in the very modest house she had built with her first husband, Baguette, the drummer of Bourbon Street. The property was listed in the name of "Drumstick's widow." Giard's home was catercorner from lot 137, until recently owned by a smuggler deported on *Les Deux Frères*, Marie Michel.[62] The eastern end of Bourbon Street was jam-packed with survivors: Manon Fontaine, on lot 230; Marie Angélique Dimanche, on lot 218 at the corner of St. Ann; Marie Daudin, on lot 173; Jeanne Coroy, on lot 171—just across the street from lot 246, the home Marie Daudin's daughter would later acquire.

Properties, including those of widows, were listed in the husband's name. Two lots—226 on Orléans Street, 241 on St. Ann—were in the name of Manon Fontaine's husband, Bourguignon. Right next door to the St. Ann Street property was lot 240, owned by Julien Gautier, soon to become Angélique Reffe's fourth husband.[63] Other properties also belonged to deported women—we know, for example, that Manon Fontaine owned two additional lots. In all, of the roughly two hundred privately owned properties in the city, between 8 and 10 percent were in the hands of women banished from France and still officially pronounced undesirable in their new homeland.[64]

Only one married woman was acknowledged as a property owner in her own right: lot 230 on Bourbon Street had been granted "to the woman named Bourguignon." That acknowledgment could be seen as an implicit recognition of one key facet of the identity that New Orleans acquired in its first decade. It became the only settlement in Louisiana where deported women were able to exert true power and influence. They made the city theirs in various ways—by working alongside men to shape it, by acquiring so much of the new urban space. Rather than passively accepting their fates and the definitions imposed on them by men in positions of authority, they attempted to redirect their lives—and even to take political action. In how many places in the world would any of this have been possible in the 1720s? In Paris, it was only in 1789 that lowborn women so actively tried to shape the course of history, and even then, such interventions were all too rare.

New Orleans was the place where the mutinous women could reinvent themselves most strikingly. And so it is fitting that, even though some deported women had larger lots and others terrain on more prominent streets, none owned more pieces of New Orleans than Manon Fontaine—the Flower Girl become major property owner.

Chapter 11

Women on the Verge in Natchitoches, Illinois, and Arkansas

THE MOST INTREPID SURVIVORS OF ALL MAY HAVE BEEN THE handful of women who quickly put as much distance as possible between themselves and the misery that reigned at Louisiana's southern limit, the Gulf Coast. Despite all they had already suffered, these deported women chose not to end their journey in New Orleans or any nearby settlement, but instead to travel on. Women who had just survived the horrors of the deportation process endured still more hardship, long and difficult journeys, overland and by water, before they reached the northern limits of the French territory in the Lower Mississippi Valley, where they found the polar opposite of the crowding at Biloxi: spaces so wide-open that small groups of inhabitants lived in almost total isolation. They also discovered a more welcoming climate and terrain far more propitious for farming. Some also found a life as hardscrabble as anywhere else.

These borderland settlements were established early on, sometimes during explorations in the 1690s, but there was only minimal construction before the very end of Louis XIV's reign. The women adventurous enough to travel there reached outposts consisting almost exclusively of rudimentary military installations. Deported women were often among their very first female inhabitants.

This was certainly true in the post that is today the oldest permanent settlement in the modern state of Louisiana: Natchitoches. In the early eighteenth century, it was a significant international geopolitical marker. At the time when French expansion into the Lower Mississippi Valley was chiefly viewed as a necessary counterforce between English and Spanish possessions, early explorers chose a site about four hundred miles north of New Orleans to mark the western limit of French colonization. The Spanish soon established a mission and a fort only twenty miles away to indicate the northeastern limit of Spanish Texas. Natchitoches thus became a contact zone between these two major European empires.

But this strategic spot was never afforded the resources it both deserved and desperately required. Inhabitant and future historian Dumont, who knew the region well, described Natchitoches as a post created "to serve as a barrier against the Spanish to prevent them from entering Louisiana."[1] In this light, it seems astonishing that French authorities never made the investment necessary for an even remotely serious defense of their territory.

Sometime in 1714, the location for a fort was determined. In September 1715, when the individual who dominated Natchitoches's early history, Louis Juchereau de Saint-Denis, made a stopover during a voyage of exploration that eventually took him into what is now Mexico, he described the newly named Fort Saint-Jean-Baptiste: "A tiny space roughly 60 feet by 50, surrounded by 8-foot-high stakes."

He concluded by stressing his astonishment at the ramshackle structure he found: "And we call this a fortress."[2]

Construction on improved defenses, barracks, and a storehouse began in 1721, and bastions were added in 1723. By 1725, all these installations were crumbling. Soldiers hewed new stakes, but by 1726, they, too, were disintegrating. Rather than provide additional funds for Natchitoches's defenses, however, the Indies Company instead sought ways of cutting the settlement's budget. And rather than sending more soldiers, as commander Saint-Denis persistently requested, the company reduced the garrison's size from twenty-nine to twenty, a number its directors pronounced more than sufficient. During all the years of Indies Company stewardship, the site seen as France's ultimate defense against Spanish aggression was nothing more than an enclosure built of rotten stakes, equipped with non-functioning cannons, and defended by a mere handful of men. In contrast, in order to "prevent the French from getting anywhere near Mexico," the Spanish counted on a proper fort with six working cannons and a garrison of one hundred.[3]

At Natchitoches, the Indies Company missed out on an opportunity that just might have helped make the colony profitable. Saint-Denis believed that Louisiana could only pay for itself through commerce and promoted Natchitoches as uniquely positioned to develop trade with Spanish Texas. The Spanish, he reasoned, had something sorely lacking in cash-poor Louisiana: coin. And they were eager to purchase French goods, particularly textiles, which they badly needed. Saint-Denis's proposal was bandied about but never seriously explored.[4]

Although those in power failed to heed his advice or offer help, Saint-Denis stuck with Natchitoches, where he served as commander until 1744, all the while proving himself perhaps the sole official representative of the French government ever to be universally appreciated and admired in Louisiana. One long-time inhabitant acclaimed him as a great military man and explorer, trusted and esteemed by all, and stressed his extensive knowledge of Native American languages, before concluding, "He should have been named governor."[5]

Despite the Indies Company's refusal to encourage its development, under such capable leadership Natchitoches survived and sometimes even prospered. The post's proponents pointed out that food staples such as corn and beans flourished in its fertile soil, that indigo grew better there than at Natchez, and that in nearby fields cattle "became extraordinarily plump."[6]

Such advantages, however, were counterbalanced by the settlement's location: Natchitoches was hard to reach in times of flooding and virtually inaccessible during the long months every year when water levels in the Mississippi and its tributaries were low. Since some 420 miles of river transport separated Natchitoches from New Orleans, its inhabitants had little contact with the colony's other French residents.

The isolated settlement, too small to be self-sustaining, was dependent on the numerous nearby Native American villages to supplement its food supply. The French colonists' Indigenous neighbors also introduced them to the commodity that became settlers' major source of income: bear oil.

In Louisiana's climate, butter and even olive oil spoiled quickly in Indies Company storehouses. Settlers found a substitute in bear oil. An early historian who knew Louisiana well touted its virtues "for every cooking need." He pronounced bear oil "as good as the finest olive oil and can be used in the same way." Already in 1719, settlers from Natchitoches were transporting bear oil to New Orleans, where, when supply was abundant, the popular commodity fetched as much as French white wine and, in years of scarcity, twelve times more.[7]

In May 1722, when Natchitoches was first included in a census, sixty-two were recorded as living there, including soldiers in the garrison: thirty-four Europeans, twenty enslaved Africans, eight enslaved Native Americans. Of the ten Frenchwomen, two had traveled on *La Mutine*: Marie Anne Benoist, passenger 80, and Jeanne

Longueville, number 114. Both figured as "wife of a soldier," indicating that their husbands were not on duty at the fort itself but deployed nearly five hundred miles further north.

When they married in New Orleans on March 24, 1721, Parisian Jeanne Longueville, born in the Faubourg Saint-Jacques and thus the only deported woman to have grown up near the Salpêtrière, and Lyonnais Pierre Pichon described themselves as living in "an unspecified place on the Mississippi"—a settlement so new that it had not yet been named. The two had met soon after Longueville reached the mainland and Pichon arrived in the colony in August 1720. They visited the capital only to marry and then made the long journey to Natchitoches, where Jeanne Longueville remained during Pierre's detachment, and where she died in the deadly mid-1720s.

In 1723, the first two survivors to settle in Natchitoches were joined by a third, Jeanne Pouillot. After the death at Natchez of her first husband, soldier Jean Marchand, Jeanne, by then about thirty-six, married for the second time in Louisiana, in New Orleans on July 7, 1723. She and Étienne Chagneau, a widower from La Rochelle who had traveled voluntarily to Louisiana to work on a land grant, moved to Natchitoches. By January 1726, Étienne and Jeanne and a five-year-old daughter from her first marriage, Marie Anne Marchand, were living on one of Natchitoches's largest farms, at 8.5 acres. Chagneau's children from his first marriage lived independently.

In September 1734, those two families forged a new alliance. Étienne Chagneau's son from his previous marriage, François, age twenty-six and French-born, and Marie Anne Marchand, by then just shy of thirteen, married. The couple had numerous children, including a daughter named "Jeanne" and another named "Marie Jeanne." We don't know if Jeanne Pouillot had children from her marriage with a Chagneau, but her DNA lived on in the Chagneau line through Marie Anne's offspring.[8]

By 1726, the number of European colonists in the settlement had grown from thirty-four to ninety-six. Three of those new inhabitants

were the children of one of the two founding survivors in Natchitoches, Marie Anne Benoist. In Paris, Marie Anne, daughter of a
deceased day laborer at Les Halles market, had worked as an *ouvrière
en linge*, cleaning and repairing the many different kinds of linen in a
grand household. If anything went missing, "linen workers" were as
vulnerable as laundresses to accusations of theft. And in 1716 that is
what happened to Marie Anne and a fellow "linen worker," Françoise
Renault. Marie Anne was sentenced to seven years in the Salpêtrière
and had served at least two years of her time when Pancatelin drew
up her list of candidates for deportation. Even though next to Benoist's name, royal lawyer Joly de Fleury pointed out the obvious, "in
Benoist's case, it would not be just to transport her for more than five
years," Marie Anne became passenger 80 on *La Mutine*.[9] None of
those who deported her gave a moment's thought to how Marie Anne
might have returned to France after five years across the Atlantic.

In fact, Marie Anne Benoist resided in Natchitoches for thirty-
four years, until her death in 1754. In Natchitoches, she married soldier Pierre Rachal. Rachal was known as "Saint-Denis" because of
his birth at Saint-Denis-d'Oléron on an island off the coast of La
Rochelle. He served as a corporal in Natchitoches's garrison and gar-
nered praise from his commanders as a "good officer." Marie Anne
and Pierre played a key role in the process by which Natchitoches became a true settlement rather than a mere military installation when
they helped a community take shape near the garrison.

Marie Anne and Pierre had many children, at least seven. Most
lived to adulthood, married, and had numerous offspring of their
own—and when it came to large families, few equaled the Rachals.
Sons Louis and Barthélémy had nine children each, while daughter Marie Louise had eight, and others did their part as well. In
the next generation, Marie Anne's grandchildren continued the tra-
dition and had eight, nine, even eleven children. Each successive
census showed Natchitoches's modest but consistent growth. Each
time, Rachals and the families of those who had married Rachal

daughters accounted for ever more of its inhabitants. The Rachals have been called "the most prolific family in the northern half of Louisiana."[10]

Shortly after Louisiana was proclaimed a state in 1812, a hamlet emerged twenty miles south of Natchitoches. "Cloutierville" was named not for a prince of the blood or a government minister, as would have been traditional under French rule, but for Alexis Cloutier, great-grandson of survivor Marie Anne Benoist's daughter Marie Louise. Another deported woman thereby left a tangible mark on the landscape of modern Louisiana.

Not far north of Cloutierville and Natchitoches now runs the border between the states of Louisiana and Arkansas. At the moment when survivors came upriver in the early 1720s, Louisiana ended well beyond "*le poste des Arkansaw*," "the Arkansas post." The colony's northern boundary was situated in an area called "*le pays des Illinois*," "the Illinois country." This was a loosely defined region of the Middle Mississippi Valley that comprised portions of the modern states of Illinois and Missouri. For decades, this territory was part of the Upper Mississippi Valley and was governed from Canada. In 1718, John Law made "the Illinois" officially part of the Lower Mississippi Valley. For once, Law had Louisiana's best interests at heart.

Early travelers to the region praised the Illinois farmland for its temperate climate and rich soil, and above all because the commodity most ardently desired by French inhabitants flourished there: wheat. More than anything else, the lack of locally grown wheat explains the massive food shortages of early Louisiana. Wheat did not grow lower down the Mississippi, and without wheat there could be no proper French flour, and the staple of every Frenchman's diet—bread—could not be made as it was in France. Law made Illinois part of Louisiana so that its wheat could be sent downriver to feed residents.

By the 1730s, when Law had long since departed from the French political scene, his idea of joining Illinois to the Lower Mississippi

Valley at last truly paid off. Veritable flotillas of large flat-bottomed boats loaded with flour from Illinois wheat, accompanied by pirogues and guarded by soldiers on horseback, were rowed and towed biannually down the more than twelve hundred miles of river that separated Illinois from New Orleans, a journey that required three to four weeks. There, the boats were loaded with various imported goods, above all textiles, before making the three-to-four-month trip back upriver. In 1730, when one hundred thousand pounds of flour reached New Orleans from Illinois, for the first time the till-then chronic subsistence crises were alleviated. In 1732, thirty boats carried two hundred thousand pounds. By the 1740s, in good years Illinois exported over eight hundred thousand pounds of flour annually to feed the capital and the Gulf Coast. Ham and salt pork from Illinois pigs were also sent south in quantity.[11]

The wheat bonanza encouraged steady population growth, as did the massive development of farming of all kinds in the 1720s and 1730s. In 1718, only a few fur traders used Illinois as a base, but from 1719 on, a series of villages began to take shape there.[12] As a result, by 1726, when "the Illinois" was first included on a census of Louisiana, 280 European settlers called it home and were farming nearly two thousand acres. Those acres were the first extensive grain fields of what was to become the American Midwest. Two deported women had found their way to these rich fields, where they were among the forty-two Frenchwomen who arrived there from France and Canada in the years between 1715 and 1730 and who were among the very first Frenchwomen to reach Illinois.[13]

These survivors helped turn the region into a story of economic prosperity unimaginable in most of the Lower Mississippi Valley, a success on the model of the English colonies that the Indies Company so desperately hoped to emulate. During survivors' years there, Illinois became a wonder in French Louisiana, a remarkably stable outpost and a self-sustaining economy—a rare settlement where colonists found it easy to make good lives for themselves.

Marie Marguerite Moule, born in France's breadbasket, the Beauce, came to Louisiana's breadbasket with her first husband, Jacques Joseph Catherine, known to all as "Captain." Captain arrived in Louisiana shortly before *La Mutine* landed, having volunteered to work on a concession. In Illinois, the couple farmed 3.5 acres of their own. There, they both witnessed and participated in the most remarkable period of growth in the history of French Illinois.[14]

A second deported woman was among Moule's neighbors. In France, Marie Jeanne Goguet had been transferred from a prison near her hometown of Arras to the Salpêtrière on May 18, 1719. She had been arrested for smuggling salt and thereby depriving of tax revenue the same Indies Company that ruled Louisiana's economy.[15] Then, in dizzying succession in barely a year's time, the young woman from northern France had been taken from Paris to Rochefort, had been deported to Louisiana, and had traveled to New Orleans, where she married land grant settler Pierre Texier on July 27, 1720.

Goguet and Texier began their life together on Richard Cantillon's small concession near New Orleans. After Cantillon realized some 30 million *livres* in profits on Law's stock, he made a sizeable investment in Law's colony. Initially, some forty recruits worked his land; by early 1722, after Cantillon had shared in Law's disgrace, only ten were left.[16] The others had moved on, Texier among them. Goguet and Texier traveled further and further north, eventually settling far from the Gulf Coast's heat.

By 1726, Marie Jeanne Goguet and Pierre Texier had had a child and relocated to "the Illinois country," where they farmed just under seven acres. Goguet was among sixty-two women in Illinois; her child had ninety-five potential playmates. Their family had a quality of life shared by few of Goguet's fellow survivors: "Life is easy and sweet in this land," in the words of someone who knew the entire colony well.[17]

One supposed Illinois treasure never enriched settlers' lives: the territory's much-vaunted silver mines. The vision of silver-rich Louisiana, constantly promoted by the Parisian press during the year of the women's deportation, was based on nothing more than unverified reports claiming that ore samples from Illinois sent to France for testing had been found to have spectacularly high silver content.[18] In the end, even though "the Illinois country" did manage to help feed Louisiana's inhabitants, it failed to provide the stupendous riches that the Indies Company and its investors had been guaranteed.

One survivor knew life in a true frontier community, a place both isolated from population centers and itself sparsely populated: Marie Françoise Le Coustelier de Jouy de Palsy, the sole aristocrat deported.

Marie Françoise's almost equally aristocratic husband, Gabriel Prévost de La Chaume, had arrived penniless in the colony and, in his own words, been "obliged to enlist" in order to survive. Gabriel soon left the army for more lucrative work, as an officially licensed *traiteur*—a use of the term invented in Louisiana to designate "those who trade with Indians." In fact, the man who persistently spoke of himself as "a person of quality" and evoked his many relations with influence at the French court was authorized by the Indies Company to negotiate with the Native American nation the French saw as their fiercest enemies, the Chickasaw.

The Chickasaw traded actively with the English, and the French couldn't, or wouldn't, compete. The English, for example, paid far more for deerskin than the French were willing to offer. Through the years, French officials in Louisiana sought "to keep the Indians on our side constantly at war with the Chickasaw." Local authorities paid, and paid well, for every Chickasaw scalp and every enslaved Chickasaw warrior brought in by allied nations such as the Choctaw.[19] Someone who agreed to deal with the Chickasaw in those conditions must have been unflinching and afraid of nothing—the perfect match for the woman he married.

At age sixteen, Marie Françoise had run away from a dead-end life in the great château that her impecunious family could not afford to maintain, sold her clothing in a village market, jumped on a raft of logs, and sailed straight into the heart of Paris. Across the Atlantic, she knew the kind of hinterland existence no other survivor experienced.

The couple married in Mobile, and La Chaume's trade soon took them to regions dependent on a place whose French origins are often overlooked today: Arkansas. The Arkansas post was 600 miles from New Orleans and some 180 miles from the nearest settlement. There, Marie Françoise faced travel at least as arduous and dangerous as riding a log train on the Seine. On his way from Mobile to fight the Natchez, Commander Joseph de Lusser, a combat veteran who'd seen it all, crossed some of the same territory and carefully detailed a torturous journey—fording rivers and bayous and negotiating canebrakes, cypress swamps, and bogs.[20]

The post itself was the most modest of all French installations in the Lower Mississippi Valley, virtually inconspicuous in the vastness of the surrounding wilderness. The place the French called "Arcansaw" or "Arcanças" was originally John Law's personal domain. Land there was considered so promising that Law reserved the spot for himself—it was said that he had intended to make it a duchy and himself the Duke of Arkansas.[21] The May 1722 census, the first to include Arkansas, tabulated solely "the workers on Monsieur Law's concession": fourteen men and one woman. There was at first a token military presence, a garrison with a mere eight soldiers. In 1725, when there was no longer any need to please "Monsieur Law," the Indies Company closed the garrison in a cost-cutting move, and its inhabitants relocated closer to New Orleans.

In 1726, the Arkansas post was still populated by just fourteen inhabitants, only three of whom were women. One long-time resident of the colony described post-Law Arkansas as a cluster of four or five houses and a hut used as a storehouse. That hut was actually the post's raison d'être, for Arkansas became a depository, a stop-off point where merchants moving between the capital and Illinois could store goods.²² Traders like La Chaume could stockpile textiles for the Chickasaw and bear oil destined for New Orleans. Life was hard in Arkansas, among the poorest of all posts. Inhabitants survived only through hunting and trade with Native Americans in surrounding villages.

A military presence was reinstated in 1735, when the minuscule post was assigned a new mission, as the principal defense against the Chickasaw. In 1742, another young man with a taste for adventure, Anne Françoise Rolland's second Sarazin son, François, was stationed in Arkansas's garrison. He served there during critical years in the long-running conflict that pitted the French and the Choctaw against the British and the Chickasaw. And François was very much in the thick of things, because in his role as "the king's interpreter at the Arkansas post," he negotiated communications with Native Americans.

Probably on May 30, 1763, Lieutenant François Sarazin was killed in battle with the Chickasaw. That July, a solemn Mass was celebrated in his honor at Pointe Coupée, the post downriver where his mother then lived.

François's death was truly senseless, since nearly three months before he died, on February 10, 1763, the Treaty of Paris had put an end to the French and Indian War that from 1754 on had pitted the colonies of British America against those of France. Even though army officers in Louisiana had surely not yet received the news, by the time François was killed defending the country that had deported his mother, France officially no longer had a military presence in mainland North America. In the long run, decades of war and attempts to set one Native American population against another proved pointless.

In February 1725 in New Orleans, a dying woman gave the priest administering the last rites the version of her life under which she wished to pass into posterity: "Marie Françoise Delachaume, daughter of Monsieur de Jouy and Madame de Jouy, of the parish of

Jouy, bishopric of Sausse [Sens] in Burgundy, age 25, came here on *Les Deux Frères*, commanded by Monsieur Ferret."[23] Marie Françoise Le Coustelier de Jouy de Palsy neglected to mention that she had "come over" because "Madame de Jouy" had had her only daughter locked away for "insolent behavior inappropriate to her social status," and because the French monarchy's representatives had not hesitated to deport a woman whose ancestors had enjoyed great favor at Louis XIV's court. The relatives living on the family fiefdom of Palsy could never have foreseen that the younger sister whose deportation they "unanimously" approved would die an ocean away, after having helped found a would-be fiefdom: the erstwhile duchy of Arkansas.

Chapter 12

Louisiana's Garden on the German Coast

T HE SETTLEMENT OF THE AREA ON THE MISSISSIPPI JUST ABOVE
New Orleans that came to be known as "the German Coast"
was yet another repercussion of John Law's ill-considered colonial experiment. The German Coast took shape when and as it did because
of the failure of Arkansas.

Law awarded himself two sizeable tracts of land in Louisiana—
one on the Mississippi near New Orleans, the other on the lower part
of its tributary, the Arkansas. But Law's plans for their development
were unlike those of other concession holders.

Law fully shared the scorn of the Indies Company officials who
dismissed French colonists as lazy and incompetent. For his concessions, he wanted none of this. Instead, in 1720, he initiated a second propaganda campaign, promoting Louisiana with the same

enticements employed in 1719 to attract French settlers and sell Indies Company stock: the colony's gold and silver mines, its fine farmland, its amazing new capital city. But the second campaign targeted specifically those Law considered superior colonists: German and Swiss farmers.[1]

This promotion succeeded brilliantly. Lured by the siren song, thousands signed up. These aspiring inhabitants then traveled from Germany and Switzerland to French ports, where they had been promised transport. To anyone familiar with the deported women's story, what transpired next was all too predictable.

Because no one had prepared in any way for the influx, the would-be inhabitants spent months biding their time in makeshift camps in France and in conditions resembling those on Biloxi beach. After outbreaks of pestilence in squalid encampments, many died on French soil, while still awaiting transport. When ships did sail, infected passengers carried disease on board, and many more died at sea. After a crossing on *Les Deux Frères* that departed the French port of L'Orient in January 1721 transporting 213 German and Swiss passengers, only 40 were alive upon reaching the Gulf Coast in March. For the Germans and Swiss who did survive, their first months in Louisiana were a replay of what they'd already endured in France.[2]

Back in Europe, the French economy was in free fall. By the time anyone remembered the settlers waiting on the Gulf Coast and still hoping for transport to Law's concessions, Law had fled France, and Louisiana was governed by the Indies Company. Its directors decided against Law's costly plan of taking new inhabitants all the way to the Arkansas River. As a result, Arkansas never became a duchy whose German and Swiss inhabitants were ruled by their duke, John Law.

The Indies Company chose instead to cut costs by settling Law's Germans closer to the Gulf Coast, principally on land that had been granted to Étienne Demeuves II, a Parisian financier who was ruined in the stock market crash.[3] The Indies Company appropriated Demeuves's bankrupt concession and turned it into the German settlement Law had dreamed of. With Bienville's approval, the Indies Company allotted each German land fronting on the Mississippi.

Accordingly, at the same time as Louisiana's new capital was emerging from the brush and about thirty miles north of the place soon to become New Orleans, beginning in early 1722 a small German territory was taking shape. The area quickly became known as "*les Allemands*," "the Germans." People spoke of traveling "to the Germans," "*aux Allemands*," or "from the Germans," "*des Allemands*." Today, a lake, a bayou, and a community are all known by the name "Des Allemands," and the entire area is called "the German Coast." In comparison with most other areas, that bit of Mississippi coastline flourished and soon represented, after New Orleans, the largest European population in the Lower Mississippi Valley.

This was due in large part to the efforts of Karl Friedrich D'Arensbourg, the German officer put in charge by the Indies Company in 1721. For a half century, D'Arensbourg kept "les Allemands" on a steady course. Under his supervision, hamlets took shape, positioned one after another for about fifteen miles along the river.

So many acres of natural floodplain have been drained in modern times to make way for farmland and towns that it's hard to get a sense today of the place that its original settlers discovered. In the early eighteenth century, inhabitants lived not only by the water but surrounded by vast expanses of naturally flooded forests, wetlands created when the river regulated itself. To go virtually anywhere, residents traveled in dugout canoes, on the Mississippi or its tributaries, including the "small canals" that the French, in their attempt to render the Choctaw "*bayuk*," first named "*bajoues*" or "*bayouks*," later "*bayous*."[4] With bayous came fauna such as alligators, rattlesnakes, and water moccasins, all profoundly unfamiliar to Europeans. The lives of the first New Orleanians were staid in comparison.

Whereas in New Orleans, most deported women had relatively little firsthand knowledge of the Mississippi, on the German Coast life revolved around the river. When settlement began in the spring of 1722, the name of the waterway that ruled their lives, like virtually every-thing in the colony, was in flux. Seventeenth-century French explor-ers christened it *"fleuve Colbert,"* "Colbert's river," after their country's finance minister. In 1712, however, a royal edict proclaimed, "From now on, it will be called *la rivière de Saint-Louis,"* "Saint Louis's river," the name found on most early maps and the name that the German Coast's original residents would have used. For the French, the river definitively became "the Mississippi" only much later. In the 1750s, the earliest historians of the colony still evoked "the Saint-Louis river or the Mississippi." The deported women both witnessed and participated in the process as a result of which the waterways that surrounded their new home on the German Coast—large and small, bayous and river alike—acquired the names still in use today.[5]

On the German Coast, river frontage was essential. The area be-came one of Louisiana's few success stories because of the soil along the Mississippi's banks, an accumulation of mud and silt deposited with each overflow. Since this strange, black soil was the most fertile in the colony, in good years, settlers' farms yielded bounteous har-vests.[6] But that bounty came at a price.

The rich land lay below water level. During what one administra-tor called *"les grandes eaux,"* "the high waters," farms were regularly submerged, and flooding was possible from late March to the end of July. Inundations after hurricanes were even worse—the great storm of September 1722 wiped most of the original holdings off the map.

More than anywhere else, settlers on the German Coast depended on effective *levées*, or levees, embankments built to help prevent flooding. Royal engineers working under Le Blond de La Tour's di-rection drew up grand projects but had no workers to carry them out. In 1728, when New Orleans was finally surrounded by a proper em-bankment, a plan was in effect to build a levee running unbroken for sixty miles on each bank of the river upstream from the city, an am-bitious project that was never carried out. Finally, in 1732, residents were ordered to build their own embankments at least six feet thick.[7]

NOT ALL INHABITANTS OF THE GERMAN COAST WERE GERMAN: AFter Jacques Massicot and Marie Daudin's son Jacques married Geneviève Grevenberg, the young couple resided and raised a family on the coast. Jacques was among D'Arensbourg's successors in governing the settlement. All through the final decades of the eighteenth century, Jacques Massicot, the son of a woman outlawed from France, served as the chief judicial authority on the German Coast.

From the start, high mortality was a fact of life on the German Coast.[8] In April 1721, Bienville sent a dispatch announcing the imminent arrival on the concessions near New Orleans of many who had long been begging to escape the encampments on Biloxi beach. Upon reaching their destination, however, the new inhabitants learned that they had exchanged one disastrous situation for another, and Bienville before long warned authorities that those who were already living on what soon became known as the German Coast "are dying every day from hunger and poverty."[9]

Among those who pulled through was the second-youngest of all survivors, Geneviève Bettemont, deported when John Law changed the rules for French investors and her mother was no longer able to make ends meet. In Louisiana, Geneviève's fate was determined when one of those who had profited most from the system that impoverished her family in Paris himself faced sudden bankruptcy.

Geneviève married Jacques Antoine Le Borne (or Borne), an *engagé* or enlistee who had come voluntarily to the colony, to cultivate land on the concession of financier Demeuves. When Demeuves was ruined, along with a group of Germans, Geneviève and Jacques Antoine developed a site on the Mississippi known as *"Anse aux Outardes,"* a name translated today as "Bustard's Cove," though its original settlers, Canadians, surely had in mind a type of *outarde* more familiar to them, Canada geese.

In 1727, the couple had a first surviving child; by 1731, three children. By 1751, when her last child was born, Geneviève had given birth to at least ten. For much of that time, Geneviève and Jacques

Antoine lived in a small, close-knit community of eight families, four of them German and four French. Their son Jacques Antoine married Marianne Haydel, one of many unions that united Germans and French.

Geneviève and her husband became respected members of the area dominated by the Germans who found refuge there in the wake of John Law's debacle. When their church was finally completed, Jacques Antoine became a trustee. And when their daughter Geneviève Marguerite married in 1754, D'Arensbourg, still the commander of the German Coast, was a witness.

The status of property on the German Coast was even more confused than in early New Orleans. After the Indies Company promised the first inhabitants a fixed amount of land in return for clearing and farming it, a brouhaha about the measurement of river frontage ensued. In 1725, two surveyors arrived from France, but they were soon dismissed, because Pauger found fault with their work. The company next decided to reduce individual allotments and guaranteed residents "definitive titles" once they had had new surveys carried out to make certain that they were respecting the revised dimensions.[10]

Some inhabitants lost hope. Volunteers like Jacques Le Borne had signed three-year contracts that guaranteed free return passage, and in the early 1720s, when those began to expire, many wanted to go home. Few ships were then traveling to Louisiana; their captains, knowing full well that the Indies Company would never reimburse their expenses, refused to honor its pledge. In the end, only a handful of volunteers managed to get out.[11]

Jacques Antoine Le Borne bided his time. In about 1731, when the Indies Company admitted defeat and returned Louisiana to the Crown, a record of property owners along the river was drawn up, including the bases for their claims. Some had been granted land; others had purchased it from a concession. Le Borne owned his land "by possession," because of a deal cut with the Indies Company. In exchange for renouncing the return passage to France legally due him, he was granted "possession" of land. Jacques and Geneviève raised a family on the farm thus acquired, 10 arpents or 8.5 acres, the third-largest holding in their community.[12]

It would not have been an easy life, but in good years these farms could be solidly profitable. Every bountiful harvest became an indispensible source of sustenance for New Orleans, so much so that Dumont referred to Des Allemands as "the garden of the capital."[13] Indeed, New Orleans may well not have survived without the help of other areas. Illinois provided grain for the city's inhabitants. Natchitoches and Arkansas gave the capital bear oil to cook with. And the German Coast sent, above all, vegetables, and also chickens. Thirty miles in a dugout was an arduous journey, but from 1724 on, farmers from the German Coast accomplished it in pirogues loaded with farm goods. New Orleanians desperate for fresh produce rushed to the riverbank and bought directly off the boat as soon as they heard of a landing. Even though authorities tried to regulate the frantic commerce by ordering farmers to display their offerings on the central square, a map of New Orleans in the late 1720s by Dumont, reproduced in Figure 13, shows "*le marché*," "the market" (number 19), right by the Saint-Louis river, adjacent to the levee (number 17) and the landing for small boats (number 16).[14]

THE MAP ALSO DEPICTS, IMMEDIATELY BEHIND THE CITY, NOT ONLY wilderness but still more waterways, notably, along the map's northern edge, a tributary that provided another route to the Mississippi, the "*grand bayou de Saint-Jean*." "Bayou Saint-Jean," today a New Orleans neighborhood known as Bayou St. John, was in the eighteenth century the province of *voyageurs*. By giving the quickest access for traders seeking to take goods directly to Biloxi and Mobile from Lake Pontchartrain, the waterway became essential to the circulation of local commodities within the colony.

Marie Avril's husband Jacques Tarascon surely navigated Bayou Saint-Jean during the years of their marriage. After Marie's death in

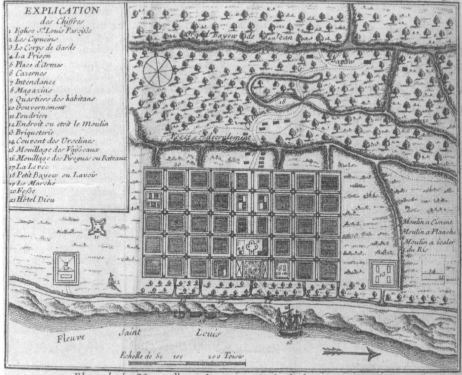

EXPLICATION
des Chiffres
1 Eglise S.t Louis Paroisse
2 Les Capucins
3 Le Corps de Garde
4 La Prison
5 Place d'Armes
6 Casernes
7 Intendance
8 Magazins
9 Quartiers des habitans
10 Gouvernement
11 Poudriere
12 Endroit ou etoit le Moulin
13 Briqueterie
14 Couvent des Urselines
15 Mouillage des Vaisseaux
16 Mouillage des Pirogues ou Bateaux
17 La Levée
18 Petit Bayou ou Lavoir
19 Le Marché
20 Fossé
21 Hôtel Dieu

Plan de la Nouvelle Orleans Capitale de la Louisiane

Figure 13. Dumont's map showing the landing place for pirogues or dugout canoes (number 16), the nearby market where inhabitants of the German Coast sold their produce (number 19), and, at the top edge, the Grand Bayou de Saint-Jean.

1738, Tarascon left Mobile for the area along the bayou, which prospered as the German Coast developed. Avril, an adept of France's smallest canals, would have understood well the canal-filled terrain where her children spent their adult lives.

Marie Avril's oldest son, Charles, married into the Girardy family of Canadians, among the original inhabitants of Gentilly, the bayou village nearest New Orleans. Her second son, Jacques II, married the granddaughter of *La Mutine* survivor Marie Anne Fourchet, named Marie Louise in honor of her godmother, survivor Marie Louise Balivet, and they prospered on Bayou Saint-Jean. In 1772, Jacques

acquired the 650-acre tract now called the Lorreins-Tarascon plantation. The house that Marie Avril's son built on this land in 1780, today usually known as the Old Spanish Customs House, is considered
among the oldest in New Orleans and a construction of exceptional
architectural significance.[15] A third survivor from Mobile's "established community" had also founded a dynasty—in her case, one that
flourished and became influential on the outskirts of New Orleans.
And there, near Bayou Saint-Jean, another survivor's child acquired
property now part of Louisiana's cultural heritage.

THE TRAJECTORY OF MARIE AVRIL'S DAUGHTER PÉLAGIE TARASCON
illustrates vividly the prosperity that land in the countryside near
New Orleans could bring. When Pélagie's first husband, Jean Baptiste Brazilier, died in 1775, he bequeathed her his entire estate, "as
they have secured their property together." The couple had in fact
"secured" so much property of all kinds that a legal suit disputing
the will dragged on for years. In 1779, Pélagie married André Jung, a
New Orleans businessman who had been a major trader with fellow
merchants in his hometown of Bordeaux since the 1730s.[16]

On September 7, 1781, Pélagie died at the home of her brother
Jacques, to whom she left the bulk of her considerable holdings.
Four days earlier, Pélagie had composed a detailed will, dispos-
ing of her land on Bayou Saint-Jean, "formerly the site of the king's
warehouse." Still more property once essential to French control over
Louisiana had been acquired by the daughter of a survivor.

Pélagie's assets were so numerous and so varied that over eighty
pages of legalese accompanied her short and thoughtful testament. To
her niece, Françoise Lorreins, Pélagie left "the contents of her armoire."
The silver stored there, so heavy that they had to remove bags from a
chest and load them individually into a pirogue, was taken, following
Pélagie's instructions, to her niece. Her brother Charles was so affluent
that he didn't need anything more; she asked Jacques to share with
Charles, "should he ever lose his fortune."[17] The wealth accumulated by

these grandchildren of a gardener in France would have been staggering to their cousins in the Old Country.

On April 7, 1739, Jeanne Mahou and her second husband, carpenter Jacques Dureau, also relocated along the river. That day, the couple signed an agreement with Nicolas Chauvin de Léry Boisclair, a
document as carefully considered as the inventory Jeanne had drawn
up after her first husband's death. The couple agreed to manage Boisclair's estate near the settlement called "Cannes Brûlées," "Burnt
Canes." Dureau promised to build a shed with a palmetto-frond roof,
as well as two "complete" *indigoteries*, multilevel structures for the
extraction of indigo blue dye.[18]

While such contracts were usually concluded exclusively between
male parties, this arrangement specified a full partnership. Except
for carpentry, Dureau's field, all responsibilities were to be shared "by
Dureau and his wife." With her experience farming near Fort Toulouse, this was labor that Jeanne Mahou knew well. In exchange for
their work as estate managers, the couple was allowed to keep a third
of the rice harvest. They were not landowners, but the arrangement
allowed them to profit from the German Coast's agricultural bounty.

On February 10, 1743, a baptism was celebrated in the German
Coast's still-new first church: the christening of Jacques, born to
Jeanne Mahou, by then forty-one, and Jacques Dureau. At least a full
day's travel by pirogue would have been necessary to cover the roughly
fifteen miles separating Cannes Brûlées, where they lived, and the
church.[19] It would have been easier to reach New Orleans, where in
1744, Jeanne Mahou signed an apprenticeship for her son from her
first marriage, Joseph Laurent, to learn the locksmith's trade.[20]

In 1743, Jeanne Mahou chose to make the longer journey between
two small settlements on the German Coast because of an enduring
friendship. Twenty-three years after *La Mutine* landed them on Massacre Island, the baby's mother and the woman she asked to serve as
his godmother, Geneviève Bettemont, by then the wife of one of the
church's trustees, remained united by their shared past.

In 1744, Geneviève Bettemont also traveled to New Orleans. She made the trip in order to join other survivors such as Marie Anne Dinan who, from 1738 on, attempted to recover money owed them by the families who had banished them to John Law's colony. Geneviève Bettemont's struggle to obtain what was lawfully hers was exceptionally protracted, the hardest-fought of any such claims.

On December 29, 1744, both Geneviève and Antoine were present to consult royal notary Augustin Chantalou. Other survivors initiated such procedures only when they were assured that relatives were deceased, but Geneviève was being farsighted. She had had no contact with Charlotte Delormel, the mother who had not seen fit to protect her, nor, it appears, had the person who provided the information she did possess, perhaps her only surviving sibling, Pierre, who lived still in Paris. She didn't know her mother's current abode, though she did know that Delormel had remarried, had again been widowed, and had once resided in Clermont-en-Beauvaisis in northern France. Geneviève believed her mother was still alive, but *"en cas de décès de Delormel,"* "in the event of Delormel's demise," she formally requested that "a full and complete inventory of her estate be drawn up."[21]

This was only the beginning of Geneviève's patient and methodical campaign to obtain her due. Twenty years later, on November 26, 1764, Geneviève and Antoine were once again in New Orleans, meeting with a notary to draw up a kind of document specific to the colonial context. In order to secure "funds due her as sole heir to her father and mother and to obtain all necessary papers proving her claims," the notary required a colleague in Paris to act on Geneviève's behalf, so she signed a blank power of attorney, authorizing *"Sieur* [name to be filled in] to recover from Paris's City Hall the capital and all back interest due on an annuity of 7,200 *livres."*[22]

Geneviève surely sensed that it ultimately wasn't necessary to demand an inventory of her mother's property because, in 1764, the sum total of all assets belonging to the estate of Pierre Bettemont and Charlotte Delormel remained precisely what it had been in 1719, when she had been deported: an annuity purchased with the life savings of Geneviève's great-aunt and bequeathed by her to the couple's children, of whom, in 1764, Geneviève was the sole survivor. In their entire lives, Geneviève's parents had acquired nothing on their own.

But she did learn something from the inquiry, since two facts came to light because of that 1764 petition. Geneviève learned that her mother was still alive. She also learned that her mother had done something expressly forbidden by Geneviève's great-aunt and had sold the principal on the annuity to a merchant in Bordeaux, who all through the decades had paid Charlotte Delormel interest.[23]

Geneviève continued to monitor the situation. She learned that in January 1767, her mother had collected interest on the annuity.[24] Sometime between then and March 6, 1769, Charlotte Delormel died. At that point, Geneviève, by then a widow, had a new petition drawn up in her name alone. On it, she was identified as "*Dame* Geneviève Bethemont." The spelling of her family name was that found in official Parisian documents, while the honorific reflected the respect accorded Geneviève after a half-century of exemplary life in the colony to which she had been deported as an impoverished fourteen-year-old.[25] The money eluded her still, but Geneviève was not one to give up.

On February 15, 1775, after a thirty-one-year-long struggle, Geneviève Bettemont, by then seventy, at last profited from her legacy—precisely seventy years after her great-aunt had drawn up the will she had hoped would guarantee a good life for her great-niece Geneviève, then but an infant. The investment landscape in France had stabilized after the collapse of Indies Company stock, and when interest on annuities was raised to pre-devaluation levels, the funds became once again an attractive investment. As a result, nearly a century after her aunt had purchased the annuity that had determined the course of Geneviève's life in France, Geneviève was able to find a buyer willing to take over the investment. The 2,300 *livres* she cleared from the transaction settled her score with her family in France.[26]

Figure 14. With this "receipt," the king of France officially decreed that Geneviève Bettemont and Jacques Antoine Le Borne had won their lawsuit and would receive the inheritance rightfully hers.

On February 4, 1778, nearly sixty years after *La Mutine* landed, Geneviève's score with the French monarchy was settled as well. On that day, "*le Roi*," Louis XVI, the grandson of the king who had presided over her exile, officially approved the sale of the annuity, clearing the way for a deported woman to receive funds on which her life had once depended. A royal *quittance*, or receipt, was drawn up, an incontrovertible proclamation of the fact that the money was Geneviève's legal due.[27]

By then, Geneviève was a wealthy woman, among the wealthiest of all the survivors. In 1784, after sixty-four years in John Law's colony, at age seventy-nine Dame Geneviève Bettemont died. On November 25, a "full and complete" inventory of her belongings, the kind of detailed accounting of which Geneviève would have approved, was drawn up. The inventory was directed by Marie Daudin's son Jacques Massicot, then the German Coast's legal authority and considered a close neighbor geographically, even though he lived seven and a half miles away. Geneviève's surviving children, Antoine and Geneviève, were present; François Verret represented his brother Joseph and his wife, Marguerite Le Borne.[28]

The inventory is a clear indication of Geneviève Bettemont's status in her community. Geneviève had had dealings with the German

Coast's elite residents: the estate of D'Arensbourg himself owed money to Geneviève's. It reveals above all her prosperity. Since 1763, when France was defeated in the Seven Years' War, the German Coast had been under Spanish rule, so the valuation was done in *piastres*, pieces of eight. Total value: 14,978 *piastres* or between 75,000 and 90,000 *livres*, far surpassing even Marie Daudin's handsome aggregate.[29] Like Marie Daudin's, Geneviève Bettemont's estate left her many grandchildren provided for. In Louisiana, she accomplished what her great-aunt had hoped to do in Paris.

THE FERTILE SOIL AND ABUNDANT HARVESTS OF "THE CAPITAL'S garden" made farmland the foundation of the wealth accumulated by

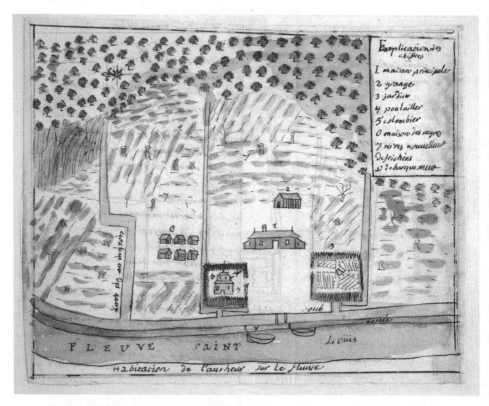

Figure 15. Dumont's depiction of the *habitation* or small farm on the German Coast where he lived in 1730.

the survivors who resided on the German Coast. In the early 1730s, Dumont lived there briefly and left a representation, shown in Figure 15, of what was called in French a *habitation*, a place where *habitants* or inhabitants resided. Like all *habitations* on the German Coast, it fronted on the river that Dumont and other early residents referred to as "Saint-Louis." At the start, *habitations* along the German Coast were for the most part simply small farms with acreage so modest that inhabitants could choose to cultivate them on their own.[30] The July 1727 census shows that Jacques Antoine Le Borne and Geneviève Bettemont did just that, working their fields alone, with no *engagés*, or indentured workers, and no enslaved Africans.

By the early 1730s, after the Indies Company's exit from the colony and the ensuing redistribution of property along the German Coast, on virtually all *habitations*, that of the Le Borne family included, the situation had changed. By 1731, not only were their holdings more extensive, but the couple had three children, and their family was still growing. Geneviève no longer had much time for farming. Jacques Antoine had turned to an outside labor force and now worked their land with the advantage of four European men who had chosen to come to Louisiana as indentured workers and four enslaved Africans.

On the one hand, Le Borne's arrangement was representative of his region. On the German Coast, where a small number of residents maintained extensive stretches of land along the Mississippi, by 1731, not a single inhabitant continued to farm alone, as Jacques had done until very recently. On the other hand, however, Le Borne's method was also distinctive. Typically, German Coast farmers with modest holdings had no indentured servants, or one at most. They instead relied exclusively on the labor of enslaved Africans, commonly at least seven or eight. Only two other small landowners in the area made the choice Le Borne did, to farm alongside a larger cohort of indentured workers and fewer enslaved Africans. It's easy to see in his decision a desire to give a chance to other men who had come to Louisiana as he had, voluntarily as *engagés*. He wanted to afford these workers

313

indentured for a fixed period of time the same opportunity to prosper that he had found. Le Borne's choice could also have reflected a desire to avoid as much as possible the dependence on the labor of enslaved Africans that was becoming ever more evident along the German Coast in the 1730s.

No matter what its motivation, Le Borne's decision had not been easily realized. By 1731, in the entire colony, almost no European indentured workers were left. In fact, only 119 *engagés* were employed in all the prosperous holdings on the German Coast, where they made up less than 3 percent of its labor force. The four men who farmed alongside Jacques Antoine themselves represented nearly 3.5 percent of the indentured workers on the entire German Coast. In contrast, by 1731, the German Coast was farmed almost exclusively by over twenty-five hundred enslaved Africans.[31] By then, just as John Law had decreed when he dictated that Louisiana's economy would be driven by tobacco alone and dependent on the labor of enslaved Africans, a mandate consistently upheld by the Indies Company, farming in this colony with few French inhabitants was almost entirely carried out by enslaved Africans.[32]

In Dumont's depiction of a *habitation*, he represented a main house no larger or more sophisticated than Jeanne Mahou and Laurent Laurent's contemporary dwelling near Fort Toulouse. He represented every construction on the property, from chicken coop to dovecote, to the "houses" or cabins built to house enslaved Africans. Just as he did in his history of Louisiana, Dumont chose to make slavery's presence visible.

Like early maps of New Orleans, Dumont's image features the fine line between farmland and wilderness that defined life on the German Coast. The amount of land available for planting is small; a larger quantity is marked "recently cleared." But behind the modest *habitation* lies wilderness, land that could become farmland only at great effort. In such terrain, inhabitants at first made space for no public constructions, so there were no official buildings on the early German Coast.

The German Coast's first church was completed only in 1740. That building was destroyed in a fire. A twentieth-century edifice, dedicated to Saint Charles Borromeo, now stands near today's Destrehan, Louisiana. The church faces a small road next to which rises a modern levee. On the other side lies a bayou, which perhaps two hundred feet down the road flows into the Mississippi. The original cemetery, probably begun in 1723, was soon swept away when floodwaters breached an early embankment. The remains of those buried in the 1720s resurfaced centuries later, and a section of today's cemetery was reserved for the reburial of early interments. A marble stele pays homage to those thus interred.

Many of the oldest tombs in today's graveyard are anonymous, the names of those buried there long since effaced by frequent flooding and the ravages of time. Among the nearby modern, above-ground tombs, one of the most arresting bears the name "Borne." The family founded by Jacques Antoine Le Borne and Geneviève Bettemont remains prominent still today. The couple's second son and Jacques Antoine's namesake fathered eleven children, eight of whom in turn had large families—as many as twelve offspring. On and on it has gone, with families up and down the modern-day German Coast still tracing their beginnings to the family raised on land grudgingly granted in the aftermath of John Law's bankruptcy.

Chapter 13

Natchez, John Law's Folly

Long before there was a German Coast, in 1714 Bienville personally selected a site for a settlement on the Mississippi about 90 leagues, some 270 miles, north of the spot where New Orleans later developed. The new post, situated squarely in the territory of a populous Native American nation, was given their name: "*les Natchez*," "the Natchez."

In late 1715, word reached the colony that, in one of the last decisions of his long reign, Louis XIV had ordered immediate occupation of the settlement. The Sun King considered Natchez indispensable for dealing with what colonial administrators later referred to as "the trepidation that has gripped [the Native American population] at the arrival of so many Europeans." "These people are not to be underestimated," one report warned Indies Company directors, speculating that the Natchez alone had eighteen hundred warriors. Management of such a critical situation justified what it called "a substantial garrison." The report suggested 130 men—though like many goals in French Louisiana's history, it was a number never achieved. At the high point, only 80 soldiers were stationed there.[1]

In 1716, Bienville announced that the Natchez had agreed to the construction of a fortress on their land. He named it Fort Rosalie, to honor the second wife of the Comte de Pontchartrain, the navy minister who was an early advocate of Louisiana. That summer, with help from the Natchez, some ten French soldiers cleared land and built a rough-hewn fence surrounding a bark-covered storehouse, a powder magazine, and a few huts to shelter soldiers. Situated on a bluff over the river, this less than prepossessing outpost became a way station for voyagers traveling between the Upper Mississippi Valley and New Orleans.

From the start, Natchez was prized as choice terrain that, unlike territory lower down on the Mississippi, was easy to clear; as exceptionally high ground in a colony known otherwise for low-lying land; and as hilly country, with fertile soil in which seemingly any crop grew more successfully than elsewhere. With its "beautiful fields," Natchez was, in visiting Capuchin missionary Father Raphael's words, "one of the finest places to be seen." Despite such notable advantages, however, for years the outpost languished. A decade after Fort Rosalie's initial construction, for example, Father Raphael noted the disrepair, describing it to the Indies Company with disbelief: "There is a fort . . . , if, however, an enclosure of half-rotten stakes that keeps no one out can be called a fort."[2]

In these years when military life at Natchez was limited, religious life was practically nonexistent. Since the post was so small, at first no missionary was assigned to it on a permanent basis. Inhabitants wishing to marry simply gathered a few witnesses and took informal vows in their presence, but there was no one to record these ceremonies and give them true legal status. As late as 1726, Father Raphael reported, "Mass is said in a disgraceful little place . . . without a ceiling or a floor, with no windows, and with room for only about 20 persons, even though there are nearly 200 communicants."[3]

With no church and no true fort, in Natchez's early years it played little role in the colony's development and was often neglected by colonial administrators. Then, with John Law's arrival on the scene, Natchez suddenly began to matter. From 1719 on, the name "Natchez" was often on the lips of French officials, always associated with one word: "tobacco."

WITHOUT TOBACCO, THE KEYSTONE OF HIS GRAND PROJECT FOR rescuing the French economy, John Law could never have made the Indies Company into a behemoth, its stock would never have soared, the women would not have been deported, and Natchez would barely have figured in accounts of French Louisiana.

In January 1719, when Pancatelin drew up her initial list of women destined "for the islands," Law's trading company was awarded France's tobacco monopoly and given a precise mission: to regulate "the sale of Louisiana's tobacco."[4] But at that moment, tobacco was not yet grown in Louisiana because there was neither the necessary equipment nor a qualified workforce, and the colony's limited agricultural resources were insufficient to provide even basic sustenance for its small population. None of that stopped Law from making his sales pitch.

On March 27, when his company's directors met for the first time, Law informed the regent and the princes of the blood "that the tobacco produced by [Louisiana] was superior to Virginia tobacco." France then imported over six million pounds of English tobacco every year; a pound of the finest Virginia tobacco sold for 1 *livre*, 12 *sols*. Law declared that the "superior" quality of tobacco from Louisiana warranted a price of two *livres* a pound. On this basis, Law projected that Louisiana would soon realize for France a profit of a million *livres* every month from this one commodity alone.[5]

And so it was that a tiny and remote outpost that the Sun King had viewed as necessary to maintain peaceful relations with Indigenous peoples received a new raison d'être. Within months of Law's forecast for Louisiana tobacco, Indies Company stock was surging, and the company's directors had chosen Natchez as the place that would justify its stock's exorbitant price.

By the time *La Mutine* landed in early 1720, reports on the state of the colony sent to Indies Company directors spoke of Natchez solely in terms of tobacco. Administrators in Louisiana guaranteed that, since a few French workers with experience in growing tobacco had been among those exiled to the colony *de force*, beginning in 1721 harvests and quality would be exceptional.

In fact, when those much-ballyhooed trained workers reached Natchez in 1720, they learned that nothing had been prepared for their arrival. They were forced to spend their first months growing food and fighting to survive. At the time of Law's downfall in December 1720, tobacco farming had barely begun. When the first Natchez tobacco was shipped to France in late 1721, the initial harvest consisted of a meager five hundred pounds—this from a colony whose production Law had pledged would be between four million and eight million pounds annually.[6]

From then on, the disconnect between wild promises and the reality of Louisiana tobacco production remained flagrant. *Next year, the harvest will be good; next year, the quality of the tobacco will be excellent*, colonial administrators repeated tirelessly, no matter what the results of previous years had demonstrated.

Yet, when tobacco from Natchez reached New Orleans in 1724, it was pronounced "unfit for sale . . . it can neither be sent to France nor sold here."[7] By 1727, barely twenty-five thousand pounds were shipped to France—and the product's quality was considered abysmal. Louis XV's trusted adviser, Cardinal Fleury, denounced "the stench" of Natchez tobacco.

Undeterred, on November 1, 1727, Louisiana's Governor Périer wrote Indies Company directors to report that "everyone will soon cultivate this plant; next year the return from it will certainly be considerable." He guaranteed that 200,000 pounds would be exported in 1728. But by April 1728, Périer lamented that "rains have almost completely destroyed the tobacco crops" and explained that over 20,000 pounds had been washed out at his personal plantation at Natchez alone. In fact, 1728's harvest was the largest yet—150,000 pounds might actually have been shipped—but it, too, was considered atrocious. "It would be better to burn such poor stuff in Louisiana than to send it to France," the directors concluded.

Nearly a decade after Natchez had been chosen as the settlement that would make Louisiana a financial windfall for France, the outpost had yet to turn a profit.

A NUMBER OF MAJOR SHAREHOLDERS IN LAW'S COMPANY ALSO BET on Natchez. They obtained large land grants there, which they planned to devote to tobacco production. After Law's downfall, while most concessions went bankrupt, two survived: that of Swiss financier Jean Daniel Kolly and that of an investor known only by his last name, Pellerin.

An incomplete census from May 13, 1722 shows two deported women among Natchez's early residents. Marie Baron, by then nineteen, had married farmer Jean Roussin, and they had had a first child. Marie Bordeau, who had traveled on *Les Deux Frères*, deported for smuggling, had become the wife of a crucial inhabitant, Noel Soileau. Soileau, the longest-serving warehouse manager in the colony, was valued by the Indies Company for his integrity, a quality considered rare among those who held the keys to the company stores. These two survivors were soon joined by Françoise Fresson, an alleged tobacco smuggler from Picardy also deported on *Les Deux Frères*.[8] She married farmer Michel Beau, among the inhabitants most appreciated by local authorities.[9]

In Natchez, two distinct ways of farming coexisted. On the land grants' substantial acreage, the labor of enslaved Africans played an essential role in the cultivation of tobacco, just as John Law had planned from the start. Other inhabitants, such as the three deported women, lived on the small farms of between two and three acres that were allotted to the early residents not employed on concessions.[10] The women worked alongside their husbands, raising a bit of tobacco but mainly focusing on food crops. None of them used slave labor.

Natchez never fulfilled Law's promise of making France rich, but during the years when tobacco production was slowly ramping up, life was good for those who resided there, and for Marie Baron in particular. In France, Marie Baron's family had not been able to make ends meet, and her father was buried in a pauper's grave. In Natchez, in May 1722, only three years after a corrupt police officer pinned the theft of a ribbon on her and had her deported, Marie Baron was already a landowner. She and Jean Roussin raised two children and farmed their own land, just under two acres. In 1724, when Dumont began serving as an officer in the Natchez garrison and met Marie Baron, he described her as "a very wealthy inhabitant."[11]

The deported woman and the future historian crossed paths when they served as godparents, a chance encounter that shaped the history of Louisiana. Dissatisfied with what all agreed were the substandard officers' quarters at Fort Rosalie, Dumont asked if he might board with the Roussin family. Two decades later, when he composed the memoirs that formed the basis for his history of the colony, Dumont featured the couple in his account of Natchez. Marie Baron and Jean Roussin thus became two of the very rare private individuals—individuals linked in no way to the colony's official administration—to be written into the early history of Louisiana. The anecdotes Dumont recorded make it clear that, in the colony, Marie found much more than the status and financial stability that had eluded her family in France.

Marie Baron's newfound independence gave her the courage to take on the very legal system that had condemned her as a "public prostitute and a thief." The story began in 1728, with the stuff of daily life in rural communities, a dispute over a dead heifer that erupted between Roussin and Longrais, the manager of the Sainte-Catherine concession. Inhabitants viewed the garrison's commander as corrupt.

When he adjudicated in favor of Longrais, Marie Baron, in Dumont's words, "could not keep from speaking out. She said to M. de Longrais that he was acting like a scoundrel and that the judge had been paid off." For this, Marie was sentenced to the kind of public penitence to which so many deported women had been condemned in France. She was ordered to march to the manager's property and publicly "beg for forgiveness."

With Dumont's help and Roussin's participation, Marie Baron appealed the judgment. To plead his wife's case before Louisiana's Superior Council, the colony's chief judicial authority, Roussin made the nearly two-and-a-half-week journey downriver to New Orleans. According to Dumont's account, this time the verdict went against Longrais, who was ordered to pay all legal fees, as well as damages, and even interest. The judge also "prohibited the reparation of honor"—and concluded his verdict by sending greetings to Marie Baron.[12]

Had anyone been paying attention, this case, judged almost immediately after Jeanne Coroy and Manon Fontaine's desertion plot, might have given authorities cause for concern—a decade after the insurrection in the Salpêtrière, the deported women were still fighting back, and in Louisiana, their defiance was going unpunished.

DUMONT'S HISTORY OF FRENCH LOUISIANA FEATURES THE DEPICtion of Natchez shown in Figure 16. Near the center sits "the Fort," Fort Rosalie, hardly a commanding presence. While the homes of some inhabitants are in near proximity to it, most are scattered randomly among the hills and wooded areas, so that Natchez scarcely seems a proper French colonial outpost. Some farms are isolated indeed, such as, near the lower right corner, the only private dwelling identified, the "maison du Sr. Rous[s]in," "the home of *Sieur* Roussin." Dumont's view of Natchez thus gave pride of place to the home of a deported woman, Marie Baron, and awarded her husband, but a modest farmer, the honorific that official documents usually accorded only Louisiana's wealthiest and most powerful inhabitants.

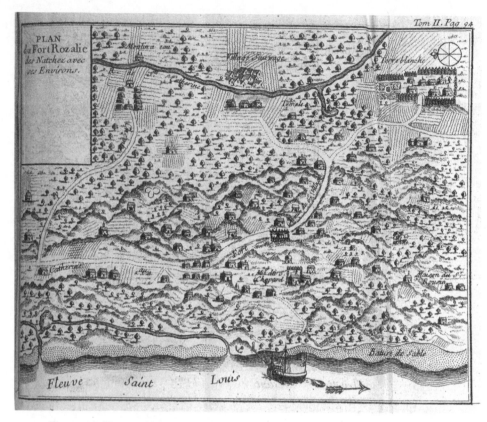

Figure 16. Dumont's depiction of the French settlement at Natchez. Just to the right of the fort, he indicated "la maison du Sr. Chepard," the home of Commander Chépart, and further to the right, "la maison du Sr. Rousin," the home shared by Marie Baron and her husband, Jean Roussin.

The image's upper corners emphasize the two large concessions that had survived the Law debacle: to the right "Terre Blanche," or "White Earth," and to the left "Sainte-Catherine." In both cases, constructions form a clear aggregate, an approximation of a village. The view's lower edge features Natchez's lifeline to the colony at large: the "fleuve Saint-Louis," the Mississippi, with what would have been a rare occurrence, a sailing ship in port.

At the top, the map highlights the outpost's other lifeline. Dumont shows a cluster of dwellings, a community rather than mere scatterings: "Village Sauvage," "Savage Village," the caption reads, using the conventional French term for Native Americans to indicate the Great Village of the Natchez nation. Just below the village and to the right the map specifies "Temple," a site much commented on by the first French visitors, who were fascinated by the sacred relics and elaborate adornments inside the Natchez temple.

As Dumont shows vividly, at "the Natchez," inhabitants lived not only on land originally that of Native Americans but also in near proximity to Native Americans. No barriers separated their farms from the dwellings of the Indigenous peoples with whom they were in constant contact.

Residents depended on their Native American neighbors in many ways. The Natchez sold the French corn flour, bread, and game; the French paid the Natchez to clear land and carry water.[13] Relations were by no means always good, and in 1722–1723, the French were often officially at war with the Natchez nation. It's impossible to know the extent to which daily life at the outpost was impacted when skirmishes between French soldiers and Native Americans took place nearby. Through it all, however, commanders of the garrison for the most part saw the wisdom of maintaining good relations with their neighbors.

In his commentary on Natchez, another early historian of the colony with firsthand knowledge of the region, Charlevoix, remarked that by the early 1720s both the Great Village and the temple were much diminished. There were fewer dwellings in the village since the French had arrived, and the temple had been stripped bare of its relics, probably, the Jesuit speculated, moved elsewhere to keep them safe from their new neighbors.[14]

Indeed, the Natchez nation itself was much diminished. Prior to the arrival of the French, its population stood at over thirty-five hundred; by the mid-1720s, it was perhaps only half as much.[15] And the same was true for nearby nations, from those the French considered their allies, such as the Choctaw, to those they saw as their enemies, such as the Chickasaw. All had suffered the devastating effects of contagious diseases introduced by Europeans and of warfare, either with Europeans or encouraged by them.

Even with vastly reduced numbers, however, Native Americans so hugely outnumbered colonists that one might have expected extreme caution on the part of French leaders in their dealings with the area's Indigenous peoples. There were at least seventeen hundred Natchez, but perhaps many more. In addition, the Choctaw totaled three thousand, according to one estimate by a French general, who counted warriors alone. Next to those numbers, the French outpost was inhabited by a garrison of eighty, of whom only twenty were permanently stationed at Fort Rosalie, and a civilian population of roughly three hundred.[16] Only a madman would have provoked the settlement's Native American neighbors.

And yet, it appears, this is just what happened in 1728. In February, a new commander took charge of Natchez's dilapidated fortress: Captain de Chépart.[17] In his depiction of Natchez, Dumont indicates "the home of M. de Chépart" just below the fort. Chépart was widely considered impulsive and unfit for such responsibility. Many called him a drunkard.

By the autumn, Chépart had decided that he wanted to share in tobacco's promised riches. Other French authorities had maintained farms at Natchez, but always on land acquired from Native Americans through some form of purchase, acquisitions that, while undocumented, were never disputed.[18] All those who first told the story of Natchez in the decades immediately following the events of 1728 and 1729 agreed that Chépart set his sights instead on fields that were sacred Natchez land, and that he made no attempt to obtain that land in any of the usual ways. Instead, in early 1729, without negotiation, he issued a peremptory order to those living there: they were to abandon their homes and immediately move elsewhere. In his published account, Dumont reported that the village leader replied "that his nation had been in possession of this village for a very long time, that the ashes of their ancestors rested there." When Chépart threatened to set fire to their temple, the Natchez begged for a delay to prepare for the move. All early accounts also agreed that the Natchez were merely gaining time in order to plot their revenge for what Dumont called demands "contrary to the basic rights of mankind."[19]

Key details of what transpired at Natchez as a result of Chépart's attempted land grab were first revealed in Dumont's 1753 history of Louisiana, and for good reason. In his history, Dumont freely admitted that he wasn't there but added that, even though he himself was not a bystander to history in the making, he had had privileged access to eyewitness testimony: "The Frenchwomen explained how [the attack] was carried out." Indeed, the testimony of one eyewitness to history ultimately proved most influential—that of a woman deported "at the King's command."

Between nine and ten on the morning of Monday, November 28, 1729, Natchez warriors settled their score with Commander Chépart. Inhabitants had gotten wind in advance of trouble brewing and warned Chépart, but he had laughed off their concerns. Before the day was out, Natchez warriors had virtually obliterated the outpost. They burned crops and buildings, from the fort to residents' homes; they killed most inhabitants. According to the first official estimate, that of Capuchin Father Philibert, the missionary by then assigned to the post and who had celebrated Mass at Natchez on November 26, 138 Frenchmen, 35 Frenchwomen, and 56 children were killed, wiping out one-tenth of Louisiana's entire European population.[20]

Among the five deported women who were perhaps residing in Natchez in 1729, Marie Bordeau alone was spared, probably because she and Noel Soileau were elsewhere at the time of the attack. Other deported women were not as fortunate. Most of the women killed died alongside their husbands. Michel Beau was among the rare Frenchmen to get out alive, while his wife, Françoise Fresson, was among the few women who died alone. Françoise perished in the fields they had farmed together, reported to be some of the finest land in Natchez.

Five deported women lost their husbands in the November attack. Ship's captain Antoine Caron, Marie Daudin's husband, had, Father Philibert reported, arrived only on November 26, piloting the company's boat. Dumont reported that Caron was the first man to die and that "the shot that killed him was the signal" that the attack was beginning.[21]

Six weeks before the Natchez uprising, in New Orleans, stonemason Pierre Caillou buried his wife, *La Mutine* survivor Marie Simone Martin. After Martin's death, Caillou immediately relocated to Natchez, where, just a month later, he and their daughter were both killed during the attack. When officials were trying to identify and record the dead, the only distinguishing detail they could recall was that "Caillou's wife came here *de force*."[22]

Irishwoman Marie Madeleine Doyart's husband, René Malain, the soldier known as "Carefree," served in the Natchez garrison and was also among the dead. Authorities identified Carefree only as "from Auvergne."[23] Doyart, the youngest of all the women deported and the youngest survivor, thus became, at age twenty-two, a young widow.

Barely a year after Marie Marguerite Moule and her husband, farmer Jacques Joseph Catherine, known as Captain, had been interrogated in connection with Jeanne Coroy and Manon Fontaine's desertion plot, Captain was killed at Natchez. In the confusion that reigned after the attack, no French authority remembered to include his name among the dead. When Marie Marguerite remarried, she identified herself as Captain's widow and added a phrase that immediately resonated with anyone who had lived through November 1729 in Louisiana: "He died at Natchez."

Marie Baron survived—but she was not spared. Instead, she was an eyewitness to the murders of her husband Jean Roussin and their eldest son. And this chapter in her life was far from over.

After news of the catastrophe reached New Orleans on December 2, the French began planning a counteroffensive. By the time it was launched, nearly two months later, those who had survived the November attack had already endured much more, as the Natchez's revenge for Chépart's greed was not quickly ended. A large group— Frenchwomen, children, enslaved Africans—was taken hostage on November 28. Spoils of war, the women were carried off individually, each by the warrior who had captured her. Many were later reunited in the home and under the protection of a female leader of the Natchez.

A list of captives was never compiled, so we'll never know their exact number—nor will we know even their names. French authorities may have wished to protect the identities of women captured and treated as "slaves," the term chosen by everyone in the colony to characterize the women's status during their captivity.

Their anonymity may also have been linked to the fact that those leading the French counteroffensive never seemed to have been much concerned with the women's fate. One French officer even contended that, for several weeks after the women's capture, French authorities made no attempt to negotiate their freedom and tried instead to make a profit by trading with their captors.[24] Army dispatches were quickly sent to New Orleans and then redirected by colonial authorities to Indies Company officials in France. Those dispatches did often discuss the whereabouts and the liberation of the enslaved Africans from the large concessions who were held by the Natchez—they were considered valuable.[25] The Natchez land grants were prized as significant developments, essential to the cultivation of tobacco, the commodity on which the Indies Company pinned any remaining hope for Louisiana. In comparison, the widows of small farmers, all of whom were in debt for purchases from the Natchez storehouse, were a financial deadweight.

The name of one hostage and one hostage alone is certain, and even this identification was never openly made in early accounts. It was, in fact, only very recently that anyone guessed the identity of the Frenchwoman who survived the ordeal and went on to become the eyewitness source on whom historian Dumont and all subsequent chroniclers relied: Marie Baron.[26]

It's because of Marie Baron that critical facts regarding the unfolding of November 28, 1729 at Natchez have survived, because of Marie Baron that details that help us understand how the women's captivity took place are known. For example, we know the fact that the women were reunited at the home of a female leader, because that leader, Dumont added, had a particular fondness for Marie Baron. An impoverished adolescent deported because of officer Bourlon's corruption guaranteed one of the few open channels of communication between the Natchez and the French during the greatest moment of crisis faced by Louisiana in the first three decades of its existence.

Some, perhaps all, the hostages knew *Mobilien*, Mobilian, the trade patois that served as a second language and facilitated dealings among settlers and Native Americans west of the Mississippi.[27] A patois like Mobilian would have been second nature to Baron. Baron could neither read nor write in French, but like all rural French of her day she had grown up bilingual, speaking predominantly the patois of her region, the Beauce, and in official contexts, French. While most French military men talked with Native Americans only through interpreters, the ability to communicate directly with the Natchez leaders who shielded her could have given Baron access to information about the attack's preparation found in Dumont's history and still repeated in histories today.

The French military presence in Louisiana was so limited that the army led by Jean Paul Le Sueur to retaliate against the Natchez was composed largely of some five hundred Choctaw warriors. They attacked at dawn on January 27, 1730, a full two months after the outpost's destruction, and soon, some alleged, "freed" roughly sixty hostages.

The women, however, were not liberated. Instead, as Marie Baron reported to Dumont, the Choctaw "seized the Frenchwomen, who thought themselves lucky to have fallen into the hands of those who came in the name of the French. But they were . . . in fact worse off among the Choctaw than they had been among the killers of their husbands." During the trench warfare and cannonading of the ensuing siege of Natchez, the women remained in Choctaw hands, still spoils of war. Near the end of February, the hostages were at last released, in exchange for gunpowder, knives, hatchets, and various items of French clothing. They were then sent by boat to New Orleans, which they reached about March 8.[28]

Missionary Father Mathurin Le Petit was an eyewitness to the scene: "No one who witnessed the arrival of the Frenchwomen could have failed to be moved. . . . The misery they had suffered was written on their faces."[29] French clothing was prized by the Native Americans, so the Choctaw had stripped their captives, and the women reached the capital "clad in little more than rags." Their misery prompted Indies Company officials to descend to new depths.

Each woman was allotted 60 *livres* credit at the company store. Whereas women sent to Louisiana as brides had been given dowries of 100 *livres*, the Natchez widows—who had lost their husbands and often children as well, their land, their homes, all their possessions— were granted a meager 60 in blood money. And even that was not a loss for the company: as Dumont explained, "its manager later made them repay." In addition, years afterward, "the poor survivors, [were] still reimbursing the company every day all the debts they owed that predated the massacre."[30] Indeed, after Antoine Caron's death in the service of the Indies Company, his widow's sole "inheritance" was money owed his employer, a debt that Marie Daudin and her second husband, Pierre La Roche, worked to pay off all during the six years of their marriage. Nearly a decade after the uprising, on January 12, 1739, Marie Marguerite Moule and her new husband, Simon Calais, finally paid the last installment of what her first husband, Captain, had owed: 1,483 *livres*, 35 *sols*.[31]

The women had spent more than three months in captivity—over two months with the Natchez and an additional month in Choctaw hands—during which time, in Dumont's words, "they were reduced to the utmost extremes of slavery."[32] By 1729, Marie Baron had extensive firsthand experience with all the degrees of unfreedom found in the colony and with various types of slavery, including that practiced by the Natchez, for whom slavery was defined above all in social rather than economic terms: slaves were excluded from the community and were thus without protection.[33] A female leader had defended Baron during her initial captivity, and her gesture may explain why at the end of the hostilities, newly freed Frenchwomen begged the French commander to spare the lives of some Natchez leaders.[34] But the women were totally defenseless during their second captivity. Whatever Dumont meant by "the utmost extremes of slavery" were almost certainly experiences they endured at that time.

It's hardly surprising that penniless, saddled with debt, and often with children to provide for, many Natchez survivors quickly remarried. Early 1730, the moment preceding their weddings, was a strange time in the history of New Orleans's Saint-Louis Church. After Anne Françoise Rolland's marriage to the warehouse keeper of Natchez, Laurent Bordelon, on February 20, there was a lull during which no new ceremonies were performed, until April 12, when, barely a month after the freed hostages had arrived in New Orleans, widows and widowers began to remarry. On April 16, Françoise Fresson's widower became one of the first among them.

On April 19, 1730, survivor and newly freed Marie Baron wed François Benjamin Dumont, future historian and son of a lawyer for the Parisian Parlement. The groom was thirty; the bride had just turned twenty-seven, and the match was one that in Paris would have been considered far above her station. Because of this April 19 wedding in Saint-Louis Church, the deported women were written into the pages of Louisiana's official history.

In April 1730, the French court at Versailles had only recently been informed of the fate of the settlement that had been the centerpiece of John Law's colonial dream. After news of what had transpired on

November 28, 1729 reached New Orleans on December 2, on December 5, Governor Périer addressed the first written account of the disaster to Navy Secretary Maurepas; the man who in November 1718 had approved Manon Fontaine's solitary confinement now had full authority over Louisiana. Even though Périer ordered a frigate to depart immediately with his dispatch, the ship reached France only on March 10, 1730. Thus it wasn't until mid-March that Périer's account reached Maurepas.

The information spread beyond court circles even more slowly. The ship carrying Father Philibert's estimate of those killed at Natchez sailed on June 10, 1730, and reached France that fall. It's not known how quickly the families of the dead might have received the news. At least weeks, perhaps even months, would have been necessary to track them down—and in the absence of an accurate tally of those killed, some families surely never learned what had transpired.

From the start, official communiqués and personal communications alike framed the story in various ways, all of them designed to lay blame or assign responsibility. In his initial account on December 5, Périer alleged that since "the attack [was] not at all characteristic of the Indians," he had no doubt that "there were some Englishmen in disguise with them." No authority ever again mentioned English infiltrators. Instead, in March 1730 Périer began evoking a "general conspiracy against the French of this colony," led by another of France's traditional enemies, the Chickasaw, who, he claimed, had convinced the Choctaw to participate and "advised the Natchez to attack us."

But already on August 7, 1730, an officer who, unlike Périer, had firsthand experience at Natchez, Ignace François Broutin, until 1727 commander at the post, wrote Indies Company officials with a radically different narrative: "I do not know the reasons that made M. Périer champion . . . a drunkard and a thoughtless man like Sieur de Chépart, who is the cause of the destruction [of Natchez]."[35] The commander at Mobile also soon sent dispatches mocking Périer's conspiracy theory. French authorities quickly came to believe that Périer had invented the conspiracy to cover up Chépart's blunders.[36]

Although news of Natchez circulated in private correspondences, the French public was officially notified of the country's loss only two years after the fact. The first account of what the Parisian press termed "the massacre" to appear in print was published in the September 1731 issue of *Le Mercure de France*, the new name for the very periodical chosen by Law in 1719 as a vehicle for his propaganda about the prosperity guaranteed all settlers in "the enchanted land" of Louisiana. Even then, the gazette glossed over "the massacre" and focused on "the defeat of the Natchez" and France's victory in the military campaign carried out in 1730 "to avenge the French nation." The account by Father Le Petit published that same year in a Jesuit periodical adopted a similar strategy.[37]

They could hardly have been expected to do otherwise. No eyewitness testimony had yet surfaced in print; no one had publicly questioned Périer's explanations. The stage seemed set for the story of Natchez to be enshrined in history as a celebration of the French triumph over Native American brutality.

Then came 1753 and the publication of Dumont's history, the first printed account with information not found in Périer's dispatches: his wife Marie Baron's memories of what had transpired.[38] The narrative opens on a preface in which Dumont promised to describe "the wars that the French were obliged to wage against the Indigenous People, whom we call Savages and who were first their friends and subsequently became their cruelest enemies, all by the fault of one man." Even Dumont's vocabulary strengthens his point that the Natchez were not naturally cruel savages and that one Frenchman alone was to blame for their attack. Rather than "*Sauvages*," or "Savages," the term used by French officials to refer to Indigenous peoples, Dumont describes the Natchez as "*les Naturels*," or "the natives or original inhabitants"—"the Originals."[39]

Still, Dumont in no way sought to minimize the extent of the Natchez's violence. Indeed, with Baron's help, he became the first to tell the story from an eyewitness perspective, to chronicle in vivid detail the torture and brutality the French inhabitants of Natchez had endured, all, he frequently repeated, because of Chépart's actions.

WHEN FATHER LE PETIT COMMENTED ON THE CEREMONIES PERformed in Saint-Louis Church in the spring of 1730, the missionary called the quick remarriages a sign that the women had "forgotten" all they had endured. Dumont offered a very different explanation for his union to Marie Baron: "I had never been able to repay [my fellow godparent] for her generosity toward me; I saw no better way to satisfy this debt."[40] In this time of crisis, when Indies Company officials were thinking only of the bottom line, Dumont conceived "debt" as what was morally right. He farmed property on the Mississippi above New Orleans and could offer Baron a chance to rebuild her life.

Marie Baron did just that.

The couple's first child, Marie Anne Françoise, was baptized on November 23, 1731. In late 1732, when Marie Baron was pregnant again, a fire destroyed their farm. They moved to New Orleans, where their son, named Jean François for his godfather, Jean François Gautreau, the new keeper of the company's storehouse, was baptized on January 5, 1733. That July 28, they buried one of the youngest Natchez survivors, Baron's son, Jean Charles Roussin, age six.

Even though Dumont insists that they "lived the life of city dwellers," theirs seems a rather bucolic existence. Dumont left an image of their property, shown in Figure 17. It was probably situated near the corner of Orléans and Dauphine at the city's northern edge, where lots faced onto the wilderness beyond.[41] Dumont depicted their house, the kitchen where an enslaved African helped prepare rice and corn flour, their extensive gardens, even a ladder concocted so that their chickens could climb up a tree to roost. Dumont sold

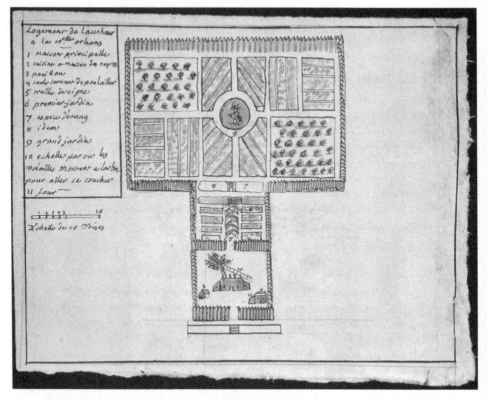

Figure 17. Dumont's rendering of the home he shared in New Orleans with his wife, Marie Baron, and their children.

vegetables. They raised turkeys, ducks, and chickens and, until 1737, led a quiet life.

That January 19, Dumont penned in his characteristic hand a petition accusing neighbors of stealing their vegetables. All spring long, he experienced various small financial headaches, because Indies Company authorities were trying to call in a debt, even though he had done work for them and had never been paid and contended that the two cancelled each other out.[42]

"Tired of living in a country like that," as he put it, at two p.m. on June 12, 1737, Dumont, Marie Baron, and their two children boarded the royal vessel the *Somme* for a return voyage to the country that had deported Baron nearly eighteen years before. Dumont had served as a commissioned officer in both the Royal Army and the Royal Navy, so his board was paid for by the nation that had exiled his wife. To feed their children, they embarked with a cow, a calf, three dozen chickens, and two dozen turkeys. On August 17, 1737, they reached Rochefort, where, in August 1719, the deportation saga had begun.

When Baron became the only deported woman known to have gone home to France, she made no attempt to conceal her identity and instead openly reclaimed her past. But there was one limit to her candor. When Dumont composed his memoirs and wished to reveal his source "for all the details" of what happened in Natchez, he said only *"mon épouse,"* "my wife," rather than using Baron's name, and he thereby avoided disclosing in print the fact that a woman exiled in perpetuity had returned to her native land.

In September, the family traveled first to the village of Le Mesnil-Thomas, where in April 1703 Marie had been born and where in May 1710 she had watched her father's burial in a pauper's grave, and then to her mother's birthplace, Verneuil, where Marie was reunited with her favorite cousin and other relatives. They spent the following year and a half in Paris, Dumont's "beloved hometown," of which Marie Baron surely had less fond memories, and where Dumont began the memoirs on which his history was based.[43]

The couple settled in Brittany, on the coast from which *La Mutine* had embarked, in Port-Louis and Lorient. On January 4, 1748, their daughter, age seventeen, married in Port-Louis—and unlike her mother, Marie Anne Françoise could sign her name. Their son followed in his father's footsteps and went to sea, and in 1749, he sailed to the Indian Ocean, to Île de France, today's Mauritius. On March 31, 1754, a year after the publication of Dumont's *Historical Memoirs on Louisiana*, he and Baron also traveled to Mauritius, on the Indies Company ship *La Paix*, the *Peace*. In contrast to the puny *La Mutine*, the *Peace* was a proper seafaring vessel, seven hundred tons. On its manifest, Dumont, passenger 171, was listed as *"à la table avec sa femme."* A woman who had first crossed an ocean chained below deck had the privilege of taking her meals at the captain's table, where she and Dumont dined alongside Captain Denis Bécard and three junior navy officers.

Their next voyage, on June 12, 1755, on an Indies Company vessel named *Le Bourbon*, took them from Mauritius to Pondicherry, where they arrived on August 3. Pondicherry (today Puducherry) in southeast India had been a French colony since the late seventeenth century. Dumont died in India in 1760, perhaps during the confrontation between French and British forces in January of that year that was the decisive battle for control over southern India in the Seven Years' War. His estate was valued at 6,486 *livres*, a sum virtually identical to the annuity Geneviève Bettemont was then fighting for, and an amount that very few French officers who died in service managed to accumulate.[44] When Dumont's father, a prominent Parisian lawyer, died in Paris in 1718, he did not leave enough to provide for Dumont, his sixth son. But Dumont and Baron, while never wealthy, had lived comfortably—and still saved money for their children. For Marie Baron, whose family in the village of her birth might have escaped starvation with even 100 *livres*, those 6,500 *livres* were surely a princely sum and tangible evidence of all she had managed to accomplish because she had never accepted that any force—poverty, police corruption, a violent uprising—could impose limits on her life.

No record survives of the death of Marie Baron, the illiterate country girl who, alone among the deported women, managed first to go home again as though the police record fabricated for her by Bourlon and Pancatelin had never existed, and then to live the kind of cosmopolitan life experienced by very few women of her day, no matter what their social class.

Neither Natchez nor French Louisiana proved as resilient as Marie Baron.

During the months that followed the widows' release from captivity, the French continued to wage war, determined to destroy the Natchez and teach allied nations a lesson.[45] On February 2, 1731,

Périer returned from the Natchez war and had a *Te Deum* sung as he proclaimed himself "victorious."[46] Only scattered groups of Natchez survived the campaign, refugees who lived in isolation from each other and their ancestral lands. The Natchez nation never recovered from the devastation unleashed by Chépart's land grab.[47]

NOVEMBER 28, 1729, THE DAY OF THE NATCHEZ UPRISING, ALSO proved a day of reckoning for the entire colony. For years, engineers in charge of "the fortifications" at Natchez had begged for the funds necessary for proper defenses. On June 3, 1729, Indies Company directors met in Paris and at last ratified a plan "to build the fort of the Natchez of bricks."[48] By the time their directive reached the colony in late 1729, however, Fort Rosalie had been destroyed in the attack.

The company never again approved significant expenses for Natchez. Fort Rosalie was reestablished near what had been the Natchez's Great Temple, but it never became a proper fort. No significant agricultural projects of any kind were ever again attempted at the outpost. In the end, no one profited from those fertile fields—not their rightful possessors, and not the European usurpers.

Even before the uprising that obliterated Natchez, the Indies Company's balance sheet had become a burning issue in Parisian financial circles. More and more financiers became convinced that Louisiana should have been returned to the Crown when Law's system collapsed. Many even contended that the Indies Company would have flourished without Louisiana. The most pessimistic of all, those arguing that the colony's tobacco production would never become profitable, found new impetus when they learned that the two major concessions at Natchez had been wiped out and that one of their own, wealthy financier Kolly, among the original "Mississippi millionaires," was on the list of the dead.

Well before Périer's devastating campaign was over, the Indies Company capitulated. On January 22, 1731, a general assembly took place in Paris. The directors reported on lengthy "deliberations" reviewing all the company had done for the colony, including the 20 million *livres* it had spent to develop it, before concluding that "the massacre at Natchez had wiped out the most flourishing part of the colony and rendered all their hopes and efforts futile." With "great reluctance," the Indies Company offered to return Louisiana to the monarchy. On January 23, the Crown accepted. The decree agreeing to retrocession was signed "d'Aguesseau, Chancellor."[49] Three decades after he had overseen all decrees concerning Manon Fontaine's trial, d'Aguesseau served as chancellor of France and controlled the kingdom's entire judicial system.

For nearly two of the colony's three-decades-long history, its development had been controlled by financiers, the investors and speculators who now had officially pronounced Louisiana unworthy of their efforts. The financial machinations that had devastated the French economy and ruined countless investors; the myriad schemes, the arrest and deportation of alleged prostitutes among them; the havoc wreaked on Indigenous peoples and their territory, had come to naught—ultimately, because of November 28, 1729, in Natchez.

The French monarchy did not, at first, abandon the dream of Louisiana tobacco. Instead, production was transferred principally to Pointe Coupée, a settlement some 120 miles north of New Orleans, roughly halfway between the capital and Natchez. By 1734, the only tobacco exported from the colony was grown at Pointe Coupée.

Marie Baron was an eyewitness to November 28, 1729, the day that brought Natchez down. In the end, the story of Natchez became the story of French Louisiana.

Chapter 14

Pointe Coupée in the Shadow of Natchez

IN DECEMBER 1721, A FEW INDENTURED WORKERS HASTILY THREW up some palmetto-thatched shacks and cleared a bit of land to plant vegetables. These were the unprepossessing beginnings of an outpost situated midway between New Orleans and Natchez, still another place without a name hoping to take root in a colony in financial meltdown.[1]

In 1722, nearby flooding cut a bend off the Mississippi, creating "Fausse Rivière," "False River," a river that goes nowhere. French inhabitants soon called first the spot where the crescent-shaped meander begins and then the adjacent outpost "Pointe Coupée," "Cut-Off Point." The 1726 census marked the till-then nameless place's official baptism, its entry into Louisiana's record books: four households were counted at Pointe Coupée, where six men, three women, eight children, and four indentured servants occupied twenty-five acres of cleared land. Initially, life at Pointe Coupée was so uneventful that when they evoked the settlement at all, early commentators simply repeated the anecdote of the Mississippi's detour to explain the outpost's odd name and then moved on to places with a story worth telling.

Then came the Natchez uprising, the event that, nearly a decade after Pointe Coupée's founding, finally put the outpost firmly on the map. From then on, colonial administrators were forced to pay attention to it. They did so for one reason alone: to keep John Law's dream of Louisiana tobacco alive.

Two years on, in 1731, the number of European settlers remained unchanged: twenty-one. However, fifteen enslaved Africans now lived at Pointe Coupée as well. Tobacco production had been displaced there from Natchez, and slavery had arrived along with tobacco, a development that in the long run determined Pointe Coupée's place in history.

In 1731, initial signs were promising, and Pointe Coupée seemed poised to realize at last the dream of making tobacco the lynchpin of Louisiana's economy. That year, the colony exported nearly 100,000 pounds of tobacco. Hope, however, soon faded: first a powerful hurricane in 1732, then a drought in 1733, followed by torrential rains and windstorms, wreaked havoc on the crop's production. As a result, the yield in 1732 was under 75,000 pounds; in 1733, it was perhaps no more than 60,000—and the situation only worsened in the second half of the decade. From 1735 on, inspectors in France began rejecting Pointe Coupée tobacco because of its "bad odor," just as Cardinal Fleury had decried "the stench" of the 1727 crop from Natchez. At its finest hour, in the early 1740s, the settlement produced no more than 150,000 to 250,000 pounds a year, a far, far cry from the millions of pounds guaranteed by John Law in 1719.[2]

By planting a variety of crops—overwhelmingly corn, then beans, and little to no tobacco—residents nonetheless fared better there than in many spots. During the early years under the monarchy, although life at Pointe Coupée could not have been called eventful, the outpost did begin to prosper. A church was completed in 1738; from then on, a missionary was in residence. In 1744, Jean Joseph Delfau, Baron de Pontalba, became commander of the garrison: a sergeant and sixteen soldiers. By 1745, Pointe Coupée had assumed the identity of an official outpost with distinct civic and religious structures.

The settlement had also known significant growth: with 260 European inhabitants, Pointe Coupée in 1745 was larger than Natchez had been in 1729. There were sixty-one households of one sort or another. Some were large, multigenerational families; in others, several small families cohabited; one widower lived alone.

The outpost had known another, even more significant, expansion. Fifteen years after the lure of tobacco forever altered Pointe Coupée's course, three-quarters of all households were slaveholders, and Europeans no longer constituted the majority of the population: 426 enslaved Africans, 20 enslaved Native Americans, and 15 enslaved individuals of mixed race were counted. There had not been a single enslaved African in 1726; there were only 15 in 1731—and then, suddenly, there were 426 in 1745. That astonishingly rapid growth—more than twice as rapid as the rise in European inhabitants—transformed Pointe Coupée's identity. By the time Pointe Coupée became an established settlement, it had already become a major slaveowning community as well. No other outpost in the Lower Mississippi Valley had from the start this kind of intimate relation with the institution of slavery. In contrast, Mobile became a true community well before slavery reached Louisiana, and Natchez, where in 1726, 56 enslaved Africans worked on the two large concessions, was obliterated before the huge rise in numbers that Pointe Coupée knew beginning in the 1730s.

Landholdings at Pointe Coupée varied greatly in size, from 7 acres to 153. Just as was the case in other settlements along the Mississippi, small farmers, with 8 to 12 acres, were not always slaveholders and never major ones, whereas the owner of 153 acres relied on the labor

of 37 enslaved Africans, and the owner of 102 acres that of 40 enslaved individuals, predominantly enslaved Africans.[3]

Pointe Coupée was like Natchez in one crucial way: it bore no re-
semblance to a traditional village. There was no agglomeration, but
instead, as was the case along the German Coast, households were
strung out at varying intervals over a twenty-mile stretch along the
Mississippi, and neighbors lived in great isolation from each other.

Among the forty-seven Frenchwomen married to inhabitants, four
had traveled on *La Mutine*. Together, they represented a cross section
of Pointe Coupée. One of the most prominent residents, just as she
had been in Mobile and New Orleans, was Anne Françoise Rolland.
Lower in the hierarchy was the woman French authorities had always
called "Marie Moule." After her first husband, Captain, was killed at
Natchez, she remarried in New Orleans on May 7, 1731. And there,
she was at last able to name herself: "Marie Marguerite Moulié."

Marie Marguerite married Simon Calais, who, like Marie Avril's
husband, Tarascon, was a *voyageur* dealing in the fur trade with Native Americans, moving goods up and down the river in his dugout
canoe. The couple relocated to Pointe Coupée, where they did so well
that in 1739, they were able to settle Captain's debt with the Indies
Company a full year ahead of schedule. From then on, they could
keep all profits from Calais's trading, rather than handing them over
to the implacable company. In 1745, Calais, forty-six, and Moulié, by
then fifty, formed a ragtag household with another couple and their
four young children. But only months after the census that counted
them all was drawn up, Marie Marguerite Moulié, the lady's maid
who had been deported because the master of the house fell madly
in love with her, was dead—twenty-five years after she had arrived
in Louisiana and seventeen years after she had participated in "the
seditious desertion plot."

In Pointe Coupée in 1745, two deported women appeared in official records for the first time since reaching the colony in 1720. Pancatelin proposed the young woman who became *La Mutine* passenger

number 71 for deportation on grounds that were unusually expansive, even for her, calling her "a libertine addicted to all sorts of vices." The prisoner she described as "Marie Brière," age seventeen, was in reality "Madeleine Brière" and only fourteen when she was placed in irons. In Pointe Coupée, Madeleine, by then forty, was living with her husband, Jean Laage, fifty-five, and raising his son from a previous marriage. On August 21, 1749, in Natchez, Madeleine Brière witnessed the marriage of her stepdaughter, Marie, to Louis Marionneau, who in 1745 had resided in Pointe Coupée with his parents. Louis's mother, Jeanne Chagneau, was the stepdaughter of *La Mutine* survivor Jeanne Pouillot.

In Pointe Coupée in 1745, a second survivor was also part of a blended family: Marie Marguerite Sara, forty-eight, and her husband, Jacques Payere, fifty-eight, lived with her son from her first marriage in Louisiana, Pierre Dupont, thirteen. Pancatelin had leveled another wild allegation at Sara, calling her "a vagabond and an outright libertine." She had also neglected to point out that Sara had a husband and children in France. One manifest for *La Mutine* got her name right: otherwise, passenger 74 was officially known as "Catherine," the name used by Pancatelin. From the time the chain of prisoners left the Salpêtrière to the moment their ship made landfall, Marie Marguerite (a.k.a. "Catherine") Sara and passenger 75, Jeanne Coroy, future leader of the desertion plot, were chained together.

Within months of the 1745 census, Jacques Payere died. Soon after, on September 7, a marriage contract was signed. That day, Sara arranged for the marriage of her daughter, also named Marie Marguerite—one of the many children who had been left behind in France when their mothers were deported. Sara was the second survivor to have managed to locate a long-lost daughter and bring her across the ocean to Louisiana. The notary drawing up the contract described the bride as "*Dame,*" and several notables of Pointe Coupée signed alongside the woman they called "their friend, Dame Marie Marguerite Sara." Rather than her husband's status, as was true for some survivors, in Sara's case that honorific recognized her loyal friendship—and perhaps also her net worth, estimated at over 4,000 *livres*.[4] In Pointe Coupée, the slate invented by Pancatelin had been wiped clean.

One other woman in Pointe Coupée was granted this honorific: Anne Françoise Rolland. In her case, "*dame*," or "lady," testified to the prominent position she had long occupied in the settlement. Indeed, it was in Pointe Coupée that Anne Françoise spent by far the greatest part of her life in Louisiana, a total of at least twenty-two years. After her marriage to Laurent Bordelon, Anne Françoise Rolland maintained the residence in New Orleans that she had shared with Nicolas Sarazin.[5] At the same time, since Bordelon retained his Indies Company position even after the colony's retrocession to the Crown, the family lived at Natchez as well. The couple's first son, also named "Nicolas," described himself as a "native of Natchez," and at least until 1733, Bordelon continued to manage the company's storehouse there. That year, in a reenactment of Sarazin's problems in New Orleans, with complaints about his dishonesty mounting up, Bordelon was recalled to the capital for an investigation. Before it began, the company's representative admitted that Bordelon was unlikely to be terminated—because he was so poorly paid. His salary was a mere 500 *livres* per annum, for a position that typically paid 900. "I don't know how I would replace him," the representative admitted, "who would accept such a remote post at such a modest remuneration?"[6]

At the time of Anne Françoise's marriage with Laurent Bordelon, four children survived from her first marriage: a daughter, Françoise, died young, but Antoine, François, and Michel Sarazin all reached maturity. Although several children with Bordelon died in infancy, two sons became adults: Nicolas and Antoine. Laurent Bordelon himself probably died shortly before February 1737, when Anne Françoise wed for the third time. With six children to raise, she would not have remained single for long.

On February 22, 1737, in Pointe Coupée, a marriage contract was signed: Anne Françoise Rolland was marrying Jean Stefan, known as "Rocancourt," a Breton from the coastal region called Cornouaille.[7] In March, the bride rented out her New Orleans property and moved her children to Pointe Coupée. The groom called himself "a resident of Pointe Coupée," though the couple may well have met in Natchez, where Stefan was living at the time of the uprising.[8]

That's the sum total of what can be learned about Stefan's life prior to his marriage with Anne Françoise Rolland. From then on, however, his name popped up regularly in court records. Stefan may simply have been more in the public eye after his prominent marriage—or he may have been trying to test his newfound status with petty lawsuits designed to prove his importance. Stefan accused neighbors of shooting his livestock; the year after their wedding, he sued his chief witness, Pierre Germain, the biggest landowner in Pointe Coupée, with whom he had boarded while he was single, for nonpayment of debt. Germain countersued, claiming that Stefan in fact owed him money. Germain produced Stefan's promissory note as proof, and the judge decided in his favor.

Nonetheless, from September to November 1738, Stefan had two suits running simultaneously against Germain, for debt recovery and for reparation of honor. He contended that Germain had accosted Anne Françoise as she was waiting at the church for the priest to arrive, and had "told her that she was the wife of a scoundrel and a crook." Stefan even asked other inhabitants to furnish "proofs of insult." Because of this public squabble, doubtless the talk of Pointe Coupée that fall, Stefan was constantly traveling back and forth between Pointe Coupée and New Orleans, where his lawsuits were heard by Louisiana's Superior Council.[9]

The scene of the alleged insult was Pointe Coupée's brand-new church, Saint-François. And the timing of Stefan's litigation was certainly odd. The couple's first child, named "Anne" after her mother, was born on October 1, 1738, and christened on November 1. On the day of the alleged confrontation, Anne Françoise was surely meeting the priest to discuss her daughter's baptism, a ceremony that was likely delayed because the baby's father left immediately after her birth in order to appear in New Orleans on October 11, to allege that "his reputation had been maligned."[10]

A second daughter, Pétronille, called "Périne," was born on April 26, 1742. The 1745 census counted the couple, their two daughters, Anne's two sons by Bordelon, and six enslaved Africans living on 24 acres. One Sarazin son, François, had already moved to the distant Arkansas post, where he would spend his adult life. Antoine Sarazin, by then twenty-four, and his brother Michel, seventeen, were in Pointe Coupée, living independently on 3.4 acres with one enslaved African.

It's hard to know if that separate household was an early sign of the discord that soon reigned. By 1752, Antoine and François Sarazin—Michel had died in 1746—officially demanded their share of property owned by their father, Nicolas Sarazin, at the time of his death. They blamed Stefan for withholding information and requested that he be obliged to provide this accounting.[11]

From the late 1740s on, Anne Françoise Rolland's children were everywhere in Pointe Coupée. First, there were marriages, beginning with the Sarazins. In 1747, Antoine was wed. In 1752, François Sarazin married in Arkansas. Next came the Bordelons: on June 2, 1753, Nicolas married, followed by Antoine on June 2, 1759. Finally, the Stefans: Anne in May 1755, Périne in October 1757.

Baptisms soon followed. Nicolas Bordelon and Adrienne Rondeau's first child, Marie Anne, was born in March 1754; she was the oldest of seven. Antoine Bordelon and Marie Anne Decuir also had seven children, beginning in 1761, and Antoine fathered four additional offspring with his second wife. The next generation of Bordelon offspring was equally prolific: Nicolas's children had eight, nine, even thirteen children of their own.

Anne Françoise's husband, Laurent, was the only Bordelon to emigrate to Louisiana. So many Bordelons descended from his two sons that a small community some fifty miles from Pointe Coupée bears the name "Bordelonville." In the end, Anne Françoise Rolland left the kind of tangible mark on Louisiana normally associated with the likes of the Comte de Pontchartrain and the Duc d'Orléans.

Anne Stefan had nine children from her marriage to Jacques Deshautels. Because of these children and those of the daughters born to Nicolas and Antoine Bordelon, Anne Françoise Rolland's dynasty grew far beyond families bearing the Bordelon name.

It's less easy to assess Anne Françoise Rolland's financial legacy: Stefan consistently made it difficult for her heirs to claim their inheritances. On January 28, 1758, "Madame Anne Rolland," age sixty-one or sixty-two, was buried in her parish cemetery.[12] Only on May 29, 1759, did Stefan resolve the suit initiated seven years earlier by her Sarazin sons: each received the 2,193 *livres* due them, he alleged, from their father's estate. Later, in order to recover their share of their mother's property with Stefan, Anne and Périne were also obliged to sue their father, who in 1771, when Pointe Coupée was under Spanish rule, settled their claim by giving each 1,000 *pesos*, about 5,000 *livres*.[13]

Since they were hardly destitute, Rolland's children initiated those suits seeking justice. When Antoine, the last Sarazin son, died, his estate was divided between his half sisters, Anne and Périne, leaving each 2,500 *livres*. When Anne Stefan's estate was settled in 1778, her children inherited over 100,000 *livres*.[14]

Parents and children; heirs and estates. During the decades when the Bordelon and Stefan lines were proliferating, there is one striking absence: the continuation of the Sarazin line. François died in 1763, leaving no heirs. When Antoine Sarazin married on June 26, 1747, he chose status, as his mother did before him. And that choice may have had enormous long-term repercussions for Pointe Coupée and for Louisiana as well.

With over fifty acres to her name, Marie Colon, Antoine's bride, was a woman of means: standing up for her at their wedding was the most important person in Pointe Coupée, the post's commander,

Pontalba. Colon had recently lost her husband of nearly three decades, Jean Rondeau. They had had at least six daughters together, two of whom still lived with their mother. Another daughter became Nicolas Bordelon's wife, while Antoine Bordelon married Marie Colon's granddaughter.

The match between Antoine Sarazin and Marie Colon was an unequal one: Colon was thirty-nine, Antoine twenty-six, barely half her deceased husband's age. Her possessions were evaluated at 19,000 *livres*, his at 5,000. She was illiterate; he wrote with ease.[15] Men rarely contracted such marriages, but women who found themselves in Antoine's situation and in similarly unbalanced partnerships were usually trying to better their lot, as Antoine's mother had done on two occasions. If this was Antoine's intention, his decision may well have come back to haunt him.

ALL DURING THE YEARS WHEN ANTOINE'S HALF SIBLINGS WERE having numerous children, including with Colon's daughter and granddaughter, Antoine and Marie had none of their own. Beginning in 1753, five years after he married, however, Antoine Sarazin did father children.

That May 29, a baby was baptized in Pointe Coupée's Saint-François Church and named Antoine. The baby's mother, Marie Jeanne, no last name given, was identified as "the slave of Antoine Sarazin." Marie Jeanne's mother was the enslaved Native American woman included on the 1745 census as the property of Jean Rondeau and Marie Colon; Marie Jeanne's father was an enslaved African. The child of enslaved persons, Marie Jeanne herself became a slave, technically the property of Marie Colon, but also that of Colon's husband, Antoine Sarazin. Baby Antoine's baptismal certificate was marked "*le père est inconnu,*" "the father is unknown," the same formula found on the baptismal record of the baby named Nicolas born to Anne Françoise Rolland in 1730, when Antoine Sarazin was about eight. This time, the father's identity was no mystery, for subsequently the child consistently referred to Antoine Sarazin as "my father."[16] Antoine Bordelon and Anne Stefan, half siblings of the baby's father, served as godparents in a ceremony close to official recognition of a multiracial child.[17]

It's impossible to determine how exceptional, or common, the situation of Anne Françoise Rolland's first Sarazin grandchild may have been. Early Pointe Coupée is frequently described as a place without a rigid social hierarchy, where racial mixing and intimate relations across racial lines were particularly prevalent, even one where acceptance of mixed-blood children was widespread, and the settlement's remoteness has been evoked to explain this blurring of categories.[18] But however accepting the world around him may have been, Antoine Sarazin's son, at birth officially classified as "mulatto," was born into slavery.

On February 25, 1764, Antoine Sarazin died.[19] His eleven-year-old son and his son's mother became the property of his half sister, Périne Stefan. In 1771, the other half sister, Anne Stefan, Antoine's aunt and godmother, purchased Antoine from Périne for 400 *piastres*, about 2,100 *livres*.[20]

By then, the colony was no longer under French control. Under the terms of the 1763 Treaty of Paris, which marked the end of the Seven Years' War, France had yielded settlements east of the Mississippi to England, while New Orleans, Pointe Coupée, and posts west of the river passed under Spanish rule. The division had various repercussions for Antoine Sarazin's son. Under Spanish law, the enslavement of Native Americans was prohibited, and in 1769, a decree published in Spanish Louisiana proclaimed that enslaved Native Americans could no longer be sold and could only be freed. Beginning in 1770, a new document came into use, a formal recognition of manumission. Thereafter, in Pointe Coupée enslaved Native Americans, and enslaved Africans as well, increasingly petitioned—often successfully— for their freedom.[21]

On September 19, 1773, the day before his owner, Anne Stefan, was buried, "Antoine Sarazin, mulatto," age twenty, initiated this process.

Calling himself "the son of her brother," Antoine argued that Stefan had forgotten to include in the will she had drawn up on September 13 a "declaration that she had often made in the presence of witnesses": "she had purchased him from M. de la Mothe [Périne's husband], her brother-in-law, solely in order to grant him his freedom."[22]

Anne Françoise Rolland's grandson made his case eloquently. When Anne Stefan was on her deathbed, he explained, she had gathered her husband; her half brother and his uncle and godfather, Antoine Bordelon; and various friends to explain "her last wishes"— that Antoine become a free man. All those present on September 19 signed a statement to this effect.

A prolonged judicial procedure ensued. One after another, those who witnessed Anne Stefan's death were called in; each testified that Antoine's statement was correct. Each was also obliged to admit, however, that Stefan had not had "a proper declaration" drawn up by a notary. Each in turn, they explained that this would not have been possible in September 1773, as no notary resided in Pointe Coupée, and the post's commander was absent. Finally, on June 14, 1775, a verdict: authorities in New Orleans had decided that the witnesses were "too intimate" with the deceased to give admissible evidence and ruled the absence of a notarized declaration decisive.

"Antoine mulatto" thus remained legally a slave—with an ambiguous status. Although in the probate inventory of Anne Stefan's property, he was described as "belonging" to her estate, Antoine was not listed with the enslaved Africans evaluated alongside other assets. Anne Rolland's Sarazin grandson is featured, however, in that lengthy document: notaries' fees incurred because of "the incident of the mulatto Antoine's pretensions to freedom" were recorded. Those 260 *livres* of debt were a mere drop in the bucket, since Stefan's children, Anne Rolland's legitimate grandchildren, inherited over 100,000 *livres*.[23]

Stefan's holdings were finally divided up in 1778, just as the wave of revolutions that swept the world in the final decades of the eighteenth century began to affect Louisiana. In that 1778 division of property, Antoine's fate is not specified, but by early 1795, Antoine Sarazin, age forty-one, was no longer in legal limbo.[24] He was the property of Julien Poydras, a New Orleans businessman with extensive holdings in Pointe Coupée.[25]

Antoine's father, like every other Sarazin, Bordelon, and Stefan, male and female, was well-educated, able to write with ease. "Antoine Sarazin, mulatto," was illiterate. However, just as he had monitored the contents of Anne Stefan's will, Antoine followed events from far-flung corners of the globe. And he knew that after the French Revolution in 1789 and the abolition of slavery by the French Republic in 1794, the institution of slavery was being openly and widely contested.

POINTE COUPÉE CAME INTO ITS OWN AS A CONSEQUENCE OF THE Natchez uprising of 1729, so it's perhaps fitting that the settlement only truly entered the pages of history because of what is known as the Pointe Coupée uprising of 1795. That attempt to bring to Louisiana the revolution ultimately led in Saint-Domingue by Toussaint Louverture, who in 1777 had obtained his legal freedom, was initiated by Antoine Sarazin.

In the aftermath of the French Revolution of 1789, Louisiana's economy went into free fall. When the market for the colony's export crops dried up suddenly, Pointe Coupée was particularly hard-hit. At the same moment, slave unrest began there, and an uprising was aborted in 1791, just before the first major revolt in Saint-Domingue. A new governor general of Spanish Louisiana, Francisco Luis Hector, Baron de Carondelet, took up his functions in December 1791. The following month, he forbade the importation of enslaved Africans from the French Caribbean, for fear that they might bring revolutionary ideas to Louisiana.[26]

By 1792, insurrectionary forces controlled a third of Saint-Domingue, and on August 29, 1793, the island's French commissioners freed some of its enslaved population. On February 4, 1794,

in Paris, the revolutionary government, the National Convention, officially abolished slavery in all French colonies. Reports of abolition
spread quickly to French possessions in the Caribbean islands, where
slave revolts broke out widely in 1795.

Word soon reached New Orleans and from there moved upriver.
Antoine Sarazin reported, for example, this conversation from early
1795: he overheard an enslaved African on a boat heading for Natchez
proclaim that "all slaves had now been freed *par le Roy*," "by order of
the king," referring to that 1794 proclamation of the National Convention.[27] Louisiana was no longer under French rule, and after Louis
XVI's execution on January 21, 1793, France was no longer governed
by a monarchy, but in the minds of former French subjects like Antoine Sarazin, that traditional phrase, *"par le Roy,"* resonated still
whenever dictates involving French subjects were proclaimed. Did
Antoine know that his paternal grandmother had been deported "by
order of the king"?

On April 9, 1795, rumors of an uprising planned for the night of
April 12 reached Captain Duparc, commander of Pointe Coupée.[28]
Antoine Sarazin was among the first to be arrested. Although en-
slaved Africans from at least five Pointe Coupée plantations, as well
as from the German Coast and spots as distant as New Orleans and
Natchez, were implicated, the landholding of Antoine's owner, Julien
Poydras, was considered the mutiny's epicenter. And the operation's
command center, where conspirators gathered to share information
about "the liberation of all slaves," was said to be *"la cabane d'Antoine
Sarazin,"* "Antoine Sarazin's cabin."[29]

A state of emergency was declared; soldiers were rushed to Pointe
Coupée from Natchez and other posts; troops from Havana were dispatched to Louisiana. After the number of arrests mounted to about
sixty, transport boats became floating prisons, and Antoine Sarazin
was held in shackles on one of them.

The process used at the dawn of the eighteenth century at Manon
Fontaine's murder trial still applied in Louisiana at the century's end:

Antoine was first interrogated and then "confronted" with other suspects. Most were identified as "André, who belonged to Colin Latour" or "Michel, who belonged to Charles Dufour." Only one other had a surname: Louis Bordelon.[30] Even though two of her grandchildren were implicated, the name of Anne Françoise Rolland was never evoked.

Unlike Manon Fontaine's, this trial ended in the manner preferred by the French judicial system: with a confession. On May 16, 1795, "the man known as Sarazin" admitted to plotting to bring the Haitian Revolution to Louisiana. In order "to accomplish what had been done *au Cap* [at Cap-Français, the capital of Saint-Domingue] to obtain freeedom for all slaves," he "had attempted to commit the crime of revolution." Antoine acknowledged that he understood that his punishment would be hanging.

In the end, some twenty-six enslaved men were convicted and executed. The first hangings took place at Pointe Coupée on May 29. A boat named *La Victoire*, the *Victory*, then left for New Orleans, and executions continued along the way. As a warning to would-be revolutionaries, the men's heads were cut off and displayed on stakes at intervals along the Mississippi from Pointe Coupée to New Orleans.

On June 1, 1795, Governor Carondelet announced measures designed to keep Louisiana safe from "the horrors that have ruined the French colonies." These ranged from banning all gatherings of enslaved persons to promising any enslaved person who reported a conspiracy being planned freedom and 1500 *livres*.[31]

By 1795, like the French before them, Spanish authorities were losing interest in a colony that still had not begun to fulfill the golden dreams of substantial revenue first spun by John Law. Since 1719, tobacco had been the focal point of those promises, and Louisiana tobacco had never proved up to snuff. In addition, tobacco's production center, Pointe Coupée, had become a hotbed of unrest, and costly measures were required to police the labor force always considered essential to tobacco's cultivation. The Pointe Coupée uprising made Spanish authorities acutely aware that the violence of Saint-Domingue could easily be reignited in Louisiana. By late 1795, Spanish withdrawal from a colony that it viewed as "cost[ing] us more than it is worth" had become inevitable.[32]

The late 1790s heightened that awareness. Uprisings broke out all over the colony. Grandchildren of many deported women—including Marie Anne Benoist, Marie Anne Fourchet, Jeanne Pouillot, and Anne Françoise Rolland—fought on various sides. Many hoped thereby to return Louisiana to French rule, hopes that were fueled by the rumors of retrocession to France that were already circulating in 1796.

Finally, on October 1, 1800, Spain signed a secret agreement with the French Republic, exchanging Spanish Louisiana for territory in Tuscany.[33] Napoleon Bonaparte then began his short-lived dream of reconstructing the French colonial empire. By the time the transfer of power became official in October 1803, however, Napoleon had also had enough.

In 1801–1802, Bonaparte sent fifty thousand soldiers to Saint-Domingue to defeat the rebels and restore both French rule and slavery, but even that immense army ultimately failed to put down the Saint-Domingue revolt. After the French incurred a final defeat in November 1803, Haitian sovereignty was soon proclaimed. Well before he was vanquished in Haiti, Napoleon had abandoned his plans to reconstruct the French empire in the Mississippi Valley.

In April 1803, an agreement was signed in Paris. With "the Sale of Louisiana," the United States acquired all French territory on the North American continent and gained free navigation on a vital trade route, the entire span of the Mississippi.

After a seditious century—New Orleans in 1728, Natchez in 1729, Pointe Coupée in 1795, with countless other uprisings, insurrections, revolts, and rebellions in between—the colony founded in 1699, the year of Manon Fontaine's arrest for that mysterious murder at Paris's Saint-Honoré gate, had come to an end.

Chapter 15

The End of the Women's Era

WELL BEFORE THE SEDITIOUS CENTURY ENDED AND AT A TIME when most of the women who had survived deportation were still alive, beginning in 1724, Indies Company officials compiled an annual list of deaths in the colony. Beginning in 1726, those tallies concluded with information about specific individuals who had traveled to Louisiana in 1719 and 1720. Having had no news of them, their families in France had asked company administrators to inquire about their fates. The reports sent back to Paris from the colony were often dire: "The man named Balmont was scalped at the Yazou post."[1]

Only once did a family inquire about a deported woman. *La Mutine* passenger 131, Anne Madeleine Dienne, was incarcerated in August 1719, after her parents, pleading "extreme poverty," alleged that "their lives were in danger" because their twenty-three-year-old daughter "had threatened to have [them] assassinated." They beseeched Machault to put Anne Madeleine away "for the rest of her days."

But in September 1728, Dienne's mother, Madeleine La Vigne, by then a widow, contacted Machault's successor, René Du Herault, with a very different request. She claimed to have accused her daughter of but "a tiny bit of wrongdoing" and feigned amazement that, for such a peccadillo, Anne Madeleine "had been taken to Mississippi or Louisiana." She begged that her only child be returned to France, because her father's sister had just died and left Anne Madeleine "a very large inheritance that no one can collect in her place." The widow explained that she needed the money "in order to live comfortably." On September 20, Herault authorized a one-off document: a "*rappel des îles*," or "return from the islands." But there could be no return for Anne Madeleine Dienne, since nothing indicates that passenger number 131 was among the women who survived the crossing on *La Mutine*.[2]

Nearly a decade after the women's arrests in the heat of investment fever, for a deported woman's mother and the Parisian police alike, the women of *La Mutine* remained just what they had been in 1719, mere "merchandise," their fates purely financial transactions.

The same was true of the territory in which the women of *Les Deux Frères* and *La Mutine* had been deposited like still more of the substandard merchandise that Indies Company officials consistently shipped to Louisiana. From the moment Louisiana caught John Law's eye, the colony was no longer valued as a geopolitical prize but instead for its potential for instant wealth. Everyone sought to maximize profits in every way possible. For this reason, whether they represented the monarchy, Crozat, or an incarnation of the Indies Company, through the decades those who administered the colony's finances tried to do so on the cheap. Even though Louisiana's governors repeated the same requests year after year, the authorities controlling the supply chain rarely sent clothing or shoes for soldiers, medicine and blankets, food for starving colonists, or basic equipment to help them grow their own. Much of what they did send had either been badly damaged in transit or was of such poor quality that it was virtually useless.

In the long run, administrators did spend considerable sums on military installations—but mainly because they had been so penny-pinching at the start. Officials in Paris kept an eye solely on the short-term bottom line and rarely concerned themselves with such basic questions as whether the garrisons at Natchez and Natchitoches were large enough or whether Mobile's fort was strong enough. As Governor Périer wrote Maurepas in November 1730, the Indies Company had consistently refused to consider that "annual repairs on [fortifications consisting of stakes driven into the ground] have cost much more than if they had been built of masonry from the start."[3]

Most critical of all, the powerful financiers who used Louisiana as a pawn in their get-rich-quick schemes never bothered to understand the basic economic realities of the commodity on which those schemes were founded. Labor was costly in Louisiana, and freight was dear. Rather than revisiting Law's predictions for a tobacco-based economy, they continued to guarantee that Louisiana tobacco could be priced to compete in the French market with Virginia tobacco, which was grown in an established colony with an experienced workforce, a colony closer to Europe and therefore with cheaper transport rates.

Those on the ground—ships' captains, for instance—saw things differently. Once tobacco production did develop, many refused to transport this financial albatross back to France. They carried instead wood from Louisiana to the French islands in the Caribbean, where they filled their vessels with the most valuable commodity in eighteenth-century Europe: sugar.

While the French government consistently subsidized the production of sugar in the Caribbean, it spent little on Louisiana's economic development.[4] When the Indies Company returned the territory to the Crown in 1731, the situation for colonists remained as dire as in the immediate aftermath of the implosion of Law's system a decade earlier.

In 1733, the commander at Mobile warned that "our farmers and merchants are dying of hunger, and those in New Orleans are no better off. Many are begging to return to France; others conspire to escape to join the Spanish at Pensacola. The colony is on the verge of being depopulated." In 1738, Louisiana's chief financial officer cautioned that many settlers had already fled and many more were sailing that year. By 1740, one of innumerable "Reports on the Colony of Louisiana" concluded, "It is too expensive to be held onto. . . . The colony is disintegrating." In March 1757, the final governor of French Louisiana, Louis Billouart de Kerlérec, advised Machault, who was still in power, that "no ship has arrived here from France for a long time. . . . The colony is in dire need of everything." By August 1758, nothing had changed, and Kerlérec warned, "Our situation is ever more critical."[5]

Already in early 1721, Franquet de Chaville, the young engineer chosen to help design New Orleans, had grasped the fundamental problems at play in Louisiana and laid the blame squarely at the feet of the Indies Company as it had taken shape under John Law's control. That "grand name" had encouraged him and his fellow engineers to trust the promises made them and believe that they would be well treated. In fact, it had all been a sham. A Law crony, newly rich on stock market gains, was in charge of supplies. He had no interest whatsoever in the colony and sought only to increase his profits. In Franquet's assessment, Law's values had doomed Louisiana. In order to survive, he argued, the colony required a complete reboot.[6]

But every time the colony changed hands, at every "retrocession," no one stepped up to redesign Louisiana's economic underpinnings and to found it on something more vital than a get-rich-quick scheme. No minister ever attempted to build an enduring colony rather than a mere mirage.

Throughout the history of French Louisiana, oversight was cruelly lacking. Just as happened when Lieutenant Général Machault simply let Pancatelin and Bourlon have their way with the deportation scheme without keeping an eye on their methods, so it was from then on. Colonists died en masse; desperately needed supplies rotted in transit; soldiers without shoes or ammunition were expected to defend crumbling forts. The occasional corrupt official was put on trial, but there seems to have been no institutional memory, and as a result, time and again the same disastrous errors were repeated. *Plus ça change.*

Rather than debating the justifications for Louisiana's existence and the investments required to meet those goals, those controlling the purse strings persistently laid the colony's failure at the feet of its inhabitants. What could anyone expect, they argued, when you were dealing with the convicts, vagabonds, ne'er-do-wells, misfits, and prostitutes who, they claimed, formed the core of Louisiana's original European population?

Against this backdrop of widespread economic disaster, survivors' achievements seem all the more remarkable. North to south, east to west, up and down the Mississippi, in all the major settlements and most of the small ones as well, survivors made lives for themselves. Some, like Marie Anne Benoist and Marie Anne Fourchet, founded dynasties with extraordinary reach: any family that traces its origins to any part of French Louisiana quite likely has ancestors who either married into one of these families or were bound to one by close ties of friendship or alliance. By now, descendants of deported women can be found all over this country. Some women, like Geneviève Bettemont and Marie Daudin, built substantial estates. Some women merely held on, and in those times, this alone was a notable achievement.

In 1731, the Indies Company gave up in defeat on the place it had promoted in 1719 as "laden with gold and silver mines," "an enchanted land where every seed one sows multiplies a hundredfold." Although New Orleans by then boasted a few buildings of more advanced construction, including a handful in brick, the map produced by Gonichon in December 1731 shows that the capital that had sprung from John Law's machinations still blended seamlessly into untamed nature, the woods and swamps that had not yet been cleared so that the city's limits could be extended. It also remained small— even in 1763, when Philadelphia boasted over seventeen thousand inhabitants, and Charleston, the destination chosen by many early deserters from Louisiana, about 11,000 residents, New Orleans had not even twenty-five hundred.[7]

In 1731, the original residents who had survived the plagues and massive food shortages of the 1720s sometimes still inhabited the rudimentary dwellings they had built with their own hands at the start. Those who, like Manon Fontaine, lived near New Orleans's northern edge were far closer to absolute wilderness than to the apex of urban civilization in Louisiana: the Place d'Armes and the surrounding public edifices, especially the biggest and grandest of them all, the no-expenses-spared headquarters of the Indies Company, a highly visible reminder of "the company's" stranglehold over the colony. That edifice even featured a costly hallmark of contemporary Parisian architecture, perhaps the sole architectural frivolity in a land where shingles and tiles remained prohibitive: elegant wrought-iron balconies. Le Blond de La Tour, chief planner of New Orleans, pronounced the result "the most beautiful building that has yet been seen in the colonies."[8]

THE HISTORY OF COLONIAL LOUISIANA IS USUALLY DELIMITED IN terms of regime change: the Crozat years, the Law years, the French monarchy's direct rule. The passing of the women who had come to the colony on *Les Deux Frères* and *La Mutine* demarcates its history in a very different manner. Their deaths denoted the endpoint of the violent and fundamentally illegal deportation that was woven into the fabric of French Louisiana.

A few of the women who had been chained together in 1719 lived long lives for the period and particularly for a colony where climate and infectious diseases cut life spans brutally short: Anne Françoise Rolland, sixty-one when she died in 1758; Marie Daudin, sixty-eight at the time of her death in 1768. Marie Anne Grise was surely in her late sixties when she died in 1767. In 1784, when Geneviève Bettemont died at age seventy-nine, she demonstrated a rare longevity.

Geneviève's death also marked the end of an era. Geneviève Bettemont was the last survivor of all, the final witness to the financial madness of 1719 that facilitated the deportation of these women who had proved crucial to the birth of a colony. Geneviève was also the last eyewitness to all they had endured—the chain gang, the shackles, starvation on Ship Island. With her passing, the founding generation of deported women came to an end.

Manon Fontaine died well before many survivors, but her death in late 1734 was another milestone—among the three participants in the alleged "uprising" in the Salpêtrière with which the entire saga began, Manon was the only one to survive the voyage. She was thus the only woman to have witnessed every step in the deportation scheme.

Manon died on land she and Bourguignon had cleared with their bare hands when the first incarnation of New Orleans was wrenched from marshes and canebrakes. Manon's plot was tiny, officially described as a half lot, situated on Bourbon Street at the corner of Sainte-Anne. She died in the modest dwelling—by then classified as "a hut in poor condition"—that the couple had constructed themselves, with a picket fence around her small domain.

In 1699, the Parisian police had been so eager to pin a murder on the woman called "*la Bouquetière*," "the Flower Girl," that they neglected to ask the standard questions: name, age, address. In 1719, Pancatelin said she was thirty-eight, and since Manon's will does not indicate her age, we'll have to accept that she was about fifty-three when she died. The Parisian police decided that her name was "Marie La Fontaine," but when Manon died in New Orleans, that matter was resolved. Her will proclaims that the woman known to her friends as "Manon," was born "Marie Anne Fontaine."

Burial records for 1734 are sketchy, so the exact date of her death is unknown.[9] On July 16, Manon sensed that the end was near. She followed legal procedure carefully, just as she had all her life when dealing with the law. She could not afford a notary's fee, so she gathered three friends as witnesses to her will.[10] One of them took dictation, and all signed, acknowledging the authenticity of the will of the woman they referred to as "Dame Marianne Fontaine." Witnesses were essential since Manon herself, "*ne sachant signer*," "not knowing how to sign her name," could only make what the will calls, using the formula required to make it legal, "her usual mark." In the case of "Dame Marianne Fontaine," this was but a simple and rudimentary cross.

The ability to sign one's name is a standard measure of literacy. Time and again, Manon Fontaine demonstrated the inadequacy of all common notions of literacy. She may have been capable of making only a rough mark, but she had a gift for language. Her unique voice always made itself heard on the rare occasions when she was allowed to speak for herself, and her testament is no exception. Manon began with the traditional reference to the soundness of her mind and body, but even there, she added her own twist, describing herself as "*de bon sang*," literally "of good blood," an uncommon phrase that signified born to honorable people, and therefore declaring herself incapable of dishonorable actions.

From itinerant flower girl to "*dame.*" This unlikely trajectory had been possible because, after fifteen years in New Orleans, her friends knew her to be just that: honorable and worthy of respect. "Nobility

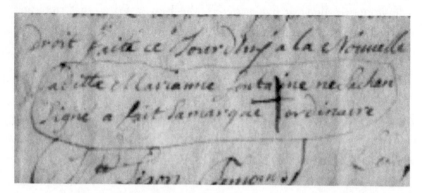

Figure 18. The mark made by Manon Fontaine on her last will and testament.

can be acquired by good acts," in the words of the official dictionary of the French language first published just when Louisiana was founded, and Manon proved that, at least in 1734 and in a land across the ocean where French was the dominant language, that idea held true.[11]

Manon's "good blood" and "fine deeds" are evident in every detail of her will. She had been a loyal friend to many; in her final years, they had loaned money and extended credit. Manon listed every debt: six *livres* to the baker who had brought her bread, 12 to fellow deportee Marie Madeleine Brière to repay a loan. To reimburse them all, she used her only treasure: land. She bequeathed the half lot and house where she lived to her executor, Hugues Marquian, son of a friend to whom she owned money, and asked him to settle her debts. Her four additional lots she parceled out: to a friend "for services rendered during her last illness," another to the friend "who continues to help me every day."

Manon knew that times had changed and that in 1734 New Orleans, property was purchased and no longer attributed in exchange for clearing the land. She affirmed that all lots belonged to her "*de bon droit*," in a valid, legal manner. After her death, Manon's land transitioned into the new system. The legitimacy of Manon's will was recognized, and on April 2, 1735, Marquian sold her home to Joseph Lequintrek for 50 *livres*.

The mid-1730s marked the end of the founding era for New Orleans as well, the moment when the few remaining rough-hewn cabins erected by its original settlers were razed to make way for more orthodox urban dwellings. But the foundation of New Orleans, the land on which those cabins had been erected and on which many newer houses have since been built, remains marked by the survivors like Manon Fontaine who had cleared it with their bare hands.

ON DECEMBER 28, 1700, WHEN A MAN WAS FOUND KNIFED TO death in Paris with those never-to-be-explained "five small pieces of raw beef" in his pocket, a process was set in motion that ended exactly thirty-four years later with the passing in another French capital of the woman falsely accused of his murder. It's ironic that the story of Manon Fontaine and ultimately of all the deported women began with a new century, one now known as the Age of Enlightenment. It's also ironic that their story began in Paris, the city always portrayed as the epicenter of a more philosophically and socially aware Europe. The finest legal minds of an age moving toward an increasingly enlightened approach to crime and its punishment never questioned the legitimacy, much less the humanity, of the brutal measures officially authorized at the highest levels of the French state to deal with the women who were shipped off to Louisiana.

It was surely obvious to such legal authorities that Marguerite Pancatelin's allegations about Manon Fontaine's responsibility for a sedition in the Salpêtrière were a fabrication. In addition, these men—all of whom had ready access to the original documents she purported to cite—could easily have verified that her pronouncement that Manon was guilty of "having knifed fifteen men to death" was a pure invention.[12] But no authority ever bothered to look into any accusation of criminal behavior. Instead, they continued to approve every successive punishment proposed for the women transported to Louisiana.

Less than a year after the "sedition" she had allegedly started in a Parisian prison, Manon Fontaine was discarded on distant shores. The rest is history, the history of the colony the French named "Louisiana." Manon and her fellow deportees on *Les Deux Frères* and *La Mutine* were forgotten, because it was more convenient for inept and ruthless administrators to invent new fictions and to claim that most died quickly, that few had married and fewer had had children, than to account for survivors who were making honorable lives in the colony.

Coda

IS A MISCARRIAGE OF JUSTICE ANY LESS GRIEVOUS BECAUSE IT TOOK place three centuries ago? Should the suffering inflicted upon Frenchwomen in 1719 remain buried if it affects the living—in this case, those among the tens of thousands descended from *La Mutine*'s convict women who are alive today? Don't their descendants deserve to know about the women who founded families and cities on these shores?

For decades, I've traveled to Paris, doing research on the period in seventeenth- and eighteenth-century France during which the deported women's lives unfolded. I always return to the Arsenal Library, usually to its signature collection, the archives of the Bastille and other Parisian prisons. One day, while looking for the file of someone arrested in 1719 whose name began with an *F*, I stumbled across a dossier marked "Fontaine (M.-A.)." Beneath that name someone had added in an ink now so faded that it is barely legible *"et autres prisonnières de la Salpêtrière pour la Louisiane"*—"and other female prisoners in the Salpêtrière for Louisiana."

I opened Fontaine (M.-A.)'s file only because of that last word: "Louisiana." What I found inside was no ordinary prison file. There was little information about the woman whose name was on the cover. Instead, the documents retraced the genesis of the deportation process—from the "sedition" in the Salpêtrière to the departure of the initial chain gang of women.

That day, I encountered for the first time vocabulary and expressions that I would soon find plastered all over key documents: "To rid the Salpêtrière of female prisoners," "to transport women to the islands." I watched as allegations that were patently ludicrous to begin with went unchallenged and became ever more inflated. I saw names appear or disappear from lists with no apparent reason. Virtually every deportation—save that of Manon Fontaine, the one woman whom Pancatelin never forgot—was a matter of chance. There was no rhyme or reason to the process, and anyone whose name was mentioned at any moment and by anyone might easily have been deported.

The manner in which the women in the Salpêtrière were described and moved about like pawns in a game shocked me then—and became only more shocking as the years went by and I began to uncover the real lives behind the names on Pancatelin's lists.

"Louisiana" jumped out at me that day for a simple reason: I grew up in southwest Louisiana not far from Pointe Coupée. As a child, I spent days on end with my paternal grandfather, a true Cajun, in his dugout canoe. I was once perhaps as comfortable in the bayous and the wetlands of that strange and fragile landscape as many deported women had grown to be over two centuries earlier.

Through the generations, everyone in my mother's family spoke French before they spoke English—until my generation, that is. I somehow became the last French speaker in a long line. This explains why, as my parents' generation aged, family members begged me to hold onto every reminder of earlier generations. No one else could read the letters and other records of our past.

I am not, however, the descendant of a deported woman. It was only years after I began reconstructing their lives that I first encountered a familiar family name: "Jean Gradenigo." In March 1766,

Gradenigo, a native of Venice who described himself as "a business-man," married Marguerite Krebs, a member of the Krebs–La Pointe dynasty of prominent, land-rich residents of the Mobile area. Two days later, Gradenigo was a witness at the next wedding celebrated in Mobile, that of Marie Anne Grise's daughter Louise Fièvre. From then on, Jean Gradenigo served as witness at the marriages of numerous descendants of survivors, including that of Céleste Roy, granddaughter of Nicolas Bordelon and Anne Françoise Rolland's great-granddaughter, in 1801.

Every time I encountered the name "Gradenigo," I remembered one such reminder of my family's past, a document that now resides in a closet of the study in which I wrote this book. It's a marriage contract, a type of record I often use in these pages to help understand the lives built by deported women in French Louisiana. One day, my favorite aunt handed me this document—or rather the crumbling fragments that remained of it—packaged in plastic wrap and asked me what it was. I had it restored so that I could transcribe it for her. I was then able to tell her about the groom, Charles François Génin. Génin, a goldsmith and watchmaker born in Mirecourt, France, a small town not far from Jeanne Mahou's birthplace, was the first of my mother's ancestors to emigrate from France. On October 25, 1825, he married Jean Gradenigo's granddaughter, Marguerite. Their wedding was celebrated in Opelousas, still another place named for a Native American nation. Opelousas became an official settlement only in about 1763, as the French were leaving Louisiana. I was born in Opelousas because Charles Génin and Marguerite Gradenigo raised a family there, as did generations of their descendants.

In French, when someone stands up for a bride or groom at their marriage, they become a *témoin* or witness. *"Ont témoigné avec nous,"* "they signed with us," was the formula traditionally used by the officiating priest just before he turned the parish register over to witnesses for their signatures. Their signatures affirm that those being married have presented themselves truthfully.

Every time Jean Gradenigo served as a witness to the identity of a deported woman's descendant, my family became an accessory to their lives. Like my distant ancestor, in the years after I discovered the prison dossier labeled "Fontaine (M.-A.)," I became a witness. I wrote this book to attest to the true identities of the deported women, to the fact that the identities recorded for them by the French judicial system were fabrications designed to serve the interests of a society corrupted by financial greed, and to the lives that survivors built against all odds in places that, as girls in France, they could never have imagined.

Acknowledgments

Every book is the product of collaboration, but a book completed during a pandemic requires, as I soon discovered, a network of collaborators both unusually large and, at times, simply unusual. As a result, the patchwork of colleagues and friends who proved indispensable in the making of this one is more far-flung and diverse than would normally have been the case. Archeologists, archivists, genealogists, librarians, experts in financial history and family history, specialists of New France and Old, long-time friends and recent ones, even a sprinkling of people I may never have the privilege of meeting in person but whom I have come to think of as friends because of their immediate and thorough willingness to help someone trying to complete a project at a moment when normal conditions suddenly became a thing of the past—all of them answered questions and offered opinions. In addition, since an essential phase of my research took place in 2020 when most libraries were shuttered and my university office was off-limits, some even scanned material to which I would otherwise not have had access. "Thank you" could never begin to cover the debt I owe them all.

Several archivists were essential to the development of this project. Karen Horton, archivist of the Archdiocese of Mobile, helped me verify numerous early sacramental records. Karen is the kind of archivist every scholar hopes to encounter: she is dedicated to her archive; she wants to help researchers get it right. I can't thank her enough for her generosity. Renée Richard and Amy Jones, archivists of the Diocese of Baton Rouge, similarly helped me check printed records against originals from the Pointe Coupée archives: without them, I would never have been sure of some intuitions. Alexandre Cojannot, Archives Nationales, had documents from the Minutier Central scanned; he personally verified that some documents were indeed missing. Claire Lesage of the Arsenal Library was a true colleague: Claire facilitated access to the Bastille Archives; she was always willing to share her knowledge and expertise. Claire helped make the many long days I spent digging in the Bastille Archives profitable and often fun as well.

Librarians helped in countless and often unexpected ways. Jane Shambra Harrison, Biloxi Public Library, shared information on subjects ranging from Ship Island to the Moran Burial Site and put me in touch with her contacts on the Gulf Coast. Jane also helped obtain scanned material for me during lockdown. Sheila Ketchum of Penn's Van Pelt Library worked miracles on more than one occasion and made resources available through Interlibrary Loan when I thought there was no hope of seeing material I needed badly. John Pollack of Van Pelt's Kislak Center had scans done for me in a hurry and made it easy for me to compare early histories of French Louisiana. Marsha Greer of the Singing River Genealogy–Local History Library, Pascagoula, managed to get an urgent scan to me during lockdown. Scott Jordon and Zachary Stein of the Edith Garland Dupré Library at the University of Louisiana at Lafayette made available digital copies from microfilms in their collections. Chris Lippa of Penn's Van Pelt Library worked magic on digital images from Paris's Archives de la Police, making it possible to read both hands in cases in which a sentence and an arrest record were superimposed. Andrea Gottschalk checked formats and prepared images. And Jim English, Cassandra Hradil, Stewart Varner, and Nicky Agate of Penn's Price Lab for the Digital Humanities devoted time and resources to the Gonichon map project.

Genealogical researchers came through on many occasions. Susan Laurent shared her extensive research, making it possible for me to double-check some of my findings. Susan's files are a wonderful resource. Robert Rousselle inspired me to investigate Jeanne Mahou's family in Saint-Dizier's archives: I thank him for encouraging me to explore lines of inquiry that I otherwise might have neglected. Robert Timon of the Société Généalogique de l'Yonne helped me trace the early lives of several women born in the Yonne—Marie Avril, Marie Daudin, Marie Grenet, Marie Francoise Le Coustelier—as well as two from distant regions—Jeanne Coroy and Jeanne Mahou—and even one woman's husband, Jean Melin. Robert's generosity is peerless, as is his scholarship.

Numerous researchers shared information of various kinds. Edmond Boudreaux graciously sent a digital copy of an important manuscript otherwise available only in an unreliable transcription. Gordon Sayre responded to many questions about Dumont's histories. The late Randall Ladnier was a wonderful interlocutor about *La Baleine*. John Styles helped me identify obscure textiles that showed up in Louisiana. Keith Luria provided important information that helped me interpret early marriage records in Mobile. Alex Dubé checked his database and found information that helped me better understand several husbands of survivors. Alex also provided an intriguing reference concerning Captain Ferret. Jeff Merrick ran names through volumes on the shelves in Paris's Archives Nationales on occasions when I wasn't able to get there. Larry Neal and François Velde answered questions about John Law and early modern finance. Colette Douroux was generous enough to photograph documents in the AG, just to help a friend of a friend.

Greg Waselkov was like a one-man, informal ILL during the lockdown of spring 2020. Greg always had answers to questions about subjects including archeological digs near Mobile, the architecture of the La Pointe–Krebs house, Louise Fièvre's property, Fort Toulouse and travel between Mobile and Fort Toulouse, the size of dugouts, building techniques in colonial Mobile—and the references to back them up. Greg shared files; he scanned books in his personal library: no one could have done more to help.

Some knew just the person I needed to contact and were happy to make introductions. Tom Klinger in particular was always obliging. Tommy Sokolosky-Wixon and his son Marks were a gold mine of information about the La Pointe–Krebs house. Erin Greenwald of the Louisiana Endowment for the Humanities put me in touch with Becky Smith of the Historic New Orleans Collection. Together, Becky and Erin helped me navigate the complexities of the Gonichon map of New Orleans.

Colleagues provided support and encouragement along the way. Lynne Farrington and John Pollack invited me to participate in a conference on frontier women. Erin Greenwald invited me to contribute work on Marie Baron to *64 Parishes*. Marc Flandreau asked me to contribute an essay to his journal, *Capitalism*.

I am lucky enough to know three researchers who seem to be able to read any early modern hand, no matter how difficult: Christian Baulez, Robert Descimon, and Philippe Florentin. In the days when I was still able to travel to Paris, whenever I was hopelessly stuck or unable to believe what I was finding, one of them was usually to be found in the reading room of Paris's Archives Nationales: they were always willing to have a go at the passage that was driving me crazy.

A number of colleagues and friends followed this project all through the years when it was taking shape. Kate Desbarats and Allan Greer answered questions, shared information and contacts, and never seemed to mind being bothered with requests. Ralph and Ellen Rosen, my pandemic picnic companions, talked me through hesitations, voted on the title, and put me in touch with Charlotte Rosen, who provided much-needed feedback on particularly delicate sections. Ralph helped me cope with many lockdown problems: he scanned books; he printed chapters—and more chapters, and still more chapters—when my home printer became uncooperative. In the end, I named Ralph this book's official printer. No friend could have been kinder or more generous. Colt Segrest and Julien Pajot were particularly supportive interlocutors during the months when I was writing and revising. They also joined me for a trip to the Gulf Coast that I'll never forget. Colt had the patience to read the manuscript as it was taking shape and to offer suggestions for making it more accessible. I am immensely grateful for his careful readings and generosity. Alan Chimacoff managed to fix a range of problems involving images: he can make the worst photograph look good.

Over the years, several Penn graduate students working as my RAs have helped with the research for this project: Pauline Carbonnel, Nathalie Lacarrière, and Kelsey Salvesen. No one could have been more diligent in helping me track the early lives in the French provinces of future passengers on *La Mutine* than Nathalie and Pauline: I so appreciated their devotion to these women. Nathalie's careful work on the archives of Le Mesnil-Thomas was particularly helpful. And Pauline provided indispensable help with archives and images and with the Gonichon map in particular.

Those who study the history of the book often stress the crucial role in the making of early books played by the men and women who printed the actual volumes that were read. Today, the editorial process has taken over from the printing process in helping an author's work take shape on the page, and at Basic Books I was in expert hands all along the way. Katie Carruthers-Busser, Kelley Blewster, Ivan Lett, Jessica Breen and her team, as well as others who worked in the background—all of them guided me through the steps that now turn a manuscript into a book. All of them responded with such energy and dedication that you'd never have guessed that much of the world seemed to be slipping into a pandemic-induced haze. And through it all, Claire Potter was there. Claire believed in the project—from the start and all along the way. She was enthusiastic, encouraging, unfailingly kind, always a pleasure to work with. She understood what I hoped to accomplish, and she did everything she could to help me get there. Claire made this a better book, and I am deeply grateful for her help.

List of Abbreviations

AAM   Archives of the Archdiocese of Mobile
AANO   Archives of the Archdiocese of New Orleans
AB   Archives de la Bastille
AD   Achives Imprimées (Archives Nationales)
AG   Archives du Ministère de la Guerre, Vincennes
AN   Archives Nationales, Paris
ANOM   Archives Nationales d'Outre-Mer, Aix-en-Provence
AP   Archives de la Police, Le Pré-Saint-Gervais
BA   Bibliothèque de l'Arsenal, Paris
E   Conseil du roi (Archives Nationales)
F   Affaires militaires (Archives Nationales)
LHQ   *Louisiana Historical Quarterly*
M   Ordres militaries et hospitaliers (Archives Nationales)
MAR   Archives de la Marine (Archives Nationales)
MC   Minutier Central des Notaires (Archives Nationales)
MPA   *Mississippi Provincial Archives* (Rowland and Sanders)
NONA   New Orleans Notarial Archives, Notarial Archives Research Center, New Orleans
O   Maison du roi (Archives Nationales)
RSCL   Records of the Superior Council of Louisiana, Louisiana State Museum, New Orleans
V   Grande Chancellerie (Archives Nationales)
X   Parlement de Paris (Archives Nationales)
Y   Châtelet de Paris (Archives Nationales)
Z   Jurisdictions spéciales (Archives Nationales)

Notes

1. FALSE ARRESTS AND TRUMPED-UP CHARGES

1. Paris was divided into districts, with officers known as *commissaires* assigned to each of them. Commissaires had administrative duties; they also directed criminal investigations, somewhat in the manner of a DCI in modern English policing.

2. "*Foutu maquereau*," literally "fucking pimp." *Foutre*'s history: DeJean 2002 (chapter 1).

3. Spelling of proper names was often fluid in eighteenth-century France: this one was written d'Autel/d'Hostel/d'Haustel. Geoffroy d'Haustel was a long-time high-level administrator for the Parisian police, *receveur des amendes*, but the victim was never identified as his son.

4. Manon's 1700–1701 trial: AN/Y//10018. The 1699 trial: AN/X/2A /1064.

5. A register eight inches thick records the decrees issued in the hundreds of cases and appeals that came before the Parisian Parlement in December 1701: AN/X/2A/514. D'Aguesseau's signature is found on only four decrees, two of which concern Manon Fontaine. Voltaire (1153).

6. Paris's population in 1700: DeJean 2014 (12). Servants in eighteenth-century Paris: Williams (192).

7. The Salpêtrière's location: Carrez (10). Conditions there: Carrez (chapters 4 and 5), Williams (233). Daily life: *Règlement pour les supérieures de la maison de la Salpêtrière*. August 1721. BA/ms. 2566/54–70. Work in La Force: Gossard (248–250). Michel Cotel: BA/AB/11,742/ 270–286.

8. Information on Pancatelin's "rule": *Mercure de France*, October 1725 (2742). Most male members of Pancatelin's family had long belonged to a dynasty of prosperous Parisian merchants, *maîtres plumassiers*, but by the early eighteenth century the Pancatelins were using their wealth to buy their way out of the merchant class. See, for example, AN/MC/ET/XXIV/421/9

December 1642 (Jacques Pancatelin) and AN/MC/ET/1/298/31 October 1720 (Jacques Pancatelin de Rochebrune).

9. Fontaine's police file: BA/AB/10,659.

10. In eighteenth-century France, it was common to speak of unmarried women, even those of about thirty-seven, as was the case for Manon in 1718, as *"filles,"* girls. Pancatelin also had in mind another use of "filles": women of easy virtue, whether married or single. The only recent scholar to discuss Manon Fontaine accepts Pancatelin's version of the police file and describes her as "a violent offender [who] had been incarcerated for committing fifteen murders" (Gould, 399).

2. JOHN LAW'S LOUISIANA GOLD RUSH

1. "Delirium": Balleroy (2:79); Voltaire (1307).

2. Law (1:204–205).

3. Company of the West: Indies Company *caissier* Du Tot's 1738 account (42–82).

4. French tobacco imports: Price (1:380).

5. Cost of clothing and salt pork: *MPA* (2:146–152); total investment in Louisiana: Hall (13).

6. Law (3:371).

7. *Nouveau Mercure Galant*, March 1719 (184–188), July (178). Additional coverage: September 1719 (96), April 1720 (179). Louisiana silver tested: Buvat (2:80).

8. Du Tot (89–90).

9. "Millionaire": *Nouveau Mercure Galant*, October 1719 (201). The newly rich: Balleroy (2:72, 84–85, 113). New millionaires purchasing land: Buvat (1:449).

10. Caumartin: Balleroy (2:79); "Mississippian": Marais (1:114); "lords . . . of Mississippi": Balleroy (2:113).

11. Population: Giraud (2:120–121).

12. March 1719 decree: AN/E//2010/149–150.

13. The fullest account of these arrests: Du Tot (86). Jacques Pancatelin, Marguerite Pancatelin's nephew, was an *officier du guet à cheval*.

14. Buvat (1:386–387).

15. *Registres d'écrou* for 1717–1720: AP/AB/178–AB/180. Valenciennes: AP/AB/180.

16. Letellier's arrests in 1712: AP/AB/251/140V; AP/AB/175. In 1719: AP/AB/180. Adrien Morel de Foucaucourt's banishment: AN/X/2A/1079. Françoise Letellier: BA/AB/10,672/27–130. Both Letelliers were *servantes de bassecour* in the Dame de Foucaucourt's residence.

17. Law's visit: Buvat (1:434).

18. Crime wave: Marais (1:254); Balleroy (2:97, 142, 151); Buvat (2:59–75); Barbier (1:23–24).

19. Gangs in 1719: BA/AB/10,671/116–139, 205–220.

20. Saint-Germain-des-Prés: AN/Z/2/3610A.

21. Boutin: BA/AB/10,638/200–202.

22. Machault's investigations: AN/O/368/28R, 38V, 87R, 90V, 132R.

23. Chevalier: BA/AB/10,655/179–192.

24. Lesage and d'Orneval (150–152).

3. "MERCHANDISE" FOR LOUISIANA

1. Pancatelin's project: BA/AB/10,659/26–76; BA/AB/12,709.

2. Porcher/Poyer's dossier: BA/AB/10,626/28–34.

3. Transportation: Ekirch, Ziegler.

4. Estimates of the number of *filles du roi* who left France, 770–850: Landry (19–44); Tuttle (96–97). Their dowries, marriages: Landry (73–78).

5. Frenchmen and Native American women: Spear 1999 (43–45).

6. "Transportation" and "deportation" were used in English in the seventeenth century when the first convicts were transported. "Deportation" first appeared in a French dictionary in the mid-eighteenth century, even then defined only with respect to ancient Roman law. Only in the late eighteenth century did French dictionaries define the term as it was used in administrative documents in 1719.

7. Furetière's 1691 dictionary includes "*déporter*" solely as a term in Roman law. The vocabulary of "deportation" entered the official dictionary of the French Academy only in 1798.

8. The first convoy: AN/O/1/63/10,20; BA/AB/10,659/53R.

9. The chain: AN/O/1/308/55R; BA/AB/12,708; BA/AB/12,709.

10. The January 1719 "rebellion": BA/AB/10,659.

11. Duclos: AP/AB/178, 28 July 1717; AN/X/2A/590, 14 January 1715; AN/X/2A/1079/2R, 2 December 1715.

12. Oudart: AP/AB/176, 8 February 1713.

13. The priest served in a village in northeastern France, Saint-Martin-sur-la-Renne. His note concludes the surviving archives for 1709.

14. The Great Winter: Lachiver.

15. Igonnet: AN/X/2A/557, 4 June 1710; AN/X/2A/1074/124R; AN/X/2A/559, 23 August 1710; AN/O/1/54/128V.

16. *Lettres de cachet*, literally "letters of the signet," orders signed by the king and countersigned by a minister and then sealed with the royal seal

or *cachet*, were sometimes obtained by families to authorize imprisonments (Farge and Foucault).

17. Le Coustelier: BA/AB/10,647/53–66.

18. Hurault: AN/Y//14914, 12 August 1710; AN/Y//10025, 5 June 1715; AP/AB/173, 25 June 1709; AP/AB/174, 16 May 1710.

19. French children today call their uncles "tonton," also slang for a police informant. While the first usage may have existed in the eighteenth century, the second usage did not.

20. LeFèvre, Paris: BA/AB/10,647/42–48; AP/AB/178, 28 July 1716; AP/AB/179, 15 November 1718; AN/X/2B/936, 23 July 1716.

21. Sara Misganelle: BA/AB/10,627/131–137.

22. Jeanne Vigneron: BA/AB/10,622/189–192.

23. Brunet: BA/AB/10,602/279–284; BA/AB/12,279; BA/AB/10,600/274–298.

24. *Affaire des poisons*: Petitfils; Tucker. Voisin's dossier: BA/AB/10,357.

25. Habit: BA/AB/10,630/304–324.

26. In 1723, Bailly succeeded Pancatelin as warden. Her corruption was notorious: inmates reported that she sought bribes for the most basic necessities.

27. The prostitute in 1719: DeJean 2019 (12–17).

28. Beaulieu's arrest in 1718: BA/AB/10,643/291R. In 1717: AP/AB/178. Her venereal disease: BA/AB/10,630/324R; BA/AB/10,659/45V.

29. Gené: AN/O/1/61/49, 26 March 1718; BA/AB/10,659/46R.

30. La Fleur: AN/Y//10023, 1 December 1713; AN/Y//10025/November 1715; AP/AB/176, 7 November 1713; AP/AB/178, 31 October 1716; BA/AB/10,659/38V.

31. Delapierre: AP/AB/176, 7 November 1713. De La Marche's 1713 trial: AN/Y//10023. Her rearrest: AP/AB/178, 31 October 1716. Joly de Fleury's decisions: BA/AB/10,659/59R, 61R. *Lettre de cachet* to transfer thirteen women to Rochefort: AN/O/1/63/59R.

32. Thirat: BA/AB/10,659/68–75; AN/MAR/B/1/41.

33. Thirat calculated in *onces*, virtually equivalent to today's ounces.

34. Louis Prince/Prins "detached": BA/AB/12,708.

35. The term *yack* to refer to some sort of vehicle is found in no contemporary dictionary. Beauharnois, Galissonière, the order to Machault: AN/MAR/B/1/42.

36. Ferret's arrival in the colony: Newberry Library/Ayer ms.293, 537.

37. Arrests for small amounts of salt: BA/AB/12,683, 25 November 1718.

38. Riots defending smugglers in 1718 and 1719: AN/E//2003/241RV, 251RV.

39. Transfers of smugglers: BA/AB/12,708.

40. *"Chaine de la Louisiane,"* July 9, 1719: BA/AB/12,683.

41. Vigneron: BA/AB/12,683/52R, 76V; AP/AB/178, 12 August 1716; AN/O/1/62/20, 3 January 1718.

42. Pinnaces: Proulx; Giraud (3:113; 4:62).

43. Correspondence about the dangers of the war with Spain: AN/MAR/B/1/43/38RV, 20V–33R.

4. THE ROUNDUP

1. Morainville: BA/AB/10,670/65–78. She was granted her freedom in January 1720: BA/AB/12,692/56R.

2. Arrest of the unidentified Irishwoman on April 4, 1719: AP/AB/180. Arrest of Marie Doyart in January 1719: AN/O/1/61/3R. Arrest of the other Irishwomen on Pancatelin's list: AN/O/1/63/70R.

3. *"Bohémien"*: Antoine Furetière's 1691 dictionary. The 1715 arrest of *"Bohémiennes"*: BA/AB/10,619/118–122. In 1719, a note was added to the dossier alleging that they had been arrested for theft. *"Bohémiens"* in early modern France: De Vaux de Foletier; Kalifa (79); Mathorez (351–365).

4. The March 1719 decree: AN/E//2010/149–150. Mercier: BA/AB/10,669/105–109.

5. Women's presence in European cities in the eighteenth century: DeJean 2014 (115, 118–120, 192–194).

6. Vaudestar: AP/AB/179, 6 March 1718. Her trial: AN/Y//10022/, 6–10 March 1718.

7. Pouillot's testimony in the trial of Babet La Fleur: AN/Y//10025, 16 November 1715.

8. Pouillot: AP/AB/176, 22 February 1714; AP/AB/178, 1 November 1717; AP/AB/179, 17 December 1718.

9. Comparison of arrests of women in Paris in 1719, 1718, and 1720: DeJean 2019.

10. Villetard: BA/AB/10,670.

11. A detailed account of one such raid is found in AN/Y//10027.

12. Transfer of Reffe, Meutrot, and Poton: AN/O/1/63/224.

13. Fontenelle: AP/AB/178, 16 December 1716; AP/AB/179, 24 October 1718; AP/AB/180, 23 August 1719.

14. Daudin: AP/AB/177, 21 April 1716; AN/Y//10617, 11 July 1716.

15. Grené: AP/AB/179, 11 September 1718; BA/AB/12,292/11V.

16. Bourlon was a lieutenant in the *Compagnie du Lieutenant Criminel de robe courte.*

17. Bourlon's 1716 arrest of Anne and Marie Maurice and Marie Antoinette Néron: BA/AB/10,623/160. Transfer to the Salpêtrière: BA/AB/10,632/123–138, 172. Picard: BA/AB/10,672/11–19, 26.

18. Number of women on the chain: BA/AB/10,672/11–19.

19. Absence of procedure: AN/O/1/368/145V–146R.

20. The October 6, 1719 *"chaine"*: AN/O/1/63/278R–279V.

21. Fouquet: BA/AB/10,659/85R.

22. Saint-Simon (7:46). "The deadly years": Lachiver (chapters 7–11).

23. Mortality in France in 1709–1710: Lachiver (381).

24. Documents on Marie Baron's life in Le Mesnil-Thomas are from parish records.

25. Baron: AP/AB/174, 12 August 1710; AP/AB/175, 16 April 1711. 1719 arrest: AP/AB/180, 9 June 1719. In 1719, Baron is a footnote in Crétin's enormous dossier: BA/AB/10,628/117–210.

26. Le Brun: AN/O/1/63/293V.

27. Chartier's case is split between two dossiers. In the first, she is called "Marie Mallet," the name used for her by Roberdeau's wife; in the second, she is "Marie Chartier." The police seem never to have connected the two dossiers: BA/AB 10,645/228–236.

28. Giard: BA/AB/12,692/1V.

29. Mahou: BA/AB/10,667/306–321. Her transfer: AN/O/1/63/288V.

30. Fourchet: BA/AB/10,659/289–294; AN/O/1/63/176. Babies born to "prostitutes": Delasselle (188, 195).

31. Damiette's *dépôt de testament* and probate inventory: AN/MC/ET/XVI/629, 20 January 1708. Election of guardians for the Bettemont children: AN/Y//4173, 25 January 1708. Average wages for workers in Paris: Baulant (483). Cost of food and the wages paid in an aristocratic household: Audiger.

32. Decree lowering the interest rate: Du Tot (121–122). Justification given for lowering the rate of return: Du Tot (111–117).

33. Rolland-Lucas marriage contract: AN/MC/ET/LIX/128, 3 November 1686. Guardians for his daughters in 1703: AN/Y//4122, 12 April 1703. Jeanne Lucas's probate inventory: AN/MC/ET/LXXXIII/235, 28 April 1703. Rolland claimed under oath that Lucas died on April 9, but on March 20, those who named him the children's guardian attested that she was already dead.

34. Anne Françoise's father signed his name with both one and two *l*'s; other family members always wrote "Rolland."

35. Rolland-Dumontel marriage contract: AN/MC/ET/LXXXIII/236, 15 July 1703. Dumontel's 1705 annuity: AN/MC/ET/LXXXIII/240, 23 June 1705. Rolland accepted reduced rate on annuity: AN/MC/ET/XLVI/229, 1 April 1719.

36. Rolland's request to Machault: AB/AB/10,673/52R–62R. Royal orders for Anne Françoise's arrest: AN/O/1/63/27V. Subsistence for a prisoner in the Salpêtrière in 1719: AN/O/1/63/20V.

37. Rate reduction: *Nouveau Mercure Galant*, February 1720 (104).

38. Documents related to Dumontel's new annuity: AN/MC/ET/CIX/437, 8 July 1719; AN/MC/ET/LXXXVII/1095, 15 July 1719. Rolland's probate inventory: AN/MC/ET/XLV/385/A, 18 September 1723. Guardians for his son: AN/Y//4331, 16 May 1720. Rolland's *clôture d'inventaire*: AN/Y//5282, 5 October 1723.

39. Loss of consumer confidence, runs on the Bank: Du Tot (140, 187–189); Faure (348).

40. *Bandouliers*: Buvat (2:77–78, 87); Balleroy (2:159–160). Revolts in Paris: Balleroy (2:159–160); Giraud (3:269–270). Decree ending deportation: AN/AD/259; Dangeau (18:274).

41. Only two petitions from 1720 request "the islands of the Mississippi" or "the colonies" for daughters: La Motte, March 1720, BA/AB/10,708/175–184; Duchemin, July 1720, BA/AB/10,701/146–157.

42. Taking profits in early 1720: Du Tot (224, 242). Law's debts: AN/V/7/254.

5. CHAINS AND SHACKLES

1. Heat in 1719: Lachiver (410–419).

2. Saint-Simon (37:257).

3. Tenon: AP/AB/180, 21 March 1719.

4. De Cercueille/De Cerceuil/Deserqueil/Cercuil: AP/AB/180, 5 August 1719; BA/AB/10,555/400–417; AN/O/1/63/198R.

5. Chantepie's arrest of Pouillot: AP/AB/179, 17 December 1718. Accused of arrests on false pretenses: Piasenza (1201, n.84). Pontchartrain: AN/O/1/367/80.

6. Forged royal orders: Cheype (6).

7. Private detentions: Cheype (35–38).

8. Testimony in the police inspectors' trial: AN/X2/B/1389–1391. Simonnet's dossier is particularly complete. Marguerite Morin, twenty-one, who sold used linen from a market stall, testified that in June 1719 an officer had demanded 6 *livres*, 10 *sols* for protection. The concept of a police inspector: Piasenza (43–45).

9. Heuret: BA/AB/10,640/395-407.

10. Boyard: BA/AB/10,627/343–353. Her mother's petition: AN/Y// 15424, 26 April 1717.

11. Accusations made by working-class Parisians against officers for abusing the homeless: AN/Y//9537, 5 May 1716.

12. Salot and Langro: BA/AB/10,647/84–91. Bazire: AP/AB/174, 24 December 1709; AP/AB/175, 1 December 1711; AP/AB/178, 29 November 1716. Bazire and Salot: BA/AB/12,692/36R. Royal orders for all three: AN/O/1/61/37.

13. Bourlon's scheme: BA/ms.7557/35V, 45V, 48V, 101R.

14. Picard: BA/AB/10,672/11–19, 26.

15. Boucher: BA/AB/10,673/312–314.

16. Gachot: AN/O/1/63/210V; BA/AB/10,660/1–6; BA/AB/10,671/ 247–255.

17. Bidault: BA/AB/10,641/141–144.

18. Lavergne: BA/AB/10,573/13, 43. The women's escape: BA/ AB/10,661/129. Their rearrest: AN/O/1/63/302R, 26 October 1719.

19. Gavelle: BA/AB/10,660/52–58. Portelaitte: BA/AB/10,672/30–47. Aubin: BA/AB/10,700/124R. Lebel/Lefebel: BA/AB/10,644/265–284; AN/O/1/63/335R.

20. Geneviève Marie: BA/AB/10,625/70; BA/AB/10,655/339. Other women released to their parents: Charlotte Trenchant (AN/O/1/368/171, AN/O/1/63/287V); Elisabeth and Marie Robitaille (AN/O/1/368/180V); Marie Pierron (AN/O/1/368/173R).

21. Monvoisin: BA/AB/10,670/58–62.

22. Henoch/Henault: BA/AB/10,661/206–208.

23. Raflon: BA/AB/10,672/176–181. Marie Boiron, passenger 154, was pardoned only on December 29, after La Mutine's departure: AN/0/1/368/196R.

24. Berthault: BA/AB/10,639/371–374. Véri: AP/AB/180, 18 June 1719. Vasseur: AP/AB/180, 29 July 1719. Lanneau: AP/AB/180, 28 September 1719. Colin: BA/AB/10,655/249–261; AN/Y//10617, 4 October 1719.

25. Lambert: AN/Z/2/3744, 2 August 1719. A case of conjugal violence: Françoise Jacquet (BA/AB/10,671/62–71; AP/AB/180, 2 September 1719).

26. Pasquier: BA/AB/10,67/297. A related case: Marie La Marche (BA/ AB/10,648/43–86, 301).

27. Blanchet: BA/AB/10,653/246–262; her release: AN/O/1/368/180V. A similar case: Judith Riette (BA/AB/10,675/224–228).

28. Olivier: BA/AB/10,648/87–126; BA/AB/10,675/289–290. Related cases: Marie Madeleine de Saint-Rémy (AN/Y//10024, 13 April 1714; AP/AB/180, 9 September 1719); Geneviève Giroux (AN/O/1/368/91V).

29. Luce: BA/AB/12,692/32V. Perronnet: BA/AB/12,690/45–52. Many of the women left in Le Havre regained Paris in February, when their files were stamped, "Freed in 1720." The women remained in the Salpêtrière until October 4, 1721, when they were released. Names of those released: BA/AB/12,692/27–30, 56R.

30. De La Cour: BA/AB/10,616/38–41.

31. The presumed earlier manifest: AN/F/5b/37. The second manifest can be found online on the website of the Service Historique de la Défense at Lorient: Rôle de la Mutine (1719–1720). Some of the discrepancies between the two manifests: the names of several escapees are found on the earlier list, and it does not contain the names of two women who did travel. It lists Marie Moule, whereas the second list does not. The second list includes Marie Denise Beaulieu and claims that she arrived in Louisiana, whereas Beaulieu was returned to the Salpêtrière.

32. *Mutin, mutine*: I quote the primary meaning given in Furetière's 1690 dictionary. Furetière also includes a secondary meaning: "*se dit aussi de celui qui se révolte contre la raison, qui est opiniâtre, querelleux.*" In the French Navy, the name was popular: frigates called *La Mutine* were in service from 1670 to 1855.

33. Of the estimated ninety-six who traveled on *La Mutine*, the origins of sixty-nine can be determined, the ages of sixty-two are known, and the alleged crimes of seventy-six are known.

34. 1726 letter: AN/M//1026.

35. Laval (2, 11).

36. Size of ships used for crossings to Louisiana: Surrey (78).

37. Complaints from Indies Company representatives: AN/MAR/B/1/43/35RV, 138RV. Beauharnois: AN/MAR/B/1/43/179RV.

38. Decree condemning bakers who shipped inferior flour: *Nouveau Mercure Galant*, February 1720 (111).

39. Seasickness: Franquet de Chaville (9).

40. "*Engagé*" was sometimes used to describe "indentured" servants or workers. Related terminology: *engagés au service de la compagnie, ouvriers serviteurs*.

41. Captains' "brutality": Franquet de Chaville (12–14); Giraud (3:115).

42. A manuscript version of the manifest for *Les Deux Frères* is available online from Library and Archives Canada. Several transcriptions exist; Tepper's version is the most faithful (1:502–509).

43. Captain's logbook from 1704: AN/MAR/B/4/23/336–392. Suicides/death rates on French slave ships: Johnson (92–95). The 1719 crossing: Giraud (3:113). April 1, 1726 voyage: Giraud (5:136). *La Mutine* was later returned to service in the African slave trade: Johnson (87, 95). On frigates: Proulx (17 and ff.), Boudriot, and Talarmin.

44. The death toll on voyages to New Orleans: Giraud (5:136–138).

45. Death toll among German passengers: Deiler (28); Langlois (107). Death tolls were also heavy among crew members on Indies Company vessels: twenty-two of fifty-three died during one 1720 crossing. Vallette de Laudun (250, 273); Giraud (3:112–113).

46. Langro: BA/AB/10,609/29–34; AN/O/1/61/37.

47. Dumont 2012 (125).

48. Le Gac (29).

49. Le Gac (18–27). Flour needed for New Orleans: *MPA* (2:311). Estimates of the population of New Orleans in 1722 vary greatly; the variations are determined by differing interpretations of census data. LaChance's estimate of 343 seems the most serious (206). Estimate of 566: *LHQ* (3:228).

50. Laval (2).

51. Franquet de Chaville (7).

52. Huron's interrogation: AN/X/2B/1391.

53. Huron's murder: Henry (155–161). Cartouche and several gang members acknowledged responsibility for Huron's death: BA/ms.7557.

54. Cartouche and Néron's marriage: Henry (133).

55. Rearrest of escapees on October 26, 1719: AN/O/1/63/302R.

56. Néron: BA/AB/10,632/172–176.

57. Néron's testimony: BA/AB/10,700/124R.

58. Testimony of Cartouche and members of his gang: BA/ms.7557/14R, 99R, 134R. Bourlon and his *mouches* were denounced by virtually everyone.

59. Gavelle's testimony: BA/ms.7557/101R, 35V, 45V. Bourlon arrested those he feared most: BA/ms.7557/103R.

60. Bourlon's confrontations: BA/ms.7557/99R.

61. Bourlon's arrest: AN/Y//16617, 8 June 1722. His trial: AN/X/2B/1352, 26 September 1722.

6. "THE ISLANDS" OF LOUISIANA

1. Bonrepos (1).

2. The 1713 publication of Henri Joutel's *Journal historique du dernier voyage que feu M. de la Sale fit dans le Golfe du Mexique* features the Gulf Coast in its title, but the journal concerns for the most part East Texas; the

accompanying map shows the Gulf Coast without a single detail. Nicolas de Fer's 1718 map depicts the Gulf Coast with no accurate details.

3. "The Mississippi": Dumont 2012 (93).

4. *Nouveau Mercure Galant*, January 1720 (199–200).

5. Detailed introduction to the colony's early years: Giraud, vols. 1–2. Naming of the colony: Villiers 1929 (2).

6. *"La grande affaire"*: Margry (4:303–305).

7. Estimates of the early population vary according to interpretations of the data in early censuses. Detailed projections: Giraud (1:29–83); LaChance (204–209); Higginbotham (538–541). Early censuses: Maduell (1–50).

8. Native American population: Usner (17). Mobilians, Choctaws: Higginbotham (42, 53); Ellis 2017 (358).

9. Failed crops: Margry (4:376).

10. Livestock: *MPA* (2:18–20).

11. Le Page du Pratz 1758 (1:9).

12. Missionary: Thwaites (66:124).

13. La Harpe (106).

14. Clothing packed with nails: *MPA* (1:60–66).

15. Trials for fraud on ships to Louisiana: AN/V/7/214.

16. Louis XIV: ANOM/B/29/278.

17. Soldiers' diet: *MPA* (1:60–66).

18. *Le Pélican*: Giraud (1:139–143).

19. Numbers of women: LaChance (208–209); Higginbotham (541).

20. Flooding in 1711: La Harpe (108).

21. Fort Louis's condition: Higginbotham (176, 243–244); Giraud (1:173, 201).

22. Soldiers lack necessities: *MPA* (2:143–144).

23. Bienville: ANOM/C/13/B/1.

24. D'Artaguiette: ANOM/C/13/A/2/641,803.

25. *Lettres patentes pour le commerce de la Louisiane*, September 1712 (articles 3–6).

26. No coin: La Harpe (111); Le Page du Pratz 1758 (1:18).

27. Families in the colony: LaChance (209). Departures from Louisiana: Giraud (1:292).

28. Economic indicators after Louis XIV's death: Earl Hamilton (51–55).

29. Population in 1717: LaChance (209). There was no official census during the Crozat years, so only estimates are possible.

30. Crozat's last years: Giraud (2:64, 98, 141, 144).

31. Administrators of Saint-Domingue: AN/MAR/B/1/20/419. Hubert: Giraud (2:144); Charlevoix (2:428).

32. Crozat's promotion of Louisiana: Giraud (3:5).

33. *Lettres patentes* (articles 2, 7, 51).

34. Shipbuilding and maritime commerce during Law's mandate: Giraud (5:101 and ff.).

35. News of war reached Louisiana; Pensacola: Dumont and Le Mascrier (2:9–11).

36. Crozat and African slavery: Giraud (3:9).

37. Slavery in New France: Trudel.

38. First enslaved Africans in Louisiana: Hall (57–58); some estimates of the number of enslaved Africans prior to June 1719 are slightly higher. Slavery in various French colonies: Pritchard (177–178).

39. Boats for Louisiana: Giraud (5:109).

40. *Nouveau Mercure Galant* in 1720, January (35–36, 59–60); February (102); August (25); October (156–157); November (141–142); December (152).

41. Pork, beef, rice: Giraud (5:144).

42. Laval (97–98).

43. Laval (97–99).

44. Value of cargo in 1726: AN/MAR/B/3/309/130RV.

45. Approximation of 2,849: LaChance (211).

46. Engineer Franquet de Chaville's memoir on his work in the colony circulated in manuscript well before its 1754 publication. Jean Baptiste Bénard de La Harpe's journal and maps based on his travels first circulated in 1720. Laval's 1720 account was published in 1728, but Laval got no further than Dauphin Island.

47. Dumont and Le Mascrier (2:32–36).

48. La Harpe makes a minimal reference to "several women from Paris's Hospital" who arrived in February 1720 (221).

7. THE DESERT ISLANDS OF ALABAMA AND MISSISSIPPI

1. Dauphin Island's renaming: Dumont and Le Mascrier (2:9); Le Page du Pratz 1758 (1:37).

2. *Robinson Crusoe*: *Nouveau Mercure Galant*, August 1720 (80–103).

3. Crew members' illnesses: Giraud (3:112).

4. *Nouveau Mercure Galant*, January 1720 (199–200). Bienville, Pauger: Villiers 1917 (xiv, 48).

5. Biloxi in 1720: Giraud (3:312–313).

6. Huts for soldiers: Franquet de Chaville (19).

7. I am grateful to Captain Louis Skrmetta for information on Ship Island through the centuries, as well as on travel in the Gulf.

8. In 1721, Franquet de Chaville traveled directly to Ship Island to draw up its first map: Giraud (4:389).

9. Dumont 2012 (125); Dumont and Le Mascrier: (1:36). Differences between the two: Sayre 2009 (426).

10. Sleeping arrangements: Dumont and Le Mascrier (2:35); Le Gac (30).

11. Cold on Ship Island: Pellerin BA/ms.4497/fol.64V; Dumont and Le Mascrier (1:9); Captain Louis Skrmetta.

12. A freshwater well was discovered only in the nineteenth century. 1720 report: AG/Registre/A/1/2592/89V. Flooding on Ship Island; no storehouse: AG/Registre/A/1/2592/25.

13. Franquet de Chaville (23). Le Page du Pratz 1758 (1:43).

14. Thévenot's *L'Art de nager*.

15. *Mémoire sur l'état de la Louisiane*: AG/Registre/A/1/2592/90.

16. Engineer Le Blond de La Tour: AG/Registre/A/1/2592/105.

17. Giraud (3:342).

18. Jean Pierre Fourchet's baptism: AAM in Calagaz (105). All references to early ceremonies performed at Mobile are to this volume.

19. Dumont 2012 (154).

20. No paper: AG/Registre/A/1/2592/130.

21. Ceremonies in 1720: Giraud (3:360).

22. The attribution of *sieur* and *dame* in Louisiana: Ingersoll (44).

23. Accusations against Sarazin: *MPA* (2:303).

24. Blavo (131, 142).

25. Repression of "licentiousness": AG/Registre-A/1/2592/31. Army officer: *MPA* (2:275). Raguet: RSCL/1724-09-02-01. La Chaise: *MPA* (2:462, 494). Accusations of prostitution: Giraud (4:180).

26. Recent specialists of French Louisiana have repeated such claims. They have argued that the women of *La Mutine* were "teenaged *debauchées*," "libertines of dubious moral fiber," who "reverted to their only means of gainful employment" in Louisiana and for whom "life was short" (Conrad 1975, 58, 31; Brasseaux 40). Since few married and fewer had children, their contribution "to the settlement of the colony seems to have been limited" (Ingersoll 12). Indeed they may even have "seriously retarded" demographic growth (Giraud 3:340). "Thieves, prostitutes, and assassins," the survivors "were parasites, accustomed to drawing sustenance from a reasonably thriving social body. Exhausted by long journeys and malnutrition,

often in advanced stages of venereal disease, they died off rapidly" (Allain 84). It has even been suggested that "being a prostitute might have been viewed as a valuable job skill in a colony with so few women" (Gould 404).

27. New government: AG/Registre/A/1/2592/32.

28. Seventeen married: Giraud (3:340). No descendants: Ingersoll (46–47). Families in 1712: Charlevoix (2:427). 1721 census: Maduell (16).

8. Biloxi's Deadly Sands

1. "New Biloxi": *MPA* (3:301); Giraud (4:123).

2. Dumont 2012 (121, 125).

3. No money for Louisiana: Giraud (4:334). Indies Company in early 1721: Giraud (4:42). Decrees abolishing Indies Company privileges: *Nouveau Mercure Galant*, January 1721 (85); February (96); May (120). Bienville: Giraud (4:132).

4. Food prices in 1720: AG/Registre/A/1/2592/35, 95V.

5. Number at New Biloxi 1720; number of deaths: AG/Registre/A/1/2592/129; Giraud (3:327, 330).

6. Pellerin: BA/ms.4492/63, 65V. Some concessions lost over 50 percent of their settlers (Giraud 4:137).

7. Death register: Conrad 1970 (2:111).

8. Dupuys: De Ville 2000 (20). Dupuys was number 148 on Pancatelin's list; on the manifest, she was confused with Marie Thérèse Dupuys.

9. Franquet de Chaville, who arrived shortly after the deported women (20–21).

10. Chapel: Wilson 1987 (109).

11. Records of marriages for which I supply a precise date can be found in either Calagaz, ed., AAM, or Nolan, ed., AANO (includes Biloxi records).

12. Arrival of *L'Alexandre* in 1720: La Harpe (234). Crossing: Giraud (3:112).

13. Manifests were drawn up only upon departure from France.

14. Pellerin: BA/ms.4497/62.

15. *"Endroit capital"*: AG/Registre/A/1/2592/118V.

16. La Croix: *LHQ* (1:103–104).

17. Bienville: AG/Registre/A/1/2592/107, 109, 110, 128.

18. *La Baleine*: La Harpe (239); Dumont and Le Mascrier (2:30–31); Ladnier.

19. Blanchard: BA/AB/10,659/12V; BA/AB/12,692/26V.

20. Letellier: RSCL/1726-02-23-02.

21. Spoiled food: Bienville: AG/Registre/A/1/2592/128, 109, 111.

22. Rains in 1721: AG/Registre/A/1/2592/113.

23. New Biloxi: Giraud (4:397).

24. Desertions: Fontaine: RSCL/1726-10-22-01; Charlevoix (6:270; 4:456).

25. *Ouragan*: La Harpe (339–340); Charlevoix (4:457–458). Crops destroyed: Giraud (4:287).

26. Moran Burial Site findings: Danforth et al. (132–179).

27. 1726 census: Maduell (61).

9. PUTTING DOWN ROOTS IN MOBILE

1. Oudart: AP/AB/174, 10 September 1710; AP/AB/176, 8 February 1713; BA/AB/10,659/38. Commissioner Bizoton: Romon (279).

2. Beaulieu: *MPA* (2:271).

3. Mahou: RSCL/1737-08-17-01; BA/AB/10,667/314.

4. Fort Louis: AG/Registre/A/1/2592/128.

5. Church: *MPA* (2:182).

6. Engineer Franquet de Chaville (28–29).

7. Livestock: Giraud (4:299).

8. Higginbotham reproduces and interprets the second map of Mobile. Construction in Mobile: Peter Hamilton (chapter 10); Wilson 1971 (81–86). Greg Waselkov provided information on archeological findings from colonial Mobile.

9. Whenever Angélique Reffe's name was recorded, it was spelled in a different manner. In those attempts to reproduce her pronunciation, Angélique's accent can be heard: "Reve," "Raive," and so forth.

10. A death certificate for Mirodot, drawn up on May 29, 1731, at Reffe's request, is found in Mobile's baptismal register.

11. Meutrot/Métrot marriage: Vidrine 1985 (40). Vivier's death: De Ville 1968 (46). Le Roy/Roy: De Ville 1968 (167).

12. Deveaux's arrest: AN/Y//10023. Her marriage: Giraud (3:343n.). I was unable to learn her husband's name and so could not trace her beyond 1721.

13. Prévost: *MPA* (2:212–214).

14. Bourguenet's arrest under the name "Bourguinet": AP/AB/178, 6 January 1717.

15. Salaries: *MPA* (2:146).

16. Fièvre: Giraud (5:254).

17. Olivier's contract: RSCL/1737-12-30-02.

18. Size of dugouts: Surrey (57); Wood (208, 243).

19. *Voyageurs*: Giraud (5:278); Brasseaux (28); Morrissey (143). Tarascon's trading: *MPA* (1:35, 48–50, 103); RSCL/1741-07-14-03; RSCL/1741-12-02-02.

20. Two-thirds of the soldiers mutinied in 1721; from then on, the garrison remained tiny: Waselkov 1989 (xxi).

21. Trade near Fort Toulouse: Waselkov 1992 and 1982.

22. Laurent inventory: RSCL/1737-08-17-01.

23. Structures in 1702: Wilson 1987 (69).

24. Parisian inventories: DeJean 2018 (234–235).

25. Marchand's death: La Harpe (343–344).

26. Fièvre's warehouse: *MPA* (2:393); Wilson 1987 (76).

27. Education in 1733: *MPA* (4:129–130). Female education and literacy in New Orleans: Clark 2007. Education and literacy in the colony: Ingersoll (49); Wilson 1987 (148–154).

28. Charles Rochon: Higginbotham (456–459).

29. La Pointe–Krebs house: Gums and Waselkov (141–142). Building materials: Giraud (1:262–263).

30. Louise Fièvre's property: Higginbotham (459n.).

31. Dumont 2012 (119).

32. Slavery and Native Americans: Libby (xii–xiii, 5). LaChance documents the decline in numbers of enslaved Native Americans. Reasons for that decline: Ellis 2017 (360–361). Enslaved Africans in April 1719: *Relation de Pénicaut* (French 146).

33. In 1721, in the entire colony there were 693 indentured servants/ workers, 950 enslaved Africans, and 183 enslaved Native Americans. By 1726, those numbers had shifted: 260; 1,401; 161. LaChance (213).

34. On April 12, 1727, Angélique Reffe was chosen as godmother by aide-major Joseph de Lusser. AAM (Calagaz 187).

35. Fourchet and La Case in New Orleans: RSCL/1725-02-10-01.

36. French families in 1764: Tate (265). The oath: *MPA* (1:121–122).

37. Saint-Louis tract: Peter Hamilton (158–159).

38. *Nouveau Mercure Galant*, August 1722 (95).

39. Storm: La Harpe (339–340).

40. In 1721, the population of Mobile stood at 572; by 1726, it had fallen to 459. In contrast, New Orleans, which in 1721 had a population of 343, had grown to 773. LaChance (213); Maduell (16, 26).

10. BUILDING A CAPITAL IN NEW ORLEANS

1. 1718: La Harpe (128); Margry (5:605). 1719: AG/Registre/A/1/2592/26R. 1720: Margry (5:623).

2. Linking Law to New Orleans's founding: Powell (24).

3. New Orleans's design: Pauger (Margry 5:634–635); Franquet de Chaville (1–46); Charlevoix (6:192–193); Langlois (in Greenwald 2018: 57–67); Giraud (4:384–412). *Nouveau Mercure Galant*, January 1720 (199–200).

4. Clearing terrain: AG/Registre/A/1/2592/36.

5. Bienville on Pauger's initial work: AG/Registre/A/1/2592/106V.

6. Le Blond de La Tour's arrival: Margry (5:656–657). Hurricane: Charlevoix (2:457–458).

7. No artisans in colony: AG/Registre/A/1/2592/32.

8. Street names: Charlevoix (1:97).

9. Caron: Margry (5:669).

10. Duflot: Tepper (1:511).

11. Procedures for granting land: Dumont and Le Mascrier (2:47–49); Giraud (3:170). Process explained to residents: AG/Registre/A/1/2592/131. A petition of the kind made by Manon Fontaine: RSCL/1723-04-03-02. Land grants: Greer (171).

12. On Pancatelin's list, Giard's name was written correctly; when the list was recopied, it was erroneously recorded "Françoise Girard," the name under which Giard appears on *La Mutine*'s manifest. Giard: BA/AB/12,692/1V; Dumont and Le Mascrier (2:36).

13. Langlois provides a breakdown of the population by occupation and street address (340–343).

14. Philbert's arrests: AP/AB/179, 14 January 1718, 30 January 1719.

15. Martin: AP/AB/178, 19 October 1717.

16. Binard's house: *LHQ* (13:227).

17. Montard: AP/AB/190, 20 January 1717; BA/AB/12,683/52R.

18. No trace of anyone named "Félix de Montfrein" survives in French archives.

19. On April 10, 1759, Jeannette Montard purchased a house and land on Toulouse Street from Marie Daudin's daughter: NONA/7417/56880–56885. The house was located between that of Jeanne Mahou and that of her son, Simon Laurent.

20. Valenciennes: AP/AB/180, 15 August 1719.

21. Doyart: AN/O/1/61/3R, 6 January 1717.

22. Lazou: *MPA* (3:449; 1:342–343; 2:655); RSCL/1723-07-09-02.

23. Balivet: RSCL/1734-08-10-01; RSCL/1737-08-23-02; *LHQ* (7:705; 8:145; 9:313).

24. 1723 plot: *MPA* (1:342–343).

25. Hospital: *MPA* (1:313).

26. Bienville: *MPA* (3:347).

27. Salot: *MPA* (3:485).

28. Automne, Ferret: ANOM/*Registres de décès*. Burial notices are found either there or in AANO (Woods and Nolan).

29. Le Fort: BA/AB/10,622/2–44.

30. Le Comte: *LHQ* (4:235).

31. Hospital in 1724: *MPA* (3:464–467).

32. Boutin: BA/AB/10,638/200.

33. Illegal establishments: Giraud (5:291).

34. Bourguignon: RSCL/1728-05-24-03. *Trépan*: Furetière's 1691 dictionary; Académie Française 1694.

35. Coroy/Cauroy: Archives Saint-Martin-sur-la-Renne; BA/AB/12,692/24V.

36. Some documents are in such poor shape that they are virtually illegible. A sometimes incorrectly transcribed summary of interrogations and RSCL numbers: *LHQ* (4:486–489; 7:686–688).

37. D'Hombourg and the Swiss: Giraud (4:302–303, 393–396). Desertions: Charlevoix (6:270).

38. Sentence: RSCL/1728-06-14-03-04. Langlois was given a token three-month prison sentence.

39. Bontemps: RSCL/1728-06-04.

40. Female merchants after 1750: White 2006.

41. Mill, church: *MPA* (2:479, 536).

42. Windows: *MPA* (1:557–558; 2:536); Giraud (5:260).

43. Sarazin affair: *MPA* (2:300–386); Giraud (5:38–40).

44. Sarazin's estate: *LHQ* (4:235; 21:1225).

45. Governor Périer: *MPA* (2:559).

46. Cariton's clothing: RSCL/1724-09-07-01.

47. Dinan's pew: *LHQ* (3:406). Pew rental: Vidal 2019 (155–157); Ingersoll (45).

48. Cariton borrowed: *LHQ* (8:686). Clothing not paid for: *LHQ* (12:304–305, 310; 13:677).

49. Dinan's petition, settlement: RSCL/1747-08-24-01; RSCL/1747-08-28-01; RSCL/1747-09-02-07; RSCL/1747-09-18-01.

50. Cariton's estate: *LHQ* (21:605–608).

51. La Roche inventory: RSCL/1736-12-22-01; debt to company: RSCL/1736-10-08-02. Indies Company obliged heirs to repay money owed: Dumont 2012 (247).

52. Massicot-Revoil: *LHQ* (18:449).

53. La Roche-Revoil: RSCL/1747-09-09-01-03.

54. La Roche house: *LHQ* (18:993).

55. Purchase of home: NONA/64632/7837.

56. Power of attorney, purchase: NONA/8 October 1773/notary Garic/ vol. 4.

57. 1767 dowry: NONA/2311.

58. Daudin's estate: NONA/90808.

59. The image in Figure 12 is a reproduction of Gonichon's 1731 map that appears in Charlevoix's 1744 history.

60. Street paving in Paris: DeJean 2014 (101-102); in New Orleans: Lalouette (5 July 1821).

61. Two slightly different versions of the map survive; each is accompanied by a chart of owners, and the two charts are not identical: one lists property owners in 1728. I include women listed on both charts. In some cases, they may no longer have been property owners in 1731.

62. Tobacco smuggler Marie Michel was a widow from Soissons in northern France. Lot 137 was listed in her name in 1728 but no longer in 1731. She may have died in the interval.

63. Gautier-Reffe marriage: AANO/9782/5 July 1738.

64. About 40 of the 253 numbered lots on Gonichon's map were official properties (royal warehouses, ateliers for construction). Since no inhabitants were listed for 12 properties, and since survivors whose husbands cannot be identified or who were misidentified surely occupied additional properties, the percentage of lots in survivors' hands was undoubtedly higher still.

11. WOMEN ON THE VERGE IN NATCHITOCHES, ILLINOIS, AND ARKANSAS

1. Dumont and Le Mascrier (2:65).

2. Saint-Denis: AG/Registre/A/1/2592/82V.

3. Natchitoches's fortifications and garrison: Margry (6:226–227); Giraud (5:408–409).

4. Trade with the Spanish: AG/Registre/A/1/2592/92; *MPA* (2:258); Le Page du Pratz 1758 (2:278).

5. Praise for Saint-Denis: Le Page du Pratz 1758 (1:299); Dumont and Le Mascrier (2:66).

6. Natchitoches's land: Le Page du Pratz 1758 (1:163).

7. Price of bear oil: Le Page du Pratz 1758 (1:207); Margry (6:382).

8. The earliest extant church records for Natchitoches date from 1734 (Elizabeth Mills 1977).

9. Benoist: BA/AB/10,659/40V, 43V.

10. Gary Mills (130).

11. Wheat: Le Page du Pratz 1758 (1:331; 2:290); Ekberg 1996 (266, 272–273); Briggs (50–51); Morrissey (142).

12. Villages: Vidal 2007b (126).

13. Frenchwomen in Illinois: Morrissey (144).

14. Captain's land grant: Ekberg 1998 (74).

15. Goguet: BA/AB/12,708.

16. Cantillon: Giraud (4:91, 222).

17. Le Page du Pratz 1758 (1:322).

18. Testing ore samples: Giraud (3:374–375).

19. Prévost: *MPA* (2:212–214); AN/F/3/241/149, 30 August 1717; Giraud (4:429). Chickasaw: *MPA* (3:303).

20. Lusser: *MPA* (1:89–110).

21. Law's "duchy": Le Page du Pratz 1758 (1:170–171).

22. Dumont and Le Mascrier (2:67–71).

23. The earliest ecclesiastical records for the Arkansas post date from 1764, so it's impossible to trace Marie Françoise's life there.

12. LOUISIANA'S GARDEN ON THE GERMAN COAST

1. 1720 campaign: Deiler (13).

2. Death tolls: Deiler (28–30); Giraud (3:154–162).

3. German colonists resettled: Giraud (4:248–249).

4. *Bajoue*: AG/Registre/A/1/2592/90V. *Bayouk*: Thwaites (68:220).

5. Dumont and Le Mascrier (1:3, "Michassipy ou Mississipy"); Le Page du Pratz 1758 (1:5, "Missicipi").

6. Black soil: Sublette (chapter 2).

7. Levees: Giraud (5:210–212, 225–229).

8. The lives of survivors who moved to the German Coast early on are not easily documented. The oldest sacramental records date from 1739. In addition, during the early years when settlers were frequently displaced at the whim of the Indies Company, government record-keeping was even spottier than elsewhere in the colony. Finally, although several attempts at a census were made in the 1720s, survivors' stories indicate that they were incomplete.

9. 1721 dispatches: AG/A/1/2592/105V, 115.

10. Systems of land attribution: *MPA* (3:447–448); Giraud (1:265; 3:321–322; 5:208, 213–216); Greer (171–173).

11. Returns to France: *MPA* (3:351); Giraud (3:177, n.2).

12. The arpent: Holmes 1983.

13. Dumont and Le Mascrier (2:69).

14. Sale of produce: Giraud (5:288–289).

15. Jacques II Tarascon's home: Wilson 1987 (374–378).

16. Jung: *MPA* (3:653).

17. Pélagie Lorreins/Tarascon estate: *LHQ* (17:213–218, 389–390; 18:478–485).

18. Mahou-Dureau contract: RSCL/1739-04-07-05.

19. River travel: Dumont 2012 (150).

20. Joseph Laurent: RSCL/1744-09-07-02.

21. Bettemont in 1744: NONA/25357/3933.

22. Bettemont in 1764: NONA/8850/75221–75222.

23. Delormel's 30 January 1714 transaction with notary François Gallois is missing from AN/MC/ET/XLVI.

24. 8 January 1767: AN/MC/ET/XIX/784.

25. Bettemont in 1769: NONA/10374/91385.

26. Bettemont in 1775: NONA/10843/100139.

27. Bettemont in 1778: AN/MC/ET/XIX/784, along with 8 January 1767 information.

28. 1784 inventory: Conrad 1974 (125–127).

29. Piece of eight-*livre/piastre* exchange in the 1780s: McCusker (283).

30. Modest size of *habitations*: Thwaites (67:282).

31. Situation in 1731: LaChance (217). *Engagés* remained a significant part of agricultural labor only in the Illinois country: Ekberg 1998 (161–162).

32. Each large landholding along the German Coast relied on the labor of sixty to two hundred enslaved Africans.

13. NATCHEZ, JOHN LAW'S FOLLY

1. 1720 report: AG/Registre/A/1/2592/91.

2. Early history of Natchez: Giraud (1:321–325; 2:151–152). Father Raphael: *MPA* (2:525).

3. Informal "marriages": Dumont 2012 (152–153). Father Raphael: *MPA* (2:527).

4. 1719 decree: AN/E//2010/19–20.

5. French imports: Price (1:380). Projected tobacco revenue: Du Tot (83).

6. "*État de la Louisiane*": AG/Registre/A/1/2592/29. Louisiana tobacco production: Price (1:308–324); Giraud (5:148–157).

7. 1724 tobacco: *MPA* (3:393).

8. Fresson's name was misrecorded on the ship's manifest as "Fressin."

9. Beau: *MPA* (2:420).

10. Settlers' farms: Libby (6).

11. Dumont 2012 (209).

12. Dumont 2012 (216). The only surviving Superior Council document dismisses the suit: RSCL/1728-11-20-11/355.

13. Natchez-French relations: Dumont and Le Mascrier (1:231); Dumont 2012 (228).

14. Charlevoix (6:174).

15. Population of Natchez nation: Usner (66); Margry (4:413).

16. Estimates of Choctaw population: AG/Registre/A/1/2592/29; *MPA* (1:116–117). The 1726 census tabulated a garrison of 80 and a civilian population (both European settlers and servants and an enslaved workforce) of some 225.

17. Chépart's first name is unknown; the spelling of his last name varies.

18. Authorities' land at Natchez: Sayre 2009 (410). Acquisition of Native American lands: Le Page du Pratz 1758 (1:126–127); Ellis 2018.

19. Dumont and Le Mascrier (2:131); Dumont 2012 (228).

20. Philibert: *MPA* (1:122–126); Giraud (5:422). Second official estimate, from 13 December 1737: ANOM/G/1/464. Marie Avril's husband, Tarascon, was among the witnesses who attested to the accuracy of the second estimate. In March 1730, de Lusser encountered Tarascon midway between Natchez and Mobile (*MPA* 2:97). Some killed appear on neither list. Other estimates: Delanglez (631–632); Sayre (Dumont 2012: 35); Usner (72).

21. Caron: Dumont 2012 (233).

22. Philibert did not include Caillou.

23. Philibert did not include Malain.

24. "Slaves": Dumont and Le Mascrier (2:236); Thwaites (68:168, 198); Vidal 2019 (109). Unconcerned with the women: Jean Baptiste Delaye (ANOM/DFC/38/33, 1 June 1730).

25. Enslaved Africans at Natchez: Johnson (113–117).

26. Dumont 2012 (236); Dumont and Le Mascrier (2:154). Dumont provided the first detailed account; much of his account was copied by, among others, Le Page du Pratz. Among recent commentators, Milne (211), Sayre (Dumont 2012: 36), and White 2013 (506) have credited Baron as Dumont's informant.

27. Mobilian: Usner (258–259).

28. Treatment by the Choctaw: Dumont 2012 (244). Release of hostages: Thwaites (68:190). Hostages reached New Orleans: Caillot (141–143).

29. Le Petit: Thwaites (68:198).

30. Women's debts: Dumont 2012 (247–248).

31. Moule: RSCL/1739-01-12-02.

32. Dumont 2012 (240).

33. The Natchez's concept of slavery: Libby (5).

34. Frenchwomen defended the Natchez: *MPA* (4:32).

35. Périer: *MPA* (1:54, 117–122, 128).

36. Doubts about Périer: Delanglez (635–637).

37. *Mercure de France*, September 1731 (2086–2104); *Lettres édifiantes et curieuses*, vol. 20 (Thwaites, 68:120–222). Charlevoix's 1744 history of the colony, the first to chronicle "the massacre," deflects blame from Chépart and follows Périer's line (2:464–469).

38. The only printed source revealing new information that was published before Dumont's history, Le Page du Pratz's articles in *Le Journal économique* in 1751–1753, contained little of the information on Natchez found in his 1758 work. In 1758, Le Page du Pratz proclaimed an unidentified French hostage, who later became his "*gouvernante*," his source. He may well have repeated details found in Dumont and Le Mascrier and supplied by Marie Baron. Sayre (2002, 2009) compares their histories.

39. Dumont and Le Mascrier (viii). "*Naturel*": Académie Française dictionary (1694).

40. Le Petit: Thwaites (68:198); Dumont 2012 (249).

41. NONA 10680, doc. 228, 19 January 1737; NONA 10681, 26 December 1737.

42. Dumont in 1737: NONA/10680/doc. 228.

43. Return to France: Dumont 2012 (276–280). Dumont's biography: Sayre (Dumont 2012: 1–57).

44. Dumont's death: Haudrère (4:1283). Estates of those who died in service: Haudrère (3:797).

45. Périer on his goals: *MPA* (4:35–38).

46. Périer "victorious": Caillot (154).

47. Importance of 1729 for the Natchez: Milne (2).

48. June 1729: *MPA* (2:649).

49. Parisian debates: Price (1:325). Retrocession decree: *MPA* (4:57–58).

14. POINTE COUPÉE IN THE SHADOW OF NATCHEZ

1. 1721: Charlevoix (6:199–200).

2. Tobacco: Price (1:335–346).

3. 1745 population: Barron (3–33).

4. Sara marriage: RSCL/1745-09-07-01.

5. The January 1732 census counted Rolland in New Orleans.

6. Bordelon: ANOM/D/2/D/10, "*Liste des employés qui servent à la Louisiane, 1733.*"

7. Variants of his names: "Stefant/Stephan/Estefand," "Roquancour/ Roquancourt." Marriage contract: RSCL/1737-02-22-01; Forsyth (47). The inventory of Rolland's possessions is missing.

8. After the uprising, a child's body was "found at Rocancourt's place."

9. Stefan vs. Germain: RSCL/1738-09-14-01; 1738-11-05-06.

10. Insults: RSCL/1738-10-11-01.

11. Sarazin-Rocancourt: RSCL/1752-10-28-02; 1753-01-13-08.

12. Rolland, born in 1697, was older than stated on the 1745 census. Date of death verified against Pointe Coupée archives.

13. Sarazin children: RSCL/1759-05-22-01. Stefan children: *LHQ* (13:687).

14. Antoine Sarazin estate: *LHQ* (13:687–693). Stefan estate: RSCL/1771-12-02-02.

15. Sarazin-Colon: RSCL/1747-06-06-01.

16. Baptismal record verified against the original in Pointe Coupée's archives (PCP:2, 90).

17. Records of marriages and baptisms in Pointe Coupée: Diocese of Baton Rouge. Records involving enslaved persons: Richard and Leumas.

18. Race relations at Pointe Coupée: Hall (238–239). Aubert (475) takes a different view.

19. Sarazin's death date was confirmed by Renée Richard.

20. 1771 sale: *LHQ* (13:690). *Piastre-livre*: McCusker (283). Marie Jeanne and her three other children, undoubtedly also fathered by Antoine Sarazin, were sold for 1,200 *piastres*.

21. Manumission in Pointe Coupée: Hall (273). Attempts by Antoine Sarazin's mother to win her freedom and his as well: Spear 2009 (166–168). Related issues and cases in Saint-Domingue: Ghachem (104, 106–111, 117–118).

22. Sarazin petition: RSCL/1774-03-07-02.

23. Stefan's estate: RSCL/1771-12-02-02.

24. Between 1778 and 1791, Antoine was sold at least three times: *LHQ* (13:689–901).

25. Beginning in 1809, Poydras played a crucial role in the process that culminated in April 1812, when Louisiana became the eighteenth state.

26. Pointe Coupée in 1791: Hall (319). Carondelet: Padgett (590).

27. The documents in Sarazin's testimony are reproduced on the website Louisiana Slave Conspiracies, Bryan Wagner, director. Location of original documents in the trial: Hall (344, 349–352nn.).

28. The conspiracy's timeline, verdicts: Holmes 1970 (345–353); Hall (344–374).

29. Antoine Sarazin as "major leader": Hall (353).

30. It's not clear if Louis, born in June 1761, was fathered by Antoine Bordelon or Nicolas Bordelon.

31. Carondelet: Padgett (593, 602–604).

32. Spanish position in 1795: Whitaker (457–459, 469–472).

33. Retrocession: Liljegren (94–95); Hall (376–379).

15. THE END OF THE WOMEN'S ERA

1. *Registre mortuaire de la Nouvelle Orléans*: ANOM/1724–1730.

2. Dienne: BA/AB/10,657/11–23. On *La Mutine*'s manifest, "Dienne" became "Dianne."

3. Forts: *MPA* (4:56–57).

4. Comparative economics of tobacco production: Price (1:357–359).

5. Louisiana in 1733–1740: ANOM/C13/A/23/136; C13/C/1/384. In 1757–1758, *MPA* (5:182, 191).

6. Franquet de Chaville (29–30).

7. Charleston: Hart (198).

8. Balconies: Caillot (78). Le Blond de La Tour: Wilson 1987 (331).

9. Burial notices for 1734 stop on August 17.

10. Fontaine will: RSCL/1734-1-16-01. Her estate: RSCL/1735-1-8-01; 1735-04-05-03.

11. "*De bon sang*": Furetière's 1691 dictionary. "*Noblesse*": 1694 Académie Française dictionary.

12. "Disorder" of November 1718: BA/AB/10,659/29R–51R.

Bibliography

Allain, Mathé. *"Not Worth a Straw": French Colonial Policy and the Early Years of Louisiana*. Lafayette: The Center for Louisiana Studies, University of Southwestern Louisiana, 1988.

Artaguiette, Diron d'. *Journal, 1722–1723*. Edited by N. Mereness. New York: MacMillan, 1916.

Aubert, Guillaume. "The Blood of France: Race and Purity of Blood in the French Atlantic World." *William and Mary Quarterly* 61, no. 3 (July 2004): 439–478.

[Audiger.] *La Maison réglée, et l'art de diriger la maison d'un grand Seigneur et autres*. Paris: Nicolas Le Gras, 1692.

Auger, Roland. "Genealogy and Immigration: Immigrants to Louisiana, 1719." *French Canadian and Acadian Genealogical Review* 1, no. 3 (Fall 1968): 197–210.

Balleroy, Marquise de. *Les Correspondants de la marquise de Balleroy*. Edited by Édouard de Barthelemy. 2 vols. Paris: Hachette, 1883.

Barbier, E. J. F. *Journal historique et anecdotique du règne de Louis XV*. Edited by A. De La Villegille. 4 vols. Paris: Jules Renouard, 1847.

Barron, Bill, ed. *The Census of Pointe Coupée, Louisiana, 1745*. New Orleans: Polyanthos, 1978.

Baulant, M. "Le Salaire des ouvriers du bâtiment à Paris de 1400 à 1762." *Annales. Économies, Sociétés, Civilisations* 26, no. 2 (March–April 1971): 463–483.

Beer, William. "Early Census Tables of Louisiana." In *Publications of the Louisiana Historical Society*. Vol. 5, 79–103. New Orleans: The Louisiana Historical Society, 1912.

Benabou, Erica. *La Prostitution et la police des mœurs au XVIIIe siècle*. Paris: Perrin, 1987.

Blavo, Yves. "La Mortalité en France de 1740 à 1829." *Population* 30 (November 1975): 123–142.

Bonrepos, Chevalier de. *Description du Mississippi, le nombre de villes et colonies établies par les Français*. Paris: Gyrin, 1720.

Borne, Clayton. "The Family Borne." *Les Voyageurs* 16, no. 3 (1996): 134–146.

Boudriot, Jean. *The History of the French Frigate, 1650–1850.* Rotherfield, UK: Jean Boudriot Publications, 1993.

Brasseaux, Carl. "The Moral Climate of French Colonial Louisiana, 1699–1763." *Louisiana History* 27, no. 1 (Winter 1986): 27–41.

Briggs, Winstanley. "Le Pays des Illinois." *William and Mary Quarterly* 47, no. 1 (January 1990): 30–56.

Buvat, Jean. *Journal de la Régence, 1715–1723.* Edited by É. Campardon. 2 vols. Paris: Plon, 1865.

Caillot, Marc Antoine. *A Company Man: The Remarkable French-Atlantic Voyage of a Clerk for the Company of the Indies.* Edited by Erin Greenwald. New Orleans: The Historic New Orleans Collection, 2013.

Calagaz, Ann, ed. *Sacramental Records of the Roman Catholic Church of the Archdiocese of Mobile.* Vol. 1, Section I, 1704–1739. Mobile, AL: Archdiocese of Mobile, 2002.

Carrez, Jean-Pierre. *Femmes opprimées à la Salpêtrière de Paris (1656–1791).* Paris: Éditions Connaissances et Savoirs, 2005.

Charlevoix, Father Pierre François Xavier de. *Histoire et description générale de la Nouvelle France.* 6 vols. Paris: Veuve Ganeau, 1744.

Cheype, Robert. *Recherches sur le procès des inspecteurs de police, 1716–1720.* Paris: Presses Universitaires de France, 1975.

Clark, Emily. "'By All the Conduct of Their Lives': A Laywomen's Confraternity in New Orleans, 1730–1744." *William and Mary Quarterly* 54, no. 4 (October 1997): 769–794.

Clark, Emily. *Masterless Mistresses: The New Orleans Ursulines and the Development of a New World Society, 1727–1834.* Chapel Hill: University of North Carolina Press, 2007.

Conrad, Glenn R. *"Émigration forcée*: A French Attempt to Populate Louisiana, 1716–1720." In *Proceedings of the Annual Meeting of the French Colonial Historical Society*, 57–66. Landham, MD: University Press of America, 1975.

Conrad, Glenn R., trans. and comp. *The First Families of Louisiana.* 2 vols. Baton Rouge: Claitor's Publishing Division, 1970.

Conrad, Glenn R. *St. Charles: Abstracts of the Civil Records of St. Charles Parish, 1700–1803.* Lafayette: University of Southwestern Louisiana, 1974.

Danforth, Marie Elaine, Danielle N. Cook, J. Lynn Funkhouser, Matthew Greer, Heather Guzik, Amanda R. Harvey, Barbara T. Hester, Harold W. Webster Jr., and Ronald Wise Jr. *Archeological and Bioarcheological*

Investigations of the French Colonial Cemetery at the Moran Site. Biloxi: Mississippi Department of Marine Resources, 2013.

Dangeau, Philippe de Courcillon, Marquis de. *Journal*. Edited by M. Feuillet de Conches. 19 vols. Paris: Didot Frères, 1854–1860.

Dawdy, Shannon. *Building the Devil's Empire: French Colonial New Orleans*. Chicago: University of Chicago Press, 2008.

Deiler, J. Hanno. *The Settlement of the German Coast of Louisiana and the Creoles of German Descent*. Philadelphia: American Germanica Press, 1905.

DeJean, Joan. *How Paris Became Paris: The Invention of the Modern City*. New York: Bloomsbury, 2014.

DeJean, Joan. "John Law's Capitalist Violence and the Invention of Modern Prostitution." *Capitalism: A Journal of History and Economics* 1, no. 1 (Fall 2019): 10–19.

DeJean, Joan. *The Queen's Embroiderer*. New York: Bloomsbury, 2018.

DeJean, Joan. *The Reinvention of Obscenity: Sex, Lies, and Tabloids in Early Modern France*. Chicago: University of Chicago Press, 2002.

Delanglez, Rev. John. "The Natchez Massacre and Governor Périer." *Louisiana Historical Quarterly* 17, no. 4 (1934): 631–641.

Delasselle, Claude. "Les Enfants abandonnés à Paris au XVIIIe siècle." *Annales. Économies, Sociétés, Civilisations* 30, no. 1 (February 1975): 187–218.

De Vaux de Foletier, François. *Les Tsiganes dans l'ancienne France*. Paris: Connaissance du Monde, 1961.

De Ville, Winston. *Calendar of Louisiana Colonial Documents*. Vol. 2, Part 1: St. Landry Parish. Baton Rouge: Louisiana State Archives and Records Commission, 1964.

De Ville, Winston. *Gulf Coast Colonials: A Compendium of French Families in Early Eighteenth-Century Louisiana*. Baltimore: Genealogical Publishing, 1968.

De Ville, Winston. *Louisiana Colonials: Soldiers and Vagabonds*. Self-published, 1963.

De Ville, Winston. *Marriage Contracts of Natchitoches, 1739–1803*. Nashville, TN: Benson Printing, 1961.

De Ville, Winston. *Selected Papers by Winston De Ville: A Collection of Articles for Colonial Genealogy and History*. Edited by Donald Pusch. Ville Platte, LA: Provincial Press, 2000.

Diocese of Baton Rouge: Catholic Church Records. Vol. 1A (1707–1769). 1978.

Dumont [de Montigny], Jean François Benjamin. *The Memoir of Lieutenant Dumont, 1715–1747*. Translated by Gordon M. Sayre. Edited by Gordon M. Sayre and Carla Zecher. Chapel Hill: University of North Carolina Press, 2012.

Dumont [de Montigny], Jean François Benjamin. "Poème en vers touchant l'état de la province de la Louisianne connue sous le nom du Missisipy avec tout ce que s'y est passé depuis 1716 jusqu'à 1741." MS 3459, Bibliothèque de l'Arsenal, Paris.

Dumont [de Montigny], Jean François Benjamin. *Regards sur le monde atlantique, 1715–1747.* Edited by Carla Zecher, Gordon M. Sayre, and Shannon Lee Dawdy. Montreal: Septentrion, 2008.

Dumont [de Montigny], Jean François Benjamin, and Jean Baptiste Le Mascrier. *Mémoires historiques sur la Louisiane, [. . .] composés sur les mémoires de M. Dumont.* 2 vols. Paris: Bauche, 1753.

Du Tot, Nicolas. *Histoire du système de John Law (1716–1720).* Edited by Antoin Murphy. Paris: Institut National d'Études démographiques, 2001.

Ekberg, Carl. "The Flour Trade in French Colonial Louisiana." *Louisiana History* 37, no. 3 (July 1996): 261–282.

Ekberg, Carl. *French Roots in the Illinois Country.* Urbana: University of Illinois Press, 1998.

Ekirch, A. Roger. *Bound for America: The Transportation of British Convicts to the Colonies, 1718–1775.* Oxford, UK: Clarendon Press, 1987.

Ellis, Elizabeth. "The Border(s) Crossed Us, Too: The Intersections of Native American and Immigrant Fights for Justice." *Emisférica* 4, no. 1 (2018).

Ellis, Elizabeth. "Dismantling the Dream of France's Peru." In *The World of Colonial America.* Edited by Ignacio Gallup-Diaz, 355–372. London: Taylor Francis, 2017.

Farge, Arlette, and Michel Foucault. *Le Désordre des familles: Lettres de cachet des Archives de la Bastille au XVIIIe siècle.* Paris: Gallimard, 1982.

Faure, Edgar. *La Banqueroute de Law: 17 juillet 1720.* Paris: Gallimard, 1977.

Forsyth, Alice, ed. *Louisiana Marriage Contracts.* New Orleans: Polyanthos, 1980.

Franquet de Chaville, Charles. "Le Voyage en Louisiane (1720–1724)." Edited by G. Musset. *Journal de la société des Américanistes de Paris.* 1902: 1–46.

French, B. F. *Historical Collections of Louisiana and Florida.* New York: J. Sabin, 1869.

Frykman, Niklas. *The Bloody Flag: Mutiny in the Age of Atlantic Revolution.* Berkeley: UC Press, 2020.

Ghachem, Malick. *The Old Régime and the Haitian Revolution.* Cambridge, UK: Cambridge University Press, 2012.

Giraud, Marcel. *Histoire de la Louisiane française*. 5 vols. Paris: Presses Universitaires de France and Harmattan, 1953–2012.

Gossard, Julia. "Breaking a Child's Will: Eighteenth-Century Parisian Juvenile Detention Centers." *French Historical Studies* 42, no. 2 (April 2019): 239–259.

Gould, Virginia. "Bienville's Brides: Virgins or Prostitutes?" *Louisiana History* 59, no. 4 (Fall 2018): 389–408.

Green, John. "Governor Périer's Expedition Against the Natchez Indians." *Louisiana Historical Quarterly* 19, no. 3 (July 1936): 547–577.

Greenwald, Erin. *Marc-Antoine Caillot and the Company of the Indies in Louisiana: Trade in the French Atlantic World*. Baton Rouge: Louisiana State University Press, 2013.

Greenwald, Erin, ed. *New Orleans, the Founding Era*. New Orleans: The Historic New Orleans Collection, 2018.

Greer, Allan. *Property and Dispossession: Natives, Empires and Land in Early Modern North America*. Cambridge, UK: Cambridge University Press, 2017.

Gums, Bonnie, and Gregory Waselkov, eds. *Archeology at the Lapointe-Krebs Plantation*. Jackson: Mississippi Department of Archives and History, 2015.

Hall, Gwendolyn Midlo. *Africans in Colonial Louisiana*. Baton Rouge: Louisiana State University Press, 1992.

Hamilton, Earl. "Prices and Wages at Paris Under John Law's System." *Quarterly Journal of Economics* 51, no. 1 (1937): 42–70.

Hamilton, Peter. *Colonial Mobile*. 1910. Reprint, Tuscaloosa, AL: University of Alabama Press, 1975.

Hardy, James, Jr. "The Transportation of Convicts to Colonial Louisiana." *Louisiana History* 7, no. 3 (Summer 1966): 207–220.

Hart, Emma. "City Government and the State in Eighteenth-Century Carolina." *Eighteenth-Century Studies* 50, no. 2 (2017): 195–211.

Haudrère, Philippe. *La Compagnie française des Indes au XVIIIe siècle, 1719–1795*. 4 vols. Paris: Librairie de l'Inde, 1989.

Hénault, Président. *Mémoires du Président Hénault*. Edited by Baron de Vigan. Paris: E. Dentu, 1855.

Henry, Gilles. *Cartouche, le brigand de la Régence*. Paris: Taillandier, 2001.

Higginbotham, Jay. *Old Mobile: Fort Louis de la Louisiane, 1702–1711*. Mobile, AL: Museum of the City of Mobile, 1977.

Hillaret, Jacques. *Gibets, piloris, et cachots du vieux Paris*. Paris: Les Éditions de Minuit, 1956.

Holmes, Jack. "The Abortive Slave Revolt at Pointe Coupée, Louisiana, 1795." *Louisiana History* 11, no. 4 (Fall 1970): 341–362.

Holmes, Jack. "The Value of the Arpent in Spanish Louisiana and West Florida." *Louisiana History* 24, no. 3 (Summer 1983): 314–320.

Ingersoll, Thomas. *Mammon and Manon in Early New Orleans: The First Slave Society in the Deep South, 1718–1819*. Knoxville: University of Tennessee Press, 1999.

Johnson, Jessica. *Wicked Flesh: Black Women, Intimacy, and Freedom in the Atlantic World*. Philadelphia: University of Pennsylvania Press, 2020.

Kalifa, Dominique. *Les Bas-fonds: Histoire d'un imaginaire*. Paris: Seuil, 2013.

LaChance, Paul. "The Growth of the Free and Slave Populations of French Colonial Louisiana." In *French Colonial Louisiana and the Atlantic World*. Edited by Bradley Bond, 204–243. Baton Rouge: Louisiana State University Press, 2005.

Lachiver, Marcel. *Les Années de misère: La Famine au temps du Grand Roi*. Paris: Fayard, 1991.

Ladnier, Randall. *The Brides of "La Baleine."* Sarasota, FL: RDL Press, 2017.

[La Harpe, Jean Baptiste Bénard de.] *Journal historique de l'établissement des Français à la Louisiane*. Paris and New Orleans: Bossange and Boismare, 1831.

Lalouette, Antoine. *Correspondance, 1821-1823*. University of Pennsylvania Libraries, Kislak Center for Special Collections.

Landry, Yves. *Les Filles du roi au XVIIe siècle: Orphelines en France, pionnières au Canada*. Montreal: Leméac, 1992.

Langlois, Gilles Antoine. *Des Villes pour la Louisiane française: Théorie et pratique de l'urbanisation coloniale au XVIIIe siècle*. Paris: L'Harmattan, 2003.

Laval, Father Antoine. *Voyage de la Louisiane, fait par ordre du roi en l'an 1720*. Paris: Mariette, 1728.

Law, John. *Œuvres complètes*. Edited by Paul Harsin. 3 vols. Paris: Librairie du Recueil Sirey, 1934.

Le Gac, Charles. *Mémoire sur la situation de la Louisiane. In Immigration and War: Louisiana 1718–1721, from the Memoir of Charles Le Gac*. Edited and translated by Glenn Conrad. Lafayette: Louisiana State University Press, 1970.

Le Page du Pratz, Antoine. "Histoire de la Louisiane." *Journal Économique* (1751–1753).

Le Page du Pratz, Antoine. *Histoire de la Louisiane*. 3 vols. Paris: Bure, Delaguette, Lambert, 1758.

Lesage, Alain René, and Jacques d'Orneval. *Arlequin, roi des ogres.* In vol. 4 of *Théâtre de la foire, ou l'Opéra comique,* 125–171. Paris: Étienne Ganeau, 1724.

Libby, David. *Slavery and Frontier Mississippi: 1720–1835.* Jackson: University of Mississippi Press, 2004.

Liljegren, Ernest. "Jacobinism in Spanish Louisiana." *Louisiana Historical Quarterly* 22 (1939): 47–97.

Maduell, Charles R., Jr. *The Census Tables for the French Colony of Louisiana from 1699 through 1732.* Baltimore: Genealogical Publishing, 1972.

Marais, Mathieu. *Journal de la Régence.* Edited by H. Duranton and R. Granderoute. 2 vols. Saint-Étienne, FR: Publications de l'Université de Saint-Étienne, 2004.

Margry, Pierre. *Mémoires et documents pour servir à l'histoire des origines françaises des pays d'outre-mer. Découverts et établissements des Français dans l'ouest et dans le sud de l'Amérique septentrionale (1683–1724).* 6 vols. Paris: Maisonneuve Frères et Ch. Leclerc, 1887.

Mathorez, J. *Les Étrangers en France sous l'Ancien Régime: Histoire de la formation de la population française.* Paris: Champion, 1919.

McCusker, John. *Money and Exchange in Europe and the Americas, 1600–1775.* Chapel Hill: University of North Carolina Press, 1978.

Milliot, Vincent. *"L'Admirable police": Tenir Paris au siècle des Lumières.* Paris: Champ Vallon, 2016.

Mills, Elizabeth. *Natchitoches: Abstracts of the Catholic Church Registers of the French and Spanish Post of St. Jean Baptiste des Natchitoches in Louisiana, 1729–1803.* New Orleans: Polyanthos, 1977.

Mills, Elizabeth. *Natchitoches Colonials.* Chicago: Adams Press, 1981.

Mills, Gary. "Backtracking a Cross-Racial Heritage in the Eighteenth and Nineteenth Centuries." *American Genealogist* 65, no. 3 (1990): 129–142.

Milne, George. *Natchez Country: Indians, Colonists, and the Landscapes of Race in French Louisiana.* Athens and London: University of Georgia Press, 2015.

Morrissey, Robert Michael. *Empire by Collaboration: Indians, Colonists, and Governments in Colonial Illinois Country.* Philadelphia: University of Pennsylvania Press, 2015.

Nolan, Charles, ed. *Sacramental Records of the Roman Catholic Church of the Archdiocese of New Orleans.* Vols. 1–3. New Orleans: Archdiocese of New Orleans, 1987–1989.

Padgett, James, ed. "A Decree for Louisiana Issued by the Baron of Carondelet, June 1, 1795." *Louisiana Historical Quarterly* 20, no. 3 (1937): 590–605.

Pellerin. *Correspondance.* MS 4497 (ff. 52–66). Bibliothèque de l'Arsenal, Paris.

Petitfils, Jean-Christian. *L'Affaire des poisons.* Paris: Perrin, 2013.

Piasenza, Paolo. "Juges, Lieutenants de police, et bourgeois à Paris aux XVIIe et XVIIIe siècles." *Annales. Économies, Sociétés, Civilisations* 45, no. 5 (October 1990): 1189–1215.

Powell, Lawrence N. *The Accidental City: Improvising New Orleans.* Cambridge, MA: Harvard University Press, 2012.

Price, Jacob. *France and the Chesapeake: A History of the French Tobacco Monopoly, 1674–1791, and of Its Relationship to the British and American Tobacco Trades.* 2 vols. Ann Arbor: University of Michigan Press, 1973.

Pritchard, James. "Population in French America, 1670–1730: The Demographic Context of Colonial Louisiana." In *French Colonial Louisiana and the Atlantic World.* Edited by Bradley Bond, 175–203. Baton Rouge: Louisiana State University Press, 2005.

Proulx, Gilles. *Between France and New France: Life Aboard the Tall Sailing Ships.* Toronto: Dundurn Press, 1984.

Richard, Renée, and Emilie Leumas, eds. *Pointe Coupée Records, 1722–1769.* Vol. 1b of *Diocese of Baton Rouge: Pointe Coupée Records.* Baton Rouge: Diocese of Baton Rouge Department of Archives, 1978.

Roche, Daniel. *Le Peuple de Paris: Essai sur la culture populaire au XVIIIe siècle.* Paris: Aubier, 1981.

Romon, Christian. "Mendiants et policiers à Paris au XVIIIe siècle." *Histoire, Économie, et Société* 1, no. 2 (1982): 259–295.

Rowland, Dunbar, and Albert Godfrey Sanders, eds. and trans. *Mississippi Provincial Archives: The French Dominion.* Vols 1–3. Jackson: Presses of the Mississippi Department of Archives and History, 1927–1932.

Rowland, Dunbar, and Albert Godfrey Sanders, eds. and trans. *Mississippi Provincial Archives: The French Dominion.* Revised and edited by Patricia Galloway. Vols. 4 and 5. Baton Rouge: Louisiana State University Press, 1984.

Rushforth, Brett. *Bonds of Alliance: Indigenous and Atlantic Slaveries in New France.* Chapel Hill: University of North Carolina Press for the Omohundro Institute of Early American History and Culture, 2012.

Saint-Simon, Louis de Rouvroy, Duc de. *Mémoires.* Edited by A. de Boislisle. 43 vols. Paris: Hachette, 1879–1930.

Sayre, Gordon. "Natchez Ethnohistory Revisited: New Manuscript Sources from Le Page du Pratz and Dumont de Montigny." *Louisiana History* 50, no. 4 (Fall 2009): 407–430.

Sayre, Gordon. "Plotting the Natchez Massacre." *Early American Literature* 37, no. 3 (2002): 381–413.

Shoemaker, Nancy. "How Indians Got to Be Red." *American Historical Review* 102, no. 3 (June 1997): 625–644.

Spear, Jennifer. *Race, Sex, and Social Order in Early New Orleans.* Baltimore: Johns Hopkins University Press, 2009.

Spear, Jennifer. "'They Need Wives': Métissage and the Regulation of Sexuality in French Louisiana." In *Sex, Love, Race: Crossing Boundaries in North American History.* Edited by Martha Hodes, 35–59. New York: NYU Press, 1999.

Sublette, Ned. *The World That Made New Orleans: From Spanish Silver to Congo Square.* Chicago: Lawrence Hill Books, 2008.

Surrey, Nancy Miller. *The Commerce of Louisiana During the French Régime, 1699–1763.* New York: Columbia University Press, 1916.

Talarmin, Marguerite. "L'Intégration des flûtes hollandaises dans la marine française, 1595–1815." Dissertation. École Nationale des Chartes, 2015.

Tate, Albert. "The French in Mobile, British West Florida, 1763–1780." *New Orleans Genesis* 22, no. 87 (July 1983): 255–268.

Tepper, Michael. *New World Immigrants: A Consolidation of Ship Passenger Lists and Associated Data from Periodical Literature.* 2 vols. Baltimore: Genealogical Publishing, 1988.

Thévenot, Melchisédech. *L'Art de nager, démontré par figures, avec des avis pour se baigner utilement.* Paris: Thomas Moette, 1696.

Thwaites, R. G., ed. *The Jesuit Relations and Allied Documents: Travels and Explorations of the Jesuit Missionaries in New France, 1610–1791.* 73 vols. Cleveland: Burrows Brothers, 1896–1901.

Trudel, Marcel. *L'Esclavage au Canada: Histoire et conditions de l'esclavage.* Québec City: Presses de l'Université de Laval, 1960.

Tucker, Holly. *City of Light, City of Poison: Murder, Magic, and the First Police Chief of Paris.* New York: Norton, 2017.

Tuttle, Leslie. *Conceiving the Old Regime: Pronatalism and the Politics of Reproduction in Early Modern France.* Oxford, UK: Oxford University Press, 2010.

Usner, Daniel. *Indians, Settlers, and Slaves in a Frontier Exchange Economy: The Lower Mississippi Valley Before 1783.* Chapel Hill: University of North Carolina Press, 1992.

[Vallette de Laudun]. *Journal d'un voyage à la Louisiane fait en 1720.* La Haye [Paris]: Musier, 1768.

Vidal, Cécile. *Caribbean New Orleans: Empire, Race, and the Making of a Slave Society.* Williamsburg, VA, and Chapel Hill: The Omohundro

Institute of Early American History and Culture and University of North Carolina Press, 2019.

Vidal, Cécile. "French Louisiana in the Age of the Companies, 1712–1731." In *Constructing Early Modern Empires, 1500–1750*. Edited by Louis Roper and Bertrand Van Ruymbeke, 134–161. Leiden, NL: Brill, 2007a.

Vidal, Cécile, ed. *Louisiana: Crossroads of the Atlantic World*. Philadelphia: University of Pennsylvania Press, 2014.

Vidal, Cécile. "Le Pays des Illinois: Six villages français au coeur de l'Amérique du Nord, 1699–1765." In *De Québec à l'Amérique française: Histoire et mémoire*. Edited by Thomas Wien, 125–138. Québec City: Presses de l'Université de Laval, 2007b.

Vidrine, Jacqueline. "A Guide to Mobile Marriages." *New Orleans Genesis* 20, no. 78 (1981): 65–70, 225–228.

Vidrine, Jacqueline. *Love's Legacy: The Mobile Marriages Recorded in French, Transcribed, with Annotated Abstracts in English, 1724–1786*. Lafayette: Center for Louisiana Studies, 1985.

Villiers, Marc de. *Histoire de la fondation de la Nouvelle Orléans (1717–1722)*. Paris: Imprimerie Nationale, 1917.

Villiers, Marc de. "La Louisiane: Histoire de son nom et de ses frontières successives." *Journal de la société des Américanistes de Paris* (1929): 1–64.

Voltaire. *Le Siècle de Louis XIV. Œuvres historiques*. Edited by René Pomeau. Paris: Gallimard, 1957.

Waselkov, Gregory. "French Colonial Trade in the Upper Creek Country." In *Calumet and Fleur-de-Lys*. Edited by John Walthall and Thomas Emerson, 34–53. Washington, DC: Smithsonian Institution Press, 1992.

Waselkov, Gregory. Introduction to *Fort Toulouse*, by Daniel Thomas, vii–xlii. Tuscaloosa: University of Alabama Press, 1989.

Waselkov, Gregory, Brian Wood, and Joseph Herbert. *Colonization and Conquest*. Auburn, AL: Auburn University, 1982.

Whitaker, Arthur. "The Retrocession of Louisiana." *American Historical Review* 39, no. 3 (April 1934): 454–476.

White, Sophie. "A Baser Commerce: Retailing, Class, and Gender in French Colonial New Orleans." *William and Mary Quarterly* 63, no. 3 (July 2006): 517–550.

White, Sophie. "Massacre, Mardi Gras, and Torture in Early New Orleans." *William and Mary Quarterly* 70, no. 3 (July 2013): 497–538.

White, Sophie. *Wild Frenchmen and Frenchified Indians: Material Culture and Race in Colonial Louisiana*. Philadelphia: University of Pennsylvania Press, 2012.

Williams, Alan. *The Police of Paris: 1718–1789*. Baton Rouge: Louisiana State University Press, 1979.

Wilson, Samuel, Jr. *The Architecture of Colonial Louisiana: The Collected Essays of Samuel Wilson, Jr.* Edited by Jean Farnsworth and Ann Masson. Lafayette: The Center for Louisiana Studies, 1987.

Wilson, Samuel, Jr. "Gulf Coast Architecture." In *Spain and Her Rivals on the Gulf Coast*. Edited by Ernest F. Dibble and Earle W. Newton, 78–126. Pensacola, FL: Historic Pensacola Preservation Board, 1971.

Wood, Peter. "Missing the Boat: Ancient Dugout Canoes in the Mississippi-Missouri Watershed." *Early American Studies* (Spring 2018): 197–254.

Woods, Earl, and Charles Nolan, eds. *Sacramental Records of the Roman Catholic Church of the Archdiocese of New Orleans*. Vol. 1 (1718–1720). New Orleans: Archdiocese of New Orleans, 1987.

Ziegler, Edith. "The Transported Convict Women of Colonial Maryland, 1718–1776." *Maryland Historical Magazine* 97, no. 1 (2002): 5–32.

Illustration Credits

Page 282 Figure 12. Father François Xavier Charlevoix. *Histoire et description générale de la Nouvelle France*. 1744. "Plan de la Nouvelle-Orléans." Engraving based on Gonichon's 1731 map. University of Pennsylvania Libraries. Kislak Center for Special Collections, Rare Books and Manuscripts.

Page 306 Figure 13. "Grand Bayou de S. Jean." "Plan de la Nouvelle Orléans, Capitale de la Louisiane." Jean François Benjamin Dumont. Dumont and Le Mascrier. *Mémoires historiques sur la Louisiane*. University of Pennsylvania Libraries. Kislak Center for Special Collections, Rare Books and Manuscripts.

Page 311 Figure 14. "Quittance." The King to Jacques Antoine Le Borne and Geneviève Bethemont. 4 February 1778. Archives Nationales, Paris. Photo prepared by Alan Chimacoff.

Page 312 Figure 15. Jean François Benjamin Dumont. "Habitation de l'auteur sur le fleuve." c. 1750. Newberry Library, Chicago, The Edward E. Ayer Collection.

Page 324 Figure 16. Jean François Benjamin Dumont. "Plan du Fort Rozalie des Natchez avec ses Environs." 1753. Dumont and Le Mascrier. *Mémoires historiques sur la Louisiane*. University of Pennsylvania Libraries. Kislak Center for Special Collections, Rare Books and Manuscripts.

Page 336 Figure 17. Jean François Benjamin Dumont. "Logement de l'auteur à la Nouvelle Orléans." c. 1750. Newberry Library, Chicago, The Edward E. Ayer Collection.

Page 364 Figure 18. Manon Fontaine. Mark. 1734. RSCL. Louisiana State Museum, New Orleans.

Index

Candace Dicarlo

Joan DeJean is Trustee Professor at the University of Pennsylvania. She is the author of twelve books on seventeenth- and eighteenth-century France, including *How Paris Became Paris* and *The Essence of Style*. She was born in southwest Louisiana and now lives in Philadelphia and Paris.